Danylo Husar Struk

UKRAINIAN FOR UNDERGRADUATES

With an "Introduction to Phonetics"

by
Edward Burstynsky

Consultant
Nicolae Pavliuc

2nd Revised Edition

KIУC
CIUS

Canadian Institute of Ukrainian Studies Press
Edmonton 1998 Toronto

Publication of this volume is made possible in part through financial assistance provided by the Stasiuk Endowment Fund.

Canadian Cataloguing in Publication Data

Struk, Danylo Husar, 1940—
Ukrainian for Undergraduates

ISBN 1-895571-26-X pa.

1. Ukrainian language — Grammar. 2. Ukrainian language — Textbooks for non-Ukrainian-speaking students — English.
1. Title.

PG3823.S87 1998 491.7'9'82421 C98-9321554-X

Cover design by Natalka Husar

2nd revised edition. Includes index

TABLE OF CONTENTS

SUGGESTIONS FOR THE USE OF THIS BOOK

1) As a minimum prerequisite for the use of this book, students should know the Ukrainian alphabet and be able to read and write in Ukrainian.

2) The instructor is strongly encouraged to spend no less than one week on the Introduction to Phonetics by Professor E. Burstynsky, paying very close attention to the differences between English and Ukrainian phonemes as well as to the students' ability to differentiate between **e** and **и**, **г** and **х** — phonemes which present particular difficulty.

3) Although the pace is certainly set by each instructor, there should be no difficulty in completing one chapter per week. The instructor should view each chapter as an integrated whole. He should encourage students to memorize the vocabulary and read the chapter before covering it in class.

4) In a four-hour week, the first hour should be devoted to an explanation of grammatical material; the second to an oral or written execution of the drills, with amplification of points which the students have difficulty in grasping. The third hour should be spent in a language laboratory; the fourth in review and, later on in the year, in supplementary reading.

5) Students should be requested to have notebooks in which to do their homework. These books should be collected and marked for errors by the instructor, but *not* corrected by him. When the notebooks are returned to the students, they must correct the marked errors. The corrections are verified by the instructor when the books are returned to him with the next homework assignment. This procedure must be maintained on a regular weekly basis, so that the homework becomes part of an educational process and not a needless chore.

PREFACE

Experience has shown that the majority of students who sign up for an introductory language course in Ukrainian are, for want of a better term, "home-speakers" of Ukrainian. That is, they use Ukrainian in their home but rarely elsewhere. Some have graduated from Ukrainian "Saturday schools", but few can be called native speakers of the language. On the whole, their language is corrupted by the overwhelming influence of English and suffers from a homebased dialect. The influence of the home dialect generally results in lexical and accentual deviations from standard literary Ukrainian, whereas the influence of English often leads to an inability to differentiate between certain phonemes (e.g., е vs и, г vs х, etc.), as well as to the withering of syntactic and morphological norms of the Ukrainian language. Furthermore, the almost total lack of knowledge of any phonetic, morphological, or syntactic rules of Ukrainian leaves these students quite unaware of the inadequacies of their Ukrainian.

The needs of these students cannot be served by an audiovisual approach, for they are too advanced in their knowledge of the language. The conversational method, on the other hand, has serious drawbacks in that it is most effective when used in concentrated time segments — a condition impossible to realize in a university schedule of three to four hours per week. Moreover, without a thorough grounding in rules, correct patterns learned by students through imitation quickly disintegrate as soon as the students leave the classroom and return to their normal language environment.

The best method, therefore, seems to be one in which the students are given basic explanations and rules governing the morphology of Ukrainian and are then asked to apply these rules in numerous grammatical drills. The main objective is not only to correct the student's defects, but also to provide them with a firm set of rules which would help them work consciously on improving and correcting their language.

Ukrainian for Undergraduates is thus primarily intended as a textbook for students with some previous knowledge of Ukrainian, whether from the home, Saturday schools, high schools, or an elementary language course at the university level. Since the proficiency level of these students will necessarily be uneven, the textbook covers all the elements of basic morphology. The organization of the material proceeds from the easiest elements (e.g., the nominative case of nouns and the past tense of verbs) to the most complex (e.g., adjectival and adverbial participles). All of the material is presented from the point of view of an English speaker learning Ukrainian.

Ukrainian for Undergraduates is divided into twenty-three chapters and an introduction to phonetics. This division readily corresponds to a lesson per week in a twenty-six week academic year, with the first two weeks devoted to phonetics, and one week remaining for testing and review. Since the aim of the textbook is to instill rules of morphology, only a basic vocabulary of approximately 1300 words is provided, sufficient to allow for grammatical pattern drills and translations. Each chapter is preceded by a vocabulary list of words to be used in the drills and explanations. A short table of contents in each chapter provides a quick reference to the morphological items covered in the lesson as well as to the equivalent terminology in Ukrainian. This, it is hoped, will facilitate a transfer to a Ukrainian language textbook in the next level of instruction.

In each lesson, each item of morphology is given a number convenient for cross-references, by indicating the chapter, the item, and the sub-item (e.g., 20.42 = lesson 20, item 4, sub-item 2). The grammatical drills are numbered consecutively throughout the book. Each lesson ends with a homework drill which is to be done outside of the class and which is intended to be a test of the student's grasp of the material covered. (See the suggestions on how to use this book.) The textbook ends with tables of paradigms of nominal, pronominal, adjectival, and verbal forms, followed by Ukrainian-English and English-Ukrainian vocabularies.

There are no dialogues or readings in *Ukrainian for Undergraduates*. This is a conscious omission. Although dialogues play an important part in any conversational approach, the aim of this book necessitates some limitations. The constraints imposed by a limited vocabulary and the relatively short time available for instruction would make dialogues both oversimplified in content and ineffective in reaching the desired goal. In place of dialogues this textbook envisions the use of language tapes to reinforce morphological forms, vocabulary, accentuation, and intonation through audio-oral drills. Suitable language tapes, together with a manual, are available. Moreover audio files are accesible through the Internet (http://lab.chass.utoronto.ca/slavic/home.html).

Despite the fact that there is great value in reading texts, no texts have been devised — again because of the limited vocabulary. Any reading texts which might be created with the minimum vocabulary given in the textbook would be of little interest, and below the intellectual level of university students. The instructor using this book, however, is strongly urged to provide reading material from literature, selecting items to suit the level and interest of a given class. The primary function of such readings is to increase the passive vocabulary of the students and to develop in them an interest and desire to read as much as possible.

The accentuation and orthography, as well as the lexical fund are based on standard literary Ukrainian as presented in H. Holoskevych, *Pravopysnyi slovnyk* (New York, 1962) and *Orfohrafichnyi slovnyk ukrains'koi movy* (Kyiv, 1995). Where the two differ, preference was usually given to Holoskevych. Parallel accents, words, and forms, however, are provided where it was felt that, although one may be preferred, others are equally correct in standard literary usage.

In conclusion, I would like to extend my deepest gratitude to all those who have made the publication of this textbook possible: to Xerox College Publishing for their kind permission to adapt their *Introductory Russian Grammar* by G. Stilman and W. Harkins as a basis for *Ukrainian for Undergraduates*; to Professor Nicolae Pavliuc, without whose help, advice, comments, corrections, and technical editing this book would be vastly inferior; to Professor Edward Burstynsky for his advice, corrections, and the excellent chapter on Ukrainian phonetics; to Professor Romana Pikulyk for her comments and suggestions; to all those teaching assistants whose use of the manuscript provided invaluable practical testing of the adaptability of this textbook to classroom situations; and to the Canadian Institute of Ukrainian Studies for publishing the manuscript.

The publication of this book was made possible by a grant from the Ministry of Culture and Recreation of Ontario.

Danylo Husar Struk

INTRODUCTION TO PHONETICS

1. **Introduction**. In the few pages that follow we hope to set out the basic principles of Ukrainian phonology. This will be done from an English point of view. That is, rather than go into all the details of Ukrainian phonology, we will concentrate on those aspects which are particularly difficult for the English-speaking beginner. Since the student will be confronted with an alphabet almost immediately, we will use the alphabet as a point of departure. Our aim, therefore, is pedagogical, not linguistic.

No student can be expected to read this chapter from beginning to end at the start of his Ukrainian studies. Rather, we anticipate that he will use it more for reference. The teacher, of course, will be expected to make frequent use of this introduction, filling out the parts where necessary.

2. **The Alphabet**. The Ukrainian language uses the Cyrillic alphabet. This alphabet, with various modifications to suit the needs of the particular languages, is used not only by Ukrainians but also by Belorussians, Russians, Bulgarians, Macedonians, and Serbs. In addition it is also used officially by Moldavians, who speak a Romance language — Romanian. However, because of the use of a separate alphabet, this Romanian dialect called Moldavian has taken on an independent status. More surprisingly, the Cyrillic alphabet is now used officially by the speakers of many non-Indo-European languages of the former U.S.S.R.

3. We give below the complete Ukrainian alphabet. The various columns will be explained in order.

4. **Column 1**. This column gives the entire Ukrainian alphabet.

5. The Ukrainian alphabet has 33 letters. In addition one usually adds the diagraphic combinations ДЖ and ДЗ to the end of the inventory to emphasize the fact that these combinations usually represent unitary phonemes. Thus the alphabet can be said to have 35 letters.

6. For students studying both Ukrainian and Russian it might be interesting to compare the two modern alphabets. The four graphemes Іі, Ґґ, Єє, Її are strictly Ukrainian and do not exist in modern Russian, while Ээ and Ыы are Russian and do not form part of the modern Ukrainian alphabet.

Ukrainian alphabet	Ukrainian phonetics	IPA and equivalents	English-based phonetics	Nearest English equivalent	Ukrainian examples
1	2	3	4	5	6
А а	а	a	a	f**a**ther	ма́сло
Б б	б	b	b	**b**a**b**y	ба́ба
В в	в ў	v w, u̯	v w	**v**ictory bo**w**, **w**in	весна́ Львів
Г г	г	h	h	per**h**aps	го́лод
Ґ ґ	ґ	g	g	**g**um	ґу́дзик
Д д	д дь	d d'	d d'	**d**ay duty	день дід
Е е	е	ɛ e	e	b**e**t	день
Є є	йе е	j ɛ ɛ e	ye e	**ye**s	гра́є тре́тє
Ж ж	ж	ʒ ž	zh	a**z**ure plea**s**ure	жа́ба
З з	з зь	z z'	z z'	**z**ink, wa**s**	зуб зять
И и	и	i'?	i	s**i**t	син
І і	і	i	ee	m**ee**t, b**ea**t	ві́тер
Ї ї	йі	ji	yee	**yea**r, **yea**st	її́
Й й	й	j	y	**y**ellow	його́
К к	к	k	k	s**k**ip, s**c**um	крі́сло
Л л	л ль	l λ	l l'	**l**ittle mi**ll**ion	ла́ска ліс

1	2	3	4	5	6
М м	м	m	m	**m**an	ма́ти
Н н	н нь	n ɳ ñ	n n'	**n**ot, si**n** **n**ews	наза́д німи́й
О о	о	o	o	m**o**re, fl**oo**r	оди́н
П п	п	P	P	s**p**in	пи́ти
Р р	р	r	r	Pete**r**, ladde**r**	рука́
С с	с сь	s s'	s s'	**s**pin, **c**ent	сад сього́дні
Т т	т ть	t t'	t t'	s**t**op **T**uesday	та́бір тя́ти
У у	у	u	oo	p**oo**r, b**oo**t	уда́р
Ф ф	ф	f	f	**f**lower **ph**one	фі́лія
Х х	х	x	kh	(Ba**ch**), lo**ch**	хата
Ц ц	ц ць	c ts ts'	ts ts'	cen**ts**	цап ціна́
Ч ч	ч	t ʃ č tš	ch	bun**ch**	чуб
Ш ш	ш	ʃ š	sh	**sh**ip	ша́пка
Щ Щ	шч	šč	shch	fre**sh ch**eese	щур
Ю ю	йу у	ju u	yoo oo	**you**, **u**se	юна́к тютю́н
Я я	йа а	ja a	ya a	**ya**rd	я́вір життя́
Ь ь	ь	'	'		
Дж дж	дж	ĵ ʤ	j	**j**am	джерело́
Дз дз	дз дзь	dz dz'	dz dz'	bi**ds**	дзе́ркало дзьоб

7. **Graphemes**. Some letters of the Ukrainian alphabet look familiar and have roughly the same phonetic values as their English counterparts.

Aa	as in f**a**ther	(not **a** as in c**a**t)
Ee	as in b**e**t	
Kk	as in s**k**y	
Mm	as in **m**an	
Oo	as in m**o**re	(not **o** as in p**o**t)
Cc	as in **c**ity	(not **c** as in **c**attle)
Tt	as in s**t**op	(not **t** as in Pe**t**er)

Other graphemes look familiar but represent completely different phonetic values than do their English counterparts.

Вв	**v** as in **v**ictory, **w** as in **w**in	(not **b** as in **b**a**b**y)
Ii	**ee** as in b**ee**t	(not **i** as in s**i**t, s**i**te)
Нн	**n** as in ma**n**y	(not **h** as in **h**appy)
Рр	**r**	(not **p** as in **p**e**pp**er)
Уу	**oo** as in p**oo**r	(not **y** as in **y**es, cit**y**)
Хх	**ch** as in lo**ch**	(not **ks** as in si**x**)

The majority of Ukrainian graphemes are completely foreign in shape to those who know only the English alphabet.

Бб	**b** as in **b**a**b**y
Гг	**h** as in per**h**aps
Ґґ	**g** as in **g**um
Дд	**d** as in **d**a**d**
Єє	**ye** as in **ye**s
Жж	**z, s** as in a**z**ure, plea**s**ure
Зз	**z** as in **z**inc
Ии	i as in s**i**t
Її	**yea** as in **yea**st
Йй	**y** as in bo**y**
Лл	**l** as in **l**ittle
Пп	**p** as in s**p**ot
Фф	**f** as in **f**un
Цц	**ts** as in cen**ts**
Чч	**ch** as in chur**ch**
Шш	**sh** as in **sh**eep
Щщ	**shch** as in fre**sh** **ch**eese
Юю	**you** as in **you**
Яя	**ya** as in **ya**rd
Ьь	

8. **Column 2 — Ukrainian Phonetics**. Although Ukrainian is said to be a "phonetic language" this is far from true. By "phonetic language" one usually means one sound, one symbol, i.e., one writes what one pronounces and one pronounces exactly what is written. We repeat that this is far from true in Ukrainian, although we must admit that the fit between spelling and pronunciation is closer in Ukrainian than it is in English.

In order to indicate the pronunciation of Ukrainian words, precisely in those cases of an imperfect fit, we will use a rather broad Cyrillic-based transcription. This transcription system is almost self-explanatory, provided one knows the Ukrainian alphabet.

сніг	[сьньіг]	"snow"
янта́р	[йанта́р]	"amber stone"
ля́мпа	[льа́мпа]	"lamp"

Taking *сніг*, the transcription [сьньіг] above makes clear the palatalization of **н** before **i**, and the palatalization of **с** due to contiguous regressive assimilation.

9. **Column 3 —** IPA. In this column we give the transcription symbols used by the IPA (International Phonetic Association), and commonly used philological variants.

10. **Column 4 — English-based Phonetics**. Since students have to cope with a new alphabet when learning Ukrainian, we thought it unwise to use an unfamiliar transcription system such as the IPA. Instead, throughout this introduction we will be using a system that follows English to a large degree. For example, the IPA [i] will be rendered by [ee] since [i] for an English student will suggest the **i** of sit, or the **i** of side. But [ee] is easier to remember since we have words such as *beet, meet,* etc. Further refinements and warnings follow.

11. **Column 5 — Nearest English Equivalents**. To say that the Ukrainian п is pronounced like the **p** of English pit is misleading and will result in a foreign accent. However, in order not to get bogged down at every turn, we have oversimplified and given what we consider to be the closest English equivalents. Precise phonetic details will be explained later.

12. **Accent Marks**. Primary stress in Ukrainian is not predictable and has to be learned with every word. In order to help the student we indicate primary stress (´) on all words of more than one syllable. Compare *я плачу́* 'I am paying' with *я пла́чу* 'I am crying'. The main difference is the placement of primary stress. But remember that normal Ukrainian texts do not show the placement of stress.

13. **Printing, Writing, and Italics**. The written forms of the graphemes are in some cases quite different from the printed forms. Beginners are also confused by italics. Below we give the three forms of the alphabet for easy reference.

14. **Transliteration**. A transliteration is a systematic graphemic substitution without regard for the niceties of pronunciation. Librarians, for example, may want to integrate Cyrillic titles into their main catalogue alphabetically. For this they will have to transliterate the Cyrillic alphabet into Latin letters. Journals will very often transliterate Cyrillic examples so that their readers may more easily comprehend the words.

In North America the most widely used system for the transliteration of the Cyrillic alphabet is the Library of Congress (LC) system. We include in the chart below the LC system of transliteration for Ukrainian with modifications which are used in other systems.

The Ukrainian Alphabet			Transliterations	
Print	Italics	Written	LC	Variations
А а	*А а*	А а	a	
Б б	*Б б*	Б б	b	
В в	*В в*	В в	v	
Г г	*Г г*	Г г	h	
Ґґ	*Ґ ґ*	Ґ ґ	g	
Д д	*Д д*	Д д	d	
Ее	*Е е*	Е е	e	
Є є	*Є є*	Є є	ie	je ye
Ж ж	*Ж ж*	Жж	zh	ž
З з	*З з*	З з	z	
Ии	*И и*	И и	y	
І і	*І і*	І і	i	
Ї ї	*Ї ї*	Ї ї	i	ji yi
Й й	*Й й*	Й й	ĭ	j y
Кк	*К к*	К к	k	
Л л	*Л л*	Л л	l	
М м	*М м*	М м	m	
Н н	*Н н*	Н н	n	
О о	*О о*	О о	o	
Пп	*П п*	П п	p	
Р р	*Р р*	Р р	r	

С с	*С с*	С с	s	
Т т	*Т т*	Т т	t	
У у	*У у*	У у	u	
Ф ф	*Ф ф*	Ф ф	f	
Х х	*Х х*	Х х	kh	x
Ц ц	*Ц ц*	Ц ц	ts	c ć
Ч ч	*Ч ч*	Ч ч	ch	č
Ш ш	*Ш ш*	Ш ш	sh	š
Щ щ	*Щ щ*	Щ щ	shch	sch šč
Ю ю	*Ю ю*	Ю ю	iu	ju yu
Я я	*Я я*	Я я	ia	ja ya
Ь ь	*Ь ь*	ь	'	

16. **Diphthongs**. A vowel which is accompanied by a change in tongue position and/or lip configuration during its articulation is a diphthong. A diphthong has two parts — a vowel (syllabic) part and semi-vowel (non-syllabic) part. The non-syllabic element is usually [w] or [y]: *buy, cow, boy*, etc. This non-syllabic element is often called a glide, and since in English it occurs after the vowel it is also called an off-glide.

Both English and Ukrainian have diphthongs. However, most English diphthongs are composed of a vowel followed by an automatic off-glide. This automatic off-glide is homorganic with the vowel — front unrounded (palatal) vowels are followed by a palatal off-glide while back rounded (velar) vowels are followed by a velar off-glide:

beet [beeyt] bait [beyt] boot [boowt] boat [bowt]

There are three English diphthongs where the glide is not homorganic:

boy [boy] sigh [say] cow [kaw]

In Ukrainian vowels are not accompanied by automatic offglides. Compare the following:

English		Ukrainian	
toot	[toowt]	тут	[toot]
sued	[soowd]	суд	[sood]
brood	[broowd]	бруд	[brood]
Pete	[peeyt]	піт	[peet]
keen	[keeyn]	кін	[keen]

Ukrainian diphthongs always have the glide element indicated in the orthography — **й** for the palatal glide, **в** for the velar glide: бій, дав, знов, був, той, мій, гай, клей

Compare the nominative plural and the feminine dative singular of the adjective *носови́й*: *носові́*, *носові́й*. English speaking students are going to pronounce both as [носовій] since in English the high front tense unrounded vowel (i) is always accompanied by an automatic off-glide and is pronounced [eey].

[eey]	бій	[beey]	[eew]	слів	[sleew]
[iy]	чий	[chiy]	[iw]	бив	[biw]
[ey]	цей	[tsey]	[ew]	лев	[lew]
[ay]	дай	[day]	[aw]	дав	[daw]
[oy]	той	[toy]	[ow]	знов	[znow]
[ooy]	дуй	[dooy]	[oow]	дув	[doow]

The off-glide in Ukrainian is more consonantal than in English.

Above all, the student must avoid inserting off-glides into Ukrainian where there is no orthographical indication.

17. **Hard** vs. **Soft Consonants**

Consonants in Ukrainian fall into two groups — hard (plain) and soft (palatalized). In many cases these can be paired.

Hard	Soft	Hard	Soft
т	ть	з	зь
д	дь	н	нь
ц	ць	л	ль
дз	дзь	р	рь
с	сь		

Not only can they be paired but minimal pairs exist.

т/ть	тест	тесть
	п'ят	п'ять
д/дь	по́від	по́відь
	груд	грудь
с/сь	трус	трусь
	ос	ось

з/зь	в'яз	в'язь
н/нь	стан	стань
	кін	кінь
л/ль	кіл	кіль

18. Palatalized consonants are pronounced like their plain counterparts, but with one important modification. In addition to the basic point of articulation, palatalized consonants are made with the middle of the tongue brought up towards the hard palate, similar to the yod sound.

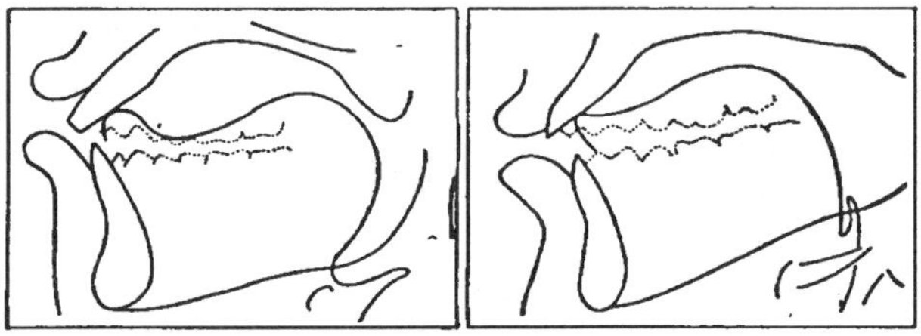

Some of these palatalized sounds have near-counterparts in English, while others are quite foreign to English.

нь — compare **news** [nyoowz] when the **n + yod** combine to form a sound similar to **gn** of French 'gagner' or **n** of Spanish 'senor'.

ль — similar to the **lli** of 'million'.

ть — similar to the **t** of 'Tuesday' [tyoowzdey] when the **t + yod** combine.

дь — similar to the **d** of 'duty' [dyoowteey].

In all the examples just given there are several ways of pronouncing the English words. The pronunciation which interests us is the one where the yod is absorbed into the preceding consonant to form a palatalized consonant.

The other palatalized consonants of Ukrainian are difficult for the English speaker and should be learned by imitation.

19. From an orthographical point of view soft consonants can be recognized in four ways:

a) by the soft sign **ь**. Any consonant followed by this sign is palatalized.

[ть]	—	на́віть, до́сить, геть, за́ворoть, ма́бу́ть, щи́рість, тьма
[дь]	—	ведмі́дь, Госпо́дь, хто-не́будь, дьо́готь, дя́дько
[ць]	—	Гриць, куць, сине́ць, мі́сяць, цьо́му, цькува́ти
[дзь]	—	ґедзь, ґудзь, дзьоб
[сь]	—	на́вскісь, десь, діду́сь, сього́дні, сьо́мий
[зь]	—	скрізь, князь, га́лузь, мазь
[нь]	—	ка́мінь, сі́чень, вого́нь, ньо́го
[ль]	—	хміль, стиль, крохма́ль, нуль, льон, льох
[рь]	—	трьох

b) a consonant followed by **і** may be palatalized, as in:

[ть]	—	ті́ло	[ты́ло]	[teelo]
[дь]	—	ді́ти	[ды́ти]	[d'eeti]
[ць]	—	ці́лий	[цы́лий]	[ts'eeliy]
[сь]	—	сіда́ти	[сыда́ти]	[s'eedati]
[зь]	—	зі́вати	[зы́вати]	[z'eevati]
[нь]	—	ніко́ли	[нико́ли]	[n'eekoli]
[ль]	—	ліс	[лыс]	[l'ees]
[рь]	—	рiка́	[рыка́]	[r'eeka]

Many Ukrainian words that have **o** in open syllables will change this **o** to **i** in closed syllables.

до Льво́ва	Львів
ножі́	ніж
со́ли	сіль
до до́му	дім

In such words (where **i** in closed syllables alternates with **o** in open syllables) the consonant before this **i** is palatalized in most Eastern Ukrainian dialects and in a few Western dialects, while in many Western dialects the consonants remain hard. The literary language admits both forms.

дім [дім] or [дым]
[deem] or [d'eem]

For those who do not palatalize before **i** coming from **o**, minimal pairs exist — one word with a hard consonant, the other with a palatalized one.

ніс	(нóса)	'nose'	[ніс]	[nees]
ніс	(нести́)	'he was carrying'	[ньіс]	[n'ees]

c) Consonants which stand before iotizing vowels become palatalized.

The Ukrainian alphabet has two sets of vowels — one set is simple, the other set is **yod + vowel**.

Plain	Iotated			
і	ї	[йі]	[yee]	as in yeast
и				
е	є	[йе]	[ye]	as in yes
а	я	[йа]	[ya]	as in yacht
о				
у	ю	[йу]	[yoo]	as in you

When the iotated vowels come at the beginning of a word or after another vowel they are pronounced according to the chart just given. For example:

її́	[йійі́]	[yeeyee]
єднáти	[йеднáти]	[yednati]
я́вір	[йáвір]	[yaveer]
Ю́рій	[йýрій]	[yooreey]
ді́я	[дьі́йа]	[d'eeya]
рукóю	[рукóйу]	[rookoyoo]

However, when these iotated vowels follow a consonant, the yod element is absorbed by the preceding consonant, yielding a soft or palatalized consonant.

ню́ня	—	[ньýньа]
	—	[n'oon'a]
дяк	—	[дьак]
	—	[d'ak]

To put this another way:

The graphemes **я, ю, є, ї** represent two different sets of phonemes.

1) When appearing after other vowels or in an initial position they represent

йа, йу, йе, йі.

2) When appearing after consonants they represent

ьа, ьу, ье, ьі.

d) Palatalized consonants may occur through regressive contiguous assimilation. A consonant which immediately precedes a palatalized consonant is itself usually palatalized.

сніг	[сьньіг]	[s'n'eeh]
сльозá	[сьльозá]	[s'l'oza]
кінський	[кіньський]	[keen's'kiy]
для	[дьльа]	[d'l'a]

There are many exceptions to assimilation based on the exact combination of consonants involved.

20. In all the examples given in this discussion of palatalized consonants, two groups of consonants are conspicuously absent. These are the labials and velars. To this we may add "r".

i) The labials (**п, б, ф, в, м**) are all hard. They have no soft counterparts. Therefore, they do not palatalize before **i**.

міра	[міра]	[meera]
вітер	[вітер]	[veeter]
філія	[фільійа]	[feel'eeya]
бідá	[бідá]	[beeda]
після	[пісьльа]	[pees'l'a]

When they stand before an iotated vowel the **yod** element does not get absorbed by the labial; the yod is pronounced. Ukrainian spelling convention inserts an apostrophe between the labial and the iotated vowel.

п'ять	[пйать]	[pyat']
в'язь	[вйазь]	[vyaz']
м'ясо	[мйасо]	[myaso]

They cannot be followed by the soft sign **ь**.

They cannot be softened by assimilation. However, note that although they are not palatalized they do not block palatalization of a preceding consonant.

сміх	[сьміх]	[s'meekh]
святи́й	[сьвйати́й]	[s'vyatiy]

ii) The velars (**к, ґ,** х) and the glottal fricative (г) do not have soft counterparts in the phonemic system of Ukrainian. Phonetically they may be semi-soft when followed by **i**. But this comes automatically to the Ukrainian speaker. The English learner should have no problem with this since English behaves similarly.

The graphemes **к, ґ,** х, г cannot be followed by the soft sign **ь**. Nor can they be followed by the palatalized vowels **ї, є, я, ю**.

iii) Although all the standard handbooks state that Ukrainian has both a hard **р** and a soft **рь**, this sound is rarely heard here in Canada except from people who come from the Eastern parts of Ukraine and who have a heavy Russian influence in their Ukrainian.

Normally what happens is that the palatalized vowels are pronounced as **yod + vowel** after **р**. In some Western dialects the **yod** disappears altogether.

	Literary, but seldom heard in Canada	More commonly		Also heard in Canada
буря́к	[бурьáк]	[бурйáк]	or	[бурáк]
рятувáти	[рьатувáти]	[рйатувáти]	or	[ратувáти]

21. iv) As has already been explained, the apostrophe is used after labials to show that the **yod** is pronounced and does not get absorbed into the preceding consonant. Its use with labials is redundant since there are no exceptions.

After consonants other than labials the use of the apostrophe is important since it has a direct bearing on pronunciation.

Without apostrophe

зять	[зьять]	[z'at']	
бу́ря	[бу́рьа]	[boor'a]	(but see preceding section)

With apostrophe

з'яви́тися	[зйави́тисьа]	[zyavitis'a]
з'їзд	[зйізд]	[zyeezd]
бур'я́н	[бурйáн]	[booryan]

22. **Unaspirated** vs. **Aspirated**

In English the phonemes (**p, t, c, k**) have two important variants each - one aspirated and the other unaspirated. Among the various positions in the word the ones most easy to identify and isolate are these : a) the aspirated varieties occur word initially; b) the unaspirated varieties occur after initial s. Aspiration sounds like a slight puff of air after the explosion of the stop.

Aspirated	Unaspirated
pot	spot
pin	spin
top	stop
truck	struck
cool	school
come	scum

The English-speaking learner is usually unaware of the phonetic difference between aspirated and unaspirated stops. He simply makes them automatically. In order to demonstrate to him the difference the following devices may be used.

a) hold the top edge of a sheet of paper about three inches from your lips, and pronounce the words **pot** and **spot**. You will notice that the air pressure after the **p** of **pot** the paper will bend much more.

b) pronounce the pairs of words given above, substituting aspiration for unaspiration and vice versa. The student should then be able to hear the difference.

In Ukrainian **п, т, ч, к** are unaspirated. It is therefore wrong to state, as many Ukrainian manuals do, that п is pronounced like **p** in English **pot**. Nothing is further from the truth. Such statements show a confusion of orthography and pronunciation and a lack of training in English and Ukrainian phonetics.

A way of illustrating the difference is to find pairs of words in both languages which are as similar as possible and pronounce these to the students.

Ukrainian unaspirated	English aspirated	Ukrainian unaspirated	English aspirated
піт	Pete	тип	tip
пай	pie	текст	text

парк	park	чіп	cheap
пейс	pace	чин	chin
порт	port	кис	kiss
там	Tom	кид	kid
ту	two	кар	car
тік	teak	кий	Kaye

Another exercise is to find pairs of words in Ukrainian which are identical except for the presence of an initial s in one of them. When pronounced one after the other it will be easy to detect if the student is aspirating one of them. Both must be unaspirated in Ukrainian.

пас	Спас	крізь	скрізь
пілка	спілка	кори́на	скори́на
пір (по́ру)	спір (спо́ру)	кіт	скіт
плат	сплат	круг	скруг
по́відь	спо́відь		
пра́ва	спра́ва	пекти́	спекти́
праве́ць	справе́ць	писа́ти	списа́ти
порт	спорт	пла́кати	спла́кати
		прийма́ти	сприйма́ти
таж	стаж	пита́ти	спита́ти
мали́й	ста́лий		
тано́к	стано́к	тасува́ти	стасува́ти
та́я	ста́я	текти́	стекти́
триб	стриб	темні́ти	стемні́ти
то	сто	те́рти	сте́рти
тільки	стільки	тріпа́ти	стріпа́ти
те́лити	сте́лити		
		копа́ти	скопа́ти
каз	сказ	каза́ти	сказа́ти
каза́ти	сказа́ти	кази́тися	скази́тися
карб	скарб	кори́ти	скори́ти
клад	склад	короти́ти	скороти́ти
ко́са	ско́са		

23. **Ukrainian [r]**

Ukrainian [r] is unlike the standard North American English **r**. In Ukrainian it is pronounced as an alveolar trill (vibrant). It is similar to an Italian or Spanish **r**.

English does have a similar sound. However, this sound functions as a **t** or **d** in the English phonological system:

la**dd**er, Pe**t**er

In Canadian English, spoken at a normal conversational speed, the **t** of Peter is pronounced as a single flap **r**.

In order to teach the students to pronounce the Ukrainian **r** we suggest the following exercise.

Have the students pronounce 'put it on' slowly. Then have them speed up the pronunciation. During the increase in tempo, they will switch over from the **t** to a **d** and finally to an alveolar trill.

In order to hear distinctly the difference between a Ukrainian **r** and an English **r** compare the words in the following list.

English	Ukrainian
rib	риб
read	рід
rod	рад
rock	рак
race	рейс
beer	бір
bar	бар
par	пар
more	мор
tour	тур

24. **Neutralization of Unstressed Vowels**

English is noted for its reduction (or neutralization) of unstressed vowels. The resulting merger is a sound of the [ə] (shwa) variety.

télegraph	but	telégraphy
[ə]		[ə]

Ukrainian also has vocalic neutralization in unstressed position although it does not go as far as English. This neutralization tends to cause difficulty in spelling.

Unstressed и and е tend to merge:

весна́, мина́є

Unstressed о and у also tend to merge:

розу́мно, буря́к

Certain speakers will insist that they keep these sounds apart in unstressed position. These are no doubt educated speakers who have a spelling pronunciation. There are certain tests which will indicate how to spell the words in question. But unfortunately those tests can only be applied by those who already know the language. We omit these from our introduction since it is for beginners.

25. **Г г**

This letter does not represent the sound of **h** in **hot**. In English **h** is usually voiceless whereas in Ukrainian it is usually voiced. Some varieties of English do have a voiced variant of **h** in words such as **perhaps**, **Sahara, inhibition,** etc. It is this sound that the student should aim at.

There is difficulty with this sound because students tend to pronounce it voiceless. A further complication arises because some students will pronounce Ukrainian **х** as [h]. This is done because English does not normally have a voiceless velar fricative. A total confusion can occur. Minimal pairs such as **хо́лод** vs. **го́лод** may help to underline the importance of keeping these two sounds apart.

26. **Geminates**

English normally does not have geminated (long) consonants although one is occasionally heard in words like **fully**. Note, however, that this takes place across morpheme boundaries.

In Ukrainian long (or geminated) consonants are more frequent. Pairs of words that are kept apart by long vs. short consonants are rare but do occur.

па́на (gen. of пан)
па́нна (nom. fem.)

27. **v/w**. The Ukrainian letter В, **в** is pronounced [v] or [u] except when it closes a syllable. In the latter case it is pronounced [w]. Or put differently, when the grapheme В is word final or pre-consonantal it is pronounced [w]. Elsewhere it is pronounced [v] or [u].

[v] or [u].	[w]
до Льво́ва	Львів
сло́во	слів
	влади́ка
	пра́вда

The choice between [v] and [u], that is between a labio-dental and a bilabial pronunciation, is a matter of dialect geography. In Canada one usually hears [v].

The difference between [v] or [u] and [w] is a very important feature of Ukrainian phonology since [w] also alternates with **l** and **oo**:

w/l	писа́в/писа́ла
w/oo	на́ша **в**чи́телька/наш **у**чи́тель

Ukrainians in Canada come from many dialect areas of Ukraine. As a result, in some cases doublets can occur. In connection with the **w/l** alternation note the following frequent doublets:

ма́впа	ма́лпа
горі́вка	горі́лка

28. **Assimilation**

Two contiguous consonants may influence each other in such a way that one will change slightly to be pronounced more like the other. English **absent** is usually pronounced [aepsnt] — the voiceless [s] influences the [b] to become its voiceless counterpart [p]. When words are pronounced slowly for emphasis, for dictation purposes, etc., assimilation tends to disappear, or rather not to take place. Many educated Ukrainians will deny the pronunciations given below, but as soon as they speak Ukrainian naturally, that is, at a fast clip, they usually make all the adjustments listed below without thinking about them.

Ukrainian exhibits assimilation. Students do not have to worry too much about certain types of assimilation because most of this will come naturally. A few types are illustrated below.

XXVI

a) assimilation of voicing:

ле́гко	[ле́хко]	(devoicing)	[гк] => [хк]
про́сьба	[про́зьба]	(voicing)	[сьб] => [зьб]
вокза́л	[воґза́л]	(voicing)	[кз] => [ґз]

b) assimilation in point of articulation:

у кни́жці	[у книзьцьі]	[жць] => [зьць]
на рі́чці	[на ріцьцьі]	[чць] => [цьць]

c) assimilation in palatalization: (see also #19d)

сніг	[сьньіг]
слід	[сьльід]

E. N. Burstynsky

CHAPTER ONE

VOCABULARY

Feminine nouns

газéта, -и	newspaper
дочкá, -й́	daughter
дружи́на, -и	wife
жíнка, -и	woman; wife
журналíстка, -и	woman journalist
кімнáта, -и	room
кни́жка, -и	book
кýхня, -і	kitchen
рікá, -и́	river
секретáрка, -и	secretary
сестрá, -и́	sister
студéнтка, -и	female student
учи́телька, -и	female teacher
шкóла, -и	school

Masculine noun

брат, -а,	brother
журналíст, -а	journalist
лист, -á	letter
словни́к, -á	dictionary
син, -а	son
студéнт, -а	male student
учи́тель, -я	male teacher
хліб, -а	bread
чоловíк, -а	man, husband

Neuter nouns

вікнó, -á	window
винó, -á	wine
мáсло, -а	butter
молокó, -á	milk
перó, -á	pen
пóле, -я	field

Adverbs and other words

вдóма	at home
вéсело	joyfully
гáрно	nicely
так	yes, so
такóж	also
тíльки	only
чи	if, whether
чомý	why
як	how
коли́	when
ось	here it is
там	there
тут	here
де	where

Some Ukrainian names

Óльга, -и	Olha
Натáлка, -и	Natalka
Бори́с, -а	Borys
Івáн, -а	Ivan
Андрíй, -я	Andriy

GRAMMAR

Articles — Чле́ни — озна́чений і неозна́чений (1.0—1.1)
Indefinite Demonstrative Word це *"this" — Вказівне́ сло́во* це *(1.2)*
"Yes" and "No" Answers — Ві́дповіді з так *і* ні *(1.3—1.31)*
Genders: Masculine, Feminine, Neuter — Ро́ди: чолові́чий, жіно́чий, сере́дній (1.4—1.41)
Hard and Soft Stems — Тверді́ і м'які́ осно́ви (1.42)
Personal Pronouns — Особо́ві займе́нники (1.5—1.51)
Possessive Pronouns — Присві́йні займе́нники (1.6—1.81)
Demonstrative Pronouns — Вказівні́ займе́нники (1.8—1.81)

1.0 In Ukrainian THERE ARE NO ARTICLES, definite or indefinite, such as "the" and "a" in English.

1.1 In the present tense a sentence can be formed in Ukrainian WITHOUT THE VERB (*Copula*) "TO BE" (*am, is, are*).

Він тут.	He is here.
Шко́ла там.	The school is there.

1.2 The INDEFINITE DEMONSTRATIVE WORD-PHRASE "THIS IS" (це) is indeclinable and is used to point out something which the rest of the sentence defines.

Це кімна́та.	**This is** a room.
Це газе́та.	**This is** a newspaper.

1.3 "YES" AND "NO" ANSWERS. In a "yes" (так) or "no" (ні) answer the question or the key word in the question is often repeated after the response of "yes" or "no".

Дочка́ тут?	Так, тут.
Is the daughter here?	Yes, here.
Це газе́та?	Ні, це не газе́та.
Is this a newspaper?	No, this is not a newspaper.
Це словни́к?	Ні, це не словни́к, це кни́жка.
Is this a dictionary?	No, this is not a dictionary, this is a book.

1.31 Do not confuse the independent word-phrase **ні** with the negative particle **не** "not".

Не тут.	Not here.
Це не шкóла.	This is not a school.

Drill #l.

Form sentences in Ukrainian based on the following model. Use the vocabulary list on page 1.

Це газéта?	Is this a newspaper?
Так, це газéта.	Yes, this is a newspaper.
Ні, це не газéта.	No, this is not a newspaper.

1.4 The Ukrainian language has THREE GENDERS: masculine, feminine, and neuter. Generally, the gender of a Ukrainian noun depends on its form and has no relation to its meaning. Names of inanimate objects or abstract nouns can be masculine, feminine, or neuter:

masc.:	стіл	table
	ум	mind
fem.:	кімнáта	room
	наýка	science
neut.:	вікнó	window
	мистéцтво	art

1.41 One can best see the pattern of gender endings by looking at the form of the THIRD PERSON SINGULAR OF THE PERSONAL PRONOUN:

masc.:	**він**	he
fem.:	**вонá**	she
neut.:	**вонó**	it

The gender of Ukrainian nouns follows the pattern of these third person pronouns. Nouns ending in a consonant (like **він**) are masculine: **стіл**. Nouns ending in the vowel **-а** (like **вонá**) are feminine: **кімнáта**. Nouns ending in the vowel **-о** (like **вонó**) are neuter: **вікнó**.

There is only one form in the plural for all three genders of the third person pronoun: **вони́** — they.

Thus, one can say that, like **він**, all masculine nouns have a stem in a consonant and a zero ending to designate gender. Neuter and feminine nouns have the consonant stem followed by gender designating endings **-о** and **-а** respectively.

1.42 Although, as seen from the above, all nouns have consonantal stems, some stems are hard and some are soft. In the following nouns the stem consonants are all hard:

брат — brother (hard consonant т + **zero** ending)
сестрá — sister (hard consonant р + а ending)
винó — wine (hard consonant н + о ending)

The following nouns, however, all have soft stems:

учи́тель — teacher (soft consonant ль + **zero** ending)
кýхня — kitchen (soft consonant нь + а ending)[1]
пóле — field (formerly soft consonant л + е ending)[2]

Drill #2

Form questions and answers on the pattern of *Шкóла тут. Вонá тут* — substituting for *шкóла* the nouns given below and using the proper form of the personal pronoun (*він, вонá, вонó*) in the second part of the pattern. Identify the gender of each noun used:

лист	журналíст	мáсло
брат	сестрá	рікá
винó	вікнó	молокó
хліб	словни́к	син
дружи́на	учи́тель	кýхня

1.5 PERSONAL PRONOUNS. Besides the third person personal pronoun presented above, Ukrainian also has the first and second personal pronouns:

---

1 Orthographically **а** after a soft consonant is written as **я**. No soft sign is necessary. (see Phonetics #19.C)

2 Although the consonant **л + е** is now hard, the former softness can be seen in other case endings of such neuter nouns as **пóле**: e.g., genitive = **пóля** (soft consonant **ль + а** ending)[1]

		Singular		Plural	
1st person:		**я**	I	**ми**	we
2nd person:		**ти**	you (thou)	**ви**	you
3rd person:	masc.	**він**	he	**вони́**	they
	fem.	**вона́**	she		
	neut.	**воно́**	it		

1.51 **Ви**, the second person plural, serves not only as the plural of **ти**, but also as the second person (sing. & plural) in formal address.

Drill #3

Replace the dots with *він, вона́, воно́* as required:

1. Це журналі́стка? — Так, це ..... .
2. Шко́ла тут? — Ні, ... там.
3. Ната́лка вдо́ма? — Так, ... вдо́ма.
4. Де кімна́та ? — Ось ..... .
5. О́льга студе́нтка? — Ні, ... вчи́телька.
6. Де перо́ ? — Ось ..... .
7. Бори́с студе́нт? — Ні, ... учи́тель.
8. Вікно́ там ? — Так, ... там.
9. Де газе́та ? — ..... тут.
10. Де словни́к? — Ось ..... .

1.6 POSSESSIVE PRONOUNS. In Ukrainian the pronouns "my", "your", and "our" are possessive in meaning and adjectival in form. They denote to whom a given object belongs and in doing so assume the gender of that object (as well as case and number). Hence they behave as adjectives normally do:

"my" and "mine"	with masc. noun:	**мій** (хліб)
	with fem. noun:	**моя́** (жі́нка)
	with neut. noun:	**моє́** (по́ле)
"your" and "yours" (informal & singular)	with masc. noun:	**твій** (лист)
	with fem. noun:	**твоя́** (секрета́рка)
	with neut. noun:	**твоє́** (вино́)
"your" and "yours" (formal and plural)	with masc. noun:	**ваш** (словни́к)
	with fem. noun:	**ва́ша** (ріка́)
	with neut. noun:	**ва́ше** (молоко́)
"our" and "ours"	with masc. noun:	**наш** (учи́тель)
	with fem. noun:	**на́ша** (вчи́телька)
	with neut. noun:	**на́ше** (вікно́)

1.61 There is no distinction in Ukrainian between "my" and "mine", "your" and "yours", etc. Thus one can say "This is my book" and "The book is mine" using the same word for both:

Це **моя́** кни́жка. Кни́жка **моя́**.

1.7 THE PRONOUN "WHOSE". In Ukrainian the interrogative pronoun "whose" is also adjectival in form. It agrees in gender with the noun whose belonging is questioned:

"whose"	with masc. noun:	**чий** (брат)
	with fem. noun:	**чия́** (сестра́)
	with neut. noun:	**чиє́** (перо́)

Drill #4

Fill in the blanks under (A) with the proper form of the interrogative *чий* and those under (B) with the proper Ukrainian form of the possessive pronoun given in English:

	(A)		(B)	
1.	.....	це газе́та?	.....	(mine)
2.	.....	це хліб?	.....	(mine)
3.	.....	це вікно́?	.....	(mine)
4.	.....	це словни́к?	.....	(yours, informal)
5.	.....	це кімна́та?	.....	(yours, informal)
6.	.....	це вино́?	.....	(yours, informal)
7.	.....	це перо́?	.....	(ours)
8.	.....	це лист?	.....	(ours)
9.	.....	це ку́хня?	.....	(ours)
10.	.....	це вікно́?	.....	(yours, formal)
11.	.....	це син?	.....	(yours, formal)
12.	.....	це ріка́?	.....	(yours, formal)

1.8 THE DEMONSTRATIVE PRONOUNS "THIS" AND "THAT". These two pronouns are also adjectival in form and agree in gender with the nouns demonstrated:

"this"	with masc. noun:	цей (стіл)
	with fem. noun:	ця (студе́нтка)
	with neut. noun:	це (вікно́)
"that"	with masc. noun:	той (чолові́к)
	with fem. noun:	та (жі́нка)
	with neut. noun:	те (ма́сло)

1.81 Do not confuse the indefinite word це (this is) with the neuter form of the demonstrative pronoun це (цей, ця, це).

Indefinite Pronoun NO AGREEMENT IN GENDER	Demonstrative Pronoun AGREEMENT IN GENDER
Це — кімна́та. This is a room.	Ця кімна́та моя́. This room is mine.
Це — перо́. This is a pen.	Це перо́ моє́. This pen is mine.
Це — стіл. This is a table.	Цей стіл мій. This table is mine.

Drill #5

Fill in the blanks, using the proper form of the words underlined in the model sentence.

Model: *Це* словни́к. *Цей* словни́к *мій.*

1. ..... кни́жка.	..... кни́жка ..... .
2. ..... перо́.	..... перо́ ..... .
3. ..... кімна́та.	..... кімна́та ..... .
4. ..... лист.	..... лист ..... .
5. ..... стіл.	..... стіл ..... .
6. ..... вікно́.	..... вікно́ ..... .

Homework

a) Memorize the vocabulary in Lesson #2;
b) Review Lesson #1;
c) Translate the following sentences into Ukrainian:

1. He is here.
2. The school is there.
3. This is a newspaper.
4. Is your brother here? No.
5. Is he a student? No, he is the teacher.
6. This is not the kitchen.
7. Is it nice here? Yes.
8. My husband is also here.
9. Only my son is there.
10. Why is the dictionary there?

CHAPTER TWO

VOCABULARY

Feminine nouns

бібліоте́ка, -и	library
вода́, -и́	water
ву́лиця, -і	street
герої́ня, -і	heroine
зима́, -и́	winter
ка́рта, -и	map
карти́на, -и	picture
кварти́ра, -и	apartment
ле́кція, -ї	lesson
ля́мпа, -и	lamp
ма́ма, -и	mother
о́пера, -и	opera
письме́нниця, -і	female writer
пого́да, -и	weather
пра́вда, -и	truth
пра́ця, -і	job
робо́та, -и	work
стіна́, -и́	wall
су́кня, -і	dress
табли́ця, -і	blackboard
ха́та, -и	house
ша́пка, -и	hat, cap

Masculine nouns

геро́й, -я	hero
горо́д, -а	garden
Ки́їв, Ки́єва	Kyiv
письме́нник, -а	male writer

Neuter nouns

а́вто, -а	automobile
кі́но, -а	cinema
крі́сло, -а	chair
лі́то, -а	summer
мі́сто, -а	city
село́, -а́	village
сло́во, -а	word
фортепія́но, -а	piano
гра́ти на фортепія́ні (*inf.*+на+*loc.case*)	to play the piano

Adjectives		Verbs	
вели́кий, -а, -е	large	**бу́ти**	to be
га́рний, -а, -е	nice	**говори́ти**	to talk
до́брий, -а, -е	good	**ду́мати**	to think
кана́дський, -а, -е	Canadian	**зна́ти**	to know
нови́й, -а́, -е́	new	**жи́ти**	to live
оста́нній, -я, -є	last	**переклада́ти**	to translate
пе́рший, -а, -е	first	**писа́ти**	to write
си́ній, -я, -є	blue	**роби́ти**	to do
стари́й, -а́, -е́	old	**слу́хати**	to listen
украї́нський, -а, -е	Ukrainian	**стоя́ти**	to stand
		чека́ти	to wait
		чита́ти	to read

Other words

але́	but
або́ . . . або́	either . . . or
бли́зько	near
вчо́ра	yesterday
дале́ко	far
за́вжди	always
ма́ло	few, little
на́віть	even
недале́ко	not far
норма́льно	normally
по-англі́йському	in English
пога́но	poorly, bad
по-украї́нському	in Ukrainian
ра́зом	together
ско́ро	fast, soon
сього́дні	today
тепе́р	now
ціка́во	interestingly
ще	still, more
ще ні	not yet
що́	what
що	that

GRAMMAR

Declensions — Відмі́нювання іме́нників (2.0—2.1)
Locative Case — Місце́вий відмі́нок (2.2—2.3)
Interrogative Pronouns **хто, що** *"Who" and "What" — Пита́льні займе́нники* **хто, що** *(2.4—2.41)*
Locative Case of possessive, demonstrative, and interrogative pronouns — Місце́вий відмі́нок присві́йних, вказівни́х і пита́льних займе́нників (2.5)
Past Tense of Verbs — Мину́лий час дієслі́в (2.6)
Negative Particle — Запере́чна ча́стка **не** *(2.7)*
Euphonic Alternation — Чергува́ння **у/в** *(2.8)*
Adjectives — Прикме́тники (2.9—2.92)
Relative Pronouns — Відно́сні займе́нники (2.10)
Exclamatory word-particle — Окли́чно-підси́лювальна ча́стка (2.11)

2.0 DECLENSIONS. Ukrainian has an extensive system of inflections, that is, nouns, adjectives, and other classes of words take different endings depending on their function in the sentence. In English this is done by word order or by the use of prepositions.

There are seven cases in Ukrainian including the nominative. The nominative may be regarded as the basic form — the form in which words appear in dictionaries or vocabularies. The most important function of the nominative case in the sentence is that of the subject.

The other cases are: genitive, dative, accusative, instrumental, locative, and vocative. Based on the set of endings nouns assume, they are classified into declensions. There are three such declensions of nouns in Ukrainian.

The first declension is by far the largest. It contains three groups of nouns — masculine, feminine, and neuter — which in turn are subdivided into three categories each: masculine hard stem nouns, masculine soft stem nouns, and masculine mixed stem nouns; feminine hard, feminine soft, and feminine mixed as well as neuter hard, soft, and mixed.

In the appendix to chapter two there are paradigms (declension sets) for each type of noun in the first declension in the singular.

2.1 There are also masculine soft stem nouns in Ukrainian which belong to the first declension but end in the semi-consonant **-й (-j)**:

Андрíй	semi-cons. **-й** + zero ending
герóй	semi-cons. **-й** + zero ending

2.2 THE LOCATIVE CASE OF NOUNS. The ending for the locative case of nouns in the first declension is the same for all three groups and all nine categories. The ending is the vowel **-i** with a few exceptions, which will be discussed later. The masculine gender in all three categories has an alternate ending: **-ові** for hard stems and **-еві** for mixed and soft stems.

2.21 The locative case is used primarily to show the location of the action of the sentence. It is never used alone but always with a preposition. Two such prepositions governing the locative case are **у/в** "in", and **на** "on" or "at".

у/в горóді	in the garden
у/в шкóлі	in the school
у/в пóлі	in the field
на столí	on the table
на робóті	at work
на вікнí	on the window

2.22 With masculine nouns ending in the semi-consonant "j", the orthographic sign for **й+і = ї, й+е = є**:

на герóї	on the hero
на герóєві	on the hero (preferred form)
на Андрíєві	on Andriy

2.23 Nouns ending in stem consonants **к, г, х** undergo an alteration known as the second palatalization where, with the addition of the locative ending **-i,** the consonants **к, г, х** change to **ц, з, с** respectively.

бібліотéка: в бібліотéці	in the library
шáпка: на шáпці	on the cap
мýха: на мýсі	on a fly
ногá: на нозí	on the foot

2.31 THE LOCATIVE CASE OF THE THIRD PERSON PRONOUN.

		Nominative	Locative
Singular:	Masc.	він	в/на ньóму (нім)
	Fem.	вонá	в/на ній
	Neut.	вонó	в/на ньóму (нім)
Plural for all genders		вони́	в/на них

Drill #6

Fill in the blanks in each of the sentences below using the locative case of the noun that occurs in the preceding sentence in the nominative:

A. Ось *мíсто.*

1. У..... ву́лиця.
2. На ..... хáта.
3. У..... кварти́ра.
4. У..... кімнáта.
5. У..... стіл.

B. Це *шкóла.*

1. У..... стінá.
2. На..... табли́ця.
3. На..... лéкція.

C. Це *бібліотéка.*

1. У..... кни́жка.
2. У..... кáрта.
3. На..... Ки́їв.
4. У..... Андрíй.

Drill #7

Translate the answers to the following questions into Ukrainian. Use the proper form of the third person pronoun.

1.	Де ваш словни́к?	It is on the window.
2.	Де Бори́с?	He is in the city.
3.	Де кáрта?	It is on the wall.
4.	Де нáша вчи́телька?	She is at school.
5.	Де мáма?	She is in the kitchen.
6.	Де вáша дочкá?	She is at work.
7.	Де твій брат?	He is in Kyiv.
8.	Де письмéнник?	He is over there, in the chair.
9.	Де шáпка?	It is in the apartment.
10.	Де моя́ су́кня?	It is on the piano.

2.4 THE INTERROGATIVE PRONOUNS "WHO" AND "WHAT", ХТО, ЩО. These pronouns are also relative pronouns when they are used in relative clauses.

The nominative **хто** "who" is used for animate nouns of all three genders; **що** "what" is used for inanimate nouns.

2.41 The locative case of **хто** and **що**.

Хто на/в кóму (кім).
Щó на/в чóму (чім).

Drill #8

Supply the proper preposition in each question and answer the question using a suitable word from the vocabulary you have learned. Follow the model.

Model: Хто в óпері? В óпері герóй.

1. Хто ..... вýлиці ? ..... .
2. Хто ..... кіні[1]? ..... .
3. Хто ..... Кúєві? ..... .
4. Хто ..... робóті ? ..... .
5. Хто ..... кімнáті ? ..... .
6. Хто ..... бібліотéці ? ..... .
7. Хто ..... селí ? ..... .
8. Хто ..... лéкції? ..... .
9. Що ..... таблúці ? ..... .
10. Що ..... мáпі? ..... .
11. Що ..... водí? ..... .

Drill #9

Substitute the proper pronoun for the noun used, according to the model.

Model: Ось картúна; на ній горóд.

---

1 The indeclinable form *кінó* is also used

1. Ось нáша хáта; в ..... мій брат.
2. Ось книжка; в ..... картúна.
3. Ось крíсло; на ..... газéта.
4. Ось фортепіяно; на ..... мій словнúк.
5. Ось нáша квартúра; в ..... таблúця.
6. Ось кýхня; в ..... мáма.

2.5 THE LOCATIVE CASE OF POSSESSIVE, DEMONSTRATIVE, AND INTERROGATIVE PRONOUNS.

		Nominative	Locative
Possessive			
Sing.	Masc.	мій	на/в моéму (моїм)
	Fem.	моя́	моїй
	Neut.	моé	моéму (моїм)
Plural,	all genders	мої	моїх
Sing.	Masc.	твій	на/в твоéму (твоїм)
	Fem.	твоя́	твоїй
	Neut.	твоé	твоéму (твоїм)
Plural,	all genders	твої	твоїх
Sing.	Masc.	наш	на/в нáшому (нáшім)
	Fem.	нáша	нáшій
	Neut.	нáше	нáшому (нáшім)
Plural,	all genders	нáші	нáших
Sing.	Masc.	ваш	на/в вáшому (вáшім)
	Fem.	вáша	вáшій
	Neut.	вáше	вáшому (вáшім)
Plural,	all genders	вáші	вáших
Interrogative/Possessive			
Sing.	Masc.	чий	на/в чийóму (чиїм)
	Fem.	чия́	чиїй
	Neut.	чиé	чийóму (чиїм)
Plural,	all genders	чиї	чиїх
Interrogative			
Sing. and Plural			
	Masc. and Fem.	хто	на/в кóму (кім)
	Neut.	щó	на/в чóму (чім)

Demonstrative

Sing.	Masc.	цей	на/в цьо́му (цім)
	Fem.	ця	цій
	Neut.	це	цьо́му (цім)
Plural, all genders		ці	цих
Sing.	Masc.	той	на/в то́му (тім)
	Fem.	та	тій
	Neut.	те	то́му (тім)
Plural, all genders		ті	тих

Drill #10

Complete the sentences below by changing the words in parentheses to the locative case:

1. Словни́к на ..... (моє́ фортепія́но).
2. Газе́та в ..... (твоя́ кімна́та).
3. На́ша кварти́ра в ..... (це мі́сто).
4. Шко́ла на..... (ця ву́лиця).
5. Ната́лка в ..... (твоя́ кімна́та).
6. О́льга тако́ж в ..... (на́ша шко́ла).

2.6 THE PAST TENSE OF VERBS. In Ukrainian the past tense of the verb is not conjugated in the true sense of the word, but instead the verb merely agrees in gender and number with its subject. Like other attributes, it has the three gender forms in the singular and one form for all in the plural.

The past tense of verbs is formed by adding the following endings to the infinitive stem: **-в** for the masculine, **-ла** for the feminine, **-ло** for the neuter, and **-ли** for the plural of all three genders.

Note that the pattern of consonant + zero ending for masculine, **-а** ending for feminine, and **-о** ending for neuter is preserved here as well.

Ukrainian verbs in the infinitive have the ending **-ти**. By subtracting this ending from the infinitive, one obtains the infinitive stem.

Infinitive		Stem
роби́ти	to do	**роби́-**
чита́ти	to read	**чита́-**
говори́ти	to speak	**говори́-**
стоя́ти	to stand	**стоя́-**

Past tense formations

Stem	Masculine	Feminine	Neuter	Plural
робú-	робúв	робúла	робúло	робúли
читá-	читáв	читáла	читáло	читáли
говорú-	говорúв	говорúла	говорúло	говорúли
стоя́-	стоя́в	стоя́ла	стоя́ло	стоя́ли

2.61 Past tense of the verb бути "to be".

Stem	Masculine	Feminine	Neuter	Plural
бу-	був	булá	булó	булú

Drill #ll

Supply the correct past tense form of the verb indicated for each of the following sections:

A. *бýти*

1. Ми вчóра ..... на óпері (п'єса)/в óпері (будúнок).
2. В кýхні ..... крíсло.
3. На крíслі ..... кнúжка.
4. На кнúжці ..... лист.
5. Іван сьогóдні ..... на робóті.

B. *жúти*

1. Він ..... у селí ? Так, він там .....
2. Хто ..... на пóлі ? Андрíй ..... там.
3. Вонú ..... в Кúєві ? Ні, вонú там не ......
4. Óльга ..... в бібліотéці ? Так, вонá там .....
5. Ти ..... там у містí ? Ні, ... там у селí.

C. *стоя́ти*

1. На вікнí ..... кнúжка.
2. У квартúрі ..... крíсло.
3. На áвті ..... герóй.
4. В пóлі ..... стінá.
5. Ми ..... на робóті рáзом.

2.7 THE NEGATIVE PARTICLE **не**. The negative particle **не** "not" affects the word which immediately follows it.

Positive statement:

Я був у кіні[1] вчора.
I went to (was at) the movies yesterday.

Different elements negated:

Я **не** був у кіні вчóра.
I did not go to the movies yesterday.

Не я був у кіні вчóра.
It wasn't I who went to the movies yesterday.

Я був **не** в кіні вчóра.
It was not to the movies that I went yesterday.

Я був у кіні **не** вчóра.
It was not yesterday that I went to the movies.

2.8 EUPHONIC RULE — **у/в** ALTERNATION. To facilitate smooth pronunciation, Ukrainian alternates the letters **в** and **у**. The alternation usually depends on the preceding word. If the word ends in a consonant, the next word, be it the preposition **в** or a word beginning with **в** like **вдома**, will alternate with **у**. If, on the other hand, a word ends in a a vowel, it will be followed by the letter **в**:

Він **у** кіні.	He is at the cinema.
Вона **в** кіні.	She is at the cinema.
Він **удóма**.	He is at home.
Вони́ **вдóма**.	They are at home.
Він **учи́тель**.	He is a teacher.
Вонá **вчи́телька**.	She is a teacher.

2.9 ADJECTIVES. Ukrainian adjectives agree in gender number, and case with the noun they modify. Adjectives, like nouns, can be hard stem or soft stem. There are different endings for hard and soft stem adjectives.

---

1 The indeclinable form **кінó** is also used.

2.91 Nominative case:

	Hard Stem	Ending	Soft stem	Ending
Masc.	нови́й	**-ий**	си́ній	**-ій**
Fem.	нова́	**-а**	си́ня	**-я**
Neut.	нове́	**-е**	си́нє	**-є**

2.92 Locative case:

	Hard stem	Ending	Soft Stem	Ending
Masc.	ново́му	**-ому**	си́ньому	**-ьому**
Fem.	нові́й	**-ій**	си́ній	**-ій**
Neut.	ново́му	**-ому**	си́ньому	**-ьому**

Examples:

на ново́му геро́єві	on the new hero
у нові́й ха́ті	in the new house
у ново́му сло́ві	in the new word
у си́ньому листі́	in the blue letter
у си́ній су́кні	in the blue dress
у си́ньому мі́сті	in the blue city

Drill #12

Supply the following adjectives with the correct endings.

нови́й	new	*вели́кий*	big
си́ній	blue	*га́рний*	nice

1. нов ..... кімна́та	1. вели́к ..... мі́сто
2. нов ..... студе́нт	2. вели́к ..... по́ле
3. нов ..... перо́	3. вели́к ..... кварти́ра
4. нов ..... крі́сло	4. га́рн ..... учи́тель
5. нов ..... ку́хня	5. га́рн ..... секрета́рка
6. си́н ..... су́кня	6. га́рн ..... вино́
7. си́н ..... лист	7. га́рн ..... пого́да
8. си́н .... словни́к	8. га́рн .... лі́то
9. си́н .... ша́пка	9. га́рн .... зима́

оста́нній last	*пе́рший* first
1. оста́нн ..... лист	1. пе́рш ..... сло́во
2. оста́нн ..... кни́жка	2. пе́рш ..... ле́кція
3. оста́нн ..... хліб	3. пе́рш ..... ву́лиця
4. оста́нн ..... сло́во	4. пе́рш ..... учи́тель

2.10 THE RELATIVE PRONOUN "WHICH", "WHAT KIND".

The relative pronoun **яки́й, яка́, яке́** "which" is declined as an adjective and agrees in gender and number with the noun it relates to. The case, however, is determined by the use of the pronoun in its own clause.

Note: In Ukrainian the relative clause is always preceded by a comma.

Ха́та, в *які́й* я жив, була́ стара́.
The house in which I lived was old.

А́вто, в *я́кому* я чека́в, було́ си́нє.
The automobile in which I waited was blue.

Very often in Ukrainian a relative clause is introduced by **що** or **хто**, when **що** or **хто** are the subjects of the relative clause.

Фортепія́но, *що* стоя́ло тут.
The piano which stood here/The piano that stood here.

It is also possible to say:

Фортепія́но, *яке́* стоя́ло тут.
The piano which stood here.

The first construction with **що** is preferred in standard Ukrainian. Similarly, in such a construction, **хто** is preferred when it refers to persons and is linked with the demonstrative pronoun **той**.

Той чолові́к, *хто* це знав.
That man who knew this.

Note: Do not confuse the interrogative **котри́й, котра́, котре́,** "which one" of a set, with **яки́й, яка́, яке́** "which":

Котри́й стіл ваш?
Which table (one of several) is yours?

Стіл, *яки́й* у кімна́ті, мій.
The table *which* is in the room is mine.

2.11 The relative pronoun **яки́й** is also used as an exclamatory word-particle in such statements as "what a beautiful...":

Яки́й га́рний день!	What a beautiful day!
Яка́ га́рна кни́жка!	What a nice book!
Яке́ га́рне а́вто!	What a pretty car!

In such constructions **яки́й** agrees in number, gender, and case with the noun it modifies. These are nominal sentences and therefore do not have a predicate.

Drill #l3

Fill in the blanks with the correct form of the word shown in the model.

Model: *Котри́й* стіл *ваш, цей* чи *той* ? *Цей мій.*

1. ..... кімна́та ....., ... чи .....? ....
2. ..... по́ле ....., ... чи .....? ....
3. ..... словни́к ....., ... чи .....? ....

Model: *Яка́* вона́ студе́нтка ? Вона́ *до́бра* студе́нтка.

1. ..... він учи́тель? Він ..... учи́тель.
2. ..... це перо́? Це ..... перо́.
3. ..... вона́ письме́нниця ? Вона́ ..... письме́нниця.
4. ..... це су́кня ? Це ..... су́кня.
5. ..... це словни́к ? Це ..... словни́к.
6. ..... це ша́пка ? Це ..... ша́пка.

Model: *Яка́ до́бра* журналі́стка!

1. .... лі́то!
2. .... зима́!
3. .... кни́жка!

4. .... погóда!
5. .... прáвда!
6. .... день!

Model: *Ваш* син таки́й *гáрний*!

1. ..... дружи́на такóж ..... !
2. ..... сýкня такóж ..... !
3. ..... місто такóж ..... !
4. ..... шáпка такóж ..... !

Drill #14

Fill in the blanks with the correct endings of the pronouns and adjectives.

1. Ми були́ на ц ..... гáрн ..... óпері.
2. Ми були́ в ц ..... украї́нськ ..... селí.
3. Ми були́ в нáш ..... остáнн ..... кімнáті.
4. Ми були́ в вáш ..... вели́к ..... горóді.

Drill #15

Transform the two sentences into one by using relative clauses with *яки́й* as in the model.

Model: Ось хáта. Ми в ній жили́.
Ось хáта, в якій ми жили́.

1. Ось місто. Ми в ньóму жили́.
2. Ось вýлиця. Ми на ній чекáли.
3. Ось кварти́ра. Ми в ній дýмали.
4. Ось áвто. Ми в ньóму говори́ли.

Drill #16

Fill in the blanks with the correct form of the words *яки́й* or *що*. Change the words in parentheses into the required case:

1. А́вто, ... стоя́ло в (твій) горо́ді, тепе́р[1] на (моє́) по́лі.
2. Кни́жка, ... була́ в (твоя́) кімна́ті, тепе́р на (твоя́) карти́ні.
3. Журналі́ст, ... був на ву́лиці, тепе́р у (на́ша) ку́хні.

Homework

a) Memorize the vocabulary in Lesson #3;
b) Review Lesson #2;
c) Translate the following sentences into English:

1. У Ки́єві ми жили́ у вели́кій нові́й ха́ті.
2. Або́ О́льга або́ Ната́лка вчо́ра була́ в га́рній си́ній су́кні.
3. Хто за́вжди жив у цій нові́й кварти́рі?
4. Ми ду́мали, що він наш украї́нський геро́й.
5. Хто там дале́ко в то́му га́рному си́ньому а́вті?
6. Сього́дні оста́нній студе́нт переклада́в, але́ ми не слу́хали.
7. Він і вели́кий кана́дський письме́нник стоя́ли ра́зом.
8. Він ціка́во грав на фортепія́ні.
9. Що роби́ти? Ще писа́ти, чита́ти і говори́ти по-украї́нському.
10. Стари́й учи́тель бли́зько? Ще ні.
11. Той, хто пога́но чита́в, ма́ло чита́в.
12. У на́шому мі́сті на́віть на́ша шко́ла недале́ко.
13. Ви ско́ро чита́ли по-англі́йському? Я чита́ла норма́льно.

APPENDIX TO CHAPTER TWO

First Declension Singular

Masculine

	Hard	Mixed	Soft
Nom.	стіл	ніж	учи́тель
Gen.	стола́	ножа́	учи́теля
Dat.	столо́ві (-у)	ноже́ві (-у)	учи́телеві (-ю)
Acc.	стіл	ніж	учи́теля
Instr.	столо́м	ноже́м	учи́телем
Loc.	(на) столі́	(на) ножі́	(на) учи́телеві (-і)
Voc.	сто́ле	но́же	учи́телю

1 = "now"

Neuter

	Hard		Mixed	Soft
Nom.	ліжко	вікно́	во́гнище	мі́сце
Gen.	ліжка	вікна́	во́гнища	мі́сця
Dat.	ліжку	вікну́	во́гнищу	мі́сцю
Acc.	ліжко	вікно́	во́гнище	мі́сце
Instr.	ліжком	вікно́м	во́гнищем	мі́сцем
Loc.	(на/у) ліжку	вікні́	(на/у) во́гнищі	(на) мі́сці
Voc.	ліжко	вікно́	во́гнище	мі́сце

Feminine

	Hard		Mixed	Soft
Nom.	кни́га	шко́ла	кру́ча	ку́хня
Gen.	кни́ги	шко́ли	кру́чі	ку́хні
Dat.	кни́зі	шко́лі	кру́чі	ку́хні
Acc.	кни́гу	шко́лу	кру́чу	ку́хню
Instr.	кни́гою	шко́лою	кру́чею	ку́хнею
Loc.	(на/у) кни́зі	(у) шко́лі	(на) кру́чі	(у) ку́хні
Voc.	кни́го	шко́ло	кру́че	ку́хне

Notes : Note that in most case forms the hardness or softness of the stem ending is preserved and is shown in spelling. In the mixed category the paradigm follows both the hard and the soft pattern. The hard pattern is followed for the endings with the vowels **a** and **y**; the soft pattern for the endings with vowels **e** and **i**.

On the whole, the vowels in Ukrainian can be arranged to correspond between hard and soft:

Hard stem takes endings with:	а	у	о	й
Mixed stem takes endings with:	а	у	е	і
Soft stem takes endings with:	я	ю	е	і

Certain changes may occur in the stem consonant due to the declension. These changes are a result of palatalization and depalatalization. For example, г changes to **з** if followed by an **і**, as in the dative case of the word кни́га “book”. To avoid a similar change of к to ц in the locative case of the word ліжко “bed”, an alternate form of the ending is employed: у which no longer necessitates the change of к to **ц**.

CHAPTER THREE

VOCABULARY

Feminine nouns

адре́са, -и	address
на́зва, -и	name of place or thing
при́ятелька, -и	girl friend
скля́нка, -и	glass
столи́ця, -і	capital
сторона́, -и́	side
ціна́, -и́	price

Masculine nouns

ве́чір, ве́чора	evening
готе́ль, -ю	hotel
день, дня	day
кіне́ць, кінця́	end
ко́лір, ко́льору	color
ко́рінь, ко́реня	root
кусо́к, куска́	piece
о́браз, -а	image, portrait
о́браз, -у	literary figure
поча́ток, поча́тку	beginning
при́ятель, -я	male friend
рестора́н, -у	restaurant
сир, -у	cheese
фунт, -а	pound
центр, -а/-у	center
час, -у	time

Adjectives

бі́лий, -а, -е	white
виѓідний, -а, -е	comfortable
гаря́чий, -а, -е	hot
деше́вий, -а, -е	cheap
дороги́й, -а́, -е́	expensive
европе́йський, -а, -е	European
зимови́й, -а́, -е́	winter (adj.)
молоди́й, -а́, -е́	young
прекра́сний, -а, -е	beautiful

приє́мний, -а, -е	pleasant
пога́ний, -а, -е	ugly
те́мний, -а, -е	dark
трудни́й, -а́, -е́	difficult
францу́зький, -а, -е	French
холо́дний, -а, -е	cool
я́сний, -а, -е	clear, bright

Verbs

ба́чити	to see
ї́сти (їв, ї́ла, ї́ло, ї́ли)	to eat
спа́ти	to sleep
пи́ти	to drink

Adverbs and other words

уве́сь/ввесь, уся́/вся, усе́/все	everything, whole, all (*pron.*)
давно́	long ago (*adv.*)
і/й	and (*conj.*)
неда́вно	not long ago (*adv.*)
пізно	late (*adv.*)
ра́но	early (*adv.*)
скільки	how much (*adv.*)
уже́/вже	already (*adv.*)
уве́чорі	in the evening (*adv.*)

Expressions

на поча́тку	at the beginning
з поча́тку	from the beginning
з поча́тку до кінця́	from beginning to end
на кіне́ць	at the end
з кінця́	from the end
ввесь день/уве́сь день	all day
яко́го ко́льору	what color
як він/вона назива́ється?	what is his/her name?
як ви назива́єтеся?	what is your (*pl.* or *formal*) name?
як ти назива́єшся?	what is your (*sg.* or *inform.*) name?

Names

Оле́нка, -и	Olenka
О́ля, -і	Olya (*dim.* of Olha)
Дани́ло, -а	Danylo
Петро́, -а́	Petro

GRAMMAR

Genitive Case of Nouns — Родови́й відмі́нок іме́нників (3.0—3.01)
The о/е - і *alternations — Чергува́ння* о, е *з* і *(3.1)*
The fleeting о/е - Ø *— Чергува́ння* о, е *з* Ø *(нуле́м зву́ка) (3.11)*
Euphonic alternation і/й *— Чергува́ння* і - й *(3.2)*
Genitive Case of the Third Person Pronoun — Родови́й відмі́нок особо́вого займе́нника тре́тьої осо́би (3.3)
Genitive Case of Modifiers — Родови́й відмі́нок прикме́тників і займе́нників (3.4)
Genitive Case with Quantities — Родови́й відмі́нок для позна́чення кі́лькостей (3.5)
The use of є *"Is" and* нема́є *"Is not" — Вжива́ння* є - нема́є *(3.6)*
Adverbs — Прислі́вники (3.7)

3.0 THE GENITIVE CASE OF NOUNS

The main function of the genitive case in Ukrainian is to denote possession, This case performs a function similar to the English "'s", e.g., John's.

Nouns of the first declension have the following endings in the Genitive case:

		Nominative	Genitive	Ending
Masc.	hard/mixed	лист	листа́	-а
	soft	учи́тель	учи́теля	-я
Neut.	hard/mixed	село́	села́	-а
	soft	по́ле	по́ля	-я
Fem.	hard	кни́жка	кни́жки	-и
	soft/mixed	ку́хня	ку́хні	-і

3.01 Masculine nouns in the first declension which refer to abstract concepts or describe things which are amorphous in shape, as well as nouns of foreign origin, have in the genitive singular the ending **-у** for hard and mixed and **-ю** for soft stems:

	Nominative	Genitive	Ending
	час	ча́су	-у
	готе́ль	готе́лю	-ю
	рестора́н	рестора́ну	-у
	о́браз (*abstract*)	о́бразу	-у
but	о́браз (*concrete*)	о́браза	-а

Drill #17

Supply the correct case forms for the nouns given in parentheses:

1. Чий це дім? Це дім..... (брат).
2. Чиє́ це перó? Це перó? ..... (сестрá)
3. Чия́ це кáрта? Це кáрта ..... (учи́тель).
4. Чиє́ це áвто? Це ..... (журналíст Козáченко).
5. Чия́ це кварти́ра? Це кварти́ра ..... (Петрó й Олéнка).
6. Чия́ це адрéса? ..... (письмéнник Петрéнко).

Drill #18

Translate the following sentences into Ukrainian:

1. This is the beginning of the lesson.
2. Where is the writer's room? It's there.
3. Whose book is this? This is Natalka's and Danylo's book.
4. Whose chair is this? It's my brother's chair.
5. Whose wife is she? She is Kozachenko's wife.
6. Who is he? He is my friend and Olya's husband.
7. Whose house is this? This is the house of the hero.

3.1 THE о AND е ALTERNATION WITH і

Due to the disappearance of certain reduced vowels during the development of the Ukrainian language, in certain words the vowels о and е change into і or vice versa. This happens when, during the course of inflection (the adding or subtracting of endings while declining), an open syllable becomes closed or a closed syllable opens. An open syllable is one where the syllable ends in a vowel; a closed syllable is one where the syllable ends in a consonant. Thus, if an о or an е in an open syllable finds itself in a closed syllable, it will change to і.

дім (*cvc-closed*)	—	дóму	(*cv/cv-open*)
мід (*cvc-closed*)	—	мéду	(*cv/cv-open*)
вéчір (*cv/cvc-closed*)	—	вéчора	(*cv/cv/cv-open*)
кóрінь (*cv/cvc-closed*)	—	кóреня	(*cv/cv/cv-open*)

3.11 THE "FLEETING" o or e

Due to the same historical process, in some nouns the vowels o and e which precede the final consonant in the nominative case disappear or alternate with zero when the word is declined. Such disappearance will remain throughout the whole declension of the noun in all cases but the nominative, and the accusative if the latter is the same as the nominative:

Nominative	Genitive	Locative	
кіне́ць	кінця́	на кінці́	"end"
кусо́к	куска́	у куску́	"piece"
день	дня	у дні	"day"

Since there is no ready way of knowing when these changes will occur, it is best to memorize the nominative and the genitive forms of the nouns. If there is a change between the nominative and the genitive, this change will be maintained throughout the declension of the given noun.

3.2 EUPHONIC RULE OF і AND й

Based on the same principle as the alternation of у and в, the conjunction і and some words which begin with the vowel і like *іти́* "to go", change to й when preceded by a word ending in a vowel:

Він і вона́ (н + і)	He and she.
Вона́ й він (а + й)	She and he.

3.3 THE GENITIVE CASE OF THE THIRD PERSON PRONOUN

	Nominative	Genitive
Masc.	він	його́
Neut.	воно́	його́
Fem.	вона́	її́
Pl. for all	вони́	їх

3.31 The genitive form of the third person pronoun serves another function, that of the indeclinable possessive "his", "hers", and "its". Note the difference between the two uses:

Я не знав його́.	I didn't know **him**. (genitive)
Я знав його́ бра́та.	I knew **his** brother. (possessive)

Unlike the possessive pronouns for the first and second persons — *мій, твій, ваш, наш* — which agree with the noun possessed in case, number, and gender, the third person possessives — *його́, її́, їх* — are indeclinable.

3.4 THE GENITIVE CASE OF MODIFIERS

Modifiers take the following endings in the genitive case:

	Hard stem	Soft stem	-**j**-(-й) stem
Masc.	**-ого**	**-ього**	**-його**
Neut.	**-ого**	**-ього**	**-його**
Fem.	**-ої**	**-ьої**	**-еї**

Unfortunately, the genitive forms of the different classes of modifiers are not all regular and consistent with the endings presented above. They are given below and some should be memorized as irregular. The regular expected form will be given in parentheses and is often a secondary and dialectal form.

	Nominative Masc. and Neut.		Genitive Masc. and Neut.
Adj.	**білий**	**біле**	**білого**
	си́ній	**си́нє**	**си́нього**
Poss. pron.	**мій**	**моє́**	**мого́ (мо́його)**
	твій	**твоє́**	**твого́**
	наш, ваш	**на́ше, ва́ше**	**на́шого, ва́шого**
Dem. pron.	**той**	**те**	**того́**
	цей	**це**	**цього́ (це́го́)**
Interr. pron.	**чий**	**чиє́**	**чийо́го**

	Fem.	Fem.
Adj.	**біла**	**білої**
	си́ня	**си́ньої**
Poss. pron.	**моя́, твоя́**	**моє́ї, твоє́ї**
	на́ша, ва́ша	**на́шої, ва́шої**

Dem. pron.	та ця	тіє́ї (тóї) ціє́ї (цéї)
Interr. pron.	чия́	чиє́ї

Drill #19

Supply the correct forms of the words given in parentheses. Then reword the sentence by substituting a pronoun in the genitive case, as in the model:

Model: Чий це дім? Це дім *мого́ бра́та*. Це *його́ дім.*

1. Чиє́ це а́вто? Це а́вто (мій син) ..... Це .....
2. Чиє́ це перó? Це перó (моя́ дружи́на) ..... Це .....
3. Чия́ це кімна́та? Це кімна́та (наш син) ..... Це.....
4. Чий це при́ятель? Це при́ятель (мій чоловíк) ..... Це .....
5. Це кварти́ра (ваш учи́тель і його́ дружи́на). Це .....
6. Це газéта (Коза́ченко). Це .....
7. Це крíсло (твій ста́рший брат). Це .....
8. Це кни́жка (наш га́рний учи́тель). Це .....
9. Це журна́л (на́ша нова́ вчи́телька). Це .....
10. Це нова́ су́кня (моя́ приє́мна сестра́). Це .....

Drill #20

Change the words in the right-hand column into the genitive case:

1.	Яка́ ціна́? (What is the price of)	цей си́ній óбраз це га́рне перó ця стара́ кни́жка це вели́ке пóле
2.	Яка́ на́зва? (What is the name of)	ваш вигíдний ресторáн ця дешéва кни́жка її́ нова́ столи́ця
3.	Яка́ адрéса? (What is the address of)	ва́ша прекра́сна при́ятелька наш остáнній учи́тель його́ францу́зький при́ятель той європéйський готéль

3.5 THE GENITIVE CASE WITH EXPRESSIONS OF QUANTITY

The genitive case is used with expressions of quantity, especially with such adverbs as **багáто** "much, many" **мáло** "little, few", and the pronoun **скíльки** "how much, how many".

Скíльки хлíба буló в кýхні?
У кýхні буló багáто хлíба.

How much bread was there in the kitchen?
There was a lot of bread in the kitchen.

The verb in the past tense is always neuter singular with such expressions.

The genitive case is also used in a partitive sense with such words as **кусóк** "piece", **фунт** "pound", **склянка** "glass":

У кýхні був кусóк хлíба.
In the kitchen there was a piece of bread.

Here, however, the verb is no longer neuter singular, but agrees with the subject. The subject is **кусóк**.

Drill #21

Fill in the correct case forms of the nouns given in parentheses:

1. У склянці буló мáло (водá).
2. Скíльки (сир) в ресторáні? В ресторáні мáло (сир), алé багáто (хліб).
3. Скíльки тут (молокó) ? Тут тíльки склянка (молокó).
4. Скíльки (сир) у кýхні? В кýхні фунт (сир).
5. На вікнí тíльки склянка (винó).
6. Нáзва (та кни́жка) "Початок і кінéць".
7. Це почáток (лéкція).
8. Це кінéць (гаряче лíто).
9. Я бáчив тíльки бíлий кусóк (хліб) в (кýхня).

3.6 THE USE OF є AND немáє/немá "is" AND "is not"

Since the verb "to be" is usually omitted in the present tense, the word є "there is, there are" when included in the sentence is used to express the existence or availability of something or someone:

Що є в цьóму місті ? У цьóму місті є óпера, гóтель і нáвіть є бібліотéка.

What is there in this city? In this city there is an opera, a hotel, and there is even a library.

The negative form of the word є is **немáє/немá**. Nouns or pronouns governed by the word **немáє/немá** take the genitive case:

Чогó **немáє** в нáшому місті ? В нáшому місті **немá** кíна й ресторáну.

What is lacking (literally—what is there not) in our city? In our city there is no cinema and no restaurant.

The past tense of the word є is the past tense of the verb "to be" **був, булó, булá, булú**. The verb agrees with the subject in gender and number.

The past tense of the word **немáє/немá** is **не булó** for all three genders in both the singular and plural. The negative **не булó** governs the genitive case, just as the word **немáє/немá**:

У бібліотéці **не булó** тiéї книжки.
That book was not in the library.

Drill #22

Translate the phrases in the left column and combine each of them with each word or phrase in the right column:

On the piano there is no	кни́жка
On the piano there was	перó
On the piano there was no	украї́нський словни́к
	украї́нська грамáтика (grammar)
	нови́й ромáн (novel)
	бíла склянка

Drill #23

Supply the correct form of the words in parentheses:

1. Сьогóдні, коли́ я булá в кýхні, (Olha was not there).
2. Як нормáльно, вчóра (Danylo was not at home).
3. На цій вýлиці (there is) францýзький ресторáн.

4. Цей францу́зький рестора́н (is on this street).
5. (Petro was not in Kyiv), коли́ я там був.
6. У бібліоте́ці мого́ бра́та (there is) вікно́, а в мої́й бібліоте́ці (there is no window).
7. На його́ стіні́ (there is) о́браз. На мої́й стіні́ (there was a picture), але́ тепе́р на ній (there is no picture).
8. У на́шому мі́сті (there was a writer), а в ва́шому мі́сті (there was no writer).
9. На поча́тку ле́кції (Ivan was not there).

3.7 THE ADVERB

Besides words which are always adverbs, adverbs can be created from adjectives by adding to the stem of the adjective the vowel о or in rare cases the vowel е.

Adjective		Adverb	
прие́мн-ий	pleasant	прие́мно	pleasantly
вигі́дн-ий	comfortable	вигі́дно	comfortably
деше́в-ий	cheap	деше́во	cheaply
дорог-и́й	expensive	до́рого	expensively
до́бр-ий	good	до́бре	well

Бори́с пога́ний студе́нт; він за́вжди пога́но перекладав.
Borys is a poor student; he always translated poorly.

In some cases there occurs a shift in stress when the adjective is made into an adverb:

happy	весе́лий, -ла, -ле	happily	ве́село
hot (adj.)	гаря́чий, -ча, -че	hotly (adv.)	га́ряче́

3.71 In Ukrainian, adverbs are used in many impersonal expressions where English uses adjectives. Impersonal expressions in Ukrainian have no subject.

It is pleasant here.	Тут прие́мно.
It is cool on the street.	На ву́лиці хо́лодно.
It's nice that you were there.	Га́рно, що ви були́ там.

In the past tense these impersonal constructions use the neuter past form of the verb:

It was cool yesterday. Вчóра булó хóлодно.

3.72 Another impersonal construction often used in Ukrainian is one with an infinitive:

Читáти по-украї́нському лéгко, алé трýдно говори́ти.
It's easy to read Ukrainian but hard to speak it.

Drill #24

Translate the following adjectives and adverbs given in parentheses:

1. Андрíй був (good) студéнт. Він зáвжди читáв (well).
2. Óля (poor) студéнтка. Вонá зáвжди читáла (little and poorly).
3. Вонá булá (beautiful) жíнка; вонá все роби́ла (beautifully).
4. Тут (it is pleasant) жи́ти. Це (a pleasant) мíсто.
5. На вýлиці (it is dark), а тут у моїй кімнáті (light and pleasant).
6. Вчóра (it was cool), а сьогóдні (hot).
7. Яки́й (cold) день!
8. Як (difficult) жи́ти в цéнтрі мíста!
9. Як тут (dark)! Це такóж (dark) кварти́ра.
10. Якá (bright) кімнáта!
11. Як (pleasant) в вáшій (bright) кімнáті!

Homework

a) Memorize the vocabulary in Lesson #4;
b) Review Lesson #3;
c) Translate the following sentences into Ukrainian:

1. What is his name? What is his young brother's name?
2. What is your sister's name? What is the name of this town?
3. On what side of the street is it always light?
4. Have you waited here long? All day.
5. What is the color of their house? Their house is white.
6. This is the end of winter.
7. We ate bread in the evening. Now it is time to sleep.
8. It was still evening, but it was dark in the street.
9. It was hot and I drank a lot of water. It was already late.
10. What is the title of the book which you read from the beginning to the end?

CHAPTER FOUR

VOCABULARY - СЛОВНИ́К

Feminine nouns — Іме́нники жіно́чого ро́ду

Аме́рика, -и	America
балери́на, -и	ballerina
бльонди́нка, -и	blonde
брюне́тка, -и	brunette
вечі́рка, -и	evening party
грама́тика, -и	grammar
ді́вчина, -и	girl
Кана́да, -и	Canada
крамни́ця, -і	store
му́зика, -и	music
непра́вда, -и	lie, untruth
пласти́нка, -и	record
по́друга, -и	friend
поли́ця, -і	shelf
Украї́на, -и	Ukraine

Masculine nouns — Іме́нники чолові́чого ро́ду

бале́т, -у	ballet
блонди́н, -а	blond
брюне́т, -а	brunet
відпочи́нок, -нку	rest
гість, го́стя	guest
друг, -а	friend
журна́л, -у	journal
кабіне́т, -у	study
конце́рт, -у	concert
Львів, Льво́ва	Lviv
мі́сяць, -я	month, moon
музе́й, -ю	museum
Нью-Йорк, -у	New York
профе́сор, -а	professor
рома́н, -у	novel
стіл, стола́	table
теа́тр, -у	theater
ти́ждень, ти́жня	week

Adjectives — Прикме́тники

вузьки́й, -а́, -е́	narrow
ко́жний, -а, -е	every, each
мали́й, -а́, е́	small
моло́дший, -а, -е	younger
неприє́мний, -а, -е	unpleasant
нудни́й, -а́, -е́	dull, boring
ста́рший, -а, -е	older
ти́хий, -а, -е	quiet
товсти́й, -а́, -е́	fat, thick
ці́лий, -а, -е	whole
черво́ний, -а, -е	red

Verbs — Дієслова́

відпочива́ти	to rest
відчиня́ти	to open
гра́ти	to play
зачина́ти	to begin
зачиня́ти	to close
кінча́ти	to finish
купува́ти	to buy
пита́ти	to ask
поя́снювати	to explain
працюва́ти	to work
розумі́ти	to understand

Adverbs and other words —
Прислівники та інші словá

шви́дко	quickly (*adv.*)
більше	more (*adv.*)
всі	all (*pron.*)
дýже	very (*adv.*)
інколи	sometimes (*adv.*)
іноді	sometimes (*adv.*)
мáйже	almost (*adv.*)
мéнше	less (*adv.*)
напри́клад	for example (*adv.*)
повóлі	slowly (*adv.*)
томý	therefore (*adv.*)

Expressions — Ви́рази

мáйже ніщó	hardly anything (*subj.*)
мáйже нічóго	hardly anything (*obj.*)
мáйже ніхтó	hardly anyone (*subj.*)
мáйже нікóго	hardly anyone (*obj.*)

Names — Іменá

Гáня, -і	Hanya
Івáнко, -а	Ivanko
Íгор, -я	Ihor
Микóла, -и	Mykola (*masc.*)

GRAMMAR

Accusative Case of Nouns and Modifiers — Знахі́дний відмі́нок іме́нників, прикме́тників, присві́йних та вказівни́х займе́нників (4.0)
Accusative Singular of Personal and Interrogative Pronouns — Знахі́дний відмі́нок одни́ни особо́вих і пита́льних займе́нників (4.14)
Accusative with Expressions of Time — Знахі́дний відмі́нок при ви́разах ча́су (4.2)
Present Tense of Verbs — Тепе́рішній час дієслі́в (4.3—4.33)
Negative Expressions — Запере́чні ви́рази (4.4)
Declension of Numeral оди́н "One" — Відмі́нювання числі́вника оди́н *(4.5)*
The Use of Word пови́нен *"Must/Should" — Вжива́ння сло́ва* пови́нен *(4.6)*

4.0 THE ACCUSATIVE CASE OF NOUNS AND MODIFIERS

The accusative case is the case of the direct object. The direct object is the person or thing which is directly affected by the action of the verb in the sentence. Verbs which have a direct object are called transitive verbs. In English, direct objects are often determined by word order in the sentence: "John saw Peter", *Peter* is the direct object. In Ukrainian, Peter would be in the accusative case:

Іва́н ба́чив Петра́.

Neuter nouns in the accusative case have the same form as in the nominative. This is also true of modifiers referring to neuter nouns.

Я ба́чив твоє́ си́нє перо́.
I saw your blue pen.

Feminine nouns in the accusative case have the following endings: **-у** and **-ю**, for hard/mixed and soft stems respectively. The same endings are used for modifiers which relate to feminine nouns:

Я ба́чив твою́ га́рну си́ню ха́ту.
I saw your nice, blue house.

Masculine nouns in the accusative case may have either the form of the genitive or the form of the nominative, depending on whether the noun is animate (persons or animals) or inanimate (things and abstract concepts). The same rule applies to all modifiers of masculine nouns:

Я ба́чив то́го до́брого чолові́ка.
I saw that good man.

Я ба́чив ваш до́брий стіл.
I saw your good table.

To summarize the accusative case for nouns and their modifiers:

Я ба́чив його́ бра́та.	(*masc. animate-like genitive*)
Я ба́чив мій стіл.	(*masc. inanimate-like nominative*)
Я ба́чив моє́ вікно́.	(*neut.-like nominative*)
Я ба́чив мою́ сестру́.	(*fem. hard stem*)
Я ба́чив мою́ ку́хню.	(*fem. soft stem*)

4.1 ACCUSATIVE SINGULAR OF PRONOUNS

All personal pronouns have the accusative identical in form with the genitive:

Nom.	я	ти	він, воно́	вона́	ми	ви	вони́
Gen.	мене́	тебе́	його́	її́	нас	вас	їх
Acc.	мене́	тебе́	його́	її́	нас	вас	їх

4.11 INTERROGATIVE PRONOUNS хто? AND що?

Nom.	хто?	що́?
Gen.	кого́?	чого́?
Acc.	кого́?	що́?

Drill #25

Translate into English:

1. Коли́ тут був украї́нський бале́т, ми ба́чили балери́ну Оле́ну.
2. Мико́ла тако́ж її́ ба́чив.
3. Ми вчо́ра слу́хали нову́ пласти́нку. Іва́нко тако́ж її́ слу́хав.
4. Я так давно́ вас не ба́чив.

5. Ви чита́ли кана́дську газе́ту? Так, я її чита́в.
6. Він слу́хав нас.
7. Де журна́л "Суча́сність"? Я вже його́ чита́в.
8. То пра́вда, що ти тепе́р ба́чив Га́ню? Ні, це непра́вда, я ба́чив її вчо́ра.
9. Коли́ ви ба́чили О́льгу й Іва́нка ? Я їх ба́чив сього́дні.

Drill #26

Fill in the form of the direct object of the pronoun which corresponds to the subject of the first sentence, as in the model:

Model: Він був у Льво́ві. Я **його́** там ба́чив.

1. Кни́жка була́ в кабіне́ті. Я ..... там ба́чив.
2. Журна́л був на столі́. Я ..... там ба́чив.
3. Вони́ були́ в Аме́риці. Я ..... там ба́чив.
4. І́гор був у Ки́єві. Я ..... там ба́чив.
5. Їх ма́ма була́ на конце́рті. Я ..... там ба́чив.
6. О́ля й Дани́ло були́ на конце́рті. Я ..... там ба́чила.

Drill #27

Fill in the direct object of the given pronouns, as in the model:

Model: Чому́, коли́ **вона́** говори́ла, ти **її** не слу́хав ?

1. Чому́, коли́ **ми** говори́ли, ти ..... не слу́хав?
2. Чому́, коли́ **я** говори́в, ти ..... не слу́хав ?
3. Чому́, коли́ **ви** говори́ли, він ..... не слу́хав?
4. Чому́, коли́ **ти** говори́в, він ..... не слу́хав?
5. Чому́, коли́ **вони́** говори́ли, ти ..... не слу́хав?
6. Чому́, коли́ **Га́ня** говори́ла, ти ..... не слу́хав?
7. Чому́, коли́ **Бори́с** говори́в, ти ..... не слу́хав?

Drill #28

Put the words in parentheses into the correct case and translate the whole sentence into English.

1. Я вже чита́в (ця кни́жка).
2. Андрі́й писа́в (нови́й рома́н).
3. Ми вчо́ра ба́чили (О́льга Зари́цька).
4. Я ба́чила (вона́) на ле́кції.

5. Ми зна́ли (він).
6. Профе́сор Коза́че́нко знав (вони́).
7. Вони́ зна́ли (профе́сор Коза́че́нко).
8. Ми чита́ли ("Мару́ся Богусла́вка").
9. Моя́ ма́ма зна́ла (цей стари́й письме́нник). Вона́ ба́чила (він) у Льво́ві.
10. Де газе́та? Я ба́чив (вона́) в кабіне́ті.
11. Де журна́л? Я ба́чила (він) на столі́.
12. Де Андрі́й? Я ба́чив (він) на ву́лиці.
13. Де ти ба́чив (я) ? Я ба́чив (ти) на о́пері.
14. Я ба́чив (гість), що їв у готе́лі.
15. Я до́бре знав (ва́ша дочка́ О́льга) й (ваш ста́рший син Іва́нко).
16. Хто знав (той те́мний брюне́т) ?
17. Ми вчо́ра ба́чили (твій стари́й друг).

Drill #29

Translate into Ukrainian.

1. Did you see the hero of our capital when he was in your city?
2. No, but I saw him when I was in the capital.
3. Where did Shevchenko write the book *Kobzar*?[1]
4. Have you read Shevchenko's book, the *Kobzar*?
5. Yes, I have read it.
6. Where did you see us?
7. I saw you in a store, but you didn't see me.
8. Whom did you know there? I knew only their sister.
9. Did you see our brother? Yes, I saw him.
10. Have you seen my novel? Yes, I saw it.
11. Have you seen my dictionary? No, I haven't seen it.

4.2 THE ACCUSATIVE CASE WITH TIME EXPRESSIONS

Besides serving as the case of the direct object, the accusative case is used to designate the period of time in which an action is carried out:

Вони́ працюва́ли ціли́й день.
They worked the whole day.

---

1 When a title is used with a noun which identifies it as book, play, poem, etc., only the identifying noun is declined.

Ми працювáли ти́ждень.
We worked a week.

4.3 PRESENT TENSE OF VERBS

As nouns are arranged into declensions, Ukrainian verbs are arranged into conjugations when they are in the present tense. There are basically two conjugations in Ukrainian.

The first conjugation is designated by the "theme" vowel **-е/-є** which appears in the endings of all but the 1st person singular and 3rd person plural.

The second conjugation is designated by the "theme" vowel **-и/-ї** which appears in the endings of all but the 1st person singular and 3rd person plural.

The first conjugation has the theme vowel (**-е/-є**) ending in the 3rd person singular and the 3rd person plural ends in **-уть/-ють**.

The second conjugation has the 3rd person singular ending **-ить/-їть** and the 3rd person plural ends in **-ать/-ять**.

4.31 The endings of the two conjugations in the present tense are added to the present stem of the verb. In many cases the present stem of the verb is derived by subtracting the infinitive ending **-ти**. This is not, however, always the case and often the present stem of the verb must be memorized along with the infinitive.

	First Conjugation Singular	Second Conjugation Singular
1st pers.	**-у,**[1] **-ю**	**-у,**[1] **-ю**
2nd pers.	**-еш, -єш**	**-иш -їш**
3rd pers.	**-е, -є**	**-ить, -їть**
	Plural	Plural
1st pers.	**-емо, -ємо**	**-имо, -їмо**
2nd pers.	**-ете, -єте**	**-ите, -їте**
3rd pers.	**-уть,**[1] **-ють**	**-ать,**[1] **-ять**

1 **-у, -уть, -ать** are used after sibilants and some other consonants.

Infinitive:	писа́-ти	чита́-ти	ба́чи-ти	стоя́-ти
Pres. Stem	пиш-	чита-	бач-	сто-
1st pers.	пиш-у́	чита́-ю	ба́ч-у	сто-ю́
2nd pers.	пи́ш-еш	чита́-єш	ба́ч-иш	сто-ї́ш
3rd pers.	пи́ш-е	чита́-є	ба́ч-ить	сто-ї́ть
1st pers. pl.	пи́ш-емо	чита́-ємо	ба́ч-имо	сто-їмо́
2nd pers. pl.	пи́ш-ете	чита́-єте	ба́ч-ите	сто-їте́
3rd pers. pl.	пи́ш-уть	чита́-ють	ба́ч-ать	сто-я́ть

4.32 THE PRESENT STEM OF **-ува** VERBS.

Verbs which have the suffix **-ува/-юва** in the infinitive drop the **-ва** in forming the present stem and in conjugating in the present tense:

Infinitive	Past Tense	Present Stem	2nd pers. sing.
поя́снювати	поя́снював	поя́сню-	поя́снюєш
працюва́ти	працюва́в	працю́-	працю́єш
турбува́ти	турбува́в	турбу́-	турбу́єш

4.33 SECOND CONJUGATION VERBS (Continued)

Second conjugation verbs with stems ending in the labial consonants **-б, -в, -м, -п, -ф** have an л inserted after the labial consonant in the first person singular and the third person plural:

to sleep:	спа́ти — сплю, спиш . . . сплять
to like:	люби́ти — люблю́, лю́биш . . . лю́блять

Drill #30

Translate into English:

1. Я зачина́ю розумі́ти, що́ ви гово́рите.
2. Я відпочива́ю, коли́ я слу́хаю му́зику.
3. Всі все розумі́ють, коли́ ви не ду́же ско́ро гово́рите.
4. Коли́ я не розумі́ю, пита́ю вчи́теля.
5. Де ви купу́єте сир? Я купу́ю його́ в малі́й крамни́ці на мої́й ву́лиці.
6. Ми кінча́ємо нову́ ле́кцію.
7. Вони́ кінча́ють чита́ти нудну́ кни́жку, але́ я ще не зачина́в її́.

8. Мій моло́дший брат купу́є нову́ пласти́нку ма́йже ці́лий день.
9. Його́ ста́рша сестра́ слу́хає ти́ху му́зику.
10. Я говорю́ або́ по-украї́нському або́ по-англі́йському.

Drill #31

Fill in the correct endings of the verbs:

1. Я шви́дко працю́ .....
2. Що ти пита́ ..... ?
3. Що вони́ гово́р ..... ?
4. Ми вас слу́ха .....
5. Вони́ відпочива́ .....
6. Він гово́р ..... по-англі́йському.
7. Чому́ ти кінча́ ..... кни́жку?
8. Я не розумі́ ....., що ти гово́р .....
9. Ви до́бре поя́сню ..... грама́тику.
10. Що вони́ гра́ ..... ?
11. Вони́ гово́р ..... по-украї́нському.
12. Ми зачина́ ..... розумі́ .....

Drill #32

Change the infinitives in parentheses to the correct forms of the present tense and translate the sentences into English:

1. Вони́ ду́же (працюва́ти).
2. Де ви (купува́ти) газе́ту?
3. Вони́ (говори́ти) ду́же пові́лі.
4. Я (розумі́ти) все, що ти (говори́ти).
5. Я його́ (пита́ти), де він (працюва́ти).
6. Чому́ ти не (слу́хати), коли́ (говори́ти) ?
7. Я за́вжди (слу́хати), коли́ ти (говори́ти).
8. Іва́нко (зачиня́ти) вікно́, а ви (відчиня́ти) його́.
9. Що ви (роби́ти) ? Я (зачиня́ти) вікно́.
10. Ми (зачина́ти) (чита́ти) нови́й рома́н.
11. Вони́ (кінча́ти) (писа́ти) о́перу.
12. Я і́ноді (відпочива́ти), і́нколи (працюва́ти).
13. Ви не (працюва́ти), ви (говори́ти).
14. Вони́ (відпочива́ти) в селі́.
15. Що ти (ду́мати) ? Я не (зна́ти).
16. Ви не (слу́хати), коли́ вони́ (говори́ти).

4.4 NEGATIVE EXPRESSIONS

Many negative expressions are formed in Ukrainian by prefixing **ні-** to an interrogative:

Interrogative	Negative	English translation
коли́	ніко́ли	never
хто	ніхто́	no one (*nom.*)
кого́	ніко́го	no one
що	ніщо́	nothing (*nom.*)
чого́	нічо́го	nothing
де	ніде́	nowhere
	ні . . . ні	neither . . . nor

Unlike English, Ukrainian requires the use of a double negative:

Я ніко́ли ніко́го ніде́ не ба́чив. (4 negatives)
I never saw anybody anywhere (literally: I never did not see no one nowhere).

4.5 DECLENSION OF NUMERAL оди́н "ONE"

The numeral **оди́н, одна́, одне́** declines like **той, та, те**. The **и** of the masculine nominative drops out of all oblique (other than nominative) cases:

	Masculine	Feminine	Neuter
Nom.	**оди́н**	**одна́**	**одне́, (одно́)**
Gen.	**одно́го́**[1]	**одніє́ї (одно́ї)**	**одно́го́**
Acc.	**одно́го́** **оди́н**	**одну́**	**одне́, (одно́)**
Loc.	**(на) одно́му́**	**(на) одні́й**	**(на) одно́му́**

The word оди́н sometimes has the meaning of the English "a"/"a certain".

> Я зна́ю *одного́* неприє́много чолові́ка.
> I know *a certain* unpleasant man.

---

1 The first stress is used primarily when following a preposition.

4.6 THE USE OF пови́нен "MUST/SHOULD"

The word пови́нен agrees in gender and number with the subject and is used with infinitives to mean "one must", "has to":

Masc.	він пови́нен чита́ти	he should read
Neut.	воно́ пови́нне слу́хати	it should listen
Fem.	вона́ пови́нна переклада́ти	she should translate
Pl.	вони́ пови́нні ду́мати	they should think

Він тепе́р пови́нен працюва́ти.
He must (has to) work now.

Drill #33

Translate into English:

1. Я ніч́ого не розумі́ю, коли́ ви ско́ро гово́рите.
2. Чому́ ви ніко́ли нічо́го не пита́єте?
3. Ви пови́нні мене́ пита́ти, коли́ ви не розумі́єте, що я говорю́.
4. Тут ніхто́ не гово́рить по-украї́нському.
5. Ми вчо́ра ніде́ не були́.
6. Вони́ переклада́ли одну́ кни́жку, яку́ ви до́бре зна́єте, але́ яку́ ви давно́ не чита́ли.
7. Ми жили́ у Льво́ві ма́йже ціли́й ти́ждень. Ми там ніко́го не зна́ли.
8. Я ще ніко́го тут не зна́ю.
9. Він ду́має, що він уже́ все зна́є, але́ всі зна́ють, що він ма́йже нічо́го не зна́є.
10. Íгор пови́нен бі́льше чита́ти.

Drill #34

Translate into Ukrainian:

1. You never work. You must work more.
2. Why don't you do anything?
3. Why do you never listen when I speak? You must listen!
4. We do not work today; we are resting.
5. We don't know anything.
6. They never speak Ukrainian.

7. He doesn't do anything.
8. Nowhere did I see her.
9. They do not do anything all day.
10. Today he was neither at the lesson nor at home.

Homework

a) Memorize the vocabulary in Lesson #5;
b) Review Lesson #4;
c) Translate the following sentences into Ukrainian.

1. The blond (m.) understands the blonde (f.), but the brunette (f.) does not understand her.
2. A good student should, for example, talk less and listen more.
3. Every fat red book is not a dictionary.
4. New York is not in Canada, it is in America.
5. In our museum there is one very narrow theater.
6. lhor must read a whole month.
7. One city in Ukraine, for example, is Lviv.
8. That unpleasant girl did not listen at your concert.
9. Only when I sleep do I rest. Rest[1] is very pleasant.
10. On the shelf stood a glass of wine which no one drank at the party.

---

1 Use the infinitive.

CHAPTER FIVE

СЛОВНИ́К

Іме́нники жіно́чого ро́ду

ба́йка, -и	fairy tale
впра́ва, -и	exercise
гіта́ра, -и	guitar
господи́ня, -і	landlady
істо́рія, -ї	history
кля́са, -и	class
ра́да, -и	council
ри́ба, -и	fish
телегра́ма, -и	telegram

Іме́нники чолові́чого ро́ду

а́втор, -а	author
ге́ній, -я	genius
дару́нок, -нку	gift
джаз, -у	jazz
дире́ктор, -а	director
інжене́р, -а	engineer
клас, -у	class
костю́м, -а	suit
лі́кар, -я	doctor
музика́нт, -а	musician
нача́льник, -а	chief, boss
пра́зник, -а	holiday
приві́т, -у	greeting
ра́нок, -нку	morning
телеві́зор, -а	television set
телефо́н, -у	telephone

Іме́нники сере́днього ро́ду

бю́ро, -а	office ; **бюро́** (indeclinable)
пра́вило, -а	rule
ра́діо	radio (indeclinable except in instr. case)
Торо́нто, -а	Toronto

Прикме́тники

дурни́й, -а́, -е́	foolish, stupid
ми́лий, -а, -е	nice, sweet, kind, charming
оригіна́льний, -а, -е	original

правди́вий, -а, -е	real
розу́мний, -а, -е	intelligent
сві́жий, -а, -е	fresh
спра́вжній, -я, -є	genuine
талanови́тий, -а, -е	talented
ціка́вий, -а, -е	interesting

Дієслова́

помага́ти (*помага́ю, помага́єш*)	to help
посила́ти (*посила́ю, посила́єш*)	to send
пока́зувати (*пока́зую, пока́зуєш*)	to show
дава́ти (*даю́, дає́ш*)	to give
ра́дити (*ра́джу, ра́диш*)	to counsel
телефонува́ти (*телефону́ю, телефону́єш*)	to telephone

Прислі́вники та інші слова́

а	and, but (*conj.*)
звича́йно	usually, of course (*adv.*)
рі́дко	rarely, seldom (*adv.*)
та	and (*conj.*)
це ле́гко	that's easy
ча́сто	frequently (*adv.*)

Ви́рази

Го́споди!	Oh, my God!
на ду́мку	in the opinion of
посила́ти приві́т	to send greetings

Імена́

Аско́льд, -а	Askold
Богда́н, -а	Bohdan
Васи́ль, -я́	Vasyl
Ві́ра -и	Vira
Гриць, -я	Hryts
Миро́н, -а	Myron
Окса́на, -и	Oksana
Окса́нка, -и	Oksanka (*dim.*)
Оста́п, -а	Ostap
Павло́, -а́	Pavlo
Ро́ма, -и	Roma
Сте́фа, -и	Stefa

GRAMMAR

Adverbs of Time — Прислíвники чáсу (5.0)
Dative Case of Nouns — Давáльний відмíнок имéнників (5.1)
Dative Case of Modifiers — Давáльний відмíнок прикмéтників і займéнників (5.2—5.21)
Dative of State or Condition — Давáльний відмíнок при словáх категóрії стáну (5.3)
The use of трéба — Вживáння слóва трéба *(5.4)*
First Conjugation (Cont.) — Пéрша дієвідмíна (продóв.) (5.5—5.51)
Present Tense of the Verb давáти — *Теперíшній час дієслóва* давáти *(5.6)*
The Reflexive Possessive Pronoun — Присвíйний займéнник свій *(5.7)*

5.0 ADVERBS OF TIME WITH що + GENITIVE

In Ukrainian, words which designate segments of time, like "morning", "evening", "day", "month", "year", etc., are combined with що to form adverbs which indicate repetitiveness of that segment of time: "every morning", etc. The newly formed adverb is written as one word and consists of що + the genitive case of the given word:

щорáнку	що + gen. of рáнок	every morning
щовéчора	що + gen. of вéчір	every evening
щодня́	що + gen. of день	every day
щомíсяця	що + gen. of мíсяць	every month

5.1 DATIVE CASE OF NOUNS

The dative case denotes the recipient or addressee (the indirect object) of something that is given, sent, transmitted, or communicated (the direct object). In English, the dative case is expressed by its position in the sentence or by the use of the preposition "to".

Він давáв **Івáнові** кни́жку.
He was giving **Ivan** a book. (The indirect object precedes the direct)
He was giving a book **to Ivan**. (Use of "to")

The endings of nouns in the dative case are as follows:

		Nominative	Dative	Endings
Masc.	hard	стіл	столо́ві	**-ові (-у)**
	mixed	ніж	ноже́ві	**-еві (-у)**
	soft	учи́тель	учи́телеві	**-еві (-ю)**
Fem.	hard	жі́нка	жі́нці[1]	**-і**
	mixed	межа́	межі́	**-і**
	soft	ку́хня	ку́хні	**-і**
Neut.	hard	вікно́	вікну́	**-у**
	mixed	прі́звище	прі́звищу	**-у**
	soft	по́ле	по́лю	**-ю**

Drill #35

Translate into English:

1. Щора́нку Іва́нко Світли́чний поя́снює секрета́рці, що́ (what) вона́ пови́нна роби́ти ввесь день.
2. Ма́ти щоти́жня купу́є пласти́нку і посила́є її́ си́нові.
3. Син на́шого лі́каря, що тепе́р живе́ в Торо́нті, ча́сто телефону́є Ві́рі.
4. Я помага́ю при́ятелеві в його́ нові́й кварти́рі.
5. Я посила́ю телегра́му Бори́сові.
6. Він ніко́ли не помага́є учи́телеві.

Drill #36

Put the words in parentheses into the correct case and translate each sentence.

1. Я помага́ю (брат).
2. Я слу́хаю (брат).
3. Він учо́ра ба́чив (профе́сор Кузьме́нко).
4. Він помага́є (профе́сор Кузьме́нко).
5. Я пита́ю (друг), що́ він ро́бить.
6. Коли́ ви ба́чили (лі́кар)?
7. Що ти поя́снюєш (Гриць)?

---

1 Note the change of **к** to **ц** with addition of ending **-і** (*see 2.23*).

8. Коли́ ти ба́чив (Ві́ра)?
9. Студе́нт відповіда́є (вчи́телька).
10. Він пита́є (вчи́телька), що він тепе́р пови́нен чита́ти.

Drill #37

Translate into Ukrainian:

1. Whom are you helping? I am helping my brother.
2. Whom is the student answering? He is answering the teacher who is questioning him.
3. To whom is the teacher explaining the new rule? To a girl student.
4. To whom are you giving your new suit? To Askold.
5. To whom are you sending this book? I am sending it to a friend.
6. I don't understand whom you are counseling.
7. Who was explaining this rule in class?
8. He is sending greetings to Oksanka.
9. I am sending the new journal to doctor Savchuk.
10. Whom does he know, and to whom is he sending his regards?

5.2 DATIVE OF MODIFIERS

Masculine and Neuter

		Nominative		Dative
		Masc.	Neut.	Masc./Neut.
3rd pers. pron.		**він**	**воно́**	**йому́**
Adj.	(*hard*)	**білий**	**біле**	**білому**
	(*soft*)	**си́ній**	**си́нє**	**си́ньому**
Poss. pron.		**мій**	**моє́**	**моє́му**
		твій	**твоє́**	**твоє́му**
Dem. pron.		**той**	**те**	**то́му**
		цей	**це**	**цьо́му (це́му)**
Interr. pron.		**хто?**	**що?**	**кому́? чому́?**
		чий?	**чиє́?**	**чийо́му? (чиє́му?)**

Feminine

		Nominative	Dative
3rd pers. pron.		вона́	її́й
Adj.	(*hard*)	біла	білій
	(*soft*)	си́ня	си́ній
Poss. pron.		моя́	мої́й
		твоя́	твої́й
Dem. pron.		та	тій
		ця	цій
Interr. pron.		чия́	чиї́й

5.21 Personal pronouns have the following forms in the dative case:

Nom.	я	ти	ми	ви	вони́
Dat.	мені́	тобі́	нам	вам	їм

Drill #38

Translate into English:

1. Щове́чора ма́ма чита́є ціка́ву ба́йку мені́ й мої́й мале́нькій сестрі́.
2. Кому́ ви поя́снювали на́шу украї́нську істо́рію? Я поя́снював її́ моє́му до́брому дру́гові.
3. Моя́ ма́ма посила́є приві́т тій ти́хій ми́лій ді́вчині, яку́ вона́ ба́чила в ва́шому бю́рі.
4. Ви не пови́нні поя́снювати до́брій господи́ні, де й що́ вона́ пови́нна купува́ти.
5. Як ле́гко поя́снювати грама́тику розу́мному студе́нтові.
6. Котро́му дире́кторові ви посила́єте кни́жку? На́шому.

Drill #39

Put the words in parentheses into the correct case:

1. Дани́ло гово́рить (молода́ блонди́нка), що вона́ ду́же га́рна.
2. Профе́сор поя́снює (таланови́тий музика́нт), як гра́ти на ґіта́рі.

3. Ви не пови́нні говори́ти (спра́вжній письме́нник), як писа́ти рома́н.
4. Я посила́ю приві́т (твоя́ ми́ла дружи́на).
5. Ми пока́зуємо мі́сто (украї́нська журналі́стка і кана́дський журналі́ст).
6. Ми посила́ємо дару́нок (ти й твоя́ мала́ сестра́).

Drill #40

Translate into Ukrainian:

1. He is sending the magazine to a talented young man.
2. He was saying that to your older brother.
3. We are explaining jazz to the new musician.
4. Whom is he helping? He is helping me today.
5. We always help him and his wife, but they never help us.
6. Every day I explain to my dear husband why he must write to my sister every week.

5.3 DATIVE OF STATE OR CONDITION

When states of being or condition are experienced by a person, that person is denoted by a noun or pronoun in the dative case, and the construction includes the impersonal use of the adverb (*see 3.71*).

Мені́ хо́лодно.
I am cold.

Іва́нові було́ ну́дно.
Ivan was bored.

Note the difference when an adjective is used instead of an adverb:

Іва́н нудни́й.
Ivan is boring.

5.4 THE USE OF THE WORD тре́ба

The word тре́ба followed by an infinitive expresses the idea that "it is necessary" to do something, that something "must, should, has to be done."

This construction may be used impersonally:

Тре́ба говори́ти пра́вду.
One should speak the truth.

When a person is referred to, that person is in the dative case.

The *dative case* construction + **тре́ба** + *infinitive* equals the *nominative case* + пови́нен + **infinitive** construction in its use in the Ukrainian language.

Мені́ тре́ба говори́ти пра́вду.
I must speak the truth.

Я пови́нен говори́ти пра́вду.
I should speak the truth.

Although the constructions are practically synonymous, *dative case* + тре́ба + *infinitive* implies *need*, while *nominative case* + **пови́нен** + *infinitive* implies *moral obligation.*

The word **тре́ба** can also be used with a noun. The noun which expresses that of which there is a need is in the genitive case, the one who needs is in the dative.

Мені́ тре́ба а́вта.
I need a car.

Drill #41

Translate into Ukrainian:

1. I am closing the window because my sister feels cold.
2. She was bored.
3. You need to read more.
4. Ostap must work less.
5. He was pleased (*it was pleasant for him*) to see me.
6. Are you cold?
7. It was interesting for us to listen to her.
8. It was very interesting for my son to listen to you.
9. My son is so interesting!
10. She is bored.
11. She is boring.
12. You don't need to work so much now.

5.5 FIRST CONJUGATION VERBS (Continued)

Most of the first conjugation verbs studied up till now have present stems ending in a vowel and hence take the vowel **-є-** for the indicator of the first conjugation, e.g., **чита́ти, чита́єш**. A large group of verbs, however, has a conjugation vowel **-е-** and the third person plural **-уть**, as well as first person singular ending in **-у**. These are verbs that have the present stem ending in a consonant, like **жи́ти — живу́** or in a consonant sibilant, like **писа́ти — пишу́**.

Verbs with a consonant stem in the present conjugate in the following way:

Infinitive	жи́ти	писа́ти
	Singular	
1st pers.	живу́	пишу́
2nd pers.	живе́ш	пи́шеш
3rd pers.	живе́	пи́ше
	Plural	
1st pers.	живемо́	пи́шемо
2nd pers.	живете́	пи́шете
3rd pers.	живу́ть	пи́шуть

Note that the infinitive stem of the verb **писа́ти** is **писа́-** but that the present stem is **пиш-**. Likewise for the verb **жи́ти**, the infinitive stem is **жи-** and the present stem is **жив-**. Because of such irregularities, it is necessary to memorize three forms of each verb: the infinitive (which also enables one to form the past tense), the first person singular, and the second person singular. Knowing these three forms, the student will be able to form all the required verb forms.

5.51 Verb stress:

Verbs in which the stress falls on the vowel before the infinitive ending **-а́ти, -я́ти** retain this stress on these vowels throughout the conjugation.

Many other verbs have the stress falling on the final vowel throughout the conjugation: живу́, живе́ш, живе́, живемо́, живете́, живу́ть.

5.6 THE PRESENT TENSE OF THE VERB дава́ти "TO GIVE"

Although it is not a verb with the **-ува-** suffix (*see 4.32*), the verb **давати** behaves in the same way, since in the present conjugation it drops the **-ва**. This is true of all other verbs which are formed from the same root, such as **продава́ти** "to sell", and **передава́ти** "to pass on."

	Singular	Plural
1st pers.	даю́	даємо́
2nd pers.	дає́ш	даєте́
3rd. pers.	дає́	даю́ть.

Drill #42

Put the words in parentheses into the correct case and translate the sentence:

1. Він дає́ кни́жку (профе́сор Даре́вич).
2. Я пишу́ рома́н, а Ві́ра помага́є (я).
3. Звича́йно, І́гор не слу́хає (учи́тель), але́ ча́сто ра́дить (він), як поя́снювати грама́тику.
4. Я пита́ю (сестра́), чому́ вона́ так рі́дко пи́ше.
5. Я пита́ю (Іва́н), де він (жи́ти).
6. Я гово́рю (Іва́нко), де я (жи́ти).
7. Лі́кар ра́дить (наш молоди́й друг).

Drill #43

Fill in the blanks with the suitable form of the verbs:

1. Що ви пиш ..... ?
2. Я пиш ..... кни́жку.
3. Вони́ ча́сто пи́ш .....
4. Га́ня й Ро́ма жив ..... тут. Ви тако́ж тут жив ..... ?
5. Ми щомі́сяця пи́ш .....
6. Я тепе́р жив ..... тут. Ви тако́ж тут жив ..... ?

Drill #44

Translate into Ukrainian:

1. I often give my dictionary to Pavlo and his wife.
2. I am giving my pen to Stefa.
3. Why are you giving your library to Natalka and not to Vasyl?
4. Sometimes he counsels us well.
5. There was no dictionary in the classroom.
6. Roma is giving Bohdan the teacher's dictionary.
7. My friend Myron is writing a novel.

5.7 THE REFLEXIVE POSSESSIVE PRONOUN **свій** "ONE'S OWN"

Ukrainian has a possessive reflexive pronoun **свій, своя́, своє́** "one's own," which refers back to the subject of its sentence or clause in meaning, but agrees with the noun it modifies in gender and case. **Свій** is declined like **мій**.

Я даю́ свою́ кни́жку мої́й сестрі́.
I am giving my book to my sister.

When the subject is in the first two persons, the possessive pronouns **мій, твій, наш, ваш** may be used instead of **свій**. However, this is not the case if the subject is in the third person. With the third person, **свій** must always be distinguished from **його́, її́, їх**.

Він до́бре зна́є своє́ мі́сто.
He knows *his* (*own*) city well.

Він до́бре зна́є його́ мі́сто.
He knows *his* (*someone else's*) city well.

Remember that **свій** can refer back only to the subject of its own clause. Note the following:

Він гово́рить, що його́ ма́ма вдо́ма.
He says that his mother is at home.

Here **свій** cannot be used, even though the mother is "his own", since **він**, to whom the possessive **його́** refers, is the subject of a different clause.

Drill #45

Translate into Ukrainian:

1. Myron helps his father.
2. I help Ostap and his father.
3. He is buying a present for his wife.
4. Borys is buying a present for his (*Petro's*) wife.
5. She is a good sister; she helps her brother.
6. He is a good husband; he is buying a dress for his wife.
7. He was in his wife's room.
8. He was in his (*Pavlo's*) room.
9. She is buying a present for her husband, and Hryts is also buying a present for her husband.
10. They say that their father is now living in Toronto.
11. Askold saw his friend and says that his friend is now working here.
12. He is a bad man; he never helps either his family or his brother's family.

Drill #46

Translate the English words into Ukrainian and fill in the blanks with the proper form of the Ukrainian interrogative:

1.	Who	поя́снює грама́тику?
2.	Whom	він зна́є?
3.	To whom	вони́ даю́ть той словни́к?
4.	What (which one)	студе́нтку ви ба́чили?
5.	Who	там був ?
6.	What (which one)	журна́л ви чита́єте?
7.	What (which one)	інжене́ра вона́ ба́чила?
8.	What (which one)	журналі́стка була́ на вечі́рці ?
9.	To what (which one)	журналі́стці ви сього́дні даєте́ ле́кцію?
10.	To whom	ти продає́ш твоє́ перо́?
11.	To what (which one)	студе́нтові ти поя́снюєш пра́вило ?
12.	What	ви пи́шете та переклада́єте ?
13.	What	ра́дите мені́?

Homework

a) Memorize the vocabulary in Lesson #6;
b) Review Lesson #5;
c) Translate the following sentences into Ukrainian.

1. We live in my brother's house, and they live in their sister's house.
2. To whom do you explain the exercise everyday in class?
3. Why don't you say anything to the "genius"?
4. What is he buying for you?
5. Are you sending Stefa a fish?
6. No, I am sending her a Ukrainian novel of a very talented author.
7. They never telephone us, and we never telephone them.
8. The Council counsels us to live in Canada.
9. To whom are you sending this television set?
10. I am sending it to a Canadian journalist.
11. It is hard for him always to speak Ukrainian, and therefore he often speaks English.
12. For Petro, of course, that is easy; he is Ukrainian (українець).
13. It is boring for us to listen to her.
14. Our boss gave me a radio and a TV set.
15. Why don't you explain this stupid rule to me?
16. Oh, my God! In my office there is a fish on my table where there was always a telephone.
17. In the opinion of Myron and Olha we need a holiday.
18. He is a true friend and an original author.
19. I need a guitar!

CHAPTER SIX

СЛОВНИ́К

Іме́нники жіно́чого ро́ду

війна́, -и	war
віта́льня, -і	living room
допомо́га, -и	help
голова́, -и́	head
їда́льня, -і	dining room
книга́рня, -і	bookstore
лазни́чка, -и	bathroom
му́ха, -и	fly
нога́, -и́	leg, foot
пра́ця, -і	work
соба́ка[1], -и	dog
спа́льня, -і	bedroom
сусі́дка, -и	neighbor (*f.*)
учени́ця, -і	pupil (*f.*)
ча́шка, -и	cup

Іме́нники чолові́чого ро́ду

ки́лим, -а	carpet
мир, -у	peace
обі́д, -у	dinner
олів́е́ць, -вця́	pencil
пере́клад, -у	translation
пес, пса	dog
підру́чник, -а	handbook
сусі́д, -а	neighbor (*m.*)
у́чень, у́чня	pupil (*m.*)
хара́ктер, -у	character

Іме́нники сере́днього ро́ду

бю́рко, -а	desk
горня́тко, -а	a small pot, cup
лі́жко, -а	bed
у́хо/ву́хо, -а	ear
(в у́сі/у ву́сі)	in the ear

---

1 **соба́ка**, though a feminine noun by stucture, can be used for both male and female dogs. The specific word for "bitch" is **су́ка**.

Прикме́тники

англі́йський, -а, -е	English
бага́тий, -а, -е	rich
в/у/дово́лений, -а, -е	satisfied
висо́кий, -а, -е	tall
в/у/чора́шній, -я, -є	yesterday's
зи́мний, -а, -е	cold
ліни́вий, -а, -е	lazy
невдово́лений, -а, -е	dissatisfied
низьки́й, -а́, -е́	low
пи́льний, -а, -е	diligent
потрі́бний, -а, -е	needed
ра́дий, -а, -е	glad
сього́днішній, -я, -е	today's

Дієслова́

дзвони́ти (*дзвоню́, дзво́ниш*)	to ring
могти́ (*мо́жу, мо́жеш*)	to be able
му́сити (му́сіти) (*му́шу, му́сиш*)	to be obliged (must)
хоті́ти (*хо́чу, хо́чеш*)	to want
ма́ти (*ма́ю, ма́єш*)	to have

Прислі́вники та інші слова́

без	without (*prep. + gen.*)
до	to, up to (*prep. + gen.*)
га́ряче́	hot (*adv.*)
до́сить	enough (*adv.*)
за́втра	tomorrow (*adv.*)
зи́мно	cold (*adv.*)
крім	besides, except (*prep. + gen.*)
пі́сля	after (*prep. + gen.*)
про́сто	simply, straight (*adv.*)
пря́мо	straight (*adv.*)
тоді́	then (*adv.*)
хоч/хоча́	although (*conj.*)
якщо́	if (*conj.*)

Ви́рази

бі́льше ні	no more, no longer
вели́ке спаси́бі (спаси́-біг)	many thanks
мені́ все одно́	I don't care; It's all the same to me
мо́же бу́ти	maybe, perhaps
нема́ за́що	that's nothing
не мо́же бу́ти	it can't be
що́ мені́ роби́ти?	what am I to do?
я пря́мо не зна́ю	I simply don't know

GRAMMAR

Future Tense of the Verb бу́ти *"to be" — Майбу́тній час дієсло́ва* бу́ти *(6.0—6.01)*
Direct Object in the Genitive Case — Прями́й дода́ток у родово́му відмі́нку (6.1)
Prepositions governing the Genitive Case — Прийме́нники, що керу́ють родови́м відмі́нком (6.2—6.21)
The Verb ма́ти *"to have" — Дієсло́во* ма́ти *(6.3)*
Genitive after Preposition у/в *— Родови́й відмі́нок після прийме́нника* у/в *(6.4)*
The Use of the Adjectival Participle потрі́бний *"needed" — Вжива́ння дієприкме́тника* потрі́бний *(6.5)*
Vocative Case of Nouns — Кли́чний відмі́нок іме́нників (6.6—6.63)
Helping-Auxiliary Verbs — Допоміжні́ дієслова́ (6.7)

6.0 FUTURE TENSE OF THE VERB бу́ти "TO BE"

	Singular	Plural
1st pers.	бу́ду	ми бу́демо
2nd pers.	ти бу́деш	ви бу́дете
3rd pers.	він, вона́, воно́ бу́де	вони́ бу́дуть

6.01 The conjunction якщо́ + future.

In Ukrainian якщо́ "if" requires the future tense when the action or state referred to is in the future. This construction in English is rendered by the present tense:

Якщо́ за́втра бу́де хо́лодно .....
If it is cold tomorrow .....

Drill #47

Translate into English:

1. Він ще не зна́є, де він за́втра бу́де.
2. За́втра ми ввесь день не бу́демо вдо́ма.
3. Іва́н учо́ра не був у бібліоте́ці.
4. Коли́ я був у бібліоте́ці, Іва́на там не було́.

5. Якщó зáвтра бýде гарячé, я бýду ввесь день удóма.
6. Ви дýмаєте, що там нікóго не бýде?
7. У кабінéті дзвони́в телефóн, алé там нікóго не булó.
8. Моя́ дружи́на бýде дýже рáда вас бáчити.

Drill #48

Fill in the blanks with the proper forms of the future tense of the verb "to be":

1. Де ви ..... зáвтра?
2. Зáвтра ..... вдóма.
3. Де сьогóдні ..... Івáнко?
4. Він ..... в бібліотéці.
5. Ми ..... в шкóлі. Ви такóж там .....?
6. Так, ми такóж там .....
7. Хто ще там .....?
8. Там ..... Макси́м і Натáлка.
9. Де ви ..... ? Я не знáю, де .....

Drill #49

Translate into Ukrainian:

1. There is a library here.
2. There is no library here.
3. There was a library here.
4. There will be a library here.
5. There will be no library here.
6. There is a town here.
7. There is no town here.
8. There was a town here.
9. There will be a town here.
10. There will be no town here.

6.1 DIRECT OBJECT IN THE GENITIVE CASE

As was the case with **немáє** (*see 3.6*), in Ukrainian the object of a negated verb is not in the accusative but in the genitive.

Я їв обід.	Я не їв обíду.
I ate dinner.	I did not eat dinner.

6.2 PREPOSITIONS GOVERNING THE GENITIVE CASE

The prepositions **до, після, без,** and **крім** have their object in the genitive case.

до	to, toward, till
після	after
без	without
крім	besides, except

Я йду́ до ха́ти. Після ле́кції ми йдемо́ до ха́ти всі, крім Іва́на і всі без кни́жки/книжо́к.

I am going home (to the house). After the lesson we are all going home except for Ivan and all without a book/books.

6.21 The third person pronouns in the genitive case **його́, її́, їх** prefix an **н-** when used as objects of prepositions. The stress moves one syllable forward:

без ньо́го, без не́ї, без них — у ньо́го, у не́ї, у них.
without him, without her, without them — at his (*place*), at her (*place*), at their (*place*).

його́ but до ньо́го
її́ but до не́ї

Drill #50

Translate into English:

1. Я не ба́чив його́ після війни́.
2. Де ти бу́деш після пра́ці?
3. Що́ вона́ роби́ла після обі́ду?
4. Я після цьо́го не ба́чив його́.
5. До війни́ ми ніко́ли тут не були́.
6. Хто там був, крім вас ?
7. Що ви ї́ли, крім си́ру?
8. Нам тру́дно жи́ти без не́ї.
9. Я сього́дні нічо́го не їв, крім хлі́ба й ри́би.
10. Ми були́ в цьо́му рестора́ні без Га́ні.
11. Сусі́д тепе́р живе́ без них.

Drill #51

Translate the words in parentheses:

1. Я ба́чив Павла́ (after the concert).
2. Ми бу́демо вдо́ма (after the theater).
3. Вона́ була́ там без (Mykola and Stefa).
4. Я бу́ду тут (after work).
5. Ми тепе́р живемо́ (without Oksana).
6. Хто бу́де вдо́ма, (besides Olya and Roma? Except for them), там ніко́го не бу́де.
7. Нам ну́дно жи́ти (without him and without her).
8. Вона́ бу́де там (without her brother).
9. Той журналі́ст нічо́го не ба́чив, (besides Lviv and Kyiv).
10. На столі́ нічо́го не бу́ло, (except fish), ми ї́ли ри́бу (without bread).

Drill #52

Translate into Ukrainian:

1. He never drank anything but (except for) water.
2. They never relax after work.
3. My husband was at the theater without me.
4. We will all be there after dinner.
5. Everyone was there except him.
6. Everybody was there except his son.
7. Will you be at home after the opera?
8. Where did you live till today?

6.3 THE VERB ма́ти "TO HAVE"

Ukrainian, like English, uses the verb **ма́ти (я ма́ю, ти ма́єш)** "to have" to show possession.

Я ма́ю ха́ту.
I have a house.

Я не ма́ю ха́ти.
I don't have a house.

6.4 PREPOSITION у/в + GENITIVE CASE

The construction у/в + *genitive* of the noun or pronoun is used in Ukrainian to render the meaning "at the house of":

Сьогóдні я був у сестри́.
Today I was at my sister's (place).

This construction is also used sometimes in place of the verb мáти to show possession:

У мéне є хáта.
I have a house.

У мéне немáє хáти.
I don't have a house.

У мéне не булó хáти.
I did not have a house.

Drill #53

Translate into English:

1. Остáп і Олéнка нічóго не мáють.
2. Вони́ нікóли нічóго не мáли.
3. У них нікóли нічóго не бýде.
4. Бори́с говори́ть, що він мáє дóбрий францýзький словни́к, алé він тепéр у Андрія.
5. Ти мáєш словни́к Бори́са? Так, я мáю йогó.
6. Хто мáє мою́ газéту? Óльга.
7. Хто мáє цікáву кни́жку?
8. Ніхтó не мáє цікáвої кни́жки.
9. Мирóн нікóли не мав áвта?
10. Ні, у ньóго булó áвто, алé тепéр він йогó не мáє.
11. Віра мáє хáту в селí. Вчóра всі, крім Аскóльда й Петрá, були́ в нéї.
12. У кóго живé йогó мáма? Вонá живé у своéї молóдшої сестри́.
13. У кóго працю́є ваш стáрший брат? Він працю́є в дóктора Старакá.
14. Вчóра всі були́ в нас.

15. За́втра всі бу́дуть у ново́го вчи́теля.
16. Ваш стари́й профе́сор ма́є молоду́ дружи́ну.
17. У ко́го ви ба́чили ту кни́жку?

Drill #54

Be prepared to answer, on the basis of actual fact, questions of the following type:

Ви ма́єте бра́та? — У вас є брат?
Same for: а́вто, сестра́, син, дружи́на, словни́к, перо́

Drill #55

Translate into Ukrainian:

1. Hryts has a little sister.
2. He had a little sister.
3. They had no little sister.
4. I have no little sister.
5. She had a new house.
6. We must have a house.
7. Who has a new house?
8. Her neighbor (*f.*) has a blue car.
9. His doctor has no car.
10. Oksana had a good doctor.
11. Do you have a good dog?
12. Who has a good translation?
13. I have a bad character.
14. I shall be at your place tomorrow.
15. They lived at their neighbor's (*m.*).
16. He will be at the doctor's.
17. She will be at my brother's.
18. At whose house are they living now?
19. She is working at Professor Luckyj's.
20. All, except the secretary, were at his place.
21. We lived at his son's.
22. He has no son.

6.5 THE USE OF потрі́бний "NECESSARY"

The word **потрі́бний (потрі́бна, потрі́бне, потрі́бні)** agrees in gender and number with the object needed, which is in the nominative case. The person who needs the object is in the dative case. This form of adjectival participle can be used in all three tenses: in the present tense (without auxiliary verb), in the past and future tenses (with an auxiliary verb).

Present tense:

Мені́ потрі́бне а́вто.	I need the car.
Йому́ потрі́бна пра́ця.	He needs work.
Бра́тові потрі́бний пере́клад.	Brother needs the translation.
Вони́ нам не потрі́бні.	We don't need them.

Past tense:

Мені́ потрі́бне *було́* а́вто.	I needed the car.
Мені́ потрі́бна *була́* пра́ця.	I needed work.

Future tense:

Мені́ потрі́бне *бу́де* а́вто.	I will need the car.
Мені́ потрі́бна *бу́де* пра́ця.	I will need work.

This construction is equivalent in meaning to the use of **тре́ба** with **ма́ти** and the accusative case:

Мені́ тре́ба ма́ти а́вто. I need the car;

or **тре́ба** with the genitive of that which is needed:

Мені́ тре́ба а́вта. I need a car;

or the adverb **потрі́бно** with the genitive of that which is needed:

Мені́ потрі́бно а́вта. I need a car.

Note: The use of треба or потрібно with the genitive case is used to impart the need of an indefinite object (i.e., *a* [any] car), whereas the use of the construction of **потрі́бний, -а, -е, -і** with the nominative case imparts the need for a definite object (i.e., *the* [specific] car):

Мені́ потрі́бне а́вто. (N.) I need *the* car.
Мені́ потрі́бно а́вта. (G.) I need *a* car.

Drill #56

Translate into English:

1. Ів́ан потрі́бний Оста́пові. Оста́п потрі́бний Іва́нові.
2. Вчора́шня газе́та ніко́му не потрі́бна.
3. Де Бори́с та Іва́н? Вони́ нам потрі́бні.
4. Кому́ потрі́бний мир? Він нам потрі́бний.
5. Мені́ він бі́льше не потрі́бний.
6. Хто має журна́л Василя́ ? Він потрі́бний вчи́телеві.
7. Ми за́втра бу́демо потрі́бні Іва́нові.
8. Я ду́маю, що ви йому́ були́ потрі́бні вчо́ра. Сього́дні ви йому́ бі́льше не потрі́бні.
9. Вона́ ніко́му не потрі́бна.
10. Кому́ потрі́бна сього́днішня газе́та? Вона́ мені́ бі́льше не потрі́бна.
11. Коли́ я вам бу́ду потрі́бний? Ви мені́ бу́дете потрі́бні за́втра.
12. Го́стеві потрі́бна твоя́ допомо́га.
13. За́втра мені́ потрі́бний бу́де твій словни́к.

Drill #57

Form sentences with the following words, according to the models:

Model: Я не ма́ю кімна́ти. Мені́ потрі́бна кімна́та.
Same for: кварти́ра, учи́тель, перо́, секрета́рка.

Model: Ви не ма́ли вчо́ра крі́сла. Вам тре́ба було́ крі́сла.
Same for: поли́ця, учи́телька, бюро́.

Model: Брат не ма́є хлі́ба. Йому́ потрі́бний хліб.
Same for: ша́пка, костю́м, горня́тко, лі́жко.

Model: Сестра́ за́втра не бу́де ма́ти а́вта. Їй потрі́бне бу́де а́вто.
Same for: підру́чник, пра́ця, пере́клад, ра́діо.

6.6 VOCATIVE CASE OF NOUNS

Ukrainian has a vocative case which is used for address. Although the vocative can be formed for any noun and is done so sometimes in literature, especially when an inanimate object is personified, the vocative is primarily used with animate nouns and with names of people. The masculine singular endings for the vocative case are **-е/-у** for hard and mixed stem nouns and **-ю** for soft stem nouns.

6.61 Nouns ending in the consonants **-к, -г, -х** undergo a change known as the first palatalization (*see 2.23*) where, with the addition of the ending **-е**, the final stem consonant **-к** changes to **ч, г** changes to **ж, х** changes to **ш,** and **ць to** ч:

Бог-Бóже!	God!
робíтник-робíтниче !/(ку!)	worker!
хлóпець-хлóпче!	boy!
Олéг-Óльже!/(Олéгу!)	Oleh! * (*special case*)
птах-птáше!	bird!

6.62 Vocative case of neuter nouns is the same as the nominative.

The plural vocative for all genders is the same as the plural nominative.

Adjectives take the nominative endings for the vocative case.

6.63 Vocative case for feminine nouns consists of the ending **-о** for hard and mixed stem nouns and the ending **-е/-є** and sometimes **-ю** for soft stem nouns.

As an example, here are all the names, which appeared so far in the vocabulary, in the vocative case:

Nominative	Vocative
Óльга	**Óльго!**
Натáлка	**Натáлко!**
Борúс	**Борúсе!**
Івáн	**Івáне!**
Андрíй	**Андрíю!**
Олéнка	**Олéнко!**
Óля	**Óлю!**
Данúло	**Данúле!**
Петрó	**Пéтре!**
Гáня	**Гáню!**

Іва́нко	Іва́нку![1]
Íгор	Íгорю! і Íгоре!
Мико́ла	Мико́ло!
Аско́льд	Аско́льде!
Богда́н	Богда́не!
Васи́ль	Васи́лю!
Ві́ра	Ві́ро!
Гриць	Гри́цю!
Миро́н	Миро́не!
Okса́на	Окса́но!
Окса́нка	Окса́нко!
Оста́п	Оста́пе!
Павло́	Па́вле!
Ро́ма	Ро́мо!
Сте́фа	Сте́фо!

Drill #58

Write out the vocative form for all nouns in the vocabularies in the first six lessons.

6.7 HELPING (AUXILIARY) VERBS **хоті́ти, могти́, му́сити**

The verb **хоті́ти** means "to want, wish, desire". This verb is conjugated like a first conjugation verb. Note, however, the consonant change from the infinitive to the present stem of т to ч:

Singular	Plural
я хо́чу	ми хо́чемо
ти хо́чеш	ви хо́чете
він хо́че	вони хо́чуть

The verb могти́ means "to be able, can". This is a first conjugation verb. Note, however, the consonant change from the infinitive to the present stem of г to ж. The forms of the past tense are: **міг, могла́, могло́, могли́.**

---

1 Sometimes to avoid the palatalization, an alternate ending becomes current, as in this case.

Singular	Plural
я мóжу	ми мóжемо
ти мóжеш	ви мóжете
він мóже	вонй мóжуть

The verb **мýсити (мýсіти)** means "must". This verb is declined as a second conjugation verb. Note, however, the consonant change from the infinitive to the present stem of only the first person singular of **с** to **ш**. This helping verb is often used instead of the construction **повúнен** + *the infinitive*. There is, however, a slight semantic difference between "must" — **мýшу** and "should" — **повúнен**.

Я **мýшу** зробúти це — I *must* do this.
Я **повúнен** зробúти це — I *should* do this.

Drill #59

Fill in the proper forms of the verbs indicated:

1. Він зáвжди ..... спáти. (хотíти)
2. Петрó не ..... слýхати. (мýсити)
3. Що ти..... ? Я ..... говорúти. (хотíти)
4. Хто ..... давáти костюм? Всі ..... (мýсити)
5. Що ви..... ? Я нічóго не ..... (хотíти)
6. Ми ..... знáти прáвду. Ви такóж. ..... ? Всі ..... (мýсити)
7. Сьогóдні я не ..... читáти. (могтú)
8. Чомý ти не..... ? (могтú)
9. Ми не .. ... бýти вдóма ввесь день. (мýсити)
10. Всі ..... (хотíти) це робúти і ви такóж ..... .(мýсити)
11. Івáнко не ..... бýти тут зáвтра. (могтú)
12. Вчóра Остáп не ..... бýти в клясі. (могтú)
13. Такóж вчóра Стéфа не ..... бýти в шкóлі. (могтú)
14. Ми вчóра не ..... бýти в клясі. (мýсити)
15. Ви такóж не ..... бýти вчóра в шкóлі. (мýсити)

Drill #60

Translate into Ukrainian:

1. I cannot eat.
2. He didn't have to play the piano; it was very late.
3. She wanted to work but she couldn't.

4. They must sleep but they cannot and don't want to.
5. Nobody knows what she wants.
6. What do you want? I don't want anything.
7. We have to work.
8. They don't want anything and can't do anything.
9. Why couldn't they work? They couldn't work; it was dark.
10. Although we were glad to see you, we were cold and couldn't.

Homework

a) Memorize the vocabulary in Lesson #7;
b) Review Lesson #6;
c) Translate the following sentences into Ukrainian.

1. Who has Oksana's carpet? Perhaps I have it.
2. Do you have a pen, Ivanko? I cannot write without a pen. I must have one.
3. Although my brother's house has a living room, dining room, bedroom and a bathroom, it is not very comfortable there.
4. Borys has one head and does not need any more.
5. We will not be at home tomorrow. We will be at Vira's.
6. He cannot work without me and he must; he is lazy and dissatisfied.
7. We all worked diligently after dinner in the bookstore.
8. He simply has a very low character.
9. I will soon need your help.
10. The doctor must see my foot.
11. The pupil (*f.*) needs a mother.
12. I want to see the pupil (*m.*), I must see him, but I cannot.
13. Who has a dog? They all have one, all except for Borys.
14. I don't understand why she does not want to help us.
15. She wants to but she cannot; she is not tall enough.
16. If my son needs me then I need my son.
17. The telephone is ringing (*rings*) in my study.
18. The rich English neighbor was very satisfied.
19. Do you still need me? No more.
20. I simply don't know what I am to do and I don't care.
21. Were you also at the party at their place? It can't be.
22. Vira, many thanks! Don't mention it.
23. There is a fly in my ear.

CHAPTER SEVEN

СЛОВНИ́К

Іме́нники жіно́чого ро́ду

весна́, -и́	spring
горі́лка, -и́	whiskey
ка́ва, -и́	coffee
карто́пля, -і	potato
кре́йда, -и	chalk
лю́лька, -и	pipe
межа́, -і́	boundary
па́ні	lady, Mrs. (indecl.)
пля́шка, -и	bottle
рука́, -и́	hand, arm
сала́та, -и	salad
цитри́на, -и	lemon

Іме́нники чолові́чого ро́ду

апети́т, -у	appetite
борщ, -у́	borshch (beet soup)
ві́тер, -тру	wind
го́лос, -у	voice
господар, -я	host, landlord
дива́н, -а	couch, divan
докуме́нт, -у	document
жест, -у	gesture
істо́рик, -а	historian
Кита́й, -ю	China
ніс, но́са	nose
оліве́ць, -вця́	pencil
па́лець, па́льця	finger, toe
пан, -а	lord, Mr.
папі́р, папе́ру	paper
президе́нт, -а	president
рот, -а	mouth
смак, -у́	taste
цу́кор, -кру	sugar
чай, -ю	tea

Іме́нники сере́днього ро́ду

лице́, -я́	face
мі́сце, -я	place
о́ко, -а	eye
пр́ізвище, -а	surname

Прикме́тники

голосни́й, -а́, -е́	loud
жо́втий, -а, -е	yellow
італі́йський, -а, -е	Italian
лі́вий, -а, -е	left
лі́тній, -я, -є	summer (adj.)
мале́нький, -а, -е	small (dimin.)
пра́вий, -а, -е	right
серйо́зний, -а, -е	serious
смачни́й, -а, -е	tasty
чо́рний, -а, -е	black
широ́кий, -а, -е	wide

Дієслова́

держа́ти (*держу́, де́ржиш*)	to hold
лежа́ти (*лежу́, лежи́ш*)	to lie
люби́ти (*люблю́, лю́биш*)	to like
кури́ти (*курю́, ку́риш*)	to smoke
обі́дати (*обі́даю, обі́даєш*)	to dine
прига́дувати (*прига́дую, прига́дуєш*)	to recall, to remind (+ *dative*)
розмовля́ти (*розмовля́ю, розмовля́єш*)	to converse
сиді́ти (*сиджу́, сиди́ш*)	to sit

снíдати (*снíдаю, снíдаєш*)	to breakfast
ходи́ти (*ходжу́, хóдиш*)	to walk, go
чу́ти (*чу́ю, чу́єш*)	to hear

Прислíвники та íнші слова́

бага́то	much (adv.)
всю́ди	everywhere (adv.)
дóвго	for a long time(adv.)
зóвсім	entirely (adv.)
зóвсім ні	not at all (adv.)
пóряд	alongside, nearby (adv.)
пóряд з (+instr.)	side by side (adv.)
споча́тку	at first (adv.)

Ви́рази

ах!	oh!
не мóжу не (+inf.)	I can't help
розкажíть!	tell (imper.)
що ви говóрите!	what are you saying!

Імена́

Бори́ся, -і	Borysya
Катери́на, -и	Kateryna
Лéся, -і	Lesya
Ма́рта, -и	Marta
Ори́ся, -і	Orysya
Олексíй, -я	Oleksiy

GRAMMAR

Second Conjugation Verbs (Cont.) — Дру́га дієвідмі́на (Продо́вж.) (7.0)
Instrumental Case of Nouns — Ору́дний відмі́нок іме́нників (7.1—7.11)
Instrumental Case of Pronouns and Modifiers — Ору́дний відмі́нок займе́нників і прикме́тників (7.2)
Preposition з *with Instrumental — Прийме́нник* з *з ору́дним відмі́нком (7.3—7.31)*
Predicate Instrumental — При́судок у ору́дному відмі́нку (7.4)
Instrumental of Time — Ору́дний відмі́нок при позна́ченні ча́су (7.5)

7.0 SECOND CONJUGATION VERBS (Continued)

In the second conjugation, vowels **а** and **у** are written after sibilant consonants **ж, ч, ш, щ**:

to hold:	держа́ти — держу́, де́ржиш . . . де́ржать
to see:	ба́чити — ба́чу, ба́чиш . . . ба́чать

In the second conjugation, mutations of the stem consonant affect the first person only, as in the following:

to sit:	сиді́ти — сиджу́, сиди́ш . . .
to walk:	ходи́ти — ходжу́, хо́диш . . .
to counsel:	ра́дити — ра́джу, ра́диш . . .

Drill #61

Supply the correct forms of the verbs in parentheses for the present tense:

1. Кого́ ви ..... ? Ми вас ..... . (ба́чити)
2. Кого́ Миро́н ..... ? Він ..... нас. (ба́чити)
3. Кого́ ..... ? Я ..... вчи́теля. (ба́чити)
4. Кого́ вони́ ..... ? Вони́ ..... бра́та. (ба́чити)
5. На чо́му ви ..... ? Ми ..... на крі́слі. (сиді́ти)
6. На чо́му він ..... ? Він ..... на папе́рі. (сиді́ти)
7. На чо́му ти ..... ? Я ..... на крі́слі. (сиді́ти)
8. На чо́му вона́ ..... ? Вона́ ..... на дива́ні. (сиді́ти)
9. На чо́му вони́ ..... ? Вони́ ..... на дива́ні. (сиді́ти)
10. На чо́му ..... ? Ти ..... на межі́. (сиді́ти)
11. Чому́ ти не ..... ? (спа́ти) Тому́, що я не ..... . (хоті́ти)
12. Чому́ Ори́ся не ..... ? (спа́ти) Тому́, що вона́ не ..... . (хоті́ти)

13. Чомý ви не .....? (спáти) Томý, що я не ..... . (хотíти)
14. Чомý Óля не .....? (спáти) Томý, що вонá не ..... . (могти́)
15. Чомý вони́ не .....? (спáти) Томý, що вони́ не ..... . (могти́)
16. Чомý ми не .....? (спáти) Томý, що ми не ..... . (хотíти)
17. Чомý я не .....? (спáти) Томý, що я не ..... . (хотíти)

Drill #62

Supply the correct present tense form of the verb "to like" and translate the infinitives in the parentheses:

1. Щó він .....? Він ..... . (to smoke)
2. Щó .....? Ви ..... . (to sleep)
3. Щó вони́ .....? Вони́ ..... . (to listen)
4. Щó вонá .....? Вонá ..... . (to play the piano)
5. Щó Васи́ль .....? Він ..... . (to eat)
6. Щó ти .....? Я ..... . (to sit)

Drill #63

Supply the correct present tense form of the verbs in parentheses:

1. Я нічóго не (розумíти).
2. Вони́ нічóго не (розумíти).
3. Ти нічóго не (розумíти).
4. Ми нічóго не (розумíти).
5. Вонá нічóго не (розумíти).
6. Що вонá (держáти)?
7. Що ти (держáти)?
8. Що ви (держáти)?
9. Що я (держáти)?
10. Що Óля (держáти)?

Drill #64

Translate into English:

1. Мій бáтько зáвжди дéржить цей докумéнт у своéму бю́рку.
2. Дóктор держáв Микóлу ціли́й ти́ждень удóма.
3. Ви пригáдуєте, що Васи́ль говори́в на остáнній вечíрці? Ні, не пригáдую. Я не слýхав, щó він говори́в.
4. Я не розумíю, щó ви говóрите.

5. Як ди́вно, що вони́ вас не прига́дують.
6. Чому́ ти так бага́то ку́риш ? Я не мо́жу не кури́ти.
7. Я не розумі́ю, чому́ ми вас тепе́р так рі́дко ба́чимо.
8. Що́ вам пи́ше Катери́на? Вона́ зо́всім не пи́ше.

Drill #65

Replace the infinitives in parentheses with the correct form of the present tense and translate the sentence:

1. Я не (прига́дувати), де ви (жи́ти).
2. Я не (розумі́ти), що ви (говори́ти).
3. Я не (хоті́ти) слу́хати, що вони́ (говори́ти).
4. Ти (чу́ти), що (говори́ти)?
5. Вони́ не (розумі́ти), чому́ ми їх не (чу́ти).
6. Хто (спа́ти) в тій кімна́ті? Тут я (спа́ти), а вони́ (спа́ти) у кабіне́ті.
7. А що́ ви (люби́ти)? Я (люби́ти) лежа́ти.
8. Ми не (ба́чити), що́ він (держа́ти) в руці́.
9. Я не (прига́дувати), ваш брат (кури́ти) чи ні? У мо́їй ха́ті всі (кури́ти).
10. Як ди́вно, що ви не (прига́дувати).
11. Що ти (роби́ти)? Я (сиді́ти) і (писа́ти) сестрі́.
12. Вони́ ма́йже за́вжди (сиді́ти) вдо́ма і (писа́ти).

Drill #66

Translate into Ukrainian:

1. What are you writing? I am writing a translation.
2. Do you see him often? We don't see him at all.
3. I don't recall where he lives.
4. He lives at Lesya's, and I live there too.
5. I see him almost every day.
6. We never see him.
7. I hear very well what you are saying.
8. They say that they recall us well.
9. I don't understand why you smoke!
10. Everybody smokes.
11. Why am I sitting when you are not?
12. He is holding one dictionary.
13. I often write to my sister.
14. They live far away and see their son rather seldom.

7.1 INSTRUMENTAL CASE OF NOUNS

One of the prime uses of the instrumental case is to express the means, the instrument, or the manner by which an action is performed. This construction generally corresponds to the English prepositional phrase "with + noun" in the sense of "by means of":

Я пишу́ перо́м. (*without preposition!*)
I write with (*by means of*) a pen.

		Nominative	Instrumental	Ending
Masc.	hard	стіл	столо́м	-ом
	soft	па́лець	па́льцем	-ем
	mixed	борщ	борще́м	-ем
Fem.	hard	вода́	водо́ю	-ою
	soft	ку́хня	ку́хнею	-ею
	mixed	межа́	меже́ю	-ею
Neut.	hard	перо́	перо́м	-ом
	soft	по́ле	по́лем	-ем
	mixed	прі́звище	прі́звищем	-ем

7.11 The words **вдово́лений, невдово́лений** + Instrumental

An extension of the above use of the Instrumental of means is the use of the instrumental case with the adjective "satisfied". The "means" which causes the satisfaction or dissatisfaction is in the instrumental case:

Він удово́лений перо́м.	Він невдово́лений мно́ю.
He is satisfied with the pen.	He is dissatisfied with me.

Drill #67

Put the words in parentheses into the correct case and translate the sentences:

1. Я держу́ папі́р (рука́).
2. Ми ду́маємо (голова́).
3. Профе́сор удово́лений (Га́ня).
4. Студе́нтка невдово́лена (профе́сор).
5. Ма́ма невдово́лена (Андрі́й).

6. Ми вдово́лені (лі́кар).
7. Я ніко́ли не пишу́ (олівéць).
8. Що́ він ро́бить (ногá)?
9. Що́ ти ро́биш (головá)?
10. Ми вдово́лені (гість).
11. Вони́ ду́же вдово́лені (село́).
12. Учи́тель вдово́лений (Катери́на), алé невдово́лений (О́льга).

7.2 INSTRUMENTAL CASE OF PRONOUNS AND MODIFIERS

The basic endings of the instrumental case for all modifiers are:

	Hard stem	Soft stem
Masc.	**-им**	**-ім, -їм**
Neut.	**-им**	**-ім, -їм**
Fem.	**-ою**	**-ьою, -ею, -єю**

Masculine and Neuter

	Nominative		Instrumental
3rd pers. pron.	**він**	**воно́**	**ним**
Adj.	**нови́й**	**новé**	**нови́м**
	си́ній	**си́нє**	**си́нім**
Poss.	**мій**	**моє́**	**мої́м**
	твій	**твоє́**	**твої́м**
Demonstr.	**той**	**те**	**тим**
	цей	**це**	**цим**
Interrog.	**хто**		**ким**
		що	**чим**
	чий	**чиє́**	**чиї́м**

Feminine

	Nominative	Instrumental
3rd pers. pron.	**вонá**	**нéю**
Adj.	**новá**	**ново́ю**
	си́ня	**си́ньою**

Poss.	моя́ твоя́	моє́ю твоє́ю
Demonstr.	та ця	ціє́ю ціє́ю (це́ю)
Interrog.	чия́	чиє́ю

The instrumental case of 1st and 2nd pers. personal pron.:

Nominative	я	ти	ми	ви	вони́
Instrumental	мно́ю	тобо́ю	на́ми	ва́ми	ни́ми

Drill #68

Put the words in parentheses into the correct case and translate the sentences:

1. Я пишу́ (бі́ла кре́йда).
2. Бори́с пи́ше (чо́рний олі́ве́ць).
3. Ми вдово́лені (нови́й лі́кар).
4. Я не люблю́ писа́ти (нове́ перо́).
5. Як ти мо́жеш писа́ти (лі́ва рука́) ?
6. Я не мо́жу працюва́ти (одна́ рука́).
7. Істо́рик удово́лений (нова́ секрета́рка).
8. Ми невдово́лені (нови́й словни́к).
9. Ори́ся вдово́лена (синя́ су́кня).
10. Ма́рта вдово́лена (молоди́й гість).
11. Президе́нт удово́лений (мій пе́рший рома́н).
12. Він невдово́лений (ва́ша оста́ння кни́жка).
13. А́втор говори́в (прие́мний ти́хий го́лос).

7.3 PREPOSITION з + THE INSTRUMENTAL CASE

Accompaniment in Ukrainian is rendered by the preposition з "with" and the instrumental case for its object, the meaning of the construction being "with," "along with," "together with":

Ось ма́ма з дочко́ю.
Here is mother and (with) daughter.

Чому́ ти не гово́риш зі мно́ю?
Why aren't you speaking with me?

N.B. When "with" means "by means of", no preposition is used.

7.31 Euphonic variants of the preposition з.

When the preposition з follows or precedes a consonantal cluster, it can take on any of its numerous euphonic variants: **із, зі, ізі, ізо**:

з ним		зі мнóю
with him	but	with me

Drill #69

Translate into English:

1. Я питáю вас, чомý ви не хóчете говори́ти зі мнóю?
2. Микóла хóче писáти кни́жку зі мнóю.
3. Я не люблю́ ї́ї й не мóжу з нéю працювáти.
4. Я бáчила Мирóна й ми говори́ли.
5. Я давнó з ним не говори́ла.
6. Я хóчу з вáми перекладáти ту кни́жку.
7. Я з дружи́ною вчóра бáчив прекрáсну óперу.

Drill #70

Give answers to the questions asked, supplying the correct case form of the words in the right-hand column:

1.	З чим ви ї́ли хліб?	сир
2.	Чим ви ї́ли хліб?	рот
3.	З чим ви пи́ли чай?	цитри́на
4.	З чим ви пи́ли кáву?	молокó
5.	З ким Бори́с був у Торóнті?	брат
6.	З чим ви ї́ли ри́бу?	картóпля й салáта
7.	З ким Лéся булá в Ки́єві?	пóдруга
8.	З ким ви були́ на концéрті?	лíкар
9.	З ким брат говори́в пíсля обíду?	гість
10.	З ким Дани́ло говóрить по-украї́нському?	учи́тель

Drill #71

Put the nouns and pronouns in parentheses into the correct form.

1. Ким президéнт невдовóлений? Він невдовóлений (я і ти).
2. Він хóче серйóзно говори́ти з (ти і я).
3. Ким учи́тель вдовóлений? Він удовóлений (він і вонá).

4. З ким ви хóчете працювáти? Я хóчу працювáти з (вонá) і з (ви).
5. З ким Бори́ся бáчила Бори́са? Вонá бáчила йогó з (ви) і з (ми).
6. Він хóче говори́ти з (вони́) і з (ми).
7. Хто хóче працювáти з (вони́) і з (ми) ?
8. Чомý ви не говóрите з (вонá) ?

Drill #72

Translate into Ukrainian:

1. What did you eat the bread with? I ate it with cheese.
2. With whom did you work? I worked with her and with her silly brother.
3. What do you write with in class? I write with a new pen.
4. Why don't you want to speak with me? I don't want to speak with you because I'm displeased with you.
5. I never drank coffee with sugar.
6. With whom does he talk? He talks with his young secretary and with my sister.
7. He is very pleased with Mrs. Kateryna.
8. She cannot live with her sister, and therefore she lives with mine.

7.4 PREDICATE INSTRUMENTAL

In the sentence "John was a student," the words "was a student" form the predicate, and "student" is said to be the predicate noun or noun in the predicate. Predicate nouns in Ukrainian usually take the nominative case. They take the instrumental case only when they signify an unstable, non-permanent state of being of the subject.

Óля студéнтка.
Olya is a student.

Óля булá студéнткою.
Olya was a student (*was, but is no longer*).

Óля бýде студéнткою.
Olya will be a student (*is not now, will be later*).

Sometimes adjectives are used in the predicate. The same rules apply as with nouns:

Я молоди́й.
I am young.

Коли́ я був молоди́м...
When I was young (*was, but am no longer*)...

7.5 INSTRUMENTAL OF TIME

Nouns denoting parts of the year (seasons) as well as parts of the day are put into the instrumental case to form adverbial expressions of time of the type "in the spring," "in the morning":

Nominative		Instrumental	
весна́	spring	весно́ю	in the spring
лі́то	summer	лі́том	in the summer
зима́	winter	зимо́ю	in the winter
ра́нок	morning	ра́нком	in the morning
день	day	днем	in the daytime
ве́чір	evening	ве́чором	in the evening

Note the expressions:

сього́дні ра́нком	this morning
учо́ра ве́чором	last evening
сього́дні ве́чором	tonight (this evening)

Drill #73

Translate into English:

1. Учо́ра ве́чором я з Ле́сею обі́дав у Богда́на.
2. Я хо́чу щора́нку сні́дати з ва́ми.
3. Сього́дні ра́нком Даре́вич сні́дав з на́ми.
4. Лі́том Ори́ся жи́ла в сво́го ста́ршого бра́та.
5. Ма́рта лю́бить жи́ти в селі́ зимо́ю.
6. Вчо́ра ра́нком Андрі́й не був у кля́сі.
7. Весно́ю ми бу́демо в Ки́єві.
8. Я люблю́ украї́нську весну́.
9. Учо́ра ве́чором я обі́дав з бра́том у італі́йському рестора́ні.
10. Ра́нком Олексі́й працю́є в бібліоте́ці, а днем удо́ма.

Homework

a) Memorize the vocabulary in Lesson #8;
b) Review Lesson #7;
c) Translate the following sentences into Ukrainian.

1. With whom were you there last evening? With her and her sister.
2. I am very pleased with my surname.
3. Did you speak with him this morning? Yes, and oh, how pleased I am with him!
4. At first I want to work only with you.
5. He is telling us who sat beside the host.
6. In the spring we always live at Oleksiy's.
7. Spring in China is usually nice.
8. I don't know where he was in the summer, but I know that the summer was very hot.
9. Where will you be in the winter? If the winter is nice we will be in the village.
10. Tonight the Ukrainian historian will be at the theater with his pretty wife.
11. Where were you last night? I was at the concert with my old friend.
12. She works with Mr. Borys in the morning, but in the day she works at home.
13. His summer house was without taste.
14. I don't like winter; I don't like it when it is cold and I don't like the cold wind.
15. When I work late in the evening, I don't sleep.
16. What a cold place!
17. Her son thinks that he will be a writer.
18. What are you saying! His gesture did not show that he was dissatisfied.
19. When he was a young man he lived with his wife in China.
20. He was an engineer and is a doctor now.
21. My father was a teacher and I want to be a teacher.
22. Why do you smoke? I can't help smoking.
23. The wide dark bottle held tasty whiskey.
24. Although he was old and his face was yellow, he still ate with a good appetite.
25. With my left eye I saw his right finger, and alongside his nose I saw a pipe.

CHAPTER EIGHT

СЛОВНИ́К

Іме́нники жіно́чого ро́ду

апте́ка, -и	drugstore
ві́дповідь, -і	answer
вісь, о́сі	axle
до́повідь, -і	report, speech
любо́в, -и	love
ля́мпа, -и	lamp
ма́ти, ма́тері	mother
ніч, но́чі	night
о́сінь, о́сени	autumn
па́м'ять, -і	memory
п'є́са, -и	play
підзе́мка, -и	subway
по́міч, по́мочі	help
по́шта, -и	post office, mail
роди́на, -и	relatives
сім'я́, -ї́	family
смерть, -и	death
смета́на, -и	sour cream
ста́нція, -ї	station
стаття́, -і	article
Я́лта, -и	Yalta

Іме́нники чолові́чого ро́ду

банк, -у	bank
ба́тько, -а	father
буди́нок, -нку	building
бе́рег, -а	bank, shore
Вінніпе́ґ, -у	Winnipeg
Дніпро́, -а́	Dnipro
Кавка́з, -у	Caucasus
клюб, -у	club
край, -ю	country, edge
Крим, -у	Crimea
ліс, -у	forest
па́м'ятник, -а	monument
плащ, -а́	coat, windbreaker
по́їзд, -у	train
рай, -ю	paradise
ріг, ро́га	horn, corner
рік, ро́ку	year
сад, -у	orchard
фільм, -у	film
хрущ, -а́	beetle

Іме́нники сере́днього ро́ду

вдово́лення, -я	satisfaction
дитя́, дитя́ти	child
життя́, -я́	life
зібра́ння, -я	meeting
ім'я́, і́мени	name
курча́, курча́ти	chick
метро́	subway (indecl.)
мо́ре, -я	sea
м'я́со, -а	meat
оповіда́ння, -я	tale
пальто́, -а	heavy coat
пита́ння, -я	question
пові́тря, -я	air
сніда́ння, -я	breakfast
таксі́	taxi (indecl.)
чита́ння, -я	reading
Чо́рне мо́ре, -ого, -я	Black Sea

Прикме́тники

мину́лий, -а, -е	past
про́стий, -а, -е	straight
улю́блений, -а, -е	beloved

Дієслова́

голоси́ти *(голошу́, голо́сиш)*	to voice, to weep
учи́ти/вчи́ти *(в/у/чу́, в/у/чи́ш)*	to teach

Прислі́вники та і́нші слова́

pані́ше	earlier (adu.)
спеція́льно	specially (adv.)

Ви́рази

виголо́шувати до́повідь	to deliver a speech
мину́лого ро́ку	last year
на бе́резі	on the shore
під час	during
тому́ що	because
цьо́го ро́ку	this year

Імена́

Лю́ба, -и	Lyuba
Христи́на, -и	Khrystyna
Хри́стя, -і	Khrystia
Левко́, -а́	Levko

GRAMMAR

Review of the First Declension in the Singular — Повто́рення пе́ршої відмі́ни в однині́ (8.0)
Masculine Locative in -у/-ю *— Місце́вий відмі́нок іме́нників чолові́чого ро́ду на* -у/-ю *(8.1)*
Masculine Inanimate Nouns with Genitive = Accusative — Вжива́ння родово́го відмі́нку за́мість знахі́днього відмі́нку в іме́нниках чолові́чого ро́ду на позна́чення неісто́т (8.2)
Hard Stem Masculine Nouns ending in -о *— Іме́нники чолові́чого ро́ду твердо́ї гру́пи з закі́нченням на* -о *(8.3)*
Use of Apostrophe — Вжива́ння апо́строфа (8.4)
Third Declension: Feminine Nouns ending in a Consonant — Тре́тя відмі́на: іме́нники жіно́чого ро́ду із закі́нченням на при́голосний (8.5—8.51)
Second Declension: Neuter Nouns ending in -я/-а *— Дру́га відмі́на іме́нників сере́днього ро́ду із закі́нченням на* -я/-а *(8.6)*
Indeclinable Foreign Words — Невідмі́нювані слова́ чужо́го похо́дження (8.7)
Locative Case (Cont.) — Місце́вий відмі́нок (продо́вж.) (8.8)
Preposition про *"about" — Прийме́нник* про *(8.9)*
Review of the Declension of Modifiers in the Singular — Повто́рення відмі́нювання прикме́тників і займе́нників в однині́ (8.10)

8.0 REVIEW OF THE FIRST DECLENSION IN THE SINGULAR

Masculine Nouns

Animate

	hard	mixed	soft
Nom.	пан	хрущ	у́чень
Gen.	па́на	хруща́	у́чня
Dat.	па́нові	хруще́ві	у́чневі
Acc.	па́на	хруща́	у́чня
Inst.	па́ном	хруще́м	у́чнем
Loc.	(на) па́нові	(на) хрущі́	(на) у́чневі
Voc.	па́не	хру́ще	у́чню

 CHAPTER EIGHT

Inanimate

	hard	mixed	soft
Nom.	бéрег	плащ	край
Gen.	бéрега	плащá	крáю
Dat.	бéрегові	плащéві	крáєві
Acc.	бéрег	плащ	край
Inst.	бéрегом	плащéм	крáєм
Loc.	(на) бéрезі	(на) плащí	(на) крáю
Voc.	бéрегу	плáще	крáю

Neuter Nouns

	hard	mixed	soft
Nom.	пальтó	прíзвище	мóре
Gen.	пальтá	прíзвища	мóря
Dat.	пальтý	прíзвищу	мóрю
Acc.	пальтó	прíзвище	мóре
Inst.	пальтóм	прíзвищем	мóрем
Loc.	(у) пальтí	(на) прíзвищі	(у/на) мóрі
Voc.	пальтó	прíзвище	мóре

Feminine Nouns

	hard	mixed	soft
Nom.	аптéка	межá	статтý
Gen.	аптéки	межí	статтí
Dat.	аптéці	межí	статтí
Acc.	аптéку	межý	статтю́
Inst.	аптéкою	межéю	статтéю
Loc.	(у) аптéці	(на) межí	(у) статтí
Voc.	аптéко	мéжо	статте

8.1 LOCATIVE MASCULINE IN -у/-ю

Some masculine nouns have a secondary locative ending in the singular. These nouns are mostly monosyllabic and when placed into the locative are usually end-stressed.

в/у садý	in the garden
also: в/у садí	
в/у лісý	in the woods
also: в/у лíсі	

в/у ба́нку	in the bank
в/у раю́	in paradise
на краю́	on the edge
у Криму́	in the Crimea
в/у Нью-Йо́рку	in New York
у Вінніпе́ґу	in Winnipeg
also: у Вінніпе́зі	

Drill #74

Answer in a complete sentence using the words given in the righthand column:

1.	Де ви лю́бите працюва́ти лі́том?	сад
2.	Де лежи́ть дорога́ кни́жка?	банк
3.	Де ви хо́чете бу́ти?	рай
4.	Де стої́ть ля́мпа?	стіл
5.	Де ви ба́чили Га́ню?	Нью Йорк
6.	Де Я́лта?	Крим
7.	Де ви були́ вчо́ра вдень?	мі́сто
8.	Де ви працюва́ли сього́дні ра́нком?	бібліоте́ка
9.	Де ви ба́чили журна́л?	край стіл

8.2 MASCULINE INANIMATE NOUNS WITH AN ACCUSATIVE EQUAL TO THE GENITIVE

Nouns which designate names of games, dances, as well as the noun for letter, have the accusative singular the same as the genitive singular, despite the fact that these nouns refer to inanimate things:

Я ма́ю листа́.	Я люблю́ гопака́.
I have a letter.	I like the hopak (dance).

8.3 HARD STEM MASCULINE NOUNS ENDING IN -о

There are some nouns, mostly names of masculine beings, **Павло́, Петро́, ба́тько**, which, despite their **-о** ending in the nominative singular, decline like normal first-declension, masculine, hard-stem, animate nouns:

Nom.	**Павло́**	Петро́	ба́тько
Gen.	**Павла́**	Петра́	ба́тька
Dat.	**Павло́ві**	Петро́ві	ба́тькові
Acc.	**Павла́**	Петра́	ба́тька

Inst.	Павлóм	Петрóм	бáтьком
Loc.	(на) Павлóві	(на) Петрóві	(на) бáтькові
Voc.	Пáвле	Пéтре	бáтьку

8.4 THE USE OF THE APOSTROPHE

The rules for using the apostrophe in Ukrainian are the following:

1) The apostrophe is used after the labial consonants **б, п, в, м, ф** and before the iotated vowels **я,ю,є,ї,** if the labial consonant is not preceded by another consonant which is part of the root of the word. Thus the apostrophe is used in the word **м’я́со** and not in the words **цвях, святи́й**. If the preceding consonant is a prefix, the apostrophe must be used, as in the words **зв’язáти, зв’язóк**.

2) The apostrophe is used after the letter **р** if it is at the end of a syllable which precedes an iotated vowel, as in the words: **бур’я́н, мáтір’ю**.

   The apostrophe is not used if the letter **р** begins the syllable or is within it, as in the words: **бу́/ря, бу/ря́к, пря́/мо, ряд**.

3) The apostrophe is used after prefixes before iotated vowels, as in the following words: **з’єднáти, від’ї́зд, об’єднáти, роз’єднáти**.

Drill #75

Place the apostrophe where needed in the following words. (You are not responsible for knowing these words, however, until they appear in the vocabularies of the chapters which follow.)

зї́зд	імя́	мáтірю	пять	дéвять	цвях
пяни́ця	бу́ря	зї́сти	девятнáдцять		статтé
буря́к	пря́мо	пéса	пáмять	пáмятник	вязáти
любóвю	сімя́	мя́со	ряд	рядóк	пя́вка
буря́н	бю́рко	бю́ро	лі́каря	І́горя	обєднáти

8.5 THIRD DECLENSION: FEMININE NOUNS ENDING IN A CONSONANT

Nouns which are feminine in gender and do not belong to the first declension are grouped together into the third declension. Most of these nouns end in a soft consonant. They are declined as follows:

Nom.	вісь	смерть	любóв	óсінь	ніч
Gen.	óсі[1]	смéрти[1]	любóви[1]	óсени[1]	нóчі[1]
Dat.	óсі	смéрті	любóві	óсені	нóчі
Acc.	вісь	смерть	любóв	óсінь	ніч
Inst.	віссю	смéртю	любóв'ю	óсінню	ніччю
Loc.	(на) óсі	(у) смéрті	(у) любóві	(в) óсені	(у) нóчі
Voc.	óсе	смéрте	любóве	óсене	нóче

8.51 The declension of the noun **мáти.**

The word **мáма**, used for "mother" up till now, is really part of so-called "baby talk." The "adult" word for mother in Ukrainian is **мáти**, and it would have been introduced much earlier were it not for the fact that it has an irregular declension:

Nom	мáти
Gen.	мáтері
Dat.	мáтері
Acc.	мáтір
Inst.	мáтір'ю
Loc.	(у) мáтері
Voc.	мáти

8.6 SECOND DECLENSION: NEUTER NOUNS ENDING IN -я, -а

Nouns which are neuter in gender and do not belong to the first declension are grouped together in the second declension. They are declined as follows:

	- ЕН	-ЯТ/- АТ		double cons. + я
Nom	ім'я́	дитя́	курчá	зібрáння
Gen.	íмени	дитя́ти	курчáти	зібрáння
Dat.	íмені	дитя́ті	курчáті	зібрáнню
Acc.	ім'я́	дитя́	курчá	зібрáння
Inst.	ім'я́м (íменем)	дитя́м	курчáм	зібрáнням
Loc.	íмені	(на) дитя́ті	(на) курчáті	(на) зібрáнні
Voc.	ім'я́	дитя́	курчá	зібрáння

---

1 All have a genitive in **-і** except for those nouns which have a double consonant preceding the ending and several words: **сіль, óсінь, любóв, кров, Русь.**

Drill #76

Put the nouns in parentheses into the proper case:

1. Він мáє (мáти).
2. (Óсінь) вонá живé з (мáти).
3. Хто мáє (дитя́) ?
4. У кóго є (курчá), якé хóдить з (дитя́) ?
5. Той пес не мáє (ім'я́).
6. Я покáзую (лист) (мáти).
7. Вчóра вéчором ми були́ на (зібрáння).
8. (Ніч) тéмно.

8.7 INDECLINABLE FOREIGN WORDS

Foreign nouns which do not end in a consonant or in **-а** or **-я** that is, nouns which do not automatically fit into the masculine or feminine nouns of the first declension, but which end in the vowels **-і** or **-о** are indeclinable, like the following: **таксí, вíскі, метрó, Чікáґо, рáдіо.** Note, however, that **рáдіо** is declined in the instrumental: **рáдіом.**

Some words, however, ending in **-о** which have been in use for a long time join the neuter first declension and are declined: **Торóнто, -а, кíно, -а,** as opposed to **кінó**, which is not declined.

Drill #77

Answer in complete sentences using the nouns in parentheses:

1.	Де ти був, Пéтре?	(теáтр)
2.	Де Лю́ба?	(кíно)
3.	Де ви були́ вчóра?	(концéрт)
4.	Де ви бáчили Андрíя?	(таксí)
5.	Чогó ви не мáєте?	(костю́м)
6.	Чогó не мáє Ори́ся?	(пальтó)
7.	Де ви були́ веснóю?	(Торóнто)
8.	Де працю́є ваш брат?	(Вінніпéґ)
9.	Чогó не мáє вáша сестрá?	(рáдіо)

8.8 LOCATIVE CASE (Continued)

Usually the preposition **на** "at" is used to express location with nouns which designate surfaces or activities. By inference it is also used with some other nouns instead of the preposition **в** to mean "at," "in" or "on":

на пóшті	at the post office
на стáнції	at the station
на Кавкáзі	in the Caucasus

Drill #78

Answer in complete sentences using the word given in the righthand column:

1.	Де ви живетé?	Торóнто
2.	Де працю́є Макси́м?	аптéка
3.	Де ви працю́єте?	пóшта
4.	Де живé Íгор Крику́н?	Ки́їв
5.	Де ви купу́єте хліб?	крамни́ця
6.	Де ви звичáйно бáчите Мáрту?	стáнція
7.	Де Львів?	Украї́на
8.	Де ти живéш óсінню?	Крим
9.	Де ти бу́деш сьогóдні вéчором?	теáтр
10.	Де ти звичáйно вдень працю́єш?	бібліотéка

8.9 THE PREPOSITION про "ABOUT"

The preposition **про** governs the accusative case and means "about":

про мéне	about me
про тéбе	about you
про ньóго	about him
про нéї	about her
про нас	about us
про хáту	about the house
про стіл	about the table

Drill #79

Translate the words in parentheses into Ukrainian:

1.	Щó ти знáєш?	(about me)
2.	Щó ви знáєте?	(about us)
3.	Щó ти думаєш?	(about Hryts)
4.	Ти інколи ду́маєш?	(about Borysya)
5.	Щó ти знáєш?	(about lhor and Olya)

6.	Я нічо́го не зна́ю.	(about you)
7.	Ми все зна́ємо.	(about you)
8.	Я нічо́го не ду́маю.	(about him)
9.	Так, я ча́сто ду́маю.	(about her)
10.	Я ма́ло зна́ю.	(about them)

8.10 REVIEW OF THE DECLENSIONS OF MODIFIERS IN THE SINGULAR

Adjectives

Nom.	білий/си́ній	біле/си́нє	біла/си́ня
Gen.	білого/си́нього		білої/си́ньої
Dat.	білому/си́ньому		білій/си́ній
Acc. =	Nom. or Gen.	біле/си́нє	білу/си́ню
Inst.	білим/си́нім		білою/си́ньою
Loc.	(на) білому/си́ньому		(на) білій/си́ній
Voc.	білий/си́ній	біле/си́нє	біла/си́ня

3rd pers. pron.

	Masculine	Neuter	Feminine
Nom.	він	воно́	вона́
Gen.	його́		її́
Dat.	йому́		їй
Acc.	його́		її́
Inst.	ним		не́ю
Loc.	(на) ньо́му		(на) ній
Voc.	—	—	—

Poss. pron.

Nom.	мій	моє́	моя́
Gen.	мо́го́		моє́ї
Dat.	моє́му		мої́й
Acc. =	Nom. or Gen.	моє́	мою́
Inst.	мої́м		моє́ю
Loc.	(на) моє́му		(на) мої́й
Voc.	мій	моє́	моя́

його́, її́, їх (indeclinable)

Demonstr. pron.

Nom.	той/цей	те/це	та/ця
Gen.	того́/цього́		тіє́ї/ціє́ї
Dat.	тому́/цьому́		тій/цій
Acc. =	Nom. or Gen.	те/це	ту/цю
Inst.	тим/цим		тіє́ю/ціє́ю
Loc.	(на)то́му/цьо́му		(на) тій/цій
Voc.	той	те/це	та/ця

Inter. pron.

Nom.	хто	чий	чиє́	що	чия́
Gen.	кого́	чийо́го		чого́	чиє́ї
Dat.	кому́	чийо́му		чому́	чиі́й
Acc.	кого́	чийо́го	чиє́	що	чию́
Inst.	ким	чиі́м		чим	чиє́ю
Loc.	(на) ко́му	чийо́му		чо́му	чиі́й
Voc.	—		—		чия́

Personal pronouns

Nom.	я	ти	ми	ви
Gen.	мене́	тебе́	нас	вас
Dat.	мені́	тобі́	нам	вам
Acc.	мене́	тебе́	нас	вас
Inst.	мно́ю	тобо́ю	на́ми	ва́ми
Loc.	(на) мені́	(на) тобі́	(на) нас	(на) вас

The pronoun у/ввесь

	masc.	neut.	fem.
Nom.	у/ввесь	у/все	у/вся
Gen.	у/всьо́го		у/всіє́ї
Dat.	у/всьо́му		у/всій
Acc.	у/ввесь	у/все	у/всю
Inst.	у/всім		у/всіє́ю
Loc.	у/всьо́му		у/всій

Drill #80

Put the words in parentheses into the correct case and translate the sentence:

1. Я не ма́ю (ввесь рома́н).
2. Я не ма́ю (ввесь пере́клад).

 CHAPTER EIGHT

3. Я му́шу ду́мати про (все).
4. Я ба́чила (вся сім'я́).
5. Я ба́чив (уся́ п'є́са).
6. Я пови́нен ду́мати про (вся роди́на).
7. Я вдово́лений (вся сім'я́).

Homework

a) Memorize the vocabulary in Lesson #9;
b) Review Lesson #8;
c) Translate the following sentences into Ukrainian.

1. The question is about him and his film.
2. I was in the forest in my windbreaker and saw a beetle.
3. He teaches with his mother and sister in the club.
4. We are having dinner with her and we need your help.
5. I saw Olha at the theater and her mother in the subway.
6. He lives in Lviv and works in a drugstore.
7. His daughter lives in the Crimea and works in the post office.
8. Yalta is on the shore of the Black Sea, and the air there is pleasant.
9. Their son lives in Winnipeg, and they seldom talk about him.
10. I heard this lecture yesterday at a meeting in our club.
11. Our school is in this building.
12. I have never seen the Dnipro but I have been in Ukraine.
13. I seldom write to my mother because I have no time, but I always think about her.
14. This year I saw his beloved mother on the train.
15. I know his daughter, his sister, and his relatives, but I really don't know his family.
16. She often talks about them and about their friend.
17. They were at my talk; then read my article.
18. I've heard so much about Ukraine.
19. My old dog is always next to the chair in which I am sitting.
20. He remembers everything and talks about everything. He has a good memory.
21. What did you hear about the play?
22. They are writing a book together with me; I help them and they help me.
23. Today is a fine summer day, and we can see the monument.
24. It is difficult for him to work at this station.
25. He writes all night in the orchard.
26. At night death is at the corner of the street.
27. There is no reading in this book.

CHAPTER NINE

СЛОВНИ́К

Іме́нники жіно́чого ро́ду

авдито́рія, -ї	auditorium
гора́, -и́	mountain
ді́вчинка, -и	little girl
зада́ча, -і	assignment
Іта́лія, -ї	Italy
оці́нка, -и	grade, mark
підло́га, -и	floor
пло́ща, -і	square, area
продавщи́ця, -і	salesgirl
річ, ре́чі	thing
селя́нка, -и	peasant (*f.*)
соро́чка, -и	shirt
тарі́лка, -и	plate
ша́бля, -і	sword

Іме́нники чолові́чого ро́ду

ві́дділ, -у	department
вождь, -я́	leader
гара́ж, -у	garage
громадяни́н, -а	citizen
дім, до́му	home
зо́шит, -а	notebook
листо́к, -тка́	leaf
парк, -у	park
по́суд, -у	dishes (*collective*)
продаве́ць, -вця́	salesclerk
селяни́н, -а	villager, peasant
хло́пчик, -а	little boy
череви́к, -а	shoe

Іме́нники сере́днього ро́ду

де́рево, -а	tree, wood
ли́стя, -я	leaves (*collective*)
о́зеро, -а	lake
плече́, -а́	shoulder

Множи́нні іме́нники

воро́та,ворі́т	gates
граблі́, -і́в (-бе́ль)	rake
гру́ди, -е́й	chest

две́рі, -е́й	door
ді́ти, -е́й	children
Карпа́ти, -а́т	Carpathians
лю́ди, -е́й	people
ме́блі, -ів	furniture
но́жиці, но́жиць	scissors
окуля́ри, -ів	glasses
схо́дини, схо́дин	meeting
штани́, -ів	pants

Прикме́тники

важли́вий, -а, -е	important, necessary
величе́зний, -а, -е	huge
до́вгий, -а, -е	long
гру́бий, -а, -е	fat
зеле́ний, -а, -е	green
знамени́тий, -а, -е	remarkable
істори́чний, -а, -е	historical
ки́ївський, -а, -е	Kyivan
коро́ткий, -а, -е	short
пові́льний, -а, -е	slow
радя́нський, -а, -е	Soviet
тонки́й, -а, -е	thin

Дієслова́

задава́ти (*задаю́, задає́ш*)	to assign
запи́сувати (*запи́сую, запи́суєш*)	to note down
па́дати (*па́даю, па́даєш*)	to fall

Прислі́вники

забага́то	too much
неважли́ве	unimportant, unnecessary

Числі́вники

два	two (*m.&n.*)
дві	two (*f.*)
три	three
чоти́ри	four

Імена́

Сла́вко, -а	Slavko

GRAMMAR

Nominative Plural of Nouns — Називни́й відмі́нок іме́нників у множині́ (9.0—9.05)
Nominative Plural of Modifiers — Називни́й відмі́нок прикме́тників і прикметнико́вих займе́нників у множині́ (9.1)
Plural of Nouns with the Suffix **-ин** *— Іме́нники із су́фіксом* **-ин** *у множині́ (9.2)*
Nouns in Plural Only — Множи́нні іме́нники (9.3—9.31)
Numerals 2,3,4 — Числі́вники 2, 3, 4 (9.4)
Reciprocal Construction **оди́н о́дного** *"one another" — Взає́мно зворо́тний ви́слів* **оди́н о́дного** *(9.5)*

9.0 NOMINATIVE PLURAL OF NOUNS

First declension

Masculine	Singular	Plural	Ending
Hard	стіл	столи́	-и
Mixed	гара́ж	гаражі́	-і
Soft	оліве́ць	олівці́	-і

Feminine	Singular	Plural	Ending
Hard	кни́жка	книжки́	-и
Mixed	межа́	ме́жі	-і
Soft	ку́хня	ку́хні	-і

Neuter	Singular	Plural	Ending
Hard	перо́	пе́ра	-а
Mixed	прі́звище	прі́звища	-а
Soft	по́ле	поля́	-я

9.01 Second declension

Singular	Plural	Ending
оповіда́ння	оповіда́ння	-я (same as nom. sg.)
ім'я́	імена́	-а (+ suffix -ен-)
дитя́	дитя́та	-а (+ suffix -ят-)

9.02 Third declension

Singular	Plural	Ending
ніч	нóчі	**-і**
дóповідь	дóповіді	**-і**
любóв	любóви[1]	**-и**

9.03 The noun **мáти** in nominative plural

мáти	матерí	**-і** (+ suffix **-ер-**)

9.04 THE DUAL AS THE NOMINATIVE PLURAL

Some nouns still retain the now defunct dual form as their nominative plural. Such nouns usually designate things which come as a pair. Others have both the dual and a new plural form:

плечé	плéчі (*dual*)
óко	óчі (*dual*)
рукáв	рукáва (*dual*)/рукавú (*pl.*)
вус	вýса (*dual*)/вýси (*pl.*)
пан	панóве (*dual*) /панú (*pl.*)

9.05 Feminine and neuter nouns sometimes undergo a shift of stress in the plural to differentiate the nominative plural from the genitive singular:

Nom. sing.	Gen. sing.	Nom. pl.
вікнó	вікнá	вíкна
пóле	пóля	поля́
кнúжка	кнúжки	книжкú

1 Normally such nouns as *кров, сіль,* and *любóв* are considered not to have a plural. When *любóв*, however, refers to a person (one's beloved) a plural is possible.

I had two loves. У мéне булó дві любóви.

Drill #81

Change the following nouns from the nominative singular to the nominative plural:

стіл	гість	істóрик	водá	край
сад	кýхня	інженéр	рукá	місто
бáтько	герóй	прúятель	рікá	слóво
листóк	лéкція	учúтелька	горá	пóле
кімнáта	смерть	вождь	цінá	мóре
олівéць	оповідáння	плóща	сестрá	вікнó
óбраз	крісло	дівчина[1]	дружúна	лист
мáти	будúнок	квартúра	ногá	óзеро

9.1 NOMINATIVE PLURAL OF MODIFIERS

All modifiers, possessives, demonstratives, and numerals have the nominative plural ending in **-і** or **-ї** (after vowels):

Singular	Plural
мій	мої́
твій	твої́
свій	свої́
наш	нáші
ваш	вáші
чий	чиї́
цей	ці
той	ті
одúн	одні́
ввесь (увéсь)	всі (усí)
новúй	нові́
сúній	сúні

Drill #82

Form plurals for the following:

цей розýмний студéнт	той висóкий будúнок
твоя́ пúльна ученúця	мій вузькúй черевúк
наш дурнúй хлóпчик	цей радя́нський письмéнник
ваш новúй підрýчник	твоє́ дóвге пальтó

1 Irregular plural - дівчáта.

на́ше си́нє а́вто	це вигі́дне лі́жко
це трудне́ пра́вило	украї́нський парк
чиє́ вікно́	ця кана́дська сім'я́
вся кни́га	га́рне оповіда́ння

Drill #83

Read and translate:

1. У цьо́му мі́сті є до́вгі ву́лиці.
2. Цей письме́нник пи́ше нудні́ рома́ни.
3. Це на́ші нові́ студе́нти.
4. Хто ці молоді́ письме́нники?
5. Чиї́ ті мале́нькі хло́пчики?
6. У цій шко́лі до́брі у́чні.
7. Я чита́ю рома́н "Чоти́ри ша́блі" Яно́вського.
8. Нам потрі́бні вигі́дні крі́сла.
9. Мої́ се́стри пи́шуть коро́ткі листи́.
10. У цій кімна́ті вели́кі ві́кна.
11. Які́ величе́зні поля́!
12. У на́шій кварти́рі вели́кі я́сні кімна́ти.
13. Вона́ ма́є га́рні тонкі́ ру́ки.
14. У ньо́го га́рні секрета́рки.
15. Дівча́та! Чиї́ ці нові́ зо́шити? Вони́ ва́ші? Ні, вони́ тіє́ї ді́вчини.
16. Я люблю́ низькі́ лі́жка.

Drill #84

Translate into Ukrainian:

1. What long novels!
2. Where are your pretty secretaries?
3. Everyone likes comfortable apartments.
4. In Italy we saw narrow old streets.
5. These little boys are my pupils.
6. Who are these little girls? They are my sister's pupils.
7. I love green fields.
8. My sister has slender legs.
9. Whose are these blue notebooks?
10. Where do you buy your chairs?
11. These words were his last.
12. My students are very good. They are intelligent and diligent.

9.2 PLURAL OF NOUNS WITH THE SUFFIX -ин

Some nouns drop the suffix **-ин** before forming the plural:

селяни́н	селя́ни	"peasant"
громадяни́н	громадя́ни	"citizen"

9.3 SOME NOUNS EXIST ONLY IN THE PLURAL

The following is a partial list of such nouns:

две́рі	штани́	граблі́	но́жиці	гру́ди
окуля́ри	воро́та	ме́блі	ді́ти	

9.31

Note: Do not forget that often in the formation of the plural syllables become reconstructed and one gets the **о/і** change, as in **стіл — столи́**.

Also, sometimes consonantal changes occur due to palatalization, as in **друг — друзі**.

Drill #85

Change the words in parentheses into the plural and translate the sentences:

1. На цій ву́лиці ті́льки (низьки́й дім).
2. У то́му мі́сті (до́вга ву́лиця).
3. Я люблю́ (стари́й істори́чний буди́нок).
4. У на́шій кварти́рі (вели́ка кімна́та).
5. (Цей по́їзд таки́й пові́льний).
6. (Бе́рег) Дніпра́ ду́же (га́рний).
7. У нас вчо́ра (був ки́ївський профе́сор).
8. (Чия́ ця украї́нська газе́та).
9. (Яка́ до́вга ніч).
10. На підло́зі (лежи́ть стари́й журна́л).

Drill #86

Translate into English:

1. Оле́г друг Мико́ли. Оле́г і Мико́ла дру́зі.
2. Мої́ сини́ живу́ть у Кана́ді: оди́н син живе́ в Торо́нті, а оди́н у Вінніпе́зі.

3. Селя́ни до́брі громадя́ни. Ко́жний селяни́н бага́то працю́є.
4. Уже́ о́сінь. Надво́рі па́дає ли́стя.
5. Я ба́чу оди́н га́рний черво́ний листо́к. У на́шому саду́ старі́ й товсті́ дере́ва і ті́льки одне́ де́рево ма́є жо́вті листки́.
6. Ли́стя на цьо́му де́реві жо́вте, але́ оди́н листо́к ще зеле́ний.

Drill #87

Translate into Ukrainian:

1. Where are those old forests?
2. These good students are mine.
3. I love big cities.
4. Whose are these cars?
5. The trains here are fast.
6. Do you have good teachers?
7. Do you see those red walls?
8. The shores of the Black Sea are very beautiful.
9. These doctors are very expensive.
10. She has blue eyes.
11. They say that they are our friends.
12. In what store do they give cheap chairs?
13. The leaves on this old tree are red.
14. Our friends were then in Europe.
15. Here are our husbands.
16. All mothers think that their children are remarkable.

9.4 NUMERALS 2, 3, 4

The cardinal numerals **два (дві), три, чотири** "2, 3, 4" are followed by the nominative plural of the noun. The numeral 2 has two genders: one for masculine and neuter nouns (**два**), and one for feminine nouns (**дві**). All other numerals (save for the numeral "one" — see 4.5) are without gender.

Although the numerals 2, 3, 4 are followed by the nominative plural of the noun, (only in cases where nom. = acc.) the stress of the noun after these numerals is the same as that of the genitive singular: this is the influence of the former dual stress.

Nom. sing.	Gen. sing.	Nom. pl.
кни́жка	кни́жки	книжки́

Я ма́ю книжки́.	I have books.
Я ма́ю три кни́жки.	I have three books.

N.B. If the singular and plural of a given word use different stems, then 2, 3, 4 will be followed by the *genitive singular*. E.g.:

ді́вчина — дівча́та
2 ді́вчини
люди́на — лю́ди
3 люди́ни

Drill #88

Fill in the correct form of the numerals and change the nouns in parentheses to the proper case form:

1. Ле́ся ма́є 2 (сестра́).
2. У ме́не 2 (брат).
3. Ви ма́єте 4 (ля́мпа).
4. Тут 3 (крі́сло).
5. У дире́ктора 3 (секрета́рка).
6. На бю́рку 2 (телефо́н).
7. Соба́ка ма́є 4 (нога́).
8. Бори́с ма́є 2 (перо́).

Drill #89

Translate the words in parentheses:

1. Ви ма́єте се́стри? Так, я ма́ю (two sisters).
2. В авдито́рії є ві́кна? Так, там (three windows).
3. У ва́шій кімна́ті є крі́сла? Так, у мої́й кімна́ті (four chairs).
4. У не́ї є до́чки? Так, вона́ ма́є (two daughters).
5. Тут є о́зеро? Так, тут (two lakes).
6. Всі селя́ни на схо́динах? Ні, ті́льки (one peasant).
7. Де на́ші дружи́ни? Не зна́ю, тут ті́льки (two wives).
8. Всі лікарі́ живу́ть тут? Ні, ті́льки (two doctors).

9.5 THE RECIPROCAL CONSTRUCTION **оди́н о́дного**

The reciprocal construction **оди́н о́дного, одна́ о́дної, одне́ о́дного** corresponds to the English "one another," "each other." The first word never changes, the second is declined according to its use in the sentence. It is not used in the nominative case:

	Singular			Plural
N.	— —	— —	— —	— —
G.	одна́ о́дної	оди́н о́дного	одне́ о́дного	одні́ о́дних
D.	одна́ о́дній	оди́н о́дному	одне́ о́дному	одні́ о́дним
A.	одна́ о́дну	оди́н о́дного	одне́ о́дного	одні́ о́дних
I.	одна́ о́дною	оди́н о́дним	одне́ о́дним	одні́ о́дними
L.	одна́ (на) о́дній	оди́н (на) о́дному	одне́ (на) о́дному	одні́ (на) о́дних

Вони́ лю́блять оди́н о́дного.
They like each other (*m.*).

Вони́ лю́блять одна́ о́дну.
They like each other (*f.*).

Note: If the persons involved are of different sexes, then the neuter form is used:

Вони́ лю́блять одне́ о́дного.
They like each other (*m. & f.*).

Drill #90

Translate into Ukrainian:

1. We love each other.
2. Borys and Hanya often talk with one another.
3. Do they send each other letters?
4. They do not like one another.
5. We do not understand one another.
6. They seldom talk about one another.
7. I talk with my mother.
8. We all have families, but I like to talk with my family; we like to talk with each other.
9. There were fresh meats in the store.
10. Danylo and Ostap are friends of my daughter. These are pretty names, aren't they (*is it not true*)?
11. All infants have pretty names.

Homework

a) Memorize the vocabulary in Lesson #10;
b) Review Lesson #9;
c) Translate the following sentences into Ukrainian.

1. We need good historians.
2. In summer the trees are green, but in the fall their leaves are yellow or red.
3. These students write down all that their professors say.
4. I think that this is unnecessary. They must write down only what (*that which*) is important.
5. Borys needs new suits. He says that all his expensive suits are very old.
6. Her daughters are journalists.
7. The saleswomen in this department are very good, but they say that they have too much work.
8. I think they need one more saleswoman.
9. The old cities we saw in Italy were very interesting.
10. Her sons write letters to me every week. Sometimes I answer, and sometimes I don't. But they don't care.
11. Slavko has friends who live in our house.
12. In our capital there are beautiful parks, monuments, museums, long streets, and comfortable and expensive hotels.
13. Yesterday we had company (guests)', we drank wine and talked.
14. She has beautiful eyes.
15. Do you have any brothers? Yes, I have two brothers; one is an engineer and the other a writer.
16. My brothers and their wives live in the center of Toronto.
17. He gives lectures well and his lectures are almost always interesting.
18. He likes to buy shirts, suits, and overcoats.
19. All schoolboys and schoolgirls must prepare their assignments every day.
20. Since he gives difficult assignments, these are difficult rules.
21. All students have good marks.
22. They like one another very much.
23. We often talk with each other.
24. We need white plates and blue cups.
25. We always buy furniture and china in this department.

CHAPTER TEN

СЛОВНИ́К

Іме́нники жіно́чого ро́ду

годи́на, -и	hour
гра, -и	game
мо́ва, -и	language
полови́на, -и	half (+ *gen.*)
по́милка, -и	mistake
Фра́нція, -ї	France

Іме́нники чолові́чого ро́ду

до́ляр, -а	dollar
іспит, -у	examination
ну́мер, -у	number
ро́зділ, -у	chapter
у́ступ, -у	section, part

Іме́нники сере́днього ро́ду

та́нґо, -а	tango

Прикме́тники

ди́вний, -а, -е	strange
злий, -а, -е	bad, wrong, angry
рі́зний, -а, -е	various

Дієслова́

бра́ти: взя́ти (*беру́, бере́ш; візьму́, ві́зьмеш*)	to take
гото́вити: пригото́вити (*гото́влю, гото́виш*)	to prepare

Прислі́вники та і́нші слова́

сам, сама́, саме́, самі́	self (*as in* he himself)
нега́йно, зра́зу ж	right away
зно́ву	again

Ви́рази

гра́ти в ка́рти	to play cards
гра́ти в те́ніс	to play tennis

Імена́

Ні́на, -и	Nina
Тама́ра, -и	Tamara
Юрко́, -а	Yurko
Яри́на, -и	Yaryna

N.B. The student is also responsible for the vocabulary of perfective verbs listed under Section **10.011**.

GRAMMAR

The Aspect — Вид (10.0—10.011)

10.0 THE ASPECT

Ukrainian verbs have only three tense forms: a present, a past, and a future. In addition to tenses, Ukrainian verbs also have an aspect.

There are two aspects: the imperfective and the perfective. These have nothing to do with the basic meaning of the verb. If you think of a verb as a coin, then the aspects are the two sides of the same coin: the "heads" and "tails" of the verb, as it were.

10.01 The imperfective aspect of the verb describes:

1) action in progress over a period of time without any reference to completion or termination of the action.

   Він пи́ше (писа́в, бу́де писа́ти).
   He is (was, will be) writing.

2) actions performed repeatedly.

   Він пи́ше (бу́де писа́ти, писа́в) додо́му щоти́жня.
   He writes (will write, wrote) home every week.

3) actions spoken of in general terms, without reference to an actual performance at any particular time.

   Мій ба́тько гово́рить (говори́в, бу́де говори́ти) рі́зними мо́вами.
   My father speaks (spoke, will speak) various languages.

10.02 The perfective aspect of the verb describes actions that have been or will be brought to completion or termination:

Я напишу́ тобі́ за́втра.
I will write you tomorrow.

Thus the verbal coin "to write" — **писа́ти** has two aspectual sides:

imperfective — писа́ти
perfective — написа́ти

Examples of the imperfective:

Вчо́ра він писа́в уве́сь день.
Yesterday he wrote all day.

Він писа́в щодня́.
He wrote every day.

Він ду́же га́рно писа́в по-украї́нському.
He wrote very nicely in Ukrainian.

Examples of the perfective :

Він написа́в листа́ сього́дні ра́нком.
He wrote a letter today, in the morning.

Він за́втра напи́ше О́льзі.
He will write to Olha tomorrow.

10.03 Perfective verbs speak of actions that have reached or will reach a terminal point, not of actions as a process unfolding in time. Therefore, perfective verbs can have no present tense, since the present tense implies that an action is currently in progress. Perfective verbs have only two tenses, the past and the future.

10.04 In the past tense, there are no special endings for perfective verbs. They form the past in the same way as imperfective verbs do:

Imperfective		Perfective	
писа́в	he was writing	написа́в	he wrote
писа́ла	she was writing	написа́ла	she wrote

10.05 In the future tense, perfective verbs are conjugated with the same types of endings as imperfective verbs in the present, but they are future in meaning:

Imperfective		Perfective	
пишу́	I am writing	напишу́	I will write
пи́шеш	you are writing	напи́шеш	you will write

10.06 Imperfective verbs have two future forms: the simple future and the compound future.

The simple future is formed by adding the following endings to the infinitive:

Infinitive	Endings	Conjugation	Meaning
писа́ти	-му	писа́тиму	I shall write
	-меш	писа́тимеш	you will write
	-ме	писа́тиме	he, she, it will write
	-мемо	писа́тимемо	we shall write
	-мете	писа́тимете	you will write
	-муть	писа́тимуть	they will write

The compound future is formed by adding the future tense of the auxiliary verb бути "to be" to the infinitive:

Infinitive	Conjugation	Meaning
писа́ти	бу́ду писа́ти	I shall write
	бу́деш писа́ти	you will write
	бу́де писа́ти	he, she, it will write
	бу́демо писа́ти	we shall write
	бу́дете писа́ти	you will write
	бу́дуть писа́ти	they will write

10.07 Summary of aspects.

Imperfective : Past tense — an action was in progress

він писа́в	he was writing

Present tense — an action is in progress

він пи́ше	he is writing

Future tense — an action will be in progress

він писа́тиме/бу́де писа́ти	he will be writing

Perfective: Past tense — an action has been completed

він написа́в	he wrote

Future tense — an action will be completed

він напи́ше	he will write

10.08 There is no one definite pattern to help distinguish between a perfective and an imperfective aspect of a verb. In the case of the verb **писа́ти** "to write" and **написа́ти**, the perfective has a prefix **на-** which differentiates it from the imperfective. Usually if two verbs differ only by the fact that one has a prefix and the other has none, the one with the prefix is perfective. For example:

Imperfective	Perfective
чита́ти	прочита́ти
роби́ти	зроби́ти
гото́вити	пригото́вити

10.09 Sometimes a prefix not only changes the aspect of the verb but also alters its meaning:

Imperfective	писа́ти	to write
Perfective	написа́ти	to write
Perfective	підписа́ти	*to sign*

In situations of this kind, the new perfective has no imperfective pair, and one is formed usually with the help of the suffix **-ува-**:

Perfective	підписа́ти	Imperfective	підпи́с**ува**ти

10.010 Some verbs form aspects by using different roots:

Imperfective		Perfective	
говори́ти	"to speak"	ска́зати	"to tell" (!)
бра́ти	"to take"	взя́ти	"to take"

10.011 From now on, in the vocabularies of each lesson every verb will be listed with both aspects (unless it has no perfective). The order will always be imperfective first and perfective second. Below is a list of all the verbs introduced so far and their perfective aspect. This list is part of the vocabulary of this lesson and must be memorized.

Imperfective	Perfective
ба́чити	поба́чити
бу́ти	—
виголо́шувати	ви́голосити
відпочива́ти	відпочи́ти
відчиня́ти	відчини́ти
говори́ти	сказа́ти
голоси́ти	пологоси́ти
гра́ти	загра́ти
дава́ти	да́ти
держа́ти	вде́ржати
дзвони́ти	задзвони́ти
ду́мати	поду́мати
жи́ти	пожи́ти
задава́ти	зада́ти
запи́сувати	записа́ти
зачина́ти	зача́ти
зачиня́ти	зачини́ти
зна́ти	—
ї́сти	з'ї́сти
кінча́ти	скінчи́ти
купува́ти	купи́ти
кури́ти	закури́ти
лежа́ти	поле́жати
люби́ти	полюби́ти
ма́ти	—
могти́	змогти́
му́сити	зму́сити
обі́дати	пообі́дати
па́дати	впа́сти
пита́ти	запита́ти
переклада́ти	перекла́сти
писа́ти	написа́ти
пи́ти	ви́пити
пока́зувати	показа́ти
помага́ти	помогти́
посила́ти	пісна́ти/посла́ти

поя́снювати	поясни́ти
працюва́ти	попрацюва́ти
прига́дувати	пригада́ти
ра́дити	пора́дити
роби́ти	зроби́ти
розмовля́ти	порозмовля́ти
розумі́ти	зрозумі́ти
сиді́ти	поси́діти
слу́хати	послу́хати
сні́дати	посні́дати
спа́ти	поспа́ти
стоя́ти	посто́яти
телефонува́ти	зателефонува́ти
учи́ти	навчи́ти
ходи́ти	походи́ти
хоті́ти	схоті́ти
чека́ти	зачека́ти
чита́ти	прочита́ти
чу́ти	почу́ти

Drill #91

Choose the correct form of the verb and translate the sentences:

1. Вчо́ра Ві́ра (писа́ла, написа́ла) дві годи́ни.
2. Він гово́рить, що він (напи́ше, писа́тиме) нам щодня́.
3. Я пови́нна за́втра (писа́ти, написа́ти) Бори́сові.
4. Коли́ ви (писа́тимете, напи́шете) Ні́ні про її́ дочку́?
5. Я вчо́ра (написа́в, писа́в) уве́сь день.
6. Я їй ско́ро (бу́ду писа́ти, напишу́).
7. Я (чита́тиму, прочита́ю) вам свого́ листа́.
8. Тепе́р ви пови́нні (чита́ти, прочита́ти) ті́льки по-украї́нському.
9. Яри́на (чита́ла, прочита́ла) вчо́ра пе́рший у́ступ і тепе́р бу́де чита́ти оста́нній.
10. Я пови́нен (чита́ти, прочита́ти) його́ листа́, тоді́ зна́тиму, про що він (пи́ше, напи́ше).
11. Спе́ршу (бу́ду чита́ти, прочита́ю листа́), а по́тім ми розмовля́тимемо.
12. Коли́ я бу́ду в Фра́нції, (чита́тиму, прочита́ю) ті́льки францу́зькі газе́ти.
13. Я ще не зна́ю, що (роби́тиму, зроблю́) за́втра.

14. Що ти (роби́в, зроби́в)!
15. Він до́бре перекладає Шекспі́ра, але́ цей пере́клад він (роби́в, зроби́в) пога́но.
16. Я пови́нна (роби́ти, зроби́ти) ту зада́чу. Сього́дні не ма́ю ча́су, але́ за́втра я її́ (бу́ду роби́ти, зроблю́).
17. Вчо́ра мій чолові́к (грав, загра́в) уве́сь ве́чір у ка́рти.
18. Якщо́ хо́чете, пі́сля обі́ду я (гра́тиму, загра́ю) нове́ та́нґо.
19. Хто вчо́ра (говори́в, сказа́в) на зі́бранні?
20. Хто за́втра (бу́де говори́ти, ска́же) на зібра́нню?
21. Коли́ ви (говори́тимете, ска́жете) Миро́нові, що і́спит бу́де за́втра?
22. За́втра профе́сор (говори́тиме, ска́же) про смерть Шевче́нка ці́лу годи́ну.
23. Юрко́ нам за́втра (бу́де говори́ти, ска́же), де він живе́.
24. Мину́лого ро́ку я щодня́ (брав, узяв) книжки́ в бібліоте́ці.
25. Де мій словни́к? Хто (брав, взяв) його́?
26. Вони́ за́втра (ві́зьмуть, бра́тимуть) на́ше а́вто.
27. Ми і́нколи (бра́ли, взяли́) їх а́вто.
28. Вчо́ра Мико́ла (брав, взяв) у ме́не оста́ннього до́ляра.
29. Яку́ ша́пку ви (бу́дете бра́ти, ві́зьмете) від ма́тері, бі́лу чи чо́рну?

Drill #92

Translate into English:

1. Вона́ сказа́ла, що бу́де ча́сто нам писа́ти.
2. Але́ вона́ написа́ла нам ті́льки одно́го коро́ткого листа́.
3. До війни́, коли́ Юрко́ був з ма́тір'ю в Криму́, він і́нколи писа́в Лю́бі.
4. Пі́сля війни́ він написа́в їй ті́льки два листи́.
5. Що тобі́ пи́ше Тама́ра?
6. Коли́ я прочита́ю її́ листа́, я тобі́ скажу́.
7. Я не зна́ю, що роби́ти!
8. Сього́дні я пови́нна прочита́ти цю кни́жку, але́ в ме́не так ма́ло ча́су.
9. Всі ці дні Андрі́й нічо́го не роби́в, але́ вчо́ра він, наре́шті, зроби́в усі́ зада́чі і на́віть до́вгий та трудни́й пере́клад.

10. У них ніко́ли не дзвони́в телефо́н, але́ вчо́ра, коли́ я був у них, ра́птом телефо́н задзвони́в.
11. Хто то був? То потелефонува́ли на непра́вильне число́.
12. Я потелефону́ю О́льзі після ле́кції. Я ча́сто бу́ду їй телефонува́ти: вона́ така́ ми́ла дівчина.
13. Хто взяв мій підру́чник? Я взяв його́: мені його́ бу́ло ду́же тре́ба.
14. А ти не ма́єш підру́чника? Ди́вно.
15. Звича́йно, що ма́ю, але́ Ната́лка все його́ бере́.

Drill #93

Translate into Ukrainian:

1. He wrote father a long letter.
2. The children say that they will write to us often.
3. I wrote to Orysia yesterday and will write to her again tomorrow.
4. Yaryna wrote for three hours.
5. She wrote two letters.
6. I have read only half of his letter.
7. We shall read a lot in the summer.
8. He will read us her letter.
9. I shall read you what father writes.
10. I've read only two words, but I already know what he wants.
11. I shall read less in the winter.
12. Why did you make this mistake?
13. I know that she will make this mistake again in her translation.
14. He does not know yet what he will be doing in winter.
15. I did it every day.
16. Yesterday we did all that we had to do.
17. What did you do with the letter?
18. What did you do yesterday? We read.
19. They never play cards.
20. My son played tennis with Borysya.
21. They played three games and she did not want to play any more.
22. I shall play only one game and then I shall work.
23. He will play with us this winter.

24. Who will play with him?
25. We often played cards in winter.
26. Does her little daughter talk already?
27. Who said that the concert was dull?
28. I shall tell him that his article is very good.
29. She always talks a great deal.
30. They will not tell him what the professor has said about him.
31. Natalka told me that she spoke English well.
32. He did not want to talk to me.
33. Roma took my hat. I will take yours.
34. Who took the letter which was lying on my desk?
35. He always used to take my textbooks.
36. I know that you have no dictionary, but you can always take mine.
37. They will take your records tomorrow.
38. Will you take (have) meat or fish?
39. I am going to take French lessons in the spring.

Homework

a) Memorize the vocabulary in Lesson #ll;
b) Review Lesson #10;
c) Translate the following sentences into Ukrainian.

1. When did you write this letter? I wrote it last night.
2. I'll tell you what I think about it when I read (will have read) it.
3. What are you going to do tomorrow? I am going to work.
4. He is going to tell him that in the spring I shall often take his car.
5. I am going to take my car tonight.
6. Who is going to speak about Shevchenko at the meeting?
7. She talked a great deal, but she didn't say with whom she had been at the movies.
8. I did everything yesterday, and today I will rest.
9. He read three articles before dinner.
10. I will be at home after class and will read Yanovsky all evening. I like his book, "The Four Swords," very much.
11. Whose dictionary did you take?
12. I always take Danylo's dictionary.
13. When and where did you write this wonderful novel? I wrote it in Ukraine before the war. I was writing it for four years.
14. I must write at once to my mother.
15. He made three mistakes in his translation.

CHAPTER ELEVEN

СЛОВНИ́К

Іме́нники жіно́чого ро́ду

лябората́рія, -ї	laboratory
нови́на, -и	a piece of news
Оде́са, -и	Odesa
та́йна, -и	secret
фа́брика, -и	factory
Украї́на, -и	Ukraine
шко́да, -и	loss, shame

Іме́нники чолові́чого ро́ду

гріш, гроша́	coin
гро́ші, -ей	money (pl. only)
плян, -у	plan

Іме́нники сере́днього ро́ду

в/у/бра́ння, -ння	clothing, dress

Прикме́тники

брудни́й, -а, -е	dirty
вечі́рній, -я, -є	evening
ді́йсний, -а, -е	real, genuine
дома́шній, -я, -є	of the home
дру́гий, -а, -е	second, other
надзвича́йний, -а, -е	unusual
чи́стий, -а, -е	clean

Дієслова́

виклада́ти: ви́класти (*виклада́ю, -єш: ви́кладу, -еш*)	to lecture
відповіда́ти: відпові́сти (*відповіда́ю, -да́єш: відпові́м, -віси́*)	to answer

діставáти: дістáти (*дістаю́, -є́ш; дістáну, -еш*)	to get
одéржувати: одéржати (*одéржую, -єш; одéржу, -иш*)	to receive
перепи́сувати: переписáти (*перепи́сую, -єш: перепишу́, -пи́шеш*)	to copy, transcribe
продавáти: продáти (*продаю́, -є́ш: продáм, -даси́*)	to sell
розповідáти: розповíсти (*розповідáю, -дáєш: розповíм, -віси́*)	to tell, narrate

Прислíвники та інші словá

дíйсно	really, actually (*adv.*)
звідкіля́	from where (*adv.*)
напéвно	for sure, certainly
пізнíше	later (*adv.*)
самозрозумíло	of course (*adv.*)
чому́сь	for some reason (*adv.*)
пíсля + *gen.*	after (*prep.*)

Ви́рази

в насту́пному рóці	next year
якá шкóда	what a loss
як тíльки	as soon as
спрáва/дíло в тóму	the matter is

Іменá

Мару́ся, -і	Marusya
Орéст, -а	Orest
Рóмко, -а	Romko
Уля́на, -и	Ulyana

GRAMMAR

Athematic Verbs — Атемати́чні дієслова́ (11.0)
Prepositions з *and* від *"from" + Genitive — Прийме́нники* з *і* від *з родови́м відмі́нком (11.1)*
Tenses in Reported Speech — Часо́ва послідо́вність у непрямі́й мо́ві (11.2)

11.0 ATHEMATIC VERBS

Besides the majority of Ukrainian verbs which fall into the two conjugations and have a theme vowel, there are a few verbs which have no theme vowel and hence form their own athematic conjugation. There are four such verbs. Two of them are verbs which have as a root either **-да́ти** or **-ві́сти** (the latter is used only in prefixed form).

да́ти	to give	**розпові́сти**	to narrate
прода́ти	to sell	**відпові́сти**	to answer

я	про	/да́м	я	роз/від	/пові́м
ти		/даси́	ти		/пові́си́
він		/да́сть	він		/пові́сть
ми		/дамо́	ми		/повімо́
ви		/дасте́	ви		/повісте́
вони́		/даду́ть	вони́		/повідя́ть

Drill #94

Choose the correct form of the verb and translate the sentence:

1. Я (поя́снюватиму, поясню́) вам, де я купу́ю ри́бу.
2. Я тепе́р зна́ю це пра́вило. Учи́тель до́бре (поя́снював, поясни́в) його́.
3. Як ну́дно щодня́ (поя́снювати, поясни́ти) секрета́рці, що́ вона́ пови́нна роби́ти.
4. Моя́ дружи́на не слу́хала, коли́ син (поя́снював, поясни́в) нам свій нови́й плян.
5. Мій голова́ (поя́снюватиме, поясни́ть), що мені́ тре́ба за́втра роби́ти.
6. Чому́ ви не (відповіда́ли, відпові́ли) на його́ листа́?
7. Я (бу́ду відповіда́ти, відпові́м) сьо́го́дні вве́чорі.

8. Коли́ ви (відповіда́ли, відпові́ли) на цьо́го листа́?
9. Я (відповіда́в, відпові́в) учо́ра ра́нком.
10. Якщо́ ти бу́деш мені́ писа́ти, самозрозумі́ло (відповіда́тиму, відпові́м) тобі́.
11. Ти (пита́в, запита́в) Миха́йла, де він учо́ра був?
12. Ще ні, але́ (пита́тиму, запита́ю) його́.
13. Га́ля (пита́ла, запита́ла) мене́, чому́ я не була́ на вечі́рці.
14. Я ніко́ли не (пита́ла, запита́ла) І́рку, чому́ вона́ нічо́го не чита́є.
15. Ви (бу́дете пита́ти, запита́єте) Уля́нку, де вона́ купу́є пласти́нки ?
16. За́втра я (зачина́тиму, зачну́) чита́ти нови́й у́ступ.
17. Тепе́р Ро́мко щора́нку (бу́де зачина́ти, зачне́) працюва́ти рані́ше.
18. Лі́том я ду́же ра́но (зачина́ла, зачала́) свій день.
19. Коли́ ви (зачина́тимете, зачне́те) писа́ти статтю́?
20. Я давно́ (кінча́в, скінчи́в) її́.
21. Як ті́льки я (кінча́тиму, скінчу́) цього́ листа́, я зра́зу ж (зачина́тиму, зачну́) дру́гого.
22. Тама́ра ті́льки що (кінча́ла, скінчи́ла) гото́вити свої́ ле́кції.
23. Я не люблю́ (дава́ти, да́ти) ле́кції.
24. Хто (виклада́в, ви́клав) тобі́ ле́кції зимо́ю?
25. Ро́ма (дава́ла, дала́) мені́ три ле́кції те́нісу.
26. Ба́тько (дава́тиме, дасть) мені́ гро́ші щомі́сяця.
27. Хто (дава́в, дав) тобі́ того́ до́ляра?
28. Я (дава́тиму, дам) тобі́ своє́ пальто́ за́втра ве́чором.
29. Кому́ ви (бу́дете дава́ти, дасте́) ту кни́жку?

11.1 PREPOSITIONS з/із AND від "FROM" + THE GENITIVE

The prepositions **з/із** and **від** mean "out of", "from", and "away from". The preposition **з** is used with places. The preposition **від** is used with persons.

Звідкіля́ він приї́хав? Зві́дки?	—	З Ки́єва.
From where did he come?	—	From Kyiv.
Від ко́го він приї́хав?	—	Від Мико́ли.
From whom did he come?	—	From Mykola.

Drill #95

Choose the correct form of the verb and translate the sentence:

1. Да́рко, від ко́го ви (діставáли, дістáли) той дару́нок?
2. Я (діставáла, дістáла) його́ від Аско́льда.
3. Рані́ше Петро́ ча́сто (діставáв, дістáв) дару́нки з Аме́рики.
4. Як ті́льки (бу́ду діставáти, дістáну) ві́дповідь від О́лі, я вам зателефону́ю.
5. Ба́тько ду́має, що ми рі́дко (діставáтимемо, дістáнемо) листи́ від Ромáна.

Drill #96

Translate into Ukrainian:

1. Who will explain this rule to you?
2. She explained to me why she does not want to work here.
3. The teacher was explaining the grammar but I wasn't listening.
4. If you want, I'll explain my plan to you.
5. Every day he will explain a new rule to us.
6. He never answers my letters.
7. He usually answered the teacher quickly and well.
8. He didn't answer your question.
9. Have you answered him? Not yet. I'll answer soon.
10. They will answer the letter tomorrow.
11. Why don't you answer Hanya's letter?
12. I couldn't answer that question.
13. I asked Marusya who had been at the party.
14. I shall ask my sister what she will be doing tomorrow.
15. I never ask to whom she writes and she never tells me.
16. We often ask Ostap about you.
17. Why didn't you ask Myron where he had been last night?
18. Perhaps they will ask us what we think of them.
19. If they ask, what will you tell them?
20. We must begin a new life!
21. I will start reading the second chapter at once.
22. My brothers finished their work.
23. In the fall they used to finish working quite late.
24. At first I will finish reading the letter and then I will read it to you.

25. When will you finish reading this play? I haven't started it yet.
26. Have you finished reading that novel? Not yet.
27. I started writing a letter to my mother but I haven't finished it yet.
28. I always begin working early and finish late.
29. I just gave Mykola two dollars.
30. I often gave him money.
31. Borysya will give you her textbook.
32. I'll give mine to Ostap.
33. What will you give me?
34. They will give this money to father.
35. Who gave Roma this dictionary?
36. Mother gave her good advice.
37. I will give my brother lessons every morning.
38. I often receive letters from my mother.
39. I used to receive a letter from her every week.
40. Yesterday our friend received this letter from Lviv.
41. Oksana thinks that tomorrow she will receive an answer from Kyiv.
42. When I get an answer from Borys, I will tell you.
43. Where is that telegram from?

11.2 TENSES IN REPORTED SPEECH

In Ukrainian, the tense used in reported discourse (indirect quotation) is the same as that used in the original statement. For example, Danylo says in direct speech:

> Я пишу́ листа́ своє́му бра́тові.
> I **am writing** a letter to my brother.

This statement, as reported by someone, would appear in reported speech as follows:

> Дани́ло сказа́в, що він **пи́ше** листа́ своє́му бра́тові.
> Danylo said that he **was writing** a letter to his brother.

Note that in Ukrainian the present tense is used in both the original statement and in the indirect quotation, whereas the English uses the past tense in the indirect quotation. English requires a shift in the tense of the verb in the subordinate clause from the present to the past, from the past to the past perfect, and from the future to the future perfect.

Past

Original:

> Я написа́в листа́ бра́тові.
> I **wrote** a letter to my brother.

Reported:

> Він сказа́в, що він **написа́в** (past tense, as in original) листа́ бра́тові.
> He said that he **had written** (shift to past perfect) a letter to his brother.

Future

Original:

> Я напишу́ листа́ бра́тові.
> I **will write** a letter to my brother.

Reported:

> Він сказа́в, що він **напи́ше** (future tense, as in original) листа́ бра́тові.
> He said that he would write (shift to future perfect) a letter to his brother.

Present

Original:

> Я пишу́ листа́ бра́тові.
> I **write** a letter to my brother.

Reported:

> Він сказа́в, що він **пи́ше** (present tense, as in original) листа́ бра́тові.
> He said that he **was writing** (shift to past tense) a letter to his brother.

Drill #97

Translate into English:

1. Я запита́в Оре́ста, як до́вго він живе́ в цьо́му мі́сті.
2. Він відповів, що живе́ тут три ро́ки.
3. Сього́дні ра́нком я писа́в листа́.
4. І́гор запита́в мене́, кому́ я писа́в листа́.
5. Я відповів, що пишу́ ма́тері.
6. Вчо́ра він мені́ сказа́в, що він пи́ше нови́й рома́н.
7. Вчо́ра він мені́ сказа́в, що він написа́в нови́й рома́н.
8. Вчо́ра він мені́ сказа́в, що він ско́ро напи́ше нови́й рома́н.
9. Я відповів у листі́, що він не ма́є ча́су нам помага́ти.
10. Він розказа́в нам, де він був і що́ він роби́в.
11. Він сказа́в нам, що за́втра він бу́де вдо́ма ввесь день.
12. Коли́ я ба́чив Ма́рту, вона́ мені́ сказа́ла, що вона́ чита́є Хвильово́го.

Drill #98

Underline the correct form and translate the sentence into English:

1. За́втра він (дава́тиме, дасть) мені́ оста́нню ле́кцію.
2. Моя́ учени́ця (пита́ла, запита́ла) па́на Ко́рсуня, де живе́ його́ дочка́, але́ він чому́сь їй не відповів.
3. Хто (чита́в, прочита́в) вам ле́кції ціли́й рік?
4. Коли́ я (дістава́тиму, діста́ну) від нього́ листа́, я йому́ зра́зу ж (відповіда́тиму, відпові́м).
5. За́втра по ле́кції я (пита́тиму, запита́ю) вчи́теля, коли́ в нас бу́де і́спит.
6. Ви за́вжди пови́нні (перепи́сувати, переписа́ти) ва́ші дома́шні зада́чі.
7. Він вам (пока́зував, показа́в) свій нови́й ки́лим, що він діста́в з Украї́ни? Ще ні. Він (бу́де пока́зувати, пока́же) мені́ його́ за́втра.
8. Коли́ ти (бу́деш пока́зувати, пока́жеш) мені́ свою́ статтю́?
9. Я (пока́зуватиму, пока́жу) ї́ї тобі́, як ті́льки я ї́ї (кінча́тиму, скінчу́) писа́ти.
10. Я ду́маю, що вони́ булі́ ра́ді, коли́ (діста́ли, дістава́ли) мій дару́нок.

Drill #99

Give the correct Ukrainian verb for the English verbs and translate the whole sentence:

1. Ось продавщи́ця, що *sold* мені́ ту поли́цю на книжки́.
2. Ро́ма *will work* в крамни́ці; вона́ *will sell* ме́блі.
3. Я *will tell* Миро́нові, що він пога́но *did* той пере́клад.
4. Я will sell тобі́ своє́ вечі́рнє вбра́ння.
5. Що ма́ти *answered* тобі́, коли́ ти *asked* її́, про що́ вона́ *talked* зі мно́ю?
6. Коли́ ти *will answer* (*use athematic form*) твоє́му при́ятелеві?
7. Я *will copy* мою́ зада́чу.
8. Ви вже́ *answered* ва́шому у́чневі, від яко́го ви вчо́ра *received* листа́? Так, я йому́ *answered* і *wrote* йому́ про все.
9. Хто так до́бре *explained* вам це трудне́ пра́вило?

Homework

a) Memorize the vocabulary in Lesson #12;
b) Review Lesson #11;
c) Translate the following sentences into Ukrainian.

1. When did he tell you that, before or after the lesson?
2. When they (*will*) get my letter, I shall already be in the Crimea.
3. Yesterday, at the meeting, he talked a lot, but said only one intelligent thing.
4. From whom did you get this telegram? I got it from Orysya.
5. I shall explain this to you; I like explaining.
6. They will explain to you how to do this.
7. Here is a greeting from Ukraine.
8. Where is the answer from Professor Robinson?
9. Did he write to you from Odesa?
10. He wrote in his letter that the city was very beautiful and clean.
11. He wrote to me only from Lviv.
12. Next year I shall start working in this small school.
13. I shall tell you all about my life.

14. He wrote down his address.
15. Last year we received two letters from her from Italy and one from France.
16. After dinner, when she finished talking about her son, her daughter, and her dog, she began telling us stories about her husband's mother.
17. We heard that he had received a letter from our old director, and that next year he would work in our factory.
18. They all know that she will live at home, as she lived before the war.
19. Bob always got poor grades, but yesterday he got a good one.
20. If you don't write to her at once, she will not answer you.
21. When I (*shall*) write this article, I'll give it to my daughter; she will give it to her husband, and then they will give it to you.
22. As soon as you will get it from them, you will give it to Vasyl.
23. Every month they will get new books from London and Kyiv.
24. What did you get from them? From whom? From Orest and Marta, of course. Before I used to get good things, but now I got a hat from her and nothing from him. But I don't care.
25. They told us the streets of this city were very dirty.
26. He said he would call us today.
27. They said they would answer us soon.
28. Everybody will start working early tomorrow.
29. We got your wonderful present. Many thanks.
30. When will you start working in the new office? I shall start next year.

CHAPTER TWELVE

СЛОВНИ́К

Іме́нники жіно́чого ро́ду

блю́зка, -и	blouse
вера́нда, -и	veranda
вече́ря, -і	supper
виде́лка, -и	fork
громадя́нка, -и	citizen
ка́рта, -и	card
карти́на, -и	picture
ло́жка, -и	spoon
пі́сня, -і	song
приро́да, -и	nature
розмо́ва, -и	discussion
співа́чка, -и	singer
супере́чка, -и	argument
това́ришка, -и	friend
фотогра́фія, -ї	photograph

Іме́нники чолові́чого ро́ду

анекдо́т, -а	anecdote
балько́н, -у/-а	balcony
вірш, -а	poem
воя́к, -а́	soldier
ґа́нок, -нку	porch
двір, двора́	yard, court
до́ктор, -а	doctor, PhD.
кінь, коня́, коне́й	horse
кіт, кота́	cat
коридо́р, -у	corridor
ніж, ножа́	knife
поє́т, -а	poet
птах, -а	bird
сміх, -у	laughter
співа́к, -а́	singer
това́риш, -а	friend
університе́т, -у	university
ху́тір, ху́тора	villa, farmstead
шум, -у	noise
раз, -у	time (one time, once)

Іме́нники сере́днього ро́ду

не́бо, -а	sky
небеса́, небе́с	sky (irreg. pl.)
свя́то, -а	holiday
со́нце, -я	sun

Множи́нні іме́нники

батьки́, -ів	parents

Прикме́тники

весе́лий, -а, -е	happy, cheerful
відо́мий, -а, -е	known
го́стрий, -а, -е	sharp
дерев'я́ний, -а, -е	wooden
непотрі́бний, -а, -е	not needed
ра́нній, -я, -є	early
рі́дкісний, -а, -е	rare
роже́вий, -а, -е	pink, rosy
старомо́дний, -а, -е	old-fashioned
те́плий, -а, -е	warm
шумни́й, -а, -е	noisy

Дієслова́

вече́ряти: повече́ряти (*вече́ряю, вече́ряєш*)	to sup
встава́ти: вста́ти (*встаю́, встає́ш: вста́ну, вста́неш*)	to get up
гуля́ти: погуля́ти (*гуля́ю, гуля́єш*)	to stroll
коштува́ти (*кошту́ю, кошту́єш*)	to cost
пам'ята́ти: запам'ята́ти (*пам'ята́ю, пам'ята́єш*)	to remember
плати́ти: заплати́ти (*плачу́, пла́тиш*)	to pay
рости́: ви́рости (*росту́, росте́ш*)	to grow
співа́ти: заспіва́ти (*співа́ю, співа́єш*)	to sing
стріча́ти: стрі́нути (*стріча́ю, стріча́єш: стрі́ну, стрі́неш*)	to meet
схо́дити: зійти́ (*only схо́дить: зі́йде*)	to rise (sun)
схо́дити: зійти́ (*схо́джу, схо́диш: зійду́, зі́йдеш*)	to come down

Прислі́вники та і́нші слова́

біля + *gen*	by (*prep.*)
для + *gen.*	for (*prep.*)
за + *acc.*	for (*prep.*)
за́вжди́	always (*adv.*)
кілька + *gen.*	several (*adv.*)
круго́м + *gen.*	around (*prep.*)
тому́	ago (*adv.*)
раз	once (*adv.*)
ра́зом	together (*adv.*)

NB. As part of this vocabulary memorize the cardinal numerals in 12.3 and the ordinal numerals in 12.4.

GRAMMAR

Genitive Plural of Nouns — Родовий відмінок іменників у множині (12.0—12.02)
Genitive Plural of Modifiers — Родовий відмінок прикметникових форм у множині (12.1)
Uses of the Genitive Plural — Вживання родового відмінку у множині (12.2)
The Genitive Case with Numerals — Родовий відмінок із числівниками (12.3)
Time of Day in Hours — Години дня (12.4)
Accusative Plural — Знахідний відмінок множини (12.5)

12.0 GENITIVE PLURAL OF NOUNS

First Declension

Almost all of the masculine nouns of the first declension, hard, mixed, and soft stem alike, take the ending **-ів** in the genitive plural:

Nom. Sing.	Nom. Pl.	Gen. Pl.	Ending
стіл (h.)	столи́	столі́в	**-ів**
ґара́ж (m.)	ґаражі́	гаражі́в	**-ів**
учи́тель (s.)	учителі́	учителі́в	**-ів**

Almost all of the feminine and neuter nouns of the first declension, hard, mixed, and soft stem alike, have a zero ending or rather a stem ending in the genitive plural:

Nom. Sing.	Nom. Pl.	Gen. Pl.	Ending
та́йна (h.)	та́йни	тайн	**-Ø**
межа́ (m.)	ме́жі	меж	**-Ø**
ку́хня (s.)	ку́хні	ку́хонь	**-Ø**
крі́сло (h.)	крі́сла	крі́сел	**-Ø**
лице́ (s.)	ли́ця	лиць	**-Ø**

There are some exceptions to the above:

мо́ре — мор**і́в**
кінь — ко́н**ей**
стаття́ — статте́й, статті́в

12.01 Second Declension

The second declension neuter nouns have the stem endings **-ят/ан, -ен** or **-ань** in the genitive plural, depending on the type of noun.

Nom. Sing.	Nom. Pl.	Gen. Pl.	Ending
пита́ння	пита́ння	пита́нь	**-Ø**
ім'я́	імена́	іме́н	**-Ø**
курча́	курча́та	курча́т	**-Ø**

12.02 Third Declension

The third declension feminine nouns have the genitive plural ending in **-ей:**

Nom. Sing.	Nom. Pl.	Gen. Pl.	Ending
по́вість	по́вісті	повісте́й	-ей
смерть	сме́рті	смерте́й	-ей
любо́в	любо́ви	любо́вей	-ей
ніч	но́чі	ноче́й	-ей

Drill #100

The following words are examples of the various types of the genitive plural. Give the nominative singular of each word:

рік, гір, стін, карти́н, кварти́р, дружи́н, ламп, карт, учени́ць, озе́р, студе́нток, таріло́к, ло́жок, виде́лок, громадя́нок, сусі́док, сесте́р, ві́кон, листі́в, крі́сел, поли́ць, горня́ток, студе́нтів, домі́в, лісі́в, оповіда́нь, у́чнів, батькі́в, килимі́в, геро́їв, музе́їв, ге́ніїв, при́ятелів, госте́й, письме́нників, словникі́в, днів, авт, товаришів, лікарі́в, ножі́в, піль, ко́ней, морі́в, смерте́й, ноче́й.

Drill #101

Give the genitive plural of the following nouns:

дім, гість, шко́ла, крі́сло, геро́й, ле́кція, сестра́, кни́жка, ло́жка, кіне́ць, мо́ре, словни́к, стіна́, ліс, дружи́на, зібра́ння, жі́нка, виде́лка, ба́тько, письме́нник, письме́нниця, ки́лим, музе́й, газе́та, ге́ній, тарі́лка, ніж, у́чень, учени́ця, громадя́нка, сім'я́, роди́на, на́зва, до́ктор.

12.1 GENITIVE PLURAL OF ADJECTIVES AND OTHER MODIFIERS

All hard stem modifiers have the ending **-их** in the genitive plural. All soft stem modifiers have the ending **-ix** or **-ïx** (after vowels):

нови́й: нови́х
си́ній: си́ніх
мій : мої́х

Drill #102

Change the following phrases from the nominative to the genitive plural:

нові́ вчителі́	всі нові́ а́вта
оста́нні у́ступи	всі си́ні килими́
до́брі учени́ці	на́ші висо́кі буди́нки
англі́йські журна́ли	ті широ́кі озе́ра
мої́ старі́ батьки́	на́ші га́рні дружи́ни
ва́ші ножі́	ці важні́ на́зви
ці у́чні	ці ціка́ві ле́кції
ці широ́кі поля́	чиї́ старомо́дні ме́блі

12.2 USES OF THE GENITIVE PLURAL

The genitive plural is used like the genitive singular:

1) to show possession;
2) after certain prepositions;
3) after negation of the verb — as a direct object;
4) after adverbs of quantity.

Drill #l03

Place the words in parentheses into the proper case form:

1. У нас учо́ра було́ бага́то (ціка́вий гість).
2. У цьо́му мі́сці було́ ма́ло (га́рний день).
3. В Іта́лії бага́то (старе́ мі́сто).
4. Лі́том Мару́ся прочита́ла кі́лька (ціка́вий рома́н).
5. У цьо́му рома́ні нема́є (ді́йсний геро́й).
6. Ми не ма́ємо (всі ті журна́ли).
7. Ми ма́ємо бага́то (непотрі́бна річ).
8. В їх кварти́рі кі́лька (бі́льша кімна́та).

Drill #104

Complete the following questions and answers in the plural, using the words below, as in the model:

Model:

Питання:	Відповідь:
Ви ма́єте ті книжки́?	Ні, ми не ма́ємо тих книжо́к.

словники́, зо́шити, гро́ші, нови́ни, вечі́рні газе́ти, черво́ні крі́сла, го́стрі ножі́.

Drill #105

Translate into Ukrainian:

1. There are several large windows in your living room.
2. How many sisters does he have?
3. How many pencils do you see on the table? I see only three pencils.
4. For whom did you buy these textbooks? For my students.
5. There were no new letters on my desk.
6. How many blue plates and cups do you have?
7. We have neither blue cups nor plates.
8. There are no big forests near big cities.
9. How many weeks did you stay (live) in the Crimea? We stayed there three weeks.
10. New York has several good libraries.
11. He knows many Ukrainian words, but he speaks slowly.
12. I bought these books for my friends.
13. Near those new villas there are many forests.
14. Our students have few good textbooks.

12.3 THE GENITIVE CASE WITH NUMERALS

Numerals 5 through 20 and all compound numerals where the last digit is 5 through 0 require the genitive plural of an accompanying noun when used as subjects (nominative case) or direct objects (accusative case).

Remember that numerals 2, 3, 4, and all compound numerals where the last digit is 2, 3, or 4 require the nominative plural of the accompanying noun when used as subjects or direct objects. (see 9.4).

This does not include the teens (12, 13, 14...) which are viewed as single-digit numerals, i.e., двана́дцять, трина́дцять... higher than five.

The numeral 1 and all compound numerals where the last digit is 1 behave like modifiers in that they agree with the accompanying noun in case, number, and gender.

Examples:

Удо́ма є **п'ять** (п'ятдеся́т **п'ять**) книжо́к. Я ба́чу **п'ять** (п'ятдеся́т **п'ять**) книжо́к.
There are five (fifty-five) books at home. I see five (fifty-five) books.

Удо́ма **три** (три́дцять **три**) кни́жки. Я ба́чу **три** (три́дцять **три**) кни́жки.
There are three (thirty-three) books at home. I see three (thirty-three) books.

Удо́ма **одна́** (п'ятдеся́т **одна́**) кни́жка. Я ба́чу **одну́** (п'ятдеся́т **одну́**) кни́жку.
There is (are) one book (fifty-one books) at home. I see one book (fifty-one books).

Cardinal Numerals

5	п'ять	16	шістна́дцять
6	шість	17	сімна́дцять
7	сім	18	вісімна́дцять
8	ві́сім	19	дев'ятна́дцять
9	де́в'ять	20	два́дцять
10	де́сять	21	два́дцять оди́н
11	одина́дцять	22	два́дцять два (дві)
12	двана́дцять	30	три́дцять
13	трина́дцять	40	со́рок
14	чотирна́дцять	50	п'ятдеся́т
15	п'ятна́дцять		

Drill #106

Read and translate:

1. У то́му до́мі є шість вигі́дних кварти́р.
2. Ми ма́ємо шість мале́ньких кімна́т.
3. У ба́тька в кабіне́ті є де́сять висо́ких і вели́ких поли́ць, а в ме́не ті́льки дві мале́нькі поли́ці.
4. Я куплю́ п'ятна́дцять бі́лих горня́ток.
5. У на́шій бібліоте́ці є ті́льки два́дцять францу́зьких книг.
6. Скі́льки ви заплати́ли за ту пласти́нку? Я заплати́в за не́ї п'ять до́ларів.
7. Я ніко́ли не плачу́ бі́льше. Для ко́го ви її́ купи́ли? Я купи́ла її́ для мої́х до́чок.
8. Скі́льки кошту́є кімна́та з лазни́чкою у ва́шому готе́лі? Ми пла́тимо за кімна́ту сімна́дцять до́ларів щоти́жня.
9. Скі́льки кошту́ють ва́ші череви́ки? Я заплати́ла за них три́дцять до́ларів. Я ніко́ли не плачу́ ме́нше за череви́ки.
10. У ти́жні є сім днів.
11. Скі́льки люде́й було́ на зі́бранні?
12. Скі́льки літ тому́ ви були́ в Євро́пі? Два ро́ки тому́.
13. Скі́льки разі́в ви були́ в Украї́ні? П'ять разі́в.

Drill #107

Using the words below, complete the following questions and answers in the plural, as in the model, but varying the number in the answer:

Model:

Питання:	Відповідь:
Скі́льки ви ма́єте кімна́т?	Ми ма́ємо шість кімна́т.

крі́сла, поли́ці, мале́нькі ложки́, нові́ виде́лки, си́ні тарілки́, вели́кі килими́, до́вгі столи́, широ́кі ві́кна.

Drill #108

Translate into Ukrainian:

1. I saw several blue cars in the garage.
2. My sisters bought five red chairs, and my brothers bought three green chairs.

3. At the meeting yesterday I saw six Ukrainian journalists.
4. How many knives do you see? I see eight sharp knives.
5. I lived in England for twenty years.
6. I don't know all these people.
7. In my apartment there are five bright rooms.
8. My neighbor has three bright rooms.
9. How many years have you worked here? Three years. And I have worked here nine years.
10. I have already read that book several times.
11. I've read it three times.
12. There are few soldiers at the concert.
13. There were no soldiers there.
14. I have no new shoes.

12.4 TIME OF DAY IN HOURS

Котрá годúна?	What time is it?
О котрíй годúні?	At what time?
Пéрша годúна	One o'clock
Дрýга годúна	Two o'clock
Трéтя годúна	Three o'clock
Четвéрта годúна	Four o'clock
П'ята годúна	Five o'clock
Шóста годúна	Six o'clock
Сьóма годúна	Seven o'clock
Вóсьма годúна	Eight o'clock
Дев'ята годúна	Nine o'clock
Десята годúна	Ten o'clock
Одинáдцята годúна	Eleven o'clock
Дванáдцята годúна	Twelve o'clock

Ordinal numbers are used for the names of hours in Ukrainian. Ordinal numbers are like adjectives; they are hard stem with the exception for the number **третій, -я, -є** "third".

To the question "At what time?" — the answer is **о першій, о другій** — "at one, at two". The answer is formed with **о** + the locative case. Note that "at eleven" is **об одинадцятій**, where **об** is used for euphonic reasons.

There is no A.M. or P.M. designation in Ukrainian. Instead the following expressions are used:

		Approximately...
ра́нку	in the morning;	from 6 A.M. to 11 A.M.
дня	in the day;	from 11 A.M. to 6 P.M.
ве́чора	in the evening;	from 6 P.M. to 11 P.M.
но́чі	in the night;	from 11 P.M. to 6 A.M.

шо́ста годи́на **ра́нку**
дру́га годи́на **дня**
сьо́ма годи́на **ве́чора**

двана́дцята годи́на **но́чі**
дру́га годи́на **но́чі**

Drill #109

Translate into Ukrainian:

1. In the summer I like to get up at six o'clock.
2. In the winter I usually get up later, sometimes at eight or even at nine.
3. Tomorrow is a holiday and I shall get up at ten.
4. What time is it? It is four o'clock.
5. And I thought it was already five.
6. At what time did you have supper after the theater? We had supper at eleven o'clock.
7. We usually have dinner at exactly seven o'clock.
8. Yesterday at one o'clock I had lunch with Borys and his wife.
9. At what time did you see her? At nine o'clock in the morning.
10. At ten P.M. he was not home yet.
11. It was two o'clock when I saw them.
12. It will soon be eight.

12.5 ACCUSATIVE PLURAL

All three genders have the accusative plural equal to the nominative plural if the noun refers to an inanimate object.

All animate nouns (people) have their accusative plural equal to the genitive plural.

Nouns which refer to animals and plants and which, if they are masculine, have their accusative equal to the genitive in the singular, have their accusative equal to the nominative in the plural.

Я ба́чу столи́, книжки́, пе́ра (inanimate object).
Я ба́чу хло́пців, учи́тельок, дівча́т (person).
Я ба́чу коня́, я ба́чу ко́ні (animal).

But sometimes acc.=gen. forms do exist for animals. Hence: Я ба́чу ко́ней.

Drill #110

Put the words in parentheses into the correct case form:

1. Ро́ма ба́чила (ва́ша га́рна блю́зка, ва́ша га́рна по́друга, ва́ші га́рні по́други, це мале́ньке мі́сто, цей мале́нький хло́пчик, ці мале́нькі хло́пчики, ці мале́нькі учени́ці).
2. Ми зна́ємо (ці украї́нські журналі́сти, ця украї́нська газе́та, ця украї́нська журналі́стка, ці украї́нські журналі́стки).

Drill #lll

Translate into Ukrainian:

1. I never saw such big stores.
2. He drinks no milk.
3. Nobody likes Kozachenko's daughter.
4. I didn't see his wife at the party.
5. Ulyana doesn't like cheap restaurants.
6. We didn't see any good hotels there.
7. She never buys expensive blouses.
8. He doesn't like my mother.

Drill #112

Translate into English:

Я ма́ю по́другу Лю́бу Ту́рчин. Ми зна́ємо одна́ о́дну вже до́вгі роки́: ми ра́зом ходи́ли до шко́ли, а тепе́р ми ра́зом в університе́ті. Бі́ля Ки́єва, в ду́же га́рному мі́сці, де бага́то піль і лісі́в, батьки́ Лю́би ма́ють ху́тір. Це величе́зний старомо́дний дерев'я́ний дім. Круго́м до́му — вели́кий сад, в яко́му росту́ть вели́кі старі́ дере́ва.

В то́му вели́кому до́мі бага́то вели́ких і мале́ньких кімна́т, бага́то до́вгих і вузьки́х коридо́рів, бага́то двере́й, бальбко́нів і вера́нд. Ме́блі в до́мі старомо́дні, і ніхто́ на́віть не зна́є і не пам'ята́є, хто і коли́ їх купи́в. В до́мі бага́то га́рних образі́в і книжо́к, і всю́ди по́вно рі́зних потрі́бних і непотрі́бних рече́й.

Для ме́не — це за́вжди вели́ке свя́то жи́ти в Ту́рчинів, в цих ми́лих і прие́мних люде́й. Господар до́му, пан Миро́н Ту́рчин, відо́мий письме́нник. Він написа́в па́ру до́брих рома́нів і п'єс. Ви, напе́вно, чита́ли його́ рома́ни і бага́то разі́в ба́чили його́ ім'я́ в газе́ті і чита́ли про ньо́го бага́то ціка́вих рече́й, га́рних і пога́них. Пан Ту́рчин весе́лий та те́плий чолові́к, що до́сить ди́вно для відо́мого письме́нника. Він лю́бить люде́й, псів, коне́й, діте́й. На дворі́ його́ ху́тора (двір ду́же вели́кий) чоти́ри пси, два ко́ні і па́ра коті́в. Два коти́ живу́ть у ха́ті.

Пан Ту́рчин лю́бить приро́ду. Лі́том, коли́ га́рна пого́да, він лю́бить встава́ти ра́но, коли́ вся сім'я́ і го́сті ще сплять. І́нколи він встає́ о шо́стій, а і́нколи ще рані́ше. Все круго́м ти́хо: ті́льки пта́хи співа́ють свої́ весе́лі пі́сні.

Пан Ту́рчин сиди́ть на вера́нді на своє́му улю́бленому мі́сці. Він ба́чить роже́ве не́бо, ба́чить, як схо́дить со́нце і слу́хає пісе́нь пта́хів. Яке́ га́рне ра́ннє лі́тнє не́бо!

Го́сті і ді́ти встаю́ть пізні́ше. Але́ ось він уже́ чу́є їх голоси́. У Ту́рчинів все (= за́вжди) бага́то госте́й. Па́ні Окса́на Ту́рчин, як і її́ чолові́к, лю́бить люде́й. У них за́вжди мо́жна стрі́нути письме́нників, пое́тів, музика́нтів, співакі́в та співачо́к. Там за́вжди бага́то молоди́х дівча́т, товаришо́к Лю́би, і молоди́х хло́пців, товаришів Оре́ста, си́на Ту́рчинів. У ха́ті бага́то шу́му, весе́лого смі́ху, ціка́вих супере́чок і розмо́в. Го́сті гра́ють в ка́рти на ґа́нку, гуля́ють у саду́, розка́зують одні́ о́дним бага́то стари́х і нови́х анекдо́тів. Молоді́ лю́ди гра́ють у те́ніс, співа́ють пі́сні, чита́ють ві́рші свої́х улю́блених пое́тів, гово́рять про університе́т і про пра́цю.

Ве́чором всі лю́блять сиді́ти в вели́кім кабіне́ті па́на Ту́рчина, де по́вно фотогра́фій рі́зних ціка́вих люде́й і бага́то рі́дкісних та ціка́вих книжо́к. Там го́сті чита́ють одні́ о́дним свої́ ре́чі. Як бага́то ціка́вих і до́брих оповіда́нь, ві́ршів і п'єс я там чу́ла. Я ці́ле життя́ пам'ята́тиму цей весе́лий, шумни́й дім, цю сім'ю́, і всіх відо́мих люде́й, що я там зустрі́ла.

Homework

a) Memorize the vocabulary in Lesson #13;
b) Review Lesson #12;
c) Translate the following sentences into Ukrainian.

1. How much did you pay for that shirt? I paid $5.00 for it; I never pay more for shirts.
2. I met him several times on a noisy street in Paris.
3. At what time did you meet him? I met him yesterday at 7 P.M. and I shall meet him tomorrow at 10 A.M.
4. How many Ukrainian books do you have? I have no Ukrainian books.
5. Oleh has many sisters.
6. Are there any tall houses on your street? Yes, several.
7. There were no mountains and no forests where we lived.
8. But there were many lakes, fields, and rivers.
9. How many legs does a dog have? A dog has four legs.
10. Near our house there are several good stores.
11. For whom are you writing down that address? I am writing it down for my sisters.
12. For whom did you buy these coats? I bought them for my secretaries.
13. Khvyl'ovy (Хвильовий) did not write novels; he wrote short stories.
14. Olha has never read those stories.
15. I have never seen Kulish's (Куліш) stories.
16. I never said such things.
17. He never said such things.
18. My daughters were in the Crimea eleven months ago.
19. I've told you twenty times not to do that.
20. Near the house there grow big trees.
21. All around the house there are many fields and woods.

CHAPTER THIRTEEN — ТРИНА́ДЦЯТИЙ РО́ЗДІЛ

СЛОВНИ́К

Іме́нники жіно́чого ро́ду

А́зія, -ї	Asia
А́нглія, -ї	England
аспіри́на, -и	aspirin
А́фрика, -и	Africa
бабу́ня, -і	grandmother
запи́ска, -и	note
ма́рка, -и	stamp
пора́, -и́	season, time (the right time to do something)
спра́ва, -и	matter, affair
таксі́вка, -и	taxi

Іме́нники чолові́чого ро́ду

авто́бус, -а	bus
годи́нник, -а	watch
дощ, -у́	rain
Едмонто́н, -у	Edmonton
Пари́ж, -у	Paris
трамва́й, -я	streetcar

Іме́нники сере́днього ро́ду

Ме́хіко	Mexico (Indecl.)

Множи́нні іме́нники

вака́ції, -й	vacations

Дієслова́

ходи́ти, іти́: піти́ (*ходжу́, хо́диш, іду́, іде́ш: піду́, піде́ш*)	to go on foot
ї́здити, ї́хати: пої́хати (*ї́жджу, ї́здиш: ї́ду, ї́деш: пої́ду, пої́деш*)	to go using some sort of locomotion
продо́вжувати: продо́вжити (*продо́вжую, -єш; продо́вжу, -иш*)	to continue

Прислі́вники та і́нші слова́

додо́му	homeward (*adv.*)
ві́дти/відтіля́	from there (*adv.*)
куди́	where (with verbs of motion) (*adv.*)
ну́дно	boring (*adv.*)
пра́вильно	correctly
сюди́	here (with verbs of motion) (*adv.*)
туди́	there (with verbs of motion) (*adv.*)

Ви́рази

у/в/ве́сь час	all the time
годи́нник пізни́ть	the watch is running late
годи́нник спіши́ть	the watch is running fast
Добри́день!	Good day!

Імена́

Зе́ня, -і	Zenya

GRAMMAR

Definite and Indefinite Imperfective Aspect — Ви́значений і неви́значений недоко́наний вид (13.0)
Adverbs and Prepositional Phrases of Direction — Прислі́вники і прийме́нникові констру́кції ру́ху (на́прямку) (13.3—13.1)
Verbs of Going — Дієслова́ ру́ху (13.2, 13.4, 13.5)

13.0 DEFINITE AND INDEFINITE IMPERFECTIVE ASPECT

Most Ukrainian verbs have only one form of the imperfective aspect for two kinds of meaning:

actions in progress:	він чита́є — he is reading
habitual actions:	він чита́є — he reads

But certain going and carrying verbs have two separate forms for the definite (action actually occurring) and the indefinite (action occurring without actual reference to a specific time — a habitual action). Such is the verb **іти/ходити** — "to go" (*by foot*), "to walk":

Indefinite	Definite	Perfective
ходи́ти	іти́	піти́
ходжу́	іду́	піду́
хо́диш	іде́ш	пі́деш
хо́дить	іде́	пі́де
ходи́в	ішо́в	пішо́в
ходи́ла	ішла́	пішла́

Examples:

Він **хо́дить** до бібліоте́ки щодня́.
He goes to the library **every day**. (*No specific time and habitual*)

Він **ходи́в** туди́ щодня́.
He went there **every day**. (*No specific time and habitual*)

Він бага́то **хо́дить**.
He walks a **lot**. (*Habitual*)

Їх мале́нький хло́пчик хо́дить.
Their little boy **walks**. (*Habitual condition*)

Я йду́ додо́му.
I am going home (**now**). (*Particular occurance now*)

13.1 ADVERBS AND PREPOSITIONAL PHRASES OF DIRECTION

The adverb **де** "where" refers to a place in which something is, or in which something happened or is happening:

Де ти сиди́ш?	*Where* are you sitting?

The adverb **куди́** "where" refers to the place to which someone or something is moving or moved. It is used with verbs of motion:

Куди́ ти йде́ш?	(To) *where are you going?*

The prepositions **в** and **на** + loc. express location:

в ха́ті	in the house
в по́їзді	on the train
на столі́	on the table

The prepositions **в** and **на** + acc. and a verb of motion express direction. Direction is also expressed by the construction **до** + gen.

The construction **до** + gen. is not quite synonymous with **в** + acc., but the two can be used interchangeably. One cannot, however, substitute **до** + gen. for **на** + acc.

Я йду́ на п'є́су	I am going to the play
Я йду́ в шко́лу	I am going to school
Я йду́ до шко́ли	I am going to school

In answer to the question **куди́** "where" (direction), "here, there" (coming this, that way) are expressed by **сюди́, туди́**.

In answer to the question **де** "where" (location) "here, there" are expressed by **тут, там**.

Two adverbial expressions used to express "home" are **вдо́ма** (location) and **додо́му** (direction).

Drill #113

Choose the correct form of the verb in parentheses and translate the sentence into English:

1. З ким ви звичáйно (хóдите, ідетé) до теáтру?
2. Я нормáльно (ходжý, ідý) самá.
3. Сьогóдні ввéчорі ми (хóдимо, йдемó) до кíна.
4. Івáсю, куди́ ти тепéр (хóдиш, ідéш) ? Я (ходжý, ідý) на ґáнок.
5. Як ви (хóдите, ідетé): скóро чи повóлі?
6. Я зáвжди (ходжý, ідý) скóро.
7. Я не люблю́ (ходи́ти, іти́) повóлі.
8. З ким ви (ходи́ли, йшли́) вчóра вéчором, коли́ я вас стрíнув?
9. Я (ходи́в, йшóв) з бáтьком.
10. Я вчóра стрíнув Андрíя, коли́ він (ходи́в, ішóв) у бібліотéку.
11. Веснóю бабýня щодня́ (ходи́ла, йшлá) до пáрку.
12. Ми чáсто (хóдимо, йдемó) в кінó.

Drill #114

Form two sentences as in the models using the list of words given below; use the correct prepositions and the correct case forms:

Models: Я йдý в університéт: в університéті.
Я йдý до хáти: в хáті.

концéрт, буди́нок, лéкція, сад, пóшта, фáбрика, парк, зібрáння, дім, музéй, кімнáта.

Drill #115

Choose the correct word in parentheses and translate into English:

1. Пéтре, (куди́, де) ти йдéш?
2. Нíно, (куди́, де) ти працю́єш?
3. Івáсю, (куди́, де) ти живéш?
4. (Куди́, де) ви йдетé?
5. Ми йдемó (туди́, там).
6. Ви тáкож ідетé (туди́, там)?
7. Ми снíдали (туди́, там).
8. (Куди́, де) працю́є Івáн?
9. (Куди́, де) він ідé?
10. Він ідé (тут, сюди́).
11. Він живé (тут, сюди́).

Drill #116

Translate the words in italics:

1. Куди́ *are going* ді́ти? Вони́ *are going* до шко́ли.
2. Куди́ ти *are going*? Я *am going* до шко́ли.
3. Мико́ла хо́че *go* додо́му.
4. З ким *was walking* Ві́ра? Вона́ *was walking* сама́.
5. Ми *were going* до кі́на і стрі́нули Зе́ню.
6. Вона́ та́кож *was going* туди́.
7. Ми *are going* до теа́тру.
8. Оста́п іде́ *home*.
9. Він бу́де сні́дати *at home*.
10. Ми йдемо́ *to the drugstore*. Нам потрі́бно купи́ти аспіри́ни *at the drugstore*.
11. Ми йдемо́ *to the restaurant*. Ми обі́даємо *at the restaurant*.
12. Я йду́ *to the library*. Ви та́кож ідете́ *there*? Так, я тепе́р працю́ю *there*.
13. Я ба́чу Оре́ста. Він іде́ *here*.
14. Я не знав, що він живе́ *here*.
15. Кіт за́вжди спить *here*. Ось він іде́ *here*.

13.2 THE "GO" VERBS (Continued)

The corresponding "go" verbs when one "goes" (travels) not on foot, but on an animal or in a vehicle, are:

Indefinite	Definite	Perfective
ї́здити	ї́хати	пої́хати
ї́жджу	ї́ду	пої́ду
ї́здиш	ї́деш	пої́деш
ї́здить	ї́де	пої́де
ї́здив	ї́хав	пої́хав
ї́здила	ї́хала	пої́хала

13.21 The vehicle used in travel is often expressed by the instrumental case without a preposition:

ї́хати, по́їздом, а́втом, авто́бусом, таксі́вкою, трамва́єм
to go by train, car, bus, taxi, streetcar

Location, being in something, is expressed by the construction: prep. в/у or на + loc.:

> в а́вті, у по́їзді, у трамва́ї, в авто́бусі, у таксі́, на во́зі, на велосипе́ді
> in the car, in the train, in the streetcar, in the bus, in the taxi, on the wagon, on a bicycle

Drill #117

Choose the correct form of the verb in parentheses and translate:

1. Ми сього́дні (ї́здимо, ї́демо) до Пари́жу.
2. Ми ча́сто (ї́здимо, ї́демо) туди́.
3. Я ніко́ли не (ї́жджу, ї́ду) на вака́ції.
4. Цей журналі́ст (ї́здить, ї́де) до Льво́ва па́ру разі́в у рік.
5. Добри́день! Куди́ ви за́раз (ї́здите, ї́дете)? Я за́раз (ї́жджу, ї́ду) на ста́нцію.
6. Андрі́й ніко́ли не (ї́здить, ї́де) ско́ро.
7. Ми лю́бимо (ї́здити, ї́хати).

Drill #118

Choose the correct form of the verb in parentheses and translate:

1. Васи́ль (ї́де, іде́) до села́.
2. Я за́втра (іду́, ї́ду) до Ки́єва.
3. Соба́ка (іде́, ї́де) на вера́нду.
4. Я (іду́, ї́ду) до їда́льні.
5. Ми (ідемо́, ї́демо) до Ме́хіко.
6. Я ба́чив, як Васи́ль (ішо́в, ї́хав) а́втом.
7. Коли́ ви (ідете́, ї́дете) в Украї́ну?
8. Га́ля (іде́, ї́де) до апте́ки.
9. Ма́ма (іде́, ї́де) до ку́хні.

Drill #119

Translate into Ukrainian:

1. We are going to Europe.
2. We are going to the study.
3. Who is going to the village?
4. We are all going there by car.
5. Olha was riding very fast.
6. Where are you going? I am going to Edmonton.

7. Is your wife going there too? No, she is going to grandmother's.
8. We are going to the living room.
9. My grandmother is going to the garden. She likes to be in the garden.
10. The Kozachenkos are going to Odesa. Their daughter lives in Odesa.
11. They often go to England.
12. They are going there tomorrow.
13. They usually drive fast.
14. They were driving slowly when I saw them.
15. Where do you go every summer? We go to the village.
16. We are going there soon.
17. My husband goes to work by train, and I go by car.
18. Today I too am going by train.
19. Do you often go to Kyiv?
20. I go there five or six times a year.

13.3 ADVERBS AND PREPOSITIONAL PHRASES OF MOTION (Continued)

To go to a place is expressed by prep. **на, в** + the acc., sometimes by prep. **до** + the gen.

Ми йдемó в шкóлу.
We are going to school.

Ми йдемó до шкóли.
We are going to school.

Ми йдемó на пóшту.
We are going to the post office.

To come from a place is expressed by prep. **з** + gen.:

Ми йдемó з теáтру. We are coming from the theater.

To come from a person is expressed by prep. **від** + gen.:

Ми йдемó від Остáпа. We are coming from Ostap's.

To go for something is expressed by prep. **за** + instr.:

Ми йдемó за газéтою. We are going for a newspaper.

The same meaning can be expressed by the prep. **по** + acc. in such constructions as:

Я йду́ по во́ду.	I'm going for water.

To go for someone's benefit is expressed by prep. **для** + gen.:

Ми йдемо́ для ма́ми.	We are going for mother's sake.

To go in place of someone is expressed by prep. **за** + the acc. or prep. **замість** + gen.:

Ми йдемо́ за ма́му. Ми йдемо́ за́мість ма́ми.	We are going in place (instead) of mother.

Drill #120

Translate the words in the right hand column:

1.	Ми йдемо́	from the store.
2.	Ми йдемо́	to the store for a magazine.
3.	На́дя йде́	to the post office for a stamp.
4.	О́ля йде́	from the post office.
5.	Я тепе́р працю́ю	at the post office.
6.	Ма́ма ї́де	to Stefa's.
7.	Вона́ бу́де жи́ти	at Stefa's.
8.	Ма́ма ї́де сюди́	from Stefa's.
9.	Ми йдемо́	to see Ulyana.[1]
10.	Ми йдемо́	to Ulyana's.[1]
11.	Я йду́	to see Vasyl.
12.	Я люблю́ працюва́ти	at Vasyl's.
13.	Хто йде́	to Dr. Starak.
14.	Я був учо́ра	at Dr. Starak's.
15.	Зе́ня йде́	to Orysya for a book.
16.	Вона́ тепе́р живе́	at Orysya's.
17.	Я йду́	for you.
18.	Іва́н іде́	to the factory in your place.

1 *Identical in Ukr.* The English idiom "to go to see" is translated into Ukrainian as prep. до + gen. of the person visited.

Drill #121

Translate into Ukrainian:

1. Where are you coming from now?
2. We are coming from there.
3. I am coming from Dr. Starak's.
4. They are coming from Halya's.
5. Andriy is coming from Roma's.
6. We are going to Kyiv for our father (*for our father's sake*).
7. We live in Kyiv.
8. We are coming from Kyiv.
9. Darka is going to Lviv for (*in place of*) me.
10. She lives in Lviv.
11. Where is she coming from now?
12. She is coming from Lviv now.
13. Where are they going? They are going to Ukraine.
14. They were in Ukraine.
15. They are now coming from Ukraine.
16. We are going to the concert.
17. We are now coming from the concert.
18. Whom is this letter from? Where is it from?
19. The letter is from Olha, from Toronto.

13.4 THE PERFECTIVE ASPECT OF "GO" VERBS

The perfective aspect of both the definite and the indefinite imperfective aspects of "going" and "riding" verbs is one and the same:

Indefinite	Definite	Perfective
ходи́ти	іти́	піти́
ї́здити	ї́хати	пої́хати

Note that the perfective is formed by adding the prefix **по-** to the definite imperfective.

Drill #122

Choose the correct form of the verb in parentheses and translate:

1. Мені́ було́ ну́дно і я (йшо́в, пішо́в) до Бори́са.
2. Я (йшо́в, пішо́в) до ньо́го по цій ву́лиці.
3. Ми вчо́ра (ходи́ли, пішли́) до теа́тру.
4. Коли́ ми туди́ (йшли́, пішли́), було́ хо́лодно.

5. О́лі нема́є вдо́ма. Вона́ (йшла́, пішла́) до апте́ки за аспіри́ною.
6. Я стрі́нув її́ на ву́лиці, коли́ вона́ туди́ (йшла́, пішла́).
7. Чому́ ваш чолові́к ра́птом (ї́хав, пої́хав) до Едмонто́ну?
8. Скі́льки днів він туди́ (ї́хав, пої́хав) ?
9. Коли́ ви (ї́дете, пої́дете) до А́фрики, ми (ї́демо, пої́демо) з ва́ми.
10. Я скінчу́ писа́ти той рома́н за мі́сяць, і (ї́ду, пої́ду) до Ме́хіко.
11. Вони́ ку́плять дім у Криму́ і (ї́дуть, пої́дуть) туди́ весно́ю.

Drill #123

Choose the proper form of the verbs піти́ or пої́хати:

1. Де Ро́мко? Він ..... до това́риша в Ки́їв.
2. Коли́ я скінчу́ кни́жку, ... до бібліоте́ки, а відта́к я ..... додо́му.
3. Споча́тку ми ..... в їда́льню, а по́тім в кабіне́т.
4. Де Мару́ся? Вона́ ..... на село́.
5. Хто ..... з не́ю? Вона́ ..... сама́. То я та́кож туди́ .....
6. Куди́ ма́ма ..... ? До ку́хні.

13.5 Idiomatic uses of the verb іти́ "go"

Час іде́.	Time goes by (passes).
Годи́нник іде́.	The watch is running.
Дощ іде́.	It's raining.
Фільм, п'є́са іде́.	The film, play is running.
По́їзд іде́.	The train is going.

Drill #124

Translate into Ukrainian:

1. Last year it rained almost every day.
2. My watch isn't running.
3. It rained early in the morning.
4. Without you time will go slowly.
5. The trains are not running today.
6. It took the telegram five hours to get here.
7. This play was running two years ago.
8. I don't know what is playing in this theater.
9. In the summer time goes fast.
10. Where does this train go?

Homework

a) Memorize the vocabulary in Lesson #14;
b) Review Lesson #13;
c) Translate the following sentences into Ukrainian.

1. Every spring they go to Odesa.
2. Every day I go to school.
3. He likes to drive fast.
4. Orest always walked fast.
5. When I saw her she was walking with Vasyl.
6. I saw him going to the drugstore.
7. We shall have dinner and then shall go to a movie which is next door.
8. From the movie we shall go to a restaurant.
9. Are you going home? I shall come with you.
10. Where are you going? I am going to Odesa. I'll go with you.
11. From Asia we'll go to Ukraine.
12. Where are you going?
13. We are going to the store.
14. We go to the store several times a day.
15. I have been at the store.
16. I am coming from the store.
17. Where is Yaryna going?
18. She is going to the post office.
19. She is working at the post office.
20. She is coming from the post office.
21. Where are these young men going?
22. They are going to the factory.
23. They go there every day.
24. They work at the factory.
25. Now they are coming from the factory.
26. The day after tomorrow we are going to Professor Darevych's.
27. We shall have dinner at Professor Darevych's.
28. We are coming from Professor Darevych's.
29. Petro is coming here from Lviv.
30. Here is a letter from him.
31. And where is Borysya coming from?
32. She is coming from Edmonton.
33. Here is a note from her.
34. She often goes to Edmonton.
35. She goes there several times a year.
36. She was walking along the street with her husband.
37. She went to the store for him.
38. How late it is! It's time to sleep.

ЧОТИРНА́ДЦЯТИЙ РО́ЗДІЛ

СЛОВНИ́К

Іме́нники жіно́чого ро́ду

короле́ва, -и	queen
неді́ля, -і	Sunday
прие́мність, -ности	pleasure
п'я́тниця, -і	Friday
середа́, -и	Wednesday
середи́на, -и	middle
систе́ма, -и	system
сторі́нка, -и	page
субо́та, -и	Saturday
терпели́вість, -вости	patience
хвили́на, -и	minute
це́рква, -и	church

Іме́нники чолові́чого ро́ду

вівто́рок, -ті́рка	Tuesday
добро́дій, -я	benefactor
коро́ль, -я́	king
Ло́ндон, -у	London
о́дяг, -у	clothing
по́верх, -у	storey, floor
понеді́лок, -лка	Monday
реда́ктор, -а	editor
четве́р, -рга́	Thursday

Іме́нники сере́днього ро́ду

навча́ння, -ння	study, studying
повто́рення, -ння	repetition
ре́чення, -ння	sentence
століття, -ття	century

Прикме́тники

відмі́нний, -а, -е	excellent
насту́пний, -а, -е	next
слов'я́нський, -а, -е	Slavic

Дієслова́

від'їжджа́ти: від'ї́хати (*від'їжджа́ю, -єш: від'ї́ду, -еш*)	to leave, depart
відкрива́ти: відкри́ти (*відкрива́ю, -єш: відкри́ю, -єш*)	to open
відхо́дити: віді́йти́ (*відхо́джу, -диш: віді́йду́, віді́йдеш*)	to leave, go away
запам'ято́вувати: запам'ята́ти (*запам'ято́вую, -єш: запам'ята́ю, -єш*)	to remember
означа́ти (*означа́є: it (this) means*)	to mean
повторя́ти: повтори́ти (*повторя́ю, -єш: повторю́, повто́риш*)	to repeat
позича́ти: пози́чити (*позича́ю, -єш: пози́чу, -иш*)	to borrow, lend
приїжджа́ти: приї́хати (*приїжджа́ю, -єш: приї́ду, -еш*)	to come, arrive
прихо́дити: прийти́ (*прихо́джу, -иш: прийду́, -еш*)	to come, arrive
проси́ти: попроси́ти (*прошу́, про́сиш*)	to ask

Прислі́вники

відмі́нно	excellently
прекра́сно	wonderfully
я́сно	clearly

Ви́рази

бу́дьте такі́ до́брі	be so kind
Гура́! (Ура́!)	Hurrah!
з ва́шої сторони́	on your part
па́не добро́дію	kind sir
проба́чте, проба́ч	excuse me
Що у вас ново́го?	What's new with you?

Імена́

Га́ля, -і	Halya
Оле́сь, -я	Oles

N.B. Memorize the ordinal numerals in *14.1* as part of the vocabulary.

GRAMMAR

Imperative Mood — Наказо́вий спо́сіб (14.0—14.2)
Ordinal Numerals — Порядко́ві числі́вники (14.1)
Days of the Week — Дні тижня (14.2—14.21)
Accusative of Time — Знахі́дний відмі́нок для позначе́ння ча́су (14.3—14.32)
Verbs of Going with Prefixes **при-** *and* **від-** *— Дієслова́ ру́ху з пре́фіксами* **при-** *і* **від-** *(14.4)*

14.0 IMPERATIVE MOOD

The imperative is a verb form used to express commands or requests. The imperative mood of the verb has basically three personal forms: the 2nd person singular and plural and the 1st person plural. In Ukrainian the imperative mood is formed from the present stem of the verb, i.e., the second person singular indicative minus the ending. There are four sets of endings for the imperative mood, depending on the type of stem and on the position of the stress:

1. Present stem ending in a vowel:

Stem	Imperative	Ending	
працюва́ти	працю́й	**-й**	2pers. sg.
працю́-єш	працю́йте	**-йте**	2pers. pl.
	працю́ймо	**-ймо**	1pers. pl.

2. Present stem ending in a consonant with the stress falling on the ending of the 1st person singular:

Stem	1 pers. sg. stress	Imperative	Ending	
бра́ти	беру́	бери́	**-и**	2pers. sg.
бер-е́ш		despite берí́ть	**-іть**	2pers. pl.
		бері́мо	**-імо**	1pers. pl.

3. Present stem ending in a labial, sibilant, or р with the stress not falling on the ending in the 1st person singular:

Stem	1pers. sg. stress	Imperative	Ending	
вда́рити	вда́рю	вда́р	**-Ø**	2perg. sg.
вда́р-иш		вда́рте	**-те**	2pers. pl.
		вда́рмо	**-мо**	1pers. pl.

4. Present stem ending in a dental with the stress not falling on the ending in the 1st person singular:

Stem	1pers. sg. stress	Imperative	Ending	
бу́ти	бу́ду	будь	**-(ь)**[1]	2pers. sg.
бу́д-еш		бу́дьте	**-(ь)те**	2pers. pl.
		бу́дьмо	**-(ь)мо**	1pers. pl.

14.01 The 3rd person singular and plural imperatives do exist, but they are formed from the indicative mood with the help of **хай** or **неха́й** "let":

неха́й бере́ — let (him) take
хай беру́ть — let (them) take

14.02 Verbs of both aspects form imperatives. The perfective aspect is generally used for single, definite actions, while the imperfective imperative is used for general rules, comments, or requests. It is also used for negative imperatives:

Напиши́ своє́ ім'я́!	Write your name!
Пиши́ мені́ ча́сто!	Write often to me!
Не пиши́ нічо́го!	Don't write anything!

Drill #125

Translate the words and form their imperfective and perfective imperatives:

do, read, write, explain, begin, finish, repeat, see, buy, open, shut, say, tell (narrate), show, go (*walk*), go (*ride*), take, give, be (*imperf. only*), drink

---

1 In fact, the endings are the same as in No. 3, but the stem consonant undergoes a palatalization which is indicated by **-ь**.

Drill #126

Supply imperatives according to the model:

Model: Попроси́ Бори́са (зачини́ти вікно́).
Бори́се, зачини́ вікно́, будь ла́ска.

1. Па́не добро́дію, бу́дьте такі́ до́брі, попросі́ть ва́шого сусі́да (зачини́ти вікно́). Будь ла́ска, ... вікно́.
2. Зе́ню, скажи́ Васи́леві, що він пови́нен (прочита́ти). Васи́лю, ... оста́ннє ре́чення.
3. Мару́сю, попроси́ Ро́мка (поясни́ти тобі́ це пра́вило). Ро́мку, ..., будь ла́ска.
4. Іва́не, попросі́ть Оле́ся (відкри́ти кни́жку і зача́ти чита́ти). Оле́сю, ...
5. Попроси́ батькі́в (ча́сто до нас писа́ти). Будь ла́ска, ...
6. Попросі́ть Робе́рта (розказа́ти вам це оповіда́ння). Па́не Робе́рте, про́шу, ...
7. Я хо́чу (показа́ти вам наш нови́й дім). Так, будь ла́ска, ...
8. Попроси́ Га́лю (да́ти тобі гро́ші). Га́лю, ...
9. О́лю, якщо́ ти хо́чеш (взя́ти) мою́ кни́жку, ... ї́ї.
10. Якщо́ ви хо́чете (повтори́ти) ле́кцію, ... ї́ї.
11. Якщо́ ви хо́чете (бу́ти там) о дру́гій годи́ні, ...
12. Якщо́ ви хо́чете (купи́ти) цей о́дяг, ... його́.
13. Якщо́ ви хо́чете (купува́ти) о́дяг в Пари́жі, ... його́ там.
14. Якщо́ ти пови́нен (написа́ти) до реда́ктора, ... йому́.
15. Якщо́ ти хо́чеш (писа́ти) оповіда́ння, ... його́.
16. Якщо́ ти хо́чеш (говори́ти), ...

14.1 ORDINAL NUMERALS

пе́рший, -а, -е, -і	first
дру́гий, -а, -е, -і	second
тре́тій, -я, -є, -і	third
четве́ртий, -а, -е, -і	fourth
п’я́тий, -а, -е, -і	fifth
шо́стий, -а, -е, -і	sixth
сьо́мий, -а, -е, -і	seventh
во́сьмий, -а, -е, -і	eighth
дев’я́тий, -а, -е, -і	ninth
деся́тий, -а, -е, -і	tenth

одина́дцятий, -а, -е, -і	eleventh
двана́дцятий, -а, -е, -і	twelfth
трина́дцятий, -а, -е, -і	thirteenth
чотирна́дцятий, -а, -е, -і	fourteenth
п'ятна́дцятий, -а, -е, -і	fifteenth
шістна́дцятий, -а, -е, -і	sixteenth
сімна́дцятий, -а, -е, -і	seventeenth
вісімна́дцятий, -а, -е, -і	eighteenth
дев'ятна́дцятий, -а, -е, -і	nineteenth
двадця́тий, -а, -е, -і	twentieth

Ordinal numerals are like adjectives and agree in gender, number, and case with the noun to which they refer. Only **тре́тій** "third" is a soft-stem adjective.

Drill #127

Answer the following questions in Ukrainian:

1. Скі́льки жіно́к було́ в англі́йського короля́ Ге́нріха Во́сьмого ?
2. Хто тепе́р короле́ва А́нглії?
3. На котро́му по́версі ви живете́?
4. На котро́му по́версі ми тепе́р ма́ємо ле́кцію?

Drill #128

Write out the numerals in Ukrainian:

1. Я говорю́ про свого́ (2) си́на.
2. Я пишу́ до мого́ (2) си́на.
3. Ми чита́ємо (2) ро́зділ.
4. Він був у Лондо́ні зі свое́ю (2) дружи́ною.
5. Я повто́рюю це (3) раз.
6. Я вже чита́ю (3) украї́нську кни́жку.
7. Ми купи́ли цей дім для на́шого (4) си́на.
8. Я ба́чив це сло́во на (5) сторі́нці.
9. Ми живемо́ на (14) по́версі, а Га́ля живе́ на (15).
10. Ми що́йно скінчи́ли (17) ле́кцію в на́шій кни́жці і зачина́ємо (18).
11. Ми живемо́ в (20) столі́тті.

Діяло́г: "Повто́рення — ма́ти навча́ння"

Дні ти́жня

А. Я ма́ю пога́ну па́м'ять і мені́ ва́жко запам'ята́ти дні ти́жня. Бу́дьте такі́ до́брі, й поможі́ть мені́.
Б. Це ду́же ле́гко і про́сто. Якщо́ хо́чете, я вам поможу́.
А. Це бу́де ду́же га́рно з ва́шої сторони́. Але́ для цьо́го потрі́бно бага́то ча́су і терпели́вости.
Б. Я це зроблю́ з вели́кою прие́мністю. Я ма́ю свою́ систе́му. Слу́хайте і повторя́йте. Пе́рший день ти́жня *по неді́лі*, це **понеді́лок**. Повторі́ть два ра́зи: **Понеді́лок** — пе́рший день по неді́лі.
А. (*повторя́є*)
Б. Ду́же до́бре. А тепе́р запам'ята́йте, що дру́гий день ти́жня — це вівто́рок. **Втор** — це стари́й слов'я́нський ко́рінь, що означа́є "дру́гий". Я́сно?
А. Так, це я́сно і ле́гко запам'ята́ти, якщо́ поду́мати про сло́во **повтори́ти**, що означа́є сказа́ти дру́гий раз.
Б. Так. Повторі́ть два ра́зи: **Вівто́рок** — це дру́гий день ти́жня.
А. (*повторя́є*)
Б. По вівті́ркові йде́ тре́тій день — середа́. **Середа́** — це **середи́на** ти́жня. Повторі́ть два ра́зи: **Середа́** — це середи́на ти́жня.
А. (*повторя́є*)
Б. Відмі́нно. Тепе́р **четве́ртий** день — **четве́р**. Повторі́ть три ра́зи: **Четве́р** — це четве́ртий день ти́жня.
А. (*повторя́є*)
Б. Прекра́сно. Яки́й день по четве́ртому? Зрозумі́ло, що п'я́тий. **П'я́тий** день — **п'я́тниця**. Повторі́ть па́ру разі́в: **П'я́тниця** — це п'я́тий день ти́жня.
А. (*повторя́є*)
Б. Шо́стий день — **субо́та**. Сло́во "субо́та" похо́дить (*originates*) від "Саббат". Це ле́гко запам'ята́ти, пра́вда?
А. Так, це не тру́дно.
Б. Прекра́сно. Тепе́р сьо́мий і оста́нній день — це неді́ля. **Неді́ля** — це день без ді́ла /не(ма́) **ді́ла**/ — бо це свя́то.
А. Ура́! Я все тепе́р пам'ята́ю: понеді́лок, вівто́рок, середа́, четве́р, п'я́тниця, субо́та, неді́ля. Я вам ду́же дя́кую за ва́шу по́міч.
Б. Нема́є за́що. Я за́вжди вам ра́до поможу́.

14.2 DAYS OF THE WEEK

Days of the week are nouns and follow the rules for gender and declension which apply to other nouns. They are not capitalized in Ukrainian:

понеді́лок, -а	Monday
вівто́рок, -а	Tuesday
середа́, -и́	Wednesday
четве́р, четверга́	Thursday
п’я́тниця, -і	Friday
субо́та, -и	Saturday
неді́ля, -і	Sunday

14.21 Time *when* is expressed by the preposition в/у and the acc. case:

у понеді́лок	on Monday
у неді́лю	on Sunday
у міну́лий вівто́рок	past, last Tuesday
у цей четве́р	this Thursday
у насту́пну се́реду	next Wednesday
в міну́лий понеді́лок	last Monday

This same meaning may be rendered through the genitive construction, but only if the day is modified by “this”, “next”, etc.:

міну́лого понеді́лка	last Monday
цьо́го понеді́лка	this Monday
у цей понеді́лок	
насту́пного понеді́лка	next Monday
у насту́пний понеді́лок	

14.3 ACCUSATIVE OF TIME WITH на AND за

The preposition на is used with the accusative case to specify a period of time subsequent to an action such as going, giving, taking, lending, etc.:

Вони́ поі́хали на ти́ждень.
They left for a week.

Я взяв ту кни́жку на два дні.
I took that book for two days.

Questions of this type are formed with **на як до́вго**:

На як до́вго?	For how long?
На як до́вго він поі́хав ?	For how long did he leave?

14.31 When the period of time is that of the duration of the action itself, the accusative without the preposition is used:

Як до́вго ви чита́ли? Я чита́в **три годи́ни.**
How long did you read? I read for three hours.

but

На як до́вго ви позича́єте кни́жку?
Я позича́ю **на ти́ждень.**
For how long are you borrowing this book? I am borrowing it for a week.

14.32 The preposition **за** is used with the accusative in the sense of "after", "at the end of" an action:

За ти́ждень він поі́де до Фра́нції.
In (after) a week he will go to France.

Drill #129

Translate into Ukrainian:

1. I will take Anna's car for a few days.
2. I am going to Orest's for two hours.
3. I am going to work there for two hours.
4. I will return after two hours.
5. I am going to Europe for a week.
6. For how long are you going?
7. I am going for a month.
8. How long will you stay (live) at your sister's?
9. I am going in (after) a month.
10. We lived in Ukraine for three weeks. We are going back there in four months.
11. For how many months are you going there? For two.

Drill #130

Reply to the questions in Ukrainian:

1. Котри́й день в сере́дині ти́жня?
2. У котри́й день лю́ди відпочива́ють і хо́дять до це́ркви?
3. Котри́й день похо́дить від сло́ва "Са́ббат"?
4. Котри́й п'я́тий день ти́жня?
5. О котрі́й годи́ні ви ма́єте пе́ршу ле́кцію у вівто́рок?
6. На як до́вго ви хо́дите щодня́ до шко́ли?
7. О котрі́й годи́ні ви звича́йно встає́те в понеді́лок?
8. На як до́вго ви хо́дите щодня́ до бібліоте́ки?
9. Скі́льки годи́н у день ви працю́єте?
10. О котрі́й годи́ні ви звича́йно obі́даєте?
11. Неді́ля четве́ртий день ти́жня?
12. На як до́вго ви ї́дете в Украї́ну?
13. На скі́льки днів ви взя́ли цю кни́жку?
14. Ви надо́вго ї́дете до А́фрики?
15. За я́кий час ви прии́дете?

14.4 "GOING" VERBS WITH THE PREFIXES **при-**, **від-** AND **ви-**

The prefix **при-** is added to "going" verbs to express the idea of "coming", "arriving"; the prefix **від-** is added to express "leaving", "going away"; and **ви-** is used for "coming out of", "exiting".

In creating the new verb with a prefix, the indefinite imperfective is used to form the new imperfective and the definite imperfective is used to form the new perfective.

при + *indef. imperf.*	=	**прихо́дити**	(*new imperf.*)
при + *def. imperf.*	=	**прийти́**	(*new perf.*)

The corresponding compounds for "riding" are formed with **їжджа́ти** (instead of **ї́здити**): **приїжджа́ти**, **приїзди́ти** also exists, but it is rarely used.

The same happens with the prefix **від** or **ви**:

відхо́дити, **вихо́дити**, **відійти́**, **ви́йти**	leave, depart, exit
від'їжджа́ти, **виїжджа́ти**, **від'їхати**, **ви́їхати**	leave, depart, exit

Drill #131

Choose the correct verb and translate:

Прихóдити: прийти́

1. Зимóю (прихóдив, прийшóв) додóму о шóстій.
2. Тепéр я зáвжди (прихóджу, прийдý) скорíше.
3. Гáня вчóра (прихóдила, прийшлá) до нас о трéтій годи́ні.
4. О котрíй годи́ні Андрíй сьогóдні (прийшóв, прихóдив) до бібліотéки?
5. Зáвтра я (бýду прихóдити, прийдý) до вас рáно.
6. Лíтом Івáнко (бýде прихóдити, при́йде) до нас чáсто.

Відхóдити: відійти́, вихóдити: ви́йти

1. Секретáрка сьогóдні пíзно (ви́йшла, відійшлá, відхóдила) з бюра.
2. Веснóю вонá (вихóдила, відхóдила, ви́йшла) о четвéртій годи́ні.
3. Коли́ я працювáв у фáбриці, я (відхóдив, вихóдив, відійшóв) з хáти о п'ятій.
4. Тепéр я (вихóджу, відхóджу, відійдý) з хáти о вóсьмій.
5. Бáтько сьогóдні скóро (ви́йде, відійдé, відхóдитиме) з бюра.
6. Ми тепéр щодня́ (бýдемо відхóдити, бýдемо вихóдити, відійдéмо) тóчно о дев'ятій.

Drill #132

Translate into Ukrainian:

1. She used to come to the library at 12:00.
2. She used to leave the library at 2:00.
3. On Wednesday she always comes early and always leaves late.
4. I also come here often.
5. I leave every day at five.
6. On Monday I came early and I left early.
7. I don't know yet when I shall come on Saturday and when I shall leave.

8. She went to the store.
9. I saw her going there.
10. She goes there every morning.
11. She left home ten minutes ago.
12. We shall leave soon.
13. When will you come? I shall come on Tuesday.

Drill #133

Replace the English verb in parentheses by the proper Ukrainian verb and translate:

1.	Ми вчо́ра ..... до Нью Йо́рку.	(came)
2.	Га́ня ..... з на́ми.	(came)
3.	Цьо́го ра́зу мій ба́тько ..... до мі́ста.	(didn't come)
4.	Він ..... сюди́ раз у рік.	(used to come)
5.	Га́ня за́вжди з ним	(came)
6.	Ча́сом ми ..... самі́.	(came)
7.	Я не зна́ю, коли́ ми зно́ву ..... сюди́.	(will come)
8.	Коли́ ви ..... до нас у Крим?	(will come)
9.	Ми ..... лі́том.	(will come)
10.	Ми ..... ча́сто.	(will come)
11.	Андрі́й	(left Kyiv)
12.	Вони́ ..... ра́зом.	(left)
13.	Ми ско́ро	(left)
14.	Коли́ ви	(are leaving)
15.	Коли́ Зе́ня і він	(are leaving)
16.	Я ..... за два ти́жні.	(am leaving)
17.	Вони́ ..... на два ти́жні.	(are leaving)
18.	Коли́ вони́ ....., О́ля буде́ жи́ти в їх кварти́рі.	(will leave)
19.	Якщо́ тут бу́де ду́же га́ряче́, ми	(will leave)

Drill #134

Give a suitable Ukrainian word or phrase for the English in parentheses and fill in the blanks.

1.	Ми прийдемо ..... за́втра ра́но.	(to see you)
2.	Пі́сля ле́кції він прийшо́в	(to see me)
3.	Він був ..... о тре́тій годи́ні.	(at my place)
4.	Він ско́ро	(left my place)

5. Вони́ бу́дуть ра́ді, коли́ він ..... (will leave them)
6. Коли́ ви прийдете ..... ? (to see us)
7. Бу́ло пізно, коли́ Ніна ..... (left her)
8. Якщо́ ти за́втра бу́деш удо́ма, я прийду́ ..... (to your place)
9. Я бу́ду обідати ..... (at your place)

Homework

a) Memorize the vocabulary in Lesson #15;
b) Review Lesson #14;
c) Translate the following sentences into Ukrainian.

1. Last month when he arrived from Ukraine, he came at once to see us.
2. She just came from the editor.
3. From his study she came to my room.
4. They left school early today.
5. From where did he come, from Odesa or (чи) from Lviv?
6. When I came to his room he wasn't there.
7. Next month he will get here (arrive) from Africa.
8. I am leaving in two days.
9. When they leave Toronto next year, who is going to live in their house?
10. She left the concert before the end.
11. She had just left for Mexico for a week.
12. We came here from France.
13. When did he leave there? Last Wednesday.
14. Come to see us on Monday.
15. Memorize the names of the days of the week.
16. Be so kind as to help me.
17. Excuse me, I have no time.
18. What's new with you?
19. Take this money and give it to your son.
20. Don't give money to your little daughter.

П'ЯТНА́ДЦЯТИЙ РО́ЗДІЛ

СЛОВНИ́К

Іме́нники жіно́чого ро́ду

пере́рва, -и	recess
пора́да, -и	counsel, advice
сте́ля, -і	ceiling
хма́ра, -и	cloud

Іме́нники чолові́чого ро́ду

вальс, -у	waltz
дах, -у	roof
м'ясни́к, -а́	butcher
прохі́д, -хо́ду	walk
сніг, -у	snow
цуке́рок, -рка	candy
Шопе́н, -а	Chopin

Іме́нники сере́днього ро́ду

я́блуко, -а	apple

Прикме́тники

м'яки́й, -а́, -е́	soft

Дієслова́

боя́тися: побоя́тися *(бою́ся, бої́шся)*	to fear
буди́ти: розбуди́ти *(буджу́, бу́диш)*	to awaken
в/у/бира́ти: в/у/бра́ти *(вбира́ю, вбира́єш: вберу́, вбере́ш)*	to dress
диви́тися: подиви́тися *(дивлю́ся, ди́вишся)*	to look
замика́ти: замкну́ти *(замика́ю, замика́єш: замкну́, замкне́ш)*	to close, lock
здава́тися *(здає́ться — it seems, 3rd pers. only)*	to seem
коха́ти: покоха́ти *(коха́ю, коха́єш)*	to love
ме́шкати; за/по/ме́шкати *(ме́шкаю, ме́шкаєш)*	to inhabit, dwell
ми́ти: ви/об/ми́ти *(ми́ю, ми́єш)*	to wash
надіятися *(наді́юся, наді́єшся)*	to hope, expect

одяга́ти: одягну́ти *(одяга́ю, одяга́єш: одягну̀, одя́гнеш)*	to dress, clothe
подо́батися: сподо́батися *(подо́баюся, подо́баєшся)*	to appeal
смія́тися: за/по/смія́тися *(сміюся, смієшся)*	to laugh
спізня́тися/спі́знюватися: спізни́тися *(спізня́юся, спізня́єшся* *[спі́знююся, спі́знюєшся]:* *спізню́ся, спі́знишся)*	to be late

Прислі́вники

випадко́во	by chance
в/у/ночі́	at night
в/у/поря́дку	in order
одна́ково	alike

Ви́рази

працюва́ти над	(+ *instr.*) to work at
смія́тися над	(+ *instr.*) to laugh at
смія́тися з	(+ *gen.*) to laugh at
так собі́	so-so

Імена́

Зі́рка, -и	Zirka

GRAMMAR

Verbs Ending in **-ся** — *Дієслова́ із ча́сткою* **-ся** *(15.0—15.02)*
Conjugation of **боя́тися** — *Відмі́нювання дієсло́ва* **боя́тися** *(15.1)*
Verbs (Cont.) — Дієслова́ (продо́вж.) (15.3—15.32)
Dative, Locative, and Instrumental Plural of Nouns and Modifiers — Дава́льний, місце́вий і ору́дний відмі́нки в множині́ іме́нників та слів з прикметнико́вими фо́рмами (15.4—15.41)
Time Expressions with the Instrumental Plural — Ви́рази ча́су при вжива́нні ору́дного відмі́нку множини́ (15.5—15.51)
Prepositions Governing the Instrumental Case — Прийме́нники, що керу́ють ору́дним відмі́нком (15.6)

15.0 VERBS ENDING IN **-ся**

Many Ukrainian verbs appear only with the reflexive suffixed particle **-ся**. These are all intransitive and reflexive; in other words, they do not take a direct object and refer the action back to the subject.

Some Ukrainian verbs, however, can exist both with and without the particle **-ся**.

For example, the transitive verb **зачина́ти** "to begin", e.g.,

Я зачина́ю пра́цю о сьо́мій.
I begin work at seven.

can become intransitive with the addition of the particle **-ся**:

Моя́ пра́ця зачина́ється о сьо́мій.
My work begins at seven.

Note: First conjugation verbs have **-ть** proceeding the **-ся** in the 3rd person singular:

1st pers. sing.	зачина́ю-ся
2nd pers. sing.	зачина́єш-ся
3rd pers. sing.	зачина́є-ть-ся

Other verbs which can be both transitive and intransitive are:

ми́ти	ми́тися	to wash
вбира́ти	вбира́тися	to dress
відчиня́ти	відчиня́тися	to open
замика́ти	замика́тися	to close
ба́чити	ба́читися	to see
стріча́ти	стріча́тися	to meet

15.01 Some verbs are only reflexive and intransitive in Ukrainian:

боя́тися	to fear
смія́тися	to laugh
наді́ятися	to hope
здава́тися	to seem

15.02 The 3rd person of a reflexive verb with **-ся** sometimes denotes that an action is normally or correctly done in a certain way. Such constructions are impersonal:

Як пи́шеться ці слова́?
How does one write these words?
(How are these words written?)

Ці слова́ так не гово́риться.
One does not say these words so.
(These words are not pronounced that way.)

Note: In the examples above, although **слова́** is plural the verbs remain singular in Ukrainian.

15.1 CONJUGATION OF боя́тися "TO FEAR"

Present:	1st pers.	бою́ся/сь	боїмо́ся/сь
	2nd pers.	боЇшся	боїте́ся/сь
	3rd pers.	боЇться	боя́ться

Past: боя́вся, боя́лася/сь, боя́лося/сь, боя́лися/сь

Imperative: бі́йся, бі́йтеся/сь, бі́ймося/сь

15.2 CONJUGATION OF **надіятися/сь** "TO HOPE"

Present:	1st pers.	надіюся/сь	надіємося/сь
	2nd pers.	надієшся	надієтеся/сь
	3rd pers.	надіється	надіються

Past: надіявся, надіялася/сь, надіялося/сь, надіялися/сь

Imperative: надійся, надійтеся/сь, надіймося/сь

15.21 The verb **сміятися** "to laugh" is declined in the same manner.

15.22 The particle **-ся** may alternate (but does not have to) with an euphonic variant, the particle **-сь**, but only in places where a vowel precedes the particle:

боюся/боюсь *but* боїшся

Drill #135

Answer the following questions in Ukrainian:

1. Як до́вго ви працю́єте над украї́нською мо́вою?
2. З ким ви працю́єте? З ким ви вчите́ся?
3. Чому́ ваш сусі́д смі́ється?
4. Кого́ або чого́ ви боїте́ся?
5. Що ви пови́нні роби́ти, коли́ ви встаєте́?
6. Якщо́ ви хо́чете дістава́ти до́брі оці́нки, що ви пови́нні роби́ти?
7. Що пови́нна роби́ти ма́ти ра́нком і ве́чором, якщо́ у не́ї є мале́нька дити́на?
8. Вас одяга́є ма́ти, чи ви самі́ одяга́єтеся?

Drill #136

Change the verbs in parentheses to the appropriate form of the present, past, or future, and translate:

1. Я (боя́тися) вас.
2. Ви мене́ (боя́тися).
3. На́ші ді́ти нас зо́всім не (боя́тися).
4. Ми (надія́тися), що ви до нас при́йдете. Чому́ ви не прийшли́ ?
5. Ні́на (надія́тися), що вона́ здасть і́спит.
6. Конце́рти пе́ред тим (зачина́тися) о дев'я́тій.

7. Конце́рт (зачина́тися) за п'ять хвили́н.
8. Крамни́ця тепе́р (замика́тися) о шо́стій годи́ні.
9. Я вчо́ра (збуди́тися) о сьо́мій годи́ні. Я ско́ро (вста́ти), (поми́тися), (одягну́тися).
10. Тепе́р я за́вжди (буди́тися) о во́сьмій годи́ні. Я ско́ро (встава́ти), (ми́тися), (одяга́тися).
11. Всі ле́кції звича́йно (кінча́тися) о четве́ртій годи́ні, але́ вчо́ра вони́ (закінчи́тися) о тре́тій.
12. За́втра ле́кції (закінчи́тися), як за́вжди.

Drill #137

Choose one of the following verbs ending in **-ся** and use it in the proper form as required by the context of the sentence:

боя́тися, замика́тися, здава́тися, учи́тися, наді́ятися, одяга́тися, відкрива́тися, смія́тися

1. Петро́ ще не прийшо́в, але́ ....., що він при́йде.
2. Бори́с ду́же бага́то .....; він хоті́в ді́ста́ти до́брі оці́нки.
3. Його́ ба́тько ста́рший чолові́к і ра́ніше його́ ..... Але́ тепе́р його́ бі́льше не .....
4. Пе́ред тим мені́ ....., що Бори́с до́брий студе́нт, а тепе́р мені́ ....., що він ліни́вий.
5. Всі його́ костю́ми ду́же дорогі́: він ду́же га́рно .....
6. Вони́ ....., що ви ско́ро прийдете до них.
7. О́льга ....., що ви при́йдете, але́ ви не прийшли́.
8. Чому́ ви не замкну́ли двере́й? Ті две́рі не .....
9. Чому́ ви не відкри́ли вікна́? Тому́, що воно́ не ..... Я його́ відкри́ю. Ось ба́чите, воно́ .....
10. Я ....., що він при́йде, він мені́ ду́же потрі́бний.
11. Я ....., що він не при́йде, а він мені́ ду́же потрі́бний.
12. Всі ....., що вам бу́де ну́дно на тій ле́кції.
13. Ді́ти вже вста́ли, але́ вони́ ще не ..... Вони́ ..... за де́сять хвили́н.
14. Бу́демо ....., що все впоря́дку.

15.3 VERBS (Continued)

The verb **люби́ти** means "to like", "to be fond of". It is a transitive verb. It may be used with infinitives:

Я люблю́ ма́му.
I like mother.

Я люблю́ ї́сти м'я́со.
I like to eat meat.

15.31 The transitive verb **коха́ти** means "to love".

Я коха́ю свою́ дружи́ну.
I love my wife.

15.32 The intransitive verb **подо́батися** means "to like", "to appeal". It may express judgement, impression, evaluation:

Мені подо́бається це місце.
I like this place (literally: *this place appeals to me*).

With the verb **подо́батися** the person who likes someone or something is in the dative case; the person or thing which is being liked is in the nominative:

Я йому́ подо́баюся.
He likes me (*I appeal to him*).

Drill #138

In the sentences below, use the suitable form of the following verbs, supplying a pronoun whenever needed:

подо́батися: сподо́батися
люби́ти: полюби́ти
коха́ти: покоха́ти

1. Васи́ль ..... учи́тися вночі́.
2. Ми ..... гуля́ти в лісу́.
3. Мені́ не ..... твій нови́й костю́м.
4. Коли́ я приї́хав до Ло́ндону пе́рший раз, він мені́ ду́же не .....
5. Мені́ тепе́р ..... наш профе́сор.
6. Нам ....., як ваш брат учо́ра загра́в вальс Шопе́на.
7. Наш учи́тель не ду́же ..... Шопе́на.
8. Вчо́ра на вечі́рці О́ля говори́ла з Бори́сом. Здає́ться, що він ду́же ....
9. Купи́ о́дяг, ті́льки якщо́ він ....
10. О́ля ..... цуке́рки.
11. Миро́н сказа́в Бори́сові, що він ....

Drill #139

Translate into Ukrainian:

1. I like your young friend; he is intelligent.
2. Formerly I used to like that newspaper, but now I no longer like it.
3. How do you like this cheese? So-so. I am not very fond of cheese.
4. If we don't like the high mountains, we shall go to the seashore.
5. I like to study at night; at night it is so quiet.
6. Do you like this novel? Yes, I read it not long ago and liked it very much. I like that author.
7. Our teacher is very fond of Yanovsky's (Яновський) novel "Four Swords", but his students don't like Yanovsky.
8. I liked that novel very much when I read it for the first time.
9. Last year we travelled around Europe; I liked France and Italy very much.
10. How do you like our teacher? Not very much. He likes to ask difficult questions.

15.4 DATIVE, LOCATIVE, AND INSTRUMENTAL PLURAL OF NOUNS AND MODIFIERS

These cases have only one plural form for all three genders. The endings of these case forms are:

	Nouns	3 pers. pron.	Modifiers
Dat.	-ам/-м	їм	-им/-ім(їм after vowels)
Instr.	-ами/-ями	ни́ми	-ими/-іми(їми after vowels)
Loc.	-ах/-ях	них	-их/-іх(їх after vowels)
Dat.	стола́м /пісня́м		ва́шим /си́нім /твої́м
Instr.	стола́ми/пісня́ми		ва́шими/си́німи/твої́ми
Loc.	(на) стола́х/пісня́х		(на) ва́ших/си́ніх/твої́х

15.41 The following nouns are exceptions. They have the ending **-(ь)ми** in the instrumental plural:

кіньми	horses
людьми́	people
дверми́/двери́ма	doors
дітьми́	children
грішми	money

15.5 TIME EXPRESSIONS WITH THE INSTRUMENTAL PLURAL

The instrumental plural is used for parts of the day (**вечір, ніч, ранок, день**) to express a habitual time during which something is done:

Ми за́вжди вдо́ма **вечора́ми**.
We are always at home in the evenings.

Ми працю́ємо **ноча́ми**.
We work nights.

15.51 The preposition **в** + the *acc. pl.*, however, is the construction used to express habit with days of the week:

В се́реди ми вдо́ма.
On Wednesdays we are at home.

У вівті́рки ми в шко́лі.
On Tuesdays we are at school.

Drill #140

Supply the correct form of the dative plural:

1. В тій кля́сі розу́мні студе́нти і студе́нтки. Кому́ вчи́тель поя́снює пра́вила? ..... і .....
2. Ми ма́ємо нови́х дру́зів. Кому́ ми пи́шемо листи́? .....
3. Ні́на ма́є га́рні по́други. Ні́на купу́є дару́нки .....
4. Всі мої́ профе́сори́ задаю́ть мені́ пита́ння. Я відповіда́ю .....
5. У ме́не в кля́сі шість хло́пців. Я даю́ ..... я́блука. Ко́жному хло́пцеві по я́блукові.

Drill #141

Read the question and answer it in Ukrainian in terms of the preceding statement:

1. Андрі́й ніко́ли не жив у вели́ких міста́х. В яки́х містах він жив?
2. Вона́ лю́бить дорогі́, вигі́дні готе́лі. Де вона́ лю́бить ме́шкати?
3. У то́му місті вели́кі фа́брики. Де працю́ють ті робі́тники?
4. Моя́ ма́ти лю́бить мої́х діте́й. Про ко́го вона́ за́вжди гово́рить?

Drill #142

Place the words in the right hand column into the instrumental:

1. Він це зроби́в (*чим?*)	мале́нькі ножі́ свої́ ру́ки си́ні та черво́ні олівці́ свої́ гру́бі па́льці си́льні ко́ні
2. Ми працюва́ли там з (*ким?*)	молоді́ лікарі́ радя́нські письме́нники до́брі інжене́ри розу́мні дівча́та всі вчителі́ нові́ дру́зі ва́ші сини́

15.6 PREPOSITIONS за, пе́ред, над, під, між WITH THE INSTRUMENTAL CASE

The preposition за means "behind", "beyond", "on the other side of":

За на́шою ха́тою є сад.
Behind our house there is an orchard.

За гора́ми є місто.
There is a city on the other side of the mountains.

Він ішо́в за мно́ю.
He walked behind me.

The construction **за** + the *instr.* case is sometimes used to convey the meaning of getting things (see 13.3). It is much better to use the construction of **по** + the *acc.* case in such instances to avoid the ambiguity between "getting something" and "behind" something, especially in the case of animate nouns:

Він пішóв за Івáном.
He went after Ivan. = can mean *to get* Ivan or *behind* Ivan.

Він пішóв по Івáна.
He went after Ivan. = means only *to get* Ivan.

Idioms with **за**:

за обі́дом at dinner
за столóм at the table
за кордóном abroad

15.61 The preposition **пéред** means "in front of" (*place*), "before" (*time*):

Пéред хáтою стоя́ло áвто.
In front of the house stood a car.

Пéред лéкцією булá перéрва.
Before the lesson there was a recess.

15.62 The preposition **над** means "above", "near":

Над горáми хмáри.
There are clouds *above* the mountains.

Нáша хáта стоя́ла над рікóю.
Our house stood *near* the river.

Idioms with **над**:

працювáти над	to work at / on
смія́тися над	to laugh at

15.63 The preposition **під** means "below", "under", "underneath":

Кни́жка лежáла під столóм.
The book was lying *under* the table.

Земля́ **піді** мно́ю тверда́.
The earth *below* me is hard.

15.64 The euphonic variants of **під** and **над** are **підо** (**піді**) and **на́до** (**на́ді**). They are used when the prepositions precede words beginning with a consonant cluster:

Пі́до мно́ю сніг, а **на́ді** мно́ю не́бо.
Beneath me there is snow, and *above* me is the sky.

15.65 The preposition **між** means "between":

Наш університе́т (знахо́диться) **між** ріко́ю і па́рком.
Our university is (stands) *between* the river and the park.

Це хай бу́де **між** на́ми.
Let this remain between us.

Drill #143

Fill in the suitable prepositions:

1. Моє́ лі́жко стої́ть ..... вікно́м і полі́цею.
2. ..... ха́тою гара́ж.
3. ..... на́ми дах.
4. Він працю́є ..... нови́м рома́ном.
5. Він говори́в із профе́сором ..... ле́кцією.
6. Медві́дські живу́ть ..... ро́гом.
7. Зі́рка прийшла́ ..... обі́дом, а відійшла́ ..... обі́ду.
8. Ма́ти присла́ла мене́ ..... молоко́.
9. Я прийшо́в до вас ..... пора́ду.
10. Журна́л лежа́в ..... крі́слом.

Drill #144

Put the words on the right into the proper case:

Вели́кі хма́ри були́ над/на́ді (*ким/чим?*) на́ша ріка́
мале́нькі хати́
си́ні моря́
на́ші голови́
висо́кі дере́ва

я
ти
ви
він
ми
вони́
вона́

Homework

a) Memorize the vocabulary in Lesson #16;
b) Review Lesson #15;
c) Translate the following sentences into Ukrainian.

1. The armchair is in front of us.
2. The sofa is behind us.
3. Where are you standing? I am standing between the window and the table.
4. In front of me is a yellow armchair; behind me is a green sofa.
5. I am standing behind the yellow armchair in front of the green sofa.
6. Where is the ceiling? The ceiling is above us.
7. There is a soft, expensive rug; the rug is beneath the table.
8. Our aunt needs money; she has come to us for money.
9. The mother washes and dresses her young children, but the older children already wash and dress without her help.
10. You have written these words incorrectly! These words are spelled (are written) this way.
11. Do not fear but hope.
12. Today I met my old friends by chance on the subway.
13. When will you get up tomorrow? I will get up early.
14. I have a great deal of work and I must start studying early.
15. How long did you work on this book? I worked for a long time, almost three years.
16. If you want to come and see me, tell me and I will be at home.
17. Those two girls dress alike.
18. I like this writer, but I didn't like his novel.
19. We like to read in Ukrainian, although we read very slowly.
20. He always thinks about his friends and sends money to his friends.
21. What do you do in the evenings? I work with my sisters.

ШІСТНА́ДЦЯТИЙ РО́ЗДІЛ

СЛОВНИ́К

Іме́нники жіно́чого ро́ду

америка́нка, -и	American (woman)
англі́йка, -и	Englishwoman
дити́на, -и	child
Еспа́нія, -ї	Spain
еспа́нка, -и	Spaniard (woman)
італі́йка, -и	Italian (woman)
кана́дка, -и	Canadian (woman)
ковбаса́, -и́	kovbasa
кро́мка, -и	slice of bread
математи́ка, -и	mathematics
мело́дія, -ї	melody
ні́мка, -и	German (woman)
по́дорож, -і	journey
по́лька, -и	Pole (woman)
росія́нка, -и	Russian (woman)
ски́бка, -и	slice of bread
турке́ня, -і	Turk (woman)
украї́нка, -и	Ukrainian (woman)
францу́женка, -и	Frenchwoman
шве́дка, -и	Swede (woman)

Іме́нники чолові́чого ро́ду

акто́р, -а	actor
америка́нець, -нця	American
англі́єць, -лі́йця	Englishman
біфсте́кс, -а	steak
ви́падок, -дку	occurance, event
еспа́нець, -нця	Spaniard
італі́єць, -лі́йця	Italian
кана́дець, -дця	Canadian
Мадри́д, -у	Madrid
мужчи́на, -и	male
наро́д, -у	people, nation
ні́мець, -мця	German
поля́к, -а	Pole
росія́нин, -а	Russian
селяни́н, -а	peasant, villager
слов’яни́н, -а	Slav
суддя́, -і	judge
ту́рок, -рка	Turk

украї́нець, -нця	Ukrainian
францу́з, -а	Frenchman
християни́н, -а	Christian
чужи́нець, -нця	foreigner
швед, -а	Swede

Іме́нники сере́днього ро́ду

пи́во, -а	beer
подорожува́ння, -ння	travels, traveling
прийняття́, -ття́	reception

Множи́нні іме́нники

Об'є́днані На́ції	United Nations
З'є́днані Шта́ти Аме́рики (ЗША)	U.S.A.
Сполу́чені Шта́ти Аме́рики (США)	

Прикме́тники

еспа́нський, -а, -е	Spanish
знайо́мий, -а, -е	known, acquainted
і́нший, -а, -е	other, different
чужи́й, -а́, -е́	foreign

Дієслова́

вари́ти: звари́ти *(варю́, ва́риш)*	to cook
волі́ти *(волі́ю, волі́єш)*	to prefer
знайо́мити: познайо́мити *(знайо́млю, знайо́миш)*	to acquaint
знайо́митися: познайо́митися	become aquainted with (*з* + *instr.*)
ляга́ти: лягти́ *(ляга́ю, ляга́єш: ля́жу, ля́жеш)*	to lie down
сіда́ти: сі́сти *(сіда́ю, сіда́єш: ся́ду, ся́деш)*	to sit down
става́ти: ста́ти *(стаю́, стає́ш: ста́ну, ста́неш)*	to stand, become
трапля́тися: тра́питься *(трапля́ється: тра́питься) (3rd pers. only)*	to happen

Прислі́вники

небага́то/небага́цько	not much
сті́льки	so much

Ви́рази

бага́то чого́	many things

Імена́

Макси́м, -а	Maksym

GRAMMAR

16.0 NOUN GENDER (Continued)

Some nouns may be masculine in meaning but feminine in form:

мужчи́на, -и man
суддя́, -і́ judge (*masc.* and *fem.*)
сусі́да, -и/сусі́д, -а neighbor (*both forms exist*)

Modifiers used with these nouns take masculine endings:

Цей вели́кий мужчи́на — мій до́брий сусі́да.
This big man is my good neighbor.

16.01 Declension of суддя́

	Singular	Plural
Nom.	суддя́	су́дді
Gen.	судді́	су́ддів
Dat.	судді́	су́ддям
Acc.	суддю́	су́ддів
Instr.	судде́ю	су́ддями
Loc.	(на) судді́	(на) су́ддях
Voc.	су́дде	су́дді

16.2 MISCELLANEOUS GENITIVE PLURALS

Some nouns have genitive plurals which do not correspond to the basic threefold division presented in chapter twelve (see 12.0). Here are some examples:

Nom. Sg.	Nom. Pl.	Gen. Pl.	Not the expected	
дити́на	ді́ти	діте́й	дити́н	child
люди́на	лю́ди	люде́й	люди́н	person
ма́ти	матері́	матері́в	матер	mother
статтю́	статті́	статте́й/-і́в	стать	article
сім'я́	сі́м'ї	сіме́й/-і́в	сім	family
ді́вчина	дівча́та	дівча́т	дівчи́н	girl

16.21 Note: in words where the singular stem and the plural stem differ (e.g. **люди́н-а** vs **лю́д-и**; **дити́н-а** vs **ді́т-и**; **ді́вчин-а** vs **дівча́т-а**), one must use the genitive singular forms of the words after the numerals 2, 3, and 4 (see 9.4 and 12.3).

e.g.: Я ба́чу три **ді́вчини, люди́ни, дити́ни**
I see three girls, persons, children.

Drill #145

Translate the words in the right-hand column:

1.	Ми му́симо купи́ти	new chairs
2.	Ми ма́ємо ду́же ма́ло	chairs
3.	У мої́й кімна́ті ті́льки	two chairs
4.	Скі́льки у вас .....?	chairs
5.	Ні́на ма́є па́ру	children
6.	Я не зна́ю її	children
7.	Я ма́ю три	children
8.	Чому́ всі ..... жо́вті?	leaves
9.	На то́му де́реві бага́то	leaves
10.	Чиї́ ці .....?	pens
11.	Я ба́чу ті́льки два	pens
12.	Я не ма́ю	pens
13.	У них у са́ді ма́ло	trees
14.	Бі́ля на́шої ха́ти чоти́ри	trees
15.	Я люблю́	trees
16.	Ми не ма́ємо	judges
17.	Де всі на́ші .....?	judges
18.	Ти тут ма́єш ті́льки два	neighbors
19.	Я не зна́ю їх	neighbors
20.	Ви зна́єте бага́то украї́нських	articles

16.3 NOUNS OF NATIONALITY

Ukrainian has adjectives of nationality: украї́нський "Ukrainian", кана́дський "Canadian", etc. These are used only as modifiers. When referring to persons, nouns of nationality must be used. Following is a list of some nouns of nationality:

Masc. (Males)	Fem. (Females)	Plural	
америка́нець	америка́нка	америка́нці	American
англі́єць	англі́йка	англі́йці	Englishman
еспа́нець	еспа́нка	еспа́нці	Spaniard
кана́дець	кана́дка	кана́дці	Canadian
ні́мець	ні́мка	ні́мці	German
поля́к	по́лька	поля́ки	Pole
росія́нин	росія́нка	росія́ни	Russian
ту́рок	турке́ня	ту́рки	Turk
украї́нець	украї́нка	украї́нці	Ukrainian
францу́з	францу́женка	францу́зи	Frenchman
швед	шве́дка	шве́ди	Swede

In Ukrainian these are always written with a small letter. The word **росія́нин** declines like **селяни́н**. Therefore, the genitive singular is **росія́нина**, while the plural is different in that the suffix **-ин-** is omitted. The same peculiarity applies to the following nouns:

Nom. Sg.	Nom. Pl.	Gen. Pl.	
слов'яни́н	слов'я́ни	слов'я́н	Slav
громадяни́н	громадя́ни	громадя́н	citizen
християни́н	християни	християн	Christian
росія́нин	росія́ни	росія́н	Russian

Drill #146

Translate into English:

1. На прийнятті в президе́нта було́ бага́то чужи́нців і ми ввесь ве́чір говори́ли рі́зними мо́вами.
2. Ми вчо́ра познайо́милися з одни́м францу́зом, що працю́є в Об'є́днаних На́ціях.
3. Оди́н із госте́й був мій стари́й знайо́мий, якого́ я вже не ба́чив бага́то ро́ків.
4. Я була́ ду́же ра́да зно́ву стрі́нути того́ знайо́мого.
5. Наш учи́тель матема́тики ні́мець, а його́ дружи́на францу́женка.

6. Францу́женки га́рно одяга́ються і до́бре ва́рять.
7. Мину́лого ро́ку ми ма́ли ду́же прие́мну по́дорож: ми два мі́сяці ї́здили по Еспа́нії. Нам подо́балися еспа́нці.
8. Спеція́льно нам подо́балися еспа́нські селя́ни. В Мадри́ді в теа́трі ми ба́чили па́ру га́рних еспа́нців та еспа́нок.
9. Я хо́чу вам розпові́сти про оди́н ціка́вий ви́падок.
10. Це тра́пилося під час одно́го із мо́їх подорожува́нь по А́фриці.
11. Ви співа́єте знайо́му мело́дію. Що́ то? Я сам не зна́ю.
12. У Радя́нському Сою́зі жило́ бага́то слов'я́н, але́ не всі слов'я́ни жили́ у Радя́нському Сою́зі.

Drill #147

Translate into Ukrainian:

1. Anna is English and her husband is French.
2. Is Vasyl's wife French or American? His wife is American, and he himself is Ukrainian.
3. The English like to play tennis.
4. Americans like steak.
5. Did you speak with these Swedes?
6. No, I spoke only with these Polish women and Turkish women.
7. There are many Slavs here.
8. Who are these peasants? They are Italian and they are all Christians.
9. There are many peasants in Italy.
10. I like German women.

16.4 ADJECTIVAL WORDS EXPRESSING QUANTITY

The indefinite, cardinal numerals **бага́то** "many", **небага́то** "not much", **кі́лька** "a few", and the pronouns **скі́льки** "how much", **сті́льки** "so much", have corresponding adjectival forms in only the following cases: genitive, dative, instrumental, and locative. Note how they are declined:

Nom.	бага́то	скі́льки
Gen.	багатьо́х	скількох́
Acc. =	Nom./Gen.	
Dat.	багатьо́м	скілько́м

Instr.	багатьма́/багатьома́	скількома́
Loc.	(на) багатьо́х	(у/на) скількóх

The use of these forms may be seen in the following examples:

Скі́льки музе́їв ви ба́чили в Евро́пі? (*Acc. case*)
How many museums did you see in Europe?

But:

У *скількóх* музе́ях ви були́? (*Loc. case*)
In how many museums were you?

Я ба́чив *бага́то* краї́в. (*Acc. case*)
I saw many countries.

But:

Там були́ лю́ди *з багатьóх* краї́в. (*Gen. case*)
There were people there from many countries.

16.41 When the adjectival forms **бага́то, небага́то, скі́льки,** and **сті́льки** are used in the nominative or accusative and accompanied by a noun, the noun is always in the genitive plural. In all other cases the accompanying noun is in the same case as the word of quantity. Only the noun is plural:

Я ба́чу бага́то хат.
I see many houses (*Gen. pl.*)

Я говори́в з багатьома́ хло́пцями.
I spoke with many boys (*Instr. pl.*)

У скількóх університе́тах ви вчи́лись?
In how many universities did you study? (*Loc. pl.*)

Я вчи́вся у багатьóх університе́тах.
I have studied in many universities. (*Loc. pl.*)

16.42 The word **ма́ло** "little" has no corresponding adjectival form; **небага́то** is used instead:

В небагатьóх ви́падках.
In a few cases.

Idioms: бага́то чого́ many things

Мені́ бага́то чого́ подо́бається тут.
I like many things here.

16.5 VERBS OF LYING, SITTING, STANDING

ляга́ти : лягти́	to lie
сіда́ти : сі́сти	to sit
ставáти: ста́ти	to stand

All three verbs denote the assuming of a physical position of lying, sitting, and standing.

16.51 Conjugation of **ляга́ти: лягти́** "to lie"

Present	Imperfective		Perfective	
1st pers.	ляга́ю	ляга́ємо	ля́жу	ля́жемо
2nd pers.	ляга́єш	ляга́єте	ля́жеш	ля́жете
3rd pers.	ляга́є	ляга́ють	ля́же	ля́жуть
Past				
	ляга́в, ляга́ла		ліг, ляглá	
Imperative				
	ляга́й, ляга́ймо, ляга́йте		ляж, ля́жмо, ля́жте	

16.52 Conjugation of **сіда́ти: сі́сти** "to sit"

Present	Imperfective		Perfective	
1st pers.	сіда́ю	сіда́ємо	ся́ду	ся́демо
2nd pers.	сіда́єш	сіда́єте	ся́деш	ся́дете
3rd pers.	сіда́є	сіда́ють	ся́де	ся́дуть
Past				
	сіда́в, сіда́ла		сів, сі́ла	
Imperative				
	сіда́й, сіда́ймо, сіда́йте		ся́дь, ся́дьмо, ся́дьте	

16.53 Conjugation of **ставáти: стáти** "to stand"

Present	Imperfective		Perfective	
1st pers.	стаю́	стає́мо	стáну	стáнемо
2nd pers.	стає́ш	стає́те	стáнеш	стáнете
3rd pers.	стає́	стаю́ть	стáне	стáнуть
Past				
	ставáв, ставáла		став, стáла,	
Imperative				
	ставáй, ставáймо, ставáйте		стань, стáньмо, стáньте	

The verb **стáти** means "to stand up". It also means "to become", "to step", "to stop". But it should be distinguished from **вставáти: встáти** which means "to stand up", "to get up", "to arise" (see 21.2):

Спочáтку він **стоя́в** біля мéне, а пóтім став біля Óлі.
At first he was standing beside me, but then he stood beside Olya.

Вонá **встáла** з ліжка і сіла на крісло.
She got out of bed and sat down on the chair.

16.54 When the verb **ставáти: стáти** is used in the sense of "to become", its compliment is always in the instrumental case, or an adverb:

Стає́ **хóлодно.**
It's becoming cold.

Він став **відóмою люди́ною.**
He became a famous man.

Drill #148

Translate into Ukrainian:

1. It is getting cold.
2. It got cold.
3. Soon it will get cold.
4. If you get cold, I'll shut the window.
5. Where do you prefer to sit? I prefer to sit near you.
6. Maksym, when did you (familiar) go to bed yesterday?
7. We all went to bed early.
8. Today I shall go to bed at ten P.M., and the others will go to bed at twelve P.M.

9. My son wants to become a doctor.
10. He became a famous doctor.

16.6 THE VERB ї́сти "TO EAT"

The verb **ї́сти** is athematic (see 11.0) and is conjugated as the verb **да́ти**. But **ї́сти**, unlike **да́ти**, is the imperfective form; the perfective form is **з'ї́сти**.

Present		Future
	Imperf.	Perf.
	їм	з'їм
	їси́	з'їси́
	їсть	з'їсть
	їмо́	з'їмо́
	їсте́	з'їсте́
	їдя́ть	з'їдя́ть
Past	їв, ї́ла	з'їв, з'ї́ла
Imperative	їж, ї́жмо, ї́жте	з'їж, з'ї́жмо, з'ї́жте

The verb **з'ї́сти** means "to eat up", "to consume a given quantity". Another perfective form for **ї́сти** is **пої́сти**, which means "to eat for a while", and **дої́сти**, which means "to finish eating something". **З'ї́сти** also has a secondary imperfective **з'їда́ти** which means "to eat up completely several times, or habitually":

Ви вже ї́ли? Так, їв.
Did you eat already? Yes, I ate.

Ми пої́ли і пішли́ до кі́на.
We ate and went to the show.

Ми дої́ли м'ясо і чека́ли на десе́рт.
We finished eating the meat and waited for dessert.

Я з'їв дві кро́мки хлі́ба. Звича́йно з'їда́ю ті́льки одну́.
I ate two pieces of bread. Usually I eat only one.

16.61 Nuances of meaning also exist for the verb **пи́ти, випива́ти: ви́пити** "to drink":

> Я щóйно пив кáву.
> I just drank coffee.
>
> Я щóйно ви́пив кáву.
> I just drank (up) the coffee.
>
> Я щóйно випивáв кáву.
> I was just drinking the coffee.
>
> Я ви́пив дві чáшки. Звичáйно я випивáю тíльки однý.
> I drank two cups. Usually I drink only one.

Drill #149

Translate into Ukrainian:

1. He never eats bread.
2. Myron, what are you (*familiar*) eating? I am eating meat and (*with*) potatoes.
3. Orysya, where do you usually eat? We always eat at home.
4. I ate and went to work.
5. I ate two steaks.
6. He often eats two steaks at dinner.
7. The French drink a lot of wine.
8. Some Frenchmen drink two bottles of wine a day.
9. Olya, drink up your milk.
10. I finished eating all the meat you gave me.

Homework

a) Memorize the vocabulary in Lesson #17;
b) Review Lesson #16;
c) Translate the following sentences into Ukrainian.

1. One of my friends has just returned from England.
2. How do you say that in Ukrainian?
3. At dinner we spoke about you.
4. What kind of a magazine is that?
5. I am acquainted with that Englishman.
6. Why do you think that he did not want to see you? He told me so himself.
7. My son wants to become a teacher.
8. In the fall it gets dark early and so we go to bed early.
9. Ivan works a great deal and then he goes home and reads.
10. Don't just stand there. Sit down.

СІМНА́ДЦЯТИЙ РО́ЗДІЛ

СЛОВНИ́К

Іме́нники жіно́чого ро́ду

го́ряч, -і	heat, hot weather
літерату́ра, -и	literature
наго́да, -и	opportunity
прие́мність, -ности	pleasure
спе́ка, -и	hot weather
у́часть, -и	participation

Іме́нники чолові́чого ро́ду

Берлі́н, -у	Berlin
ву́йко, -а	uncle (*mother's side*)
ді́до, -а	grandfather
зако́н, -у	rule (of law)
лі́фт, -у/-а	elevator
піджа́к, -а́	jacket
хмарочо́с, -а	skyscraper
хо́лод, -у	cold

Іме́нники сере́днього ро́ду

ді́ло, -а	matter, affair, business
пра́во, -а	law, right

Прикме́тники

міськи́й, -а́, -е́	urban, municipal
наро́дний, -а, -е	national, folk
прекра́сний, -а, -е	beautiful

Дієслова́

верта́ти: верну́ти *(верта́ю, верта́єш: верну́, ве́рнеш)*	to return (*trans.*)
верта́тися: верну́тися	to return, come back (*intrans.*)
віддава́ти: відда́ти *(віддаю́, віддає́ш: відда́м, віддаси́)*	to give back
ві́рити: пові́рити *(ві́рю, ві́риш)*	to believe
в/у/мира́ти: в/у/ме́рти *(вмира́ю, вмира́єш: вмру́, вмре́ш)*	to die

вто́млюватися: втоми́тися *(вто́млююся, вто́млюєшся: втомлю́ся, вто́мишся)*	to tire (intrans.)
дові́дуватися: дові́датися *(дові́дуюся, -єшся; дові́даюся, -єшся)*	to find out
захоті́ти: *(захо́чу, захо́чеш)*	to want (perf.)
пам'ята́ти: запам'ята́ти *(пам'ята́ю, пам'ята́єш)*	to remember
пізнава́ти: пізна́ти *(пізнаю́, пізнає́ш: пізна́ю, пізна́єш)*	to recognize
почина́ти: поча́ти *(почина́ю, почина́єш: почну́, почне́ш)*	to begin
привика́ти: приви́кнути *(привика́ю, привика́єш: приви́кну, приви́кнеш)* [*to (до + gen.)*]	to become accustomed, get used
прийма́ти: прийня́ти *(прийма́ю, прийма́єш: прийму́, при́ймеш)*	to accept, to entertain
танцюва́ти: потанцюва́ти *(танцю́ю, танцю́єш)*	to dance
ціка́витися: поціка́витися *(ціка́влюся, ціка́вишся)*	to be interested in + intsr.

Прислі́вники

напро́ти	accross
то́чно	exactly, precisely

Ви́рази

Добра́ніч!	Good night!
до́ти до́ки	until
за грани́цю	go abroad
за мі́сто	go to the country
ма́ти ра́цію	to be right
між і́ншим	by the way

Імена́

Кость, -я	Kost
Миро́ся, -і	Myrosya

GRAMMAR

Verb Review — Повтóрення дієслóва (17.0)
The Adverb мóжна, не мóжна — *Прислíвники* мóжна, не мóжна *(17.1)*
Perfective Verb захотíти — *Дієслóво докóнаного вúду* захотíти *(17.2)*
Numerals (Cont.) — Числíвники (продóвж.) (17.3)
Age — Вúрази на познáчення вíку людúни (17.4)

17.0 VERB REVIEW

1. All verbs have the infinitive ending **-ти**.

2. Ukrainian verbs have primarily three conjugations: first, second, and athematic.

3. The first conjugation has the present stem vowel **-е-/-є-** and, in the 3rd pers. pl., **-у/-ю**. There is no ending in the 3rd pers. sg. unless the particle **-ся** is added; then the ending **-ть-** is inserted before the **-ся**. For example:

писáти	читáти
пишý	читáю
пúшеш	читáєш
пúше (пишеться)	читáє (читáється)
пúшемо	читáємо
пúшете	читáєте
пúшуть	читáють

4. The second conjugation has the present stem vowel **-и/ї** and, in the 3rd pers. pl., **-а/я**. It has the ending **-ть** in the 3rd pers. sg.:

говорúти	бáчити
говорю́	бáчу
говóриш	бáчиш
говóрить	бáчить
говóримо	бáчимо
говóрите	бáчите
говóрять	бáчать

5. Palatalization of **к, г, х** to **ч, ж, ш** before front vowels is transferred by analogy to the 1st pers. sg. and 3rd pers. pl.:

пекти́	—	печу́, пече́ш . . . печу́ть
бі́гти	—	біжу́, біжи́ш . . . біжа́ть

6. Labial roots insert an **-л-** before the ending of the 1st pers. singular and the 3rd pers. pl.:

люби́ти	—	люблю́, лю́блять
терпі́ти	—	терплю́, те́рплять

7. Since it is not possible to tell either the conjugation of the verb or its present stem from the infinitive form, it is necessary to memorize not only the infinitive form but also the 2nd pers. sg., which without the ending gives the present stem of the verb:

Infinitive	2 pers. sg.	Present Stem
бра́ти	бере́ш	бер-
пли́сти	пливе́ш	плив-
рва́ти	рвеш	рв-
моло́ти	ме́леш	мел-
будува́ти	буду́єш	буду-
закрива́ти	закрива́єш	закрива-
роздава́ти	роздає́ш	розда-
лежа́ти	лежи́ш	леж-
жи́ти	живе́ш	жив-
хоті́ти	хо́чеш	хоч-

Note that the verbs with the suffix **-ва-** in the infinitive drop the **-ва-** in the present stem. This does not happen, however, with verbs that have the vowel **-и-** before the **-ва-** in the infinitive.

8. Athematic verbs are verbs without the "theme" vowel. There are only four such verbs and, of course, all of their derivations. One of them, the verb **бу́ти** "to be", has **є** in all forms of the present tense. The other three are conjugated as follows:

да́ти	ї́сти	роз/о/пові́сти
дам	їм	роз/о/пові́м
даси́	їси́	роз/о/пові́си́
дасть	їсть	роз/о/пові́сть
дамо́	їмо́	роз/о/повімо́
дасте́	їсте́	роз/о/повісте́
даду́ть	їдя́ть	роз/о/повідя́ть

9. Ukrainian has two verbal aspects: the perfective and the imperfective. The perfective has only future and past tenses. The imperfective has present, future, and past tenses.

a) Verbs of motion and carrying have separate forms for the imperfective aspect — the **indefinite** and the **definite** — to distinguish between habitual actions and actions in progress. E.g.:

ходи́ти	—	іти́ : піти́
носи́ти	—	нести́ : понести́

With prefixation the indefinite imperfective creates new imperfective verbs, while the definite creates perfective verbs. E.g.:

вхо́дити : увійти́	—	to enter
вно́сити : внести́	—	to bring in

10. Perfectives are formed:

a) From a variant of the same root: **пуска́ти: пусти́ти**
b) By the addition of **-нути**: гри́мати: гри́мнути
c) By a change of stress: здиба́ти: зди́бати
d) By adding prefixes (the most common way): писа́ти: написа́ти
e) Sometimes imperfectives are formed from perfectives by lengthening the root with the suffix **-ува-/-ва-:**

писа́ти : підписа́ти : підпи́с**ува**ти
купи́ти : куп**ува́**ти
да́ти : да**ва́**ти

f) By changing the conjugation:

позича́ти : пози́чити
позича́ю, позича́єш : пози́чу, пози́чиш

11. Since there is no definite rule as to how each verb forms aspects, it is best to learn verbs in aspectual pairs.

12. There are three future forms in Ukrainian:

a) The "present" conjugation of perfective verbs

сказа́ти — скажу́, ска́жеш . . .

b) The simple future of imperfective verbs:
infinitive + the endings **-му, -меш, -ме, -мемо, -мете, -муть**

читáтиму, читáтимеш, читáтиме . . .

c) The compound future of imperfective verbs:

future of **бýти** + inf.

бýду читáти, **бýдеш** читáти . . .

13. The past tense is formed by using the infinitive stem (drop the suffix **-ти** from the infinitive) and by adding to the infinitive stem **-в, -ла, -ло, -ли** according to the gender and number of the subject:

він	писá-**в**
вонá	писá-**ла**
вонó	писá-**ло**
вони́	писá-**ли**

14. The imperfective past denotes a repetitive action in the past. The perfective past denotes a completed action in the past.

15. Verbs whose roots end in a consonant have no **-в** in the masculine past, just the consonant ending:

рости́: ріс, but рослá

16. Verbs with roots ending in **-с**, which alternates with **-т** or **-д** in the present stem, have neither **с, т,** nor **д** before the **в, ла, ло, ли** of the past tense:

плести́	—	плетéш: плів, плелá
клáсти	—	кладéш: клав, клáла

17. Note the vowel alternations **о/і, е/і** in closed syllables:

міг	—	моглá	ріс	—	рослá
беріг	—	береглá			

18. Verbs with the suffix **-ну-** sometimes drop the **-ну-** in the past; sometimes both forms exist:

тягну́ти: тягну́в; збліднути: збліднув /зблід
збліднула/збліdла

19. The pluperfect tense is formed by the past tense of the verb + the past tense of бу́ти:

я ходи́в був, вона́ ходи́ла була́, ми ходи́ли були́

20. The present of the conditional mood[1] is formed by the past tense of the verb with the addition of particle би after consonants, or б after vowels:

я мав би, вона мала б

21. The past conditional[1] has the past tense of бу́ти added to the conditional:

я був би мав, була́ б мала

22. The imperative is formed from the present stem of the verb, and its endings are determined by the position of the stress in the 1st pers. sing. of the present tense imperfective or future tense perfective, as well as by the type of ending in the present stem:

Stem with vowel ending	Stem with consonant ending; stressed 1st pers.	Stem with labial, sibilant, or ending "р" unstressed 1st pers.	Stem with dental ending; unstressed 1st pers.
(про) чита́ю (про) чита́єш	(по) біжу́ (по) біжи́ш	вда́рю вда́риш	ся́ду ся́деш
2p.sg. -й 2p.pl. -йте 1p.pl. -ймо	-и́ -іть -імо	-Ø -те -мо	-(ь)-Ø -(ь)те -(ь)мо

1 Although the conditional mood has yet to be covered, it is presented here to give a complete review of the verbal system in Ukrainian. For more information on the conditional mood see chapter twenty.

The 3rd pers. sg. and pl. imperative is formed by the use of helping words **хай, нехáй** + the 3rd pers. indicative:

хай пи́ше, нехáй напи́шуть
хай сиди́ть, нехáй сидя́ть

Drill #150

Translate into Ukrainian:

1. You have no right to talk like that.
2. I had the pleasure of meeting your daughter.
3. We never had the opportunity to talk about this matter.
4. You ought to have an evening dress.
5. One must have friends.
6. My teacher advises me to talk less and read more.
7. Do you advise Mykhaylo and Myrosya to go to England? No, I don't advise it.
8. He likes to consult with me about everything.
9. What can they advise us to do?
10. I know what they will advise you to do.
11. I like to dance with Tamara but we dance so seldom.
12. They dance only folk dances.
13. I like to travel and I travel a great deal.
14. I am very much interested in Ukrainian folk literature.
15. He is not interested in his students.
16. What are you interested in? The theater.
17. Why don't you ever phone us? Don't we interest you? I shall call you twice a week. All right?
18. Zenya had changed so that I didn't recognize her.
19. I don't think that you will recognize us.
20. I know that she went abroad, but I must find out where she went.
21. Please, find out where she lives.
22. I am tired; I'll go to bed early.
23. Have you got used to me? Yes, we've gotten used to you.
24. Kost has gotten used to heat and cold.
25. I can't get used to this city.
26. I will return your book when I finish it. I always return books.
27. In the winter we always returned early and went to bed early.

28. I will return at 10:00 sharp. When will you come back?
29. She returned from Europe two weeks ago.
30. We always come back together.
31. I must return your newspaper; I've finished it.
32. We came back from school early today.
33. When he dies, his sons will get all his money.
34. When I die, my children will get nothing.
35. My aunt, my mother's sister, died seven years ago.
36. His grandfather died not long ago.
37. We are dying from the heat.
38. My uncle, my mother's brother, is not afraid of death, but he does not want to die.

17.1 ADVERBS мóжна AND не мóжна

The adverbs **мóжна, мóжна булó, мóжна бýде** mean "one can, one may, one is permitted". When the person is named, the person is in the dative case:

Йомý мóжна, а тобí не мóжна...
He can, but you cannot...

Їй мóжна говори́ти, а менí не мóжна.
She can (may) speak, but I cannot.

Drill #151

Translate into English:

1. Що мóжна купи́ти в тій крамни́ці? Все, що хóчете.
2. Ви дýмаєте, що мóжна бýде скóро відійти́?
3. Лíкар сказáв, що дíдові не мóжна багáто ї́сти.
4. Йомý тепéр мóжна ї́сти м'ясо тíльки раз на ти́ждень.
5. Ранíше йомý мóжна булó ї́сти, скíльки він хотíв.
6. Не мóжна сказáти, що Пéтрів дýже розýмний чоловíк.
7. Не мóжна приви́кнути до тóго шýму.
8. До всьогó мóжна приви́кнути.
9. Не мóжна зрозумíти, щó він хóче.
10. Тáту, мóжна нам узя́ти вáше áвто? Тобí мóжна, алé Марýсі не мóжна.

Drill #152

Translate into Ukrainian:

1. May I say one word? Certainly.
2. It may be said that he's a very good poet, but it can't be said that he is a good teacher.
3. It's not possible to buy even a newspaper here.
4. It will soon be possible to go to the country.
5. You (one) can't believe him.
6. Can one live here?
7. It can't be said yet what kind of a student he is.

17.2 PERFECTIVE VERB захотíти

The verb **захотíти: захóчу, захóчеш** refers to the moment when the desire is conceived:

Я захотíв плáкати.
I had an urge to cry.

17.3 NUMERALS (Continued)

	Cardinal	Ordinal
20	двáдцять	двадцятий
30	трúдцять	тридцятий
31	трúдцять одúн	трúдцять пéрший
40	сóрок	сорокóвий
50	п'ятдесят	п'ятдесятий
60	шістдесят	шістдесятий
70	сімдесят	сімдесятий
80	вісімдесят	вісімдесятий
90	дев'ятдесят/дев'янóсто	дев'ятдесятий/дев'янóстий
100	сто	сóтий

17.4 AGE

Скíльки вам (тобí) рóків?	трúдцять одúн рік.
How old are you?	thirty one.
Менí булó, бýде,	трúдцять два рóки.
(Я мáю, мав, мáтиму)	thirty two.

I'm, was, will be тридцять п'ять рóків.
thirty five.

Drill #153

Read and translate into English:

1. З тогó чáсу, як Óльга почалá новý прáцю, вонá так втóмлюється, що лягáє спáти зáраз по вечéрі.
2. Як дóвго ви бýдете сьогóдні працювáти? Я бýду працювáти до обíду, абó дóти, дóки не втóмлюся.
3. Я дотепéр не мóжу зрозуміти, як він мóже так багáто працювáти.
4. Однá моя́ знайóма еспáнка дýже гáрно танцю́є еспáнські нарóдні тáнці і співáє еспáнські піснí. Ніхтó не знáє так багáто пісéнь.
5. Ти пам'ятáєш, щó порáдив вýйкові Михáйлові прекрáсний лíкар, у якóго він був у Берлíні? Він порáдив йомý ходи́ти дві годи́ни щодня́.
6. Я сьогóдні багáто працювáв і дýже втоми́вся. Я прийшóв додóму, ви́пив дві скля́нки чáю з цитри́ною, зажи́в (прийня́в) аспіри́ну і ліг спáти.
7. Якщó я захóчу ще скля́нку чáю, попрóшу дружи́ну.
8. Я не приймý від вас ці грóші. Я віддáм їх вам.
9. Спочáтку Петрóві та Марýсі булó вáжко приви́кнути до міськóго життя́, алé тепéр воні́ не тíльки приви́кли до ньóго, алé й лю́блять йогó.
10. Сідáйте на те крíсло: на тóму крíслі дýже вигíдно сидíти.
11. Тепéр дýже скóро стає́ тéмно.
12. А, бáчите, як ужé стáло тéмно!
13. На мою́ дýмку, Васи́ль став дóбрим студéнтом.
14. Якщó вам зрóбиться хóлодно, я дам вам свій піджáк.
15. Я дýже захотíв ї́сти, а менí ще не мóжна булó.

Drill #154

Translate into Ukrainian:

1. Kotsyubynsky's (Коцюби́нський) parents had a house in which there were 40 rooms.
2. Our teacher is 27 years old and her mother is 59.
3. My grandfather was 83 when he died.

4. Some students are interested in Ukrainian literature of the nineteenth century.
5. What are you interested in? I'm interested in Ukrainian writers of the twentieth century .
6. Myrny (Ми́рний) and Levytsky (Леви́цький) lived and wrote in the nineteenth century.
7. In this skyscraper there are forty two floors.
8. I have just found out that his office is on the fortieth floor opposite the elevator.
9. I shall see him there tomorrow at eleven o'clock, when he returns from Lviv.
10. I don't remember on which street in New York my friend lives — on 102nd street or 121st street.
11. The Rovers live on 76th street and their parents on 98th.
12. I'm telling you that for the twentieth time.
13. We live in a skyscraper on the 105th floor.
14. My mother lives on the eighth floor.

Homework

a) Memorize the vocabulary in Lesson #18;
b) Review Lesson #17;
c) Translate the following sentenses into Ukrainian:

1. When will you give me my book? I shall return it in two days.
2. I returned to Kyiv after a long trip.
3. When is your husband coming back from France?
4. We live opposite the park.
5. My room is opposite Olha's room.
6. I am tired. Good night!
7. Where is mother? She's gone to bed.
8. May I take part in your conversation? No, you may not.
9. If I can, I shall find out where he lives.
10. Kudryk is abroad, he will return here next year.
11. He will let us know as soon as he returns.
12. It was very hard for me to get used to this city, but I got used to it.
13. She is not used to such noise.
14. By the way, you can take one Ukrainian book.
15. This book does not interest me.
16. I shall phone you tomorrow.

ВІСІМНА́ДЦЯТИЙ РО́ЗДІЛ

СЛОВНИ́К

Іме́нники жіно́чого ро́ду

валі́зка, -и	suitcase
вну́чка, -и	granddaughter
доро́га, -и	road, way, route
за́бавка, -и	toy
ві́тка, -и/кві́ти, -ів	flower/flowers
па́чка, -и	package, carton
пі́вніч, -ночі	north, midnight
племі́нниця, -і/брата́нка, -и/ сестрі́нка, -и	niece
цига́рка, -и	cigarette

Іме́нники чолові́чого ро́ду

внук, -а	grandson
міст, моста́/мо́сту	bridge
паку́нок, -нка	package, parcel
пасажи́р, -а	passenger
пі́вдень, -дня/полу́день, -дня	south, noon
племі́нник, -а/брата́нок, -нка/ сестрі́нок, -нка	nephew
портфе́ль, -я	briefcase, wallet
уче́ний, -ного	scholar, scientist (*adj. noun*)

Іме́нники сере́днього ро́ду

бю́рко, -а	desk

Прикме́тники

мексіка́нський, -а, -е	Mexican
мо́дний, -а, -е	fashionable
півні́чний, -а, -е	northern
тяжки́й, -а́, -е́	heavy, difficult

Дієсловá

води́ти, ве́сти́: пове́сти́ (*во́джу, во́диш: веду́, веде́ш*)	to lead
вози́ти, ве́зти́: пове́зти́ (*вожу́, во́зиш: везу́, везе́ш*)	to transport
зауважувати: заува́жити (*заува́жую, заува́жуєш: заува́жу, заува́жиш*)	to notice
знахо́дити: знайти́ (*знахо́джу, знахо́диш: знайду́, зна́йдеш*)	to find
зупиня́тися: зупини́тися (*зупиня́юся, зупиня́єшся: зупиню́ся, зупи́нишся*)	to stop
носи́ти, не́сти́: поне́сти́ (*ношу́, но́сиш: несу́, несе́ш*)	to carry
обіця́ти: пообіця́ти (*обіця́ю, обіця́єш*)	to promise
сподіва́тися (*сподіва́юся, сподіва́єшся*)	to expect *(imperf. only)*

Прислі́вники

зві́дси	from here
зві́дти	from there
півгоди́ни	half an hour

Ви́рази

сі́сти в таксі́	to get into a taxi
ви́сісти з таксі́	to get out of a taxi
найнові́ші журна́ли	the latest magazines

GRAMMAR

The Interrogative Particle чи — *Пита́льна ча́стка* чи *(18.0)*
Particles **-сь, -не́будь, -будь** *and Prefix* де- — *Ча́стки* **-сь, -не́будь, -будь** *і префікс* де- *(18.1)*
Prepositions **ми́мо** *and* **че́рез** — *Прийме́нники* **ми́мо** *і* **че́рез** *(18.2)*
Other Verbs of Motion — Íнші дієслова́ ру́ху (18.3—18.31)
Verbs of Carrying — Дієслова́ на позна́чення вози́ння (18.4—18.41)
Verbs of Leading — Дієслова́ на позна́чення веді́ння (18.5—18.51)

18.0 THE INTERROGATIVE PARTICLE

The interrogative particle **чи** has three uses:

1. When used in a direct question it signifies that the statement is in fact a question. In this capacity it is roughly equivalent to the English usage of "do":

   Чи ви зна́єте, де він живе́?
   Do you know where he lives?

   The particle may be omitted as can the "do" form in English. In such cases intonation must serve as an indicator of the interrogative mood:

   Ви зна́єте, де він живе́?
   You know where he lives?

2. Its second usage is to introduce indirect questions. In such cases the particle is similar to the English "whether":

   Я не зна́ю, **чи** він приї́хав.
   I don't know **whether** he arrived.

3. Its third use is as a substitute for the conjunction **або́** "or" when the sentence is in the interrogative mood:

   Compare: Я люблю́ пи́ти чай **або́** молоко́.
   I like to drink tea **or** milk.

   To: Чи ви лю́бите пи́ти чай **чи** молоко́?
   Do you like to drink tea **or** milk?

Drill #155

Change the following statements into indirect questions as in the model:

Model: Тут по́шта. Запита́й його́, чи тут по́шта.

1. Іва́н був у фа́бриці.
2. Це пра́вда.
3. Я живу́ тут.
4. Га́ня ма́є гро́ші.
5. Гро́ші є в Миха́йла.
6. Вони́ хо́чуть ча́ю.
7. Це наш учи́тель.
8. Тут ішо́в дощ.

Drill #156

Translate into Ukrainian:

1. Do you know if Petruk has returned from Toronto? If he has returned, I hope that he will call me.
2. Ask Olya if she needs a black dress. If she needs one, I can give her mine.
3. I don't remember whether Borys was in class today.
4. The professor asked Tetyana if she had read "Tsarivna".
5. Who knows whether she has money.
6. We don't know whether they want to go to the country. If they wish to, they can come with us.
7. Do you know whether Ivan is at home?
8. I asked him whether he worked much.
9. Did he come from Kyiv or Lviv?

18.1 THE PARTICLES **-сь, -будь, -не́будь** AND THE PREFIX **де-**

In Ukrainian indefinite pronouns and adverbs are formed with the help of the particles **-сь, -будь, -не́будь** or the prefix **де-**. The particles **-будь, -не́будь** are synonymous and are rendered in English as "any". Although the particle **-сь** and the prefix **де-** are translated as "some", they are not quite synonymous. Thus:

хтось = someone (a definite one exists but is unknown or not named)

де́хто	=	someone (a definite one or several of a given sample)
хтобу́дь/ хтоне́будь	=	anyone (no definite one is implied)

Compare:

Хтось телефонува́в сього́дні.
Someone called today. (There was a caller but he/she is unknown or not named)

Де́хто телефонува́в у цій спра́ві.
Someone/several called about this matter. (There were some/several callers out of a sample — those who were concerned with the given matter — but they are not specifically identified)

Чи **хтобу́дь/хтоне́будь** телефонува́в?
Did anyone call? (The speaker does not know if, in fact there had been any callers at all)

Купи́ мені́ **якийбу́дь/якийне́будь** журнал.
Buy me any journal (you like). (No specific journal is implied and any will do)

The particles **-сь, -не́будь** are always added to the end of a given pronoun or adverb when it is made indefinite. The particle **-будь** may be placed at the end or at the beginning of a pronoun or adverb. If it is placed at the beginning, it must be separated by a hyphen. The prefix **де-** is always written at the beginning and is not separated by a hyphen. The pronouns, of course, when made indefinite, retain their declension. Note the following:

Adverbs		Pronouns	
чому́сь	for some reason	хтось	someone
чомуне́будь	for any reason	хтоне́будь	anyone
будь-чому́	for any reason	будь-хто́	anyone
десь	somewhere[1]	де́хто	someone/ several
дебу́дь	anywhere		

---

1 Do not confuse the adverb **де** "where" with the indefinite prefix **де-**

десь somewhere (*adv.*) **де́хто** someone (*prefix*)

бýдь-де	anywhere	комýсь	to someone
куди́сь	(to) somewhere	комунéбудь	to anyone
кудинéбудь	(to) anywhere	будь-комý	to anyone
дéкуди	(to) somewhere	дéкому	to someone/ several
будь-куди́	(to) anywhere		

Drill #157

Add the particles **-сь** or **-будь/-нéбудь** according to sense:

1. Вчóра був хто ..... на лéкції Дарéвича?
2. Хто ..... менí сказáв, що ви там були́.
3. Ви мóжете розказáти менí, що ..... цікáвого?
4. Хто ..... має цигáрку?
5. Я де ..... про це вже чув.
6. Він ще не знáє, чи поїде він куди́ ..... лíтом.
7. Ви були́ де ..... вчóра вéчором?
8. Хóче хто ..... піти́ зі мнóю?
9. Сьогóдні рáно хто ..... до вас телефонувáв?
10. Я де ..... ужé йогó бáчив.
11. Я сподівáюся, що я де ..... знайдý цьогó листá.

Drill #158

Translate into Ukrainian:

1. When you go to the store, buy me something.
2. Somebody wrote to my mother about that matter.
3. Do you know anyone who has recently been in Ukraine?
4. I heard that someone has just returned from there.
5. Where is grandmother? She went somewhere.
6. He wrote to someone about that question.
7. Somebody's money is lying on the floor.
8. If you find anything interesting in the newspaper, read it to me.
9. Roma found somebody's hat.
10. Buy me some magazine or other.
11. I've lost my briefcase somewhere.
12. For some reason he doesn't like me.

18.2 PREPOSITIONS ми́мо AND чéрез

The preposition **ми́мо** is used with the genitive case to mean "by, past"; **чéрез** is used with the accusative case to mean "across", "through".

Лю́ди йшли́ че́рез міст ми́мо шко́ли.
The people walked across the bridge past the school.

18.3 OTHER VERBS OF MOTION

The basic verb "to go" — **ходи́ти, йти, піти́** — can be turned into other verbs more specific in meaning by the use of various prefixes. It is the prefix which carries the meaning of the verb:

Prefix	New verb	Meaning
в	вхо́дити: в/у/вві́йти́	to enter
під	підхо́дити: підійти́	to approach
ви	вихо́дити: ви́йти	to come out of
за	захо́дити: зайти́	to stop by, enter
пере	перехо́дити: перейти́	to cross
про	прохо́дити: пройти́	to pass by

18.31 The same system of creating new verbs of motion applies to the verb **ї́здити** (the **-їжджа́ти** form is used for prefixation), **ї́хати: пої́хати:**

в'їжджа́ти: в'ї́хати	to drive in, to enter
під'їжджа́ти: під'ї́хати	to drive up, to approach
виїжджа́ти: ви́їхати	to drive out, to leave
заїжджа́ти: заї́хати	to drive in, to arrive
переїжджа́ти: переї́хати	to drive over, across
проїжджа́ти: проїхати	to drive through, by

Drill #159

Choose the proper form of the verbs: **вихо́дити, ви́йти, виїжджа́ти, ви́їхати, вхо́дити, ввійти́**. Translate into English:

1. Ніля тільки що ..... з кімна́ти.
2. Лікар сказа́в А́нні, що їй ще не мо́жна .....
3. Щора́нку ..... о сьо́мій годи́ні.
4. Ми пови́нні ..... ду́же ско́ро, якщо́ ми хо́чемо приї́хати до Торо́нта ще сього́дні.
5. Вона́ ..... в свою́ кімна́ту і за хвили́ну ..... зві́дти.
6. Відчині́ть две́рі і ..... в мій кабіне́т.
7. Па́ні й ді́вчинка ..... в крамни́цю.

8. Я ..... з хáти за півгоди́ни.
9. Вони́ скóро ..... з крамни́ці.
10. Коли́ ви ..... з кімнáти, закри́йте двéрі.
11. Коли́ ми ..... за місто, ми зупи́немося і поснідаємо.
12. Вони́ ..... з Ки́єва в понеділок.

Drill #160

Choose the proper form of the verb **захóдити: зайти́** and translate into English:

1. Мóжна ..... до вас на п'ять хвили́н ?
2. Я тепéр чáсто ..... до ньóго по дорóзі додóму.
3. Вчóра він до мéне ..... по кни́жку.
4. Рáно Нýся ..... до при́ятельки, алé її́ не булó вдóма.
5. Вонá тепéр рідко до нас ..... .
6. Я тепéр живý бли́зько і бýду чáсто ..... до вас.
7. ..... до мéне сьогóдні ввéчорі.
8. Я ..... до вас, і ми рáзом підéмо до кіна.

Drill #161

Choose the proper form of the verbs **підхóдити: підійти́, відхóдити: відійти́**. Translate into English:

1. ..... до столá і візьміть кни́жку.
2. По лéкції він ..... до мéне, задáв мені питáння і зáраз же ..... від мéне.
3. Я нікóли не ..... до йогó бюрка.
4. Вонá ..... до табли́ці і почалá писáти, пóтім вонá ..... від табли́ці і сіла.
5. Ми чáсто їх стрічáємо, але нікóли не ..... до них.
6. Я ..... до нéї, якщó вонá бýде самá.

18.4 VERBS OF CARRYING

The verbs of carrying have a very similar pattern to the verbs of going. They have a basic set of three: indefinite and definite imperfective, and one perfective. They also form other carrying verbs with the help of prefixes. The basic form of "to carry" is:

	Imperfective Indefinite	Imperfective Definite	Perfective
Infin.	носи́ти	не́сти	поне́сти
1st pers. sg.	ношу́	несу́	понесу́
2nd pers. sg.	но́сиш	несе́ш	понесе́ш
Masc. past	носи́в	ніс (but f. несла́)	поні́с (but f. понесла́)
2nd pers. sg. imper.	носи́!	неси́!	понеси́!

The basic form of "to transport" is:

	Imperfective Indefinite	Imperfective Definite	Perfective
Infin.	вози́ти	ве́зти́	пове́зти
1st pers. sg.	вожу́	везу́	повезу́
2nd pers. sg.	во́зиш	везе́ш	повезе́ш
Masc. past	вози́в	віз (but f. везла́)	пові́з (but f. повезла́)
2nd pers. sg. imper.	вози́!	вези́!	повези́!

Other prefixed forms based on the indefinite and definite imperfective are:

вно́сити: вне́сти́	to carry in
підно́сити: підне́сти́	to pick up
вино́сити: ви́нести	to carry out
зано́сити: зане́сти́	to carry away, to take to
перено́сити: перене́сти́	to carry across, to endure
проно́сити: проне́сти́	to carry through, to wear out (clothes)
відно́сити: відне́сти́	to carry back, to take back
ввo´зити: вве́зти́	to transport in
підво́зити: підве́зти́	to give a lift
виво́зити: ви́везти	to transport out
заво́зити: заве́зти́	to transport away, to transport to
переві́зити: переве́зти́	to transport across
прово́зити: прове́зти́	to transport through, to give a ride (lift)
відво́зити: відве́зти́	to transport back

18.41 As can be seen from the above verbs, some verbs have also a figurative meaning. Thus the verb **носи́ти** can also mean "to wear"; the verb **проно́сити** "to wear out"; the verb **перено́сити** "to endure":

> Зимо́ю я ношу́ те́пле пальто́.
> In winter I wear a warm coat.
>
> Я проноси́в на колі́нах свої́ штани́.
> I wore out my pants on my knees.
>
> Я не мо́жу перене́сти́ шу́му.
> I cannot endure the noise.

Drill #162

Replace the blanks by the correct form of the verb "to carry".

1. Я ба́чив О́лю на ву́лиці. Вона́ ..... кві́ти.
2. Вона́ рані́ше за́вжди ..... зі собо́ю бага́то гро́шей.
3. Він тепе́р ча́сто ..... тяжкі́ паку́нки.
4. Я не зна́ю, куди́ він ішо́в і що він .....
5. Я не люблю́ ..... зі собо́ю бага́то книжо́к, але́ ча́сом я їх .....
6. Ми ..... ті книжки́ до бібліоте́ки.

Drill #163

Choose the correct verb in parentheses:

1. Куди́ ви ї́хали сього́дні і куди́ ви (вози́ти, ве́зти́) діте́й?
2. Ви ча́сто (вози́ти, ве́зти́) діте́й на мо́ре мину́лого ро́ку? Так, мій чолові́к ча́сто їх (вози́ти, ве́зти́).
3. Бори́с ї́хав а́втом і (вози́ти, ве́зти́) куди́сь свою́ ма́тір.
4. Чому́ ти за́вжди (носи́ти, не́сти́) зі собо́ю той тяжки́й портфе́ль?
5. Зі́рко, що ти (носи́ти, не́сти́) і що (носи́ти, не́сти́) Бори́с, коли́ я вас стрі́нув?
6. Я не ба́чу, що він (носи́ти, не́сти́).
7. За півгоди́ни я (відноси́ти, відне́сти́) книжки́ до бібліоте́ки.
8. Про́шу, (відноси́ти, відне́сти́) молоко́ до ку́хні.

9. Якщó ви ї́дете на стáнцію, (відвóзити, відвезти́) менé туди́.
10. Я тепéр щодня́ (відвóзити, відвезти́) дітéй до шкóли.
11. Ранíше він зáвжди (привóзити, привезти́) нам дéщо із-за грани́ці.
12. Він обіця́в, що коли́ він вéрнеться, він дéщо нам (привóзити, привезти́).
13. Вчóра він приї́хав і нічóго нам не (привóзити, привезти́).
14. Коли́ я верну́ся з Пари́жу, я вам дéщо (привóзити, привезти́).
15. Зáвтра він при́йде на обíд і (принóсити, принести́) винó.
16. Коли́ він прихóдить на обíд, він зáвжди (принóсити, принести́) щось.
17. Івáн від'ї́хав у Крим і (відвóзити, відвезти́) зі собóю всі свої́ книжки́.

Drill #164

Give the correct form of the verb compound: **при/від-/нóсити, -нести́, при/від-вóзити, -везти́**.

1. Він обіця́в, що приї́де зáвтра і ..... свою́ статтю́.
2. Він приї́хав, алé нічóго не .....
3. Прийди́ до нас зáвтра і ..... свою́ статтю́.
4. Якщó ти поїдеш áвтом, ти мóжеш ..... цю пáчку на пóшту.
5. Якщó я поїду áвтом, я ..... пáчку на пóшту.
6. Він обіця́в менí ..... з Пари́жу мóдний одяг.
7. Приї́дь до нас на селó і ..... твою́ сестру́.
8. Я приї́ду до вас у понедíлок і ..... сестру́.
9. Я сподівáюся, що вонá скóро звíдси від'ї́де і ..... свогó си́на.
10. Вонá від'ї́хала і ..... си́на.
11. Ми вам з Еврóпи ..... щось цікáве.
12. Що я мóжу вам ..... з Мéхіко? Менí, будь лáска, ... мексікáнську вáзу.

18.5 VERBS OF LEADING

The verbs of leading, like the verbs of going, traveling, carrying, and transporting, have one basic set of three verbs and various other verbs formed with the standard set of prefixes. The basic "to lead" verbs are: **води́ти, вéсти́: повéсти́**.

	Imperfective		Perfective
	Indefinite	Definite	
Infin.	води́ти	ве́сти́	пове́сти́
1st pers. sg.	воджу́	веду́	поведу́
2nd pers. sg.	во́диш	веде́ш	поведе́ш
Masc. past	води́в	вів (*but*	повів (*but*
2nd pers. sg.		f. вела́)	f. повела́)
imper.	води́!	веди́!	поведи́!

Prefixed forms:

в/у/во́дити: в/у/ве́сти́	to lead in, to introduce
підво́дити: підве́сти́	to accompany part way, to pick up a fallen person, to beguile, to lead astray
виво́дити: ви́вести	to lead out
заво́дити: заве́сти́	to lead to
переводити: переве́сти́	to lead across, to translate
прово́дити: прове́сти́	to accompany, to spend (as in time)
відво́дити: відве́сти́	to lead back, away
дово́дити: дове́сти́	to prove

Notice that with the verb "to lead" even more of the prefixed forms have a figurative meaning than with carrying verbs.

18.51 THE UKRAINIAN TRANSLATION OF THE ENGLISH "TO TAKE" OR "TO BRING"

"To take" is translated into Ukrainian by an appropriate verb of carrying or leading, depending on the context. One has to note whether it is something or someone that is being taken from one place to another. Inanimate objects are carried or transported; animate beings are led or transported.

Віднеси́ ці книжки́!	Відведи́ його́!
Take these books away!	Take him away!

"To take" can also mean to assume posession, to have for one's use. If such is the context, Ukrainian will use the verb **бра́ти: взя́ти**:

Я взяв від нього́ кни́жку.
I took the book from him.

Likewise, when translating the verb "to bring" one must be careful to note if the object brought is animate or inanimate. In the first instance one has to use **приво́дити**, while in the second **прино́сити** must be used. **Приво́зити** may be used for both animate and inanimate objects if a vehicle was used in the bringing process.

Drill #165

Translate the English words in the right hand column and fill in the blanks:

1.	Васи́ль ..... скля́нку молока́ з ку́хні.	brought
2.	Васи́ль ..... щось з Іта́лії.	brought
3.	Я ..... тобі газе́ту на ґа́нок.	shall bring
4.	Я ..... тобі за́втра кві́ти зі села́.	shall bring
5.	О́ля ..... при́ятельку на обі́д.	brought
6.	Вона́ за́вжди ..... кого́сь на обі́д.	brings
7.	..... цю кни́жку до бібліоте́ки.	take
8.	..... цю валі́зку на ста́нцію.	take
9.	Ма́ма ..... по́суд до ї́да́льні.	took
10.	Хто ..... моє́ пальто́?	took
11.	Я ..... за́втра а́вто Петра́.	shall take

Homework

a) Memorize the vocabulary in Lesson #19;
b) Review Lesson #18;
c) Translate the following sentences into Ukrainian:

1. I am going north and am taking my family there.
2. We shall live in New York for a year.
3. Our doctor told our granddaughter that she may not go out yet.
4. When you go out, please shut the window.
5. The old woman entered the room and came up to me.
6. Who was the tall young man who approached you on the street?
7. I shall go into the house; it is raining.

8. When I come to see you on Tuesday, I'll bring you the latest magazines.
9. He came from the west and brought a nice little toy for our son.
10. Hello, Vasyl! Where are you going and what are you carrying?
11. I am going to my grandmother's and am taking apples and candies to her.
12. Our grandson came for us and we went together to the opera.
13. She used to drop in on us quite often.
14. Yesterday she dropped in for a few minutes and brought her niece and nephew.
15. My husband was walking along our street and found a watch.
16. I never find anything.
17. When I go to school, I usually go through the park.
18. I will cross the street at the corner.
19. I don't know if my nephew is bringing me anything from northern Italy.
20. Why does this scientist always carry his briefcase with him? I didn't notice it.
21. My sister's daughter (my niece), who lives in the south, never wears hats.
22. It began to rain; I stopped a taxi, the taxi stopped, I got in, and went home.
23. Yuriy walked Oksana home.
24. I believed him, but he led me astray.
25. You have just finished translating.

ДЕВ'ЯТНА́ДЦЯТИЙ РО́ЗДІЛ

СЛОВНИ́К

Іме́нники жіно́чого ро́ду

гаря́чка, -и	fever
зви́чка, -и	habit
просту́да, -и	cold (illness)
стипе́ндія, -ї	scholarship
температу́ра, -и	temperature
твари́на, -и	animal
фа́рба, -и	paint
хворо́ба, -и	sickness

Іме́нники чолові́чого ро́ду

день наро́дження, дня наро́дження	birthday
бе́резень, -зня	March
ве́ресень, -сня	September
гру́день, -дня	December
жо́втень, -тня	October
кві́тень, -тня	April
ли́пень, -пня	July
листопа́д, -а	November
лю́тий, -того	February
ревмати́зм, -у	rheumatism
се́рпень, -пня	August
сі́чень, -чня	January
тра́вень, -вня	May
че́рвень, -вня	June
шпита́ль, -ю	hospital

Іме́нники сере́днього ро́ду

воло́сся	hair (*collective*)
здоро́в'я	health

Прикме́тники

задово́лений, -а, -е	satisfied (+ instr. = *with*)
здоро́вий, -а, -е	healthy
кучеря́вий, -а, -е	curly
хво́рий, -а, -е	sick
шкільни́й, -а́, -е́	school (*adj.*)

Дієслова́

болі́ти: поболі́ти	to hurt *(intrans.)*
(боли́ть, боля́ть)	it hurts *(3rd pers. only)*
вивча́ти: ви́вчити *(вивча́ю, вивча́єш: ви́вчу, ви́вчиш)*	to study
виклада́ти: ви́класти *(виклада́ю, виклада́єш: ви́кладу, ви́кладеш)*	to lecture
дя́кувати: подя́кувати *(дя́кую, дя́куєш)*	to thank *(intrans.)*
нарі́ка́ти: понарі́ка́ти *(нарі́ка́ю, нарі́ка́єш)*	to complain *(на + acc.)*
почува́ти себе́ / почува́тися *(почува́ю себе́, почува́єш себе́/ почува́юся, почува́єшся)*	to feel *(imperf. only & intrans.)*
почу́ти себе́ *(почу́ю себе́, почу́єш себе́)*	to hear oneself *(perf. only & intrans.)*
просту́джуватися: простуди́тися *(просту́джуюся, просту́джуєшся: простуджу́ся, просту̀дишся)*	to catch a cold *(intrans.)*
роди́тися: народи́тися *(роджу́ся, ро́дишся)*	to be born
хворі́ти: захворі́ти *(хворі́ю, хворі́єш)*	to be sick *(intrans.)*
шука́ти: пошука́ти *(шука́ю, шука́єш)*	to search

Прислі́вники

гі́рше	worse
заздалегі́дь	in advance
кра́ще	better
лі́пше	better
найбі́льше	most

Ви́рази

на жа́ль	unfortunately
наща́стя	fortunately
поді́бний до	similar to (+ *gen.*)
схо́жий на	similar to (+ *acc.*)

GRAMMAR

Months of the Year — Місяці́ ро́ку (19.0)
Reflexive Pronoun себе́ *— Зворо́тний займе́нник* себе́ *(19.1)*
Intensive Pronoun сам *— Означа́льний займе́нник* сам *у фу́нкції підси́лювального сло́ва (19.2)*
Posessive Adjectives — Присві́йні прикме́тники (19.3—19.31)
Expressions of Health — Ви́рази на позна́чення здоро́в'я (19.4)
Education Expressions — Ви́рази на позна́чення осві́ти (19.5)
Summary of Prepositions — Повто́рне зве́дення прийме́нників (19.6)

19.0 MONTHS OF THE YEAR

The months of the year in Ukrainian are all masculine in gender. Unlike English months, they are all written with a small letter. February is adjectival in form, and November is hard stem. The rest are all soft stem, masculine nouns.

сі́чень, -чня	January	ли́пень, -пня	July
лю́тий, -того	February	се́рпень, -пня	August
бе́резень, -зня	March	ве́ресень, -сня	September
кві́тень, -тня	April	жо́втень, -тня	October
тра́вень, -вня	May	листопа́д, -а	November
че́рвень, -вня	June	гру́день, -дня	December

Idioms:

в/у да́ному мі́сяці	in a given month (*в* + *loc.*)
в/у сі́чні, лю́тому і т.д.	in January, February etc. (*в* + *loc.*)
мину́лого мі́сяця	last month (*gen.*)
насту́пного мі́сяця	next month (*gen.*)
цьо́го мі́сяця	this month (*gen.*)

Drill #166

Write answers to the following questions:

1. Котри́й тепе́р мі́сяць?
2. Котри́й мі́сяць пе́рший в ро́ці, котри́й оста́нній?
3. У котро́му мі́сяці зачина́ється шкі́льни́й рік?
4. У котро́му мі́сяці він кінча́ється?

5. У котрóму мíсяці ви роди́лися?
6. У котрóму мíсяці день нарóдження Шевчéнка?
7. Котри́й мíсяць вам найбíльше подóбається?
8. У котрóму мíсяці зачинáється веснá?
9. У котрóму мíсяці зачинáється лíто?
10. Котри́й пéрший мíсяць зими́?
11. У котри́х місяця́х три́дцять днів, а в котри́х три́дцять оди́н день?

19.1 REFLEXIVE PRONOUN **себé**

The reflexive pronoun **себé** refers back to the subject of the sentence. It has no nominative case. It corresponds to all three persons and both numbers. It is the equivalent of the English "self": *myself, himself, ourselves, themselves*, etc. The reflexive pronoun **себé** is used as the object of transitive verbs which otherwise are not reflexive or, when they become reflexive with **-ся**, have a different meaning: e.g., **знáти себé** "to know oneself", **знáтися** "to know each other":

Ніхтó себé не знáє.	Ми не знáємося.
Nobody knows himself.	We don't know each other.

Nom.	=
Gen.	себé
Dat.	собí
Acc.	себé
Inst.	собóю
Loc.	(на) сóбі

Note : There is, however, no difference in meaning between **почувáти себé** and **почувáтися**:

Я почувáю себé дóбре : Я почувáюся дóбре.
I feel well.

19.2 INTENSIVE PRONOUN **сам**

The pronoun **сам** which, together with **сами́й**, is used for "alone", is often used to identify or emphasize a particular noun or pronoun. The pronoun **сам** is declined like **оди́н**.

Я *сам* знáю себé.	I *myself* know myself.

Він *сам* мені сказáв.	He *himself* told me.
Вонá *самá* це бáчила.	She *herself* saw this.

Drill #167

Translate into Ukrainian:

1. I did that myself.
2. He bought that picture for himself.
3. Tell that to the director himself!
4. They are always very satisfied with themselves.
5. My teacher told me that herself.
6. I myself don't know what I want.
7. Don't think so much about yourself. It's bad for your health.
8. Did you bring your briefcase with you?
9. Take a coat with you; it will be cold.
10. Who understands himself?
11. I shall take you along.
12. Buy yourself a new hat.

19.3 POSSESSIVE ADJECTIVES

Normally, in Ukrainian possession is shown through the use of the genitive case. Thus стипéндія студéнта shows that it is the scholarship of the student, or student's scholarship. Possession in Ukrainian, however, can be shown also by the use of a possessive adjective formed from a given noun. Any masculine or feminine noun of the 1st declension can be made into a possessive adjective by the addition of certain suffixes. Thus стипéндія студéнта can be expressed as **студéнтова** стипéндія.

Although both expressions show that the scholarship belongs to the student, the one with the possessive adjective is attributive, that is, descriptive. Since **студéнтова** is an adjective, it describes the scholarship by telling whose it is, and precedes the noun.

19.31 Possessive adjectives are formed with the help of the following suffixes: **-ів/-їв, -ин/-їн**.

1. 1st declension masculine nouns (hard, mixed, and soft stems, as well as those ending in **-о**) are converted into possessive adjectives by the addition of:

-ів, -ова, -ове	for hard stem nouns
-ів, -ева, -еве	for mixed and soft stem nouns
-їв, -єва, -єве	for "j" stem nouns

Іва́н:	Іва́нів стіл	Ivan's table
	Іва́нова кни́жка	Ivan's book
	Іва́нове перо́	Ivan's pen
ба́тько:	ба́тьків стіл	father's table
	ба́тькова кни́жка	father's book
	ба́тькове перо́	father's pen
това́риш:	това́ришів стіл	friend's table
	това́ришева кни́жка	friend's book
	това́ришеве перо́	friend's pen
учи́тель:	учи́телів стіл	teacher's table
	учи́телева кни́жка	teacher's book
	учи́телеве перо́	teacher's pen
Андрі́й:	Андрі́їв стіл	Andriy's table
	Андрі́єва кни́жка	Andriy's book
	Андрі́єве перо́	Andriy's pen

2. 1st declension feminine nouns (hard, mixed, and soft stem) as well as masculine nouns ending in *-a* are converted into possessive adjectives by the addition of:

-ин, -ина, -ине	for hard, mixed, and soft stem nouns
-їн, -їна, -їне	for "j" stem nouns

Окса́на:	Окса́нин стіл	Oksana's table
	Окса́нина кни́жка	Oksana's book
	Окса́нине перо́	Oksana's pen
О́льга:	О́льжин* стіл	Olha's table
	О́льжина кни́жка	Olha's book
	О́льжине перо́	Olha's pen
Мико́ла:	Мико́лин стіл	Mykola's table
	Мико́лина кни́жка	Mykola's book
	Мико́лине перо́	Mykola's pen

На́дя:	На́дин стіл	Nadya's table
	На́дина кни́жка	Nadya's book
	На́дине перó	Nadya's pen
Марíя:	Марíїн стіл	Mariya's table
	Марíїна кни́жка	Mariya's book
	Марíїне перó	Mariya's pen
ма́ти:	ма́терин стіл	mother's table
	ма́терина кни́жка	mother's book
	ма́терине перó	mother's pen
Марíйка:	Марíйчин* стіл	Mariyka's table
	Марíйчина кни́жка	Mariyka's book
	Марíйчине перó	Mariyka's pen

The newly formed possessive adjectives agree in case, number, and gender with the nouns they modify and decline like all other adjectives:

ба́тьків стіл, ба́тькового стола́, ба́тьковому столóві і т.д.
ба́тькова ха́та, ба́тькової ха́ти, ба́тьковій ха́ті і т.д.
ма́терин стіл, ма́теринолго стола́, ма́теринову столóві і т.д.
ма́терина ха́та, ма́теринолї ха́ти, ма́терииній ха́ті і т.д.

* Note the 1st palatalization of **к, г, х** to **ч, ж, ш** before the frontal vowel **и**.

Drill #168

Rewrite the following sentences, substituting a proper form of the possessive adjective for nouns showing possession through the genitive case.

Model:	Я ба́чу кни́жку Іва́на.	Я ба́чу Іва́нову кни́жку.
	I see the book of Ivan.	I see Ivan's book.

1. Óля ї́де а́втом актóра. В а́вті актóра — бага́то мíсця.
2. На столí лежи́ть журна́л Аскóльда, а Аскóльд узя́в журна́л бабу́сі.
3. Усí шука́ли череви́ки балери́ни.
4. Волóсся блонди́на булó кучеря́ве, а блонди́нки булó прóсте.

5. Ба́тько купи́в фа́рбу й хо́че, щоб кімна́та Богда́на була́ бі́лою, як кімна́та О́льги.
6. Я прочита́в у зо́шиті Бори́сі, що ха́та учи́тельки зеле́на.
7. Мі́сто подарува́ло шко́лі Василя́ нову́ бібліоте́ку, а шко́лі На́сті нову́ авдито́рію.
8. Мій ву́йко, брат ма́тері, пози́чив валі́зку Петра́.
9. Вірші́ Ві́ри ду́же ціка́ві, а оповіда́ння Марі́йки ду́же до́вгі.
10. Хоч гіта́ра Гри́ця дорога́, всі хо́чуть гра́ти на ґіта́рі Ната́лки.

19.4 EXPRESSIONS OF HEALTH

Expressions:

здоро́вий чолові́к	healthy man
хво́рий чолові́к	sick man

почува́ти себе́ до́бре, пога́но, гі́рше, лі́пше
to feel well, poorly, worse, better

Мені́ (я почува́юся) гі́рше, лі́пше, до́бре, пога́но.
I feel worse, better, well, poorly.

The verb **болі́ти: поболі́ти** is intransitive in meaning, and therefore that which "hurts" is in the nominative; the one who has the pain is in the accusative or the dative case.

Мене́ боли́ть голова́.	My head hurts.
Мені́ боли́ть голова́.	"
Ма́му боля́ть о́чі.	Mother's eyes hurt.
Ма́мі боля́ть о́чі.	"

Drill #169

Choose the word which makes sense and give the proper form of **болі́ти, хворі́ти, хво́рий, -а, здоро́вий, -а:**

1. Вчо́ра мене́ ..... голова́.
2. У вівто́рок Окса́ну ..... о́чі.
3. Тепе́р Іва́на ..... ву́ха.

4. Якщó її знóву щонéбудь ....., вонá не прийде.
5. У субóту менé дýже ..... прáва рукá.
6. Якщó вас ..... óчі, підíть до лікаря.
7. Бідна Гáня! Вонá булá ..... і не моглá вихóдити цілий тиждень.
8. В ту порý рóку всі .....
9. Андрíю, якщó ти зáвтра дáлі бýдеш ....., потелефонýй менí.
10. Менí сказáли, що вони старí й ..... люди.
11. Я булá ....., алé тепéр я вже зóвсім здорóва.
12. Лікар кáже, що бáтько дýже ..... чоловíк.
13. Ми мáємо весéлих, ... дітéй.
14. Вони, дякувати Бóгу, нікóли не .....
15. Івáн мав простýду, алé тепéр він ужé .....

Drill #170

Choose the proper form of the following words:
почувáти себé, менí/йомý, погáно/дóбре, лíпше/гíрше:

1. Як ви .....? Дякую, ... дóбре.
2. Як сьогóдні ..... ваш брат? Він ..... погáно.
3. Якщó ви бýдете ..... погáно, зателефонýйте лікареві.
4. Вчóра Óля ..... погáно, а сьогóдні їй .....
5. У вівтóрок Борисові булó дýже ....., і йогó відвезли до шпитáлю.
6. На жаль, йомý сьогóдні ....., і ми не знáємо, коли він змóже вийти зі шпитáлю.
7. Я сподівáюся, що зáвтра він ..... трóхи .....

19.5 EDUCATION EXPRESSIONS

To teach: **учити: навчити / навчáти: навчити**

Both verbs are used in the same way:

The person taught is in the accusative case; the subject matter is in the genitive case.

Я вчу Марýсю украї́нської мóви.
Я навчáю Марýсю украї́нської мóви.
I teach Marusya Ukrainian language.

To learn (memorize): **вивча́ти: ви́вчити**

This verb is used only when a concrete object of the learning process is mentioned. This matter being learned is in the accusative case.

Я вивча́ю матема́тику.
I am learning math.

Я вивча́ю цю кни́жку.
I am studying this book.

To learn (study): **в/у/чи́тися: навчи́тися**

This is a more general verb for studying and is used both with and without a concrete object of learning. When used with such an object, the matter being learned is in the genitive case.

Я вчу́ся украї́нської мо́ви.
I am learning (studying) Ukrainian.

Я люблю́ вчи́тися.
I like to study.

To lecture: **виклада́ти: ви́класти**

This verb is used for teaching at a higher institution. The person/s lectured to is/are in the dative case, the subject matter is in the accusative case.

Я виклада́ю украї́нську мо́ву студе́нтам в університе́ті.
I lecture on the Ukrainian language to students at the university.

Drill #171

Translate into Ukrainian:

1. My sister teaches in this school.
2. She likes to teach.
3. I am teaching him to play the piano.
4. He studied a great deal.
5. We are studying this new map.
6. I like to study in my room.

7. Dr. Smyrny studied at this university.
8. I am learning to speak Ukrainian.
9. Where did you learn to play tennis so well? Who taught you?
10. I have been studying this problem for a whole month.

19.6 SUMMARY OF PREPOSITIONS

Prepositions of Position

в	in	loc.
на	on/in	loc.
над	above, over	instr.
під	below, under	instr.
пéред	in front of	instr.
між	between	instr.
за	behind, beyond	instr.
біля	near	gen.
кóло	near	gen.
довкóла	around	gen.

Prepositions of Motion

в	into	acc.
на	onto	acc.
над	above/over	acc.
під	under	acc.
за	behind	acc.
пéред	in front of	acc.
із	out of	gen.
з	from	gen.
від	from	gen.
до	toward	gen.
між	(in) between	gen./acc.
чéрез	across	acc.
по	along	loc./dat.
по	for	acc.
від... до	from... to	gen.
з... до	from... to	gen.

Homework

a) Memorize the vocabulary in Lesson #20;
b) Review Lesson #19;
c) Translate the following sentences into Ukrainian:

1. How is your father feeling now? Thank you, fortunately, he is better today.
2. Unfortunately our grandmother is feeling worse today.
3. In the doctor's opinion she is very sick.
4. My aunt was sick and my uncle took her to the hospital, and now I've heard that my uncle himself is sick.
5. I don't feel well this evening; I have a headache.
6. Where did you study? I studied at the Kyiv University, and besides I studied for a year in England. I studied language.
7. Does your son like to study? Yes, very much.
8. Every year we spend our vacation at the seashore. We like the sea.
9. My father spent his summer in the mountains; he likes the mountains.
10. My aunt often complains of her health (*на* + *acc.*). She is a very sick woman.
11. It is impossible to tell in advance who will receive a scholarship for next year.
12. My father's birthday is in August, and my mother's in September.
13. Tell me something about yourself. I myself don't know what to tell you.
14. It is a bad habit to speak about oneself.
15. The dog is a very interesting animal.
16. Your daughter, according to my wife, looks very much like you.
17. This city resembles Paris.
18. Thank God, my grandfather is better today.
19. Fortunately, we took him to the hospital.

ДВАДЦЯ́ТИЙ РО́ЗДІЛ

СЛОВНИ́К

Іме́нники жіно́чого ро́ду

вітри́на, -и	store window, display window
кана́па, -и	sofa
парасо́ля, -і	umbrella
части́на, -и	part
ша́фа, -и	closet, cupboard
шухля́да, -и	drawer

Іме́нники чолові́чого ро́ду

Бог, -а	God
ви́бір, -бору	choice
дя́дько, -а	uncle, any older man
капелю́х, -а	hat
кут, -а́	corner (as of a room), angle (as in a triangle)
літа́к, -а́	airplane
схід, схо́ду	east

Множи́нні іме́нники

кані́кули, -кул	vacations

Прикме́тники

мо́крий, -а, -е	wet
пе́вний, -а, -е	sure
поро́жній, -я, -є	empty
сере́дній, -я, -є	middle

Дієслова́

бігати, бігти: побігти *(бі́гаю, бі́гаєш; біжу́, біжи́ш)*	to run
здава́ти: зда́ти *(здаю́, здає́ш: здам, здаси́)*	to pass (exam), to give up
здійма́ти: здійня́ти *(здійма́ю, здійма́єш: здійму́, зді́ймеш)*	to take off

знімáти: зня́ти (знімáю, знімáєш: знімý, знíмеш)	to take off
клáсти: поклáсти *(кладý, кладéш)*	to place *(in a lying position), to lay*
літáти, летíти: полетíти *(літáю, літáєш; лечý, лети́ш)*	to fly
плáвати, пли́сти: попли́сти *(плáваю, плáваєш; пливý, пливéш)*	to swim
стáвити: постáвити *(стáвлю, стáвиш)*	to place *(in a standing position)*

GRAMMAR

The Conditional Mood — Умóвний спóсіб (20.0)
Verbs of Placing — Дієсловá на markuвначення кладíння (20.1)
*Prepositions **за** and **під** — Приймéнники за і під (20.2)*
Other Verbs of Motion: Running, Flying, Swimming — Íнші дієсловá рýху: бíгати, літáти, плáвати (20.3)

20.0 THE CONDITIONAL MOOD

The conditional mood in Ukrainian is expressed by the particle **би** (after words ending in a consonant) and **б** (after words ending in a vowel). Usually this particle is placed right after the verb which in the conditional mood has the form of the past tense. The particle, however, may be placed also after the first word in the sentence. The "if" clause of a conditional statement begins with **якщó б** or **якбú**:

Якщó б я мав грóші, я б купúв хáту.
If I had money, I would buy a house.

Якбú він мені сказáв, я прийшлá б.
If he had told me, I would have come.

The conditional mood really has no tense. Thus **читáв би** "I would read" can refer to the present, future, or past. There is, however, a past conditional which adds to the conditional a past tense of the verb **бýти** "to be" agreeing in gender and number with the subject. It signifies the irrevocability of a condition and hence the fact that the condition has passed.

Якбú я мав був грóші, я був би купúв хáту.
If I had had the money, I would have bought a house.

20.01 Often **би, б** alone are used colloquially as expressions of a wish, hope, uncertainty, tentative consideration, etc.

Гáрно б поїхати кудибýдь.
It would be nice to go anywhere.

Трéба б написáти до бáтька.
I should write to father.

Де б ми пообíдали?
I wonder where we can have dinner?

20.02 A variant of the conditional construction is used in purpose-type sentences. In these constructions, the subordinate clause is introduced by the conjunction **щоб**, and the verb is either in the past tense or the infinitive. If the subject of the main clause and the subordinate clause are the same, the infinitive is used after **щоб**; if the subjects are different, the subordinate verb has the form of the past tense (not past in meaning):

Іва́н хо́че, щоб *Петро́* **прийшо́в** (*Different subjects*).
Ivan wants Petro to come (Ivan wants that Petro come).

Я дав йому́ гро́ші, щоб *він* **поїхав** (*Different subjects*).
I gave him money so that he could go.

Він вчи́вся бага́то, щоб **зда́ти** іспит (*Subjects the same*).
He studied a lot (in order) to pass his exam.

Do not confuse the purpose-type construction with the conditional. In the conditional the **б** is separate from **що** and is movable:

Що **б** було́, якби́ ми не поїхали : Що було́ **б**, якби́ ми не поїхали?
What would have been, if we had not gone?

In the purpose clause, **щоб** is one word:

Я хо́чу, **щоб** ти приїхав.
I want you to come.

Drill #172

Translate the English words into Ukrainian:

1. Ми ду́же хо́чемо, ... в субо́ту. you to come
2. Моя́ ма́ти хо́че, ... до ба́тька. me to write
3. Я не зна́ю, що зроби́ти, ... більше по-українському. that he should speak
4. Вони́ ..... ду́же ра́ді вас ба́чити. would have been
5. Було́ б га́рно, ... if he would come
6. Ви пови́нні попроси́ти його́, ... п'ятдеся́т до́ларів. that he should bring

7. ..... пере́клад, мені́ потрі́бний словни́к. in order to do
8. Він хоті́в, ... йому́ цього́ листа́. me to read
9. Вони́ так ..... поїхати в Украї́ну. would like

Drill #173

Translate into Ukrainian:

1. He said that he would buy me a present.[1]
2. If he had had the money, he would have bought me a present.
3. If he has (*will have*) the money tomorrow, he'll buy me something.
4. How nice it would have been, if you had written to Olya.
5. I would like to see him.
6. In order to see him, you must go to Kyiv.
7. Mother doesn't want me to go to Kyiv.
8. I wrote to her in (*to*) Kyiv to bring us Ukrainian books.
9. You should have written to her husband.

20.1 VERBS OF PLACING: **кла́сти: покла́сти/положи́ти** AND **ста́вити: поста́вити**

Ukrainian makes a distinction between placing something in a standing position and placing it in a lying position. Some objects can be placed only in one of the two, others in both, as, for example, a book.

Я **покла́в** цього́ листа́ на стіл, і він ще там **лежи́ть**.
I *put* this letter on the table, and it's still *lying* there.

Я **поста́вив** крі́сло в кут, і воно́ там **стої́ть**.
I *put* the chair in the corner, and it's *standing* there.

Я **поста́вив** кни́жку на поли́цю і вона́ там **стої́ть** між і́ншими книжка́ми.
I *placed* the book on the shelf and it is *standing* there among other books.

---

1 Do not confuse the English *would* (future perfect) used in indirect speech with the *would* of a conditional mood. (See 11.2)

Я **поклáв** кни́жку на поли́цю і вонá там **лежи́ть** між íншими книжкáми.
I *placed* the book on the shelf and it is *lying* there among other books.

Note that both **клáсти** and **стáвити** are considered verbs of directional motion. Hence they take prepositions and adverbs that show direction, not position.

Я кладý олівéць на стіл (*на* + *acc.*)
I place the pencil on the table.

20.2 PREPOSITIONS за AND під

When used with verbs of motion to indicate direction, these prepositions are followed by the accusative case.

Я постáвив крíсло **за** двéрі, а листá **під** кни́жку.
I put the chair *behind* the door, and the letter *under* the book.

The instrumental case is used to show location :

під кни́жкою; за двери́ма

Drill #174

Fill in the blanks with a suitable verb: **клáсти: поклáсти, стáвити: постáвити, лежáти, стоя́ти**

1. Хто ..... ті листи́ на моє́ бю́рко? Вíра ..... їх туди́.
2. Чомý ти зáвжди ..... всі листи́ на моє́ бю́рко? Я нормáльно ..... їх туди́, томý що я не знáю, куди́ їх .....
3. Чиї́ листи́ ..... на моє́му бю́рку?
4. Васи́лю, куди́ ти ..... горíлку? Я ..... її́ туди́, куди́ я зáвжди її́ .....
5. Візьмíть ці докумéнти і ..... їх у шухля́ду, а словни́к ..... на поли́цю, туди́, де ..... францýзькі книжки́.

Drill #175

Translate into Ukrainian:

1. Children, don't put empty glasses under the table.
2. And don't put them under the armchair.
3. Put them on the table.
4. Glasses should not stand under a table.
5. Borys, why did you put this old newspaper behind the sofa?
6. I don't know where to put old newspapers.
7. I've put the salt behind the bread.
8. Who has put my pencil under the dictionary?
9. Vasyl went behind the garage.
10. Why were his toys behind the garage?
11. I've put the chair behind the tree.
12. You see? The chair is standing behind the tree.

20.3 The basic form of "to run" is:

	Imperfective		Perfective
	Indefinite	Definite	
Infin.	бігати	бігти	побігти
1st pers. sg.	бігаю	біжу́	побіжу́
2nd pers. sg.	бігаєш	біжи́ш	побіжи́ш
Masc.past	бігав	біг (*but f.* бігла.)	побіг (*but f.* побігла)
2nd pers. imper.	бігай!	біжи́!	побіжи́!

The basic form of "to fly" is:

	Imperfective		Perfective
	Indefinite	Definite	
Infin.	літа́ти	леті́ти	полеті́ти
1st pers. sg.	літа́ю	лечу́	полечу́
2nd pers. sg.	літа́єш	лети́ш	полети́ш
Masc. past	літа́в	леті́в	полеті́в
2nd pers. imper.	літа́й!	лети́!	полети́!

The basic form of "to swim" is:

	Imperfective		Perfective
	Indefinite	Definite	
Infin.	пла́вати	пли́сти́/пливти́	попли́сти
1st pers. sg.	пла́ваю	пливу́	попливу́
2nd pers. sg.	пла́ваєш	пливе́ш	пopливе́ш
Masc. past	пла́вав	плив (*but* *f.* плила́/пливла́)	попли́в
2nd pers. imper.	пла́вай!	пливи́!	попливи́!

As with other verbs of motion, certain prefixes may be added to the indefinite and the definite imperfectives in order to create new verbs. During prefixation, however, the form **-пли́вати** is used instead of **пла́вати:**

вбіга́ти: вбі́гти	to run in (inside)
набіга́ти: набі́гти	to run into, converge
вибіга́ти: ви́бігти	to run out of (an enclosure)
підбіга́ти: підбі́гти	to run up to
забіга́ти: забі́гти	to drop in (in haste)
перебіга́ти: перебі́гти	to run across
пробіга́ти: пробі́гти	to run by
відбіга́ти: відбі́гти	to run away from
добіга́ти: добі́гти	to approach by running
влі́та́ти: влеті́ти	to fly (run) into
налі́та́ти: налеті́ти	to converge, to come upon from above
вилі́та́ти: ви́летіти	to fly out of
підлі́та́ти: підлеті́ти	to fly up off the ground
залі́та́ти: залеті́ти	to fly to a given destination
перелі́та́ти: перелеті́ти	to fly across
пролі́та́ти: пролеті́ти	to fly by
відлі́та́ти: відлеті́ти	to fly away
долі́та́ти: долеті́ти	to approach in flight, reach (sound)
впллива́ти: вппли́сти́	to flow/swim in
вплива́ти: впли́нути	to influence
напплива́ти: наппли́сти	to flow into
виплива́ти: ви́плисти	to flow out of, to swim out of
підплива́ти: підпли́сти	to flow up to, to swim up to

запливáти: заплúсти	to flow/swim to a given destination
перепливáти: перепливстú	to flow across, to swim across
пропливáти: проплúсти	to flow by, to swim by
відпливáти: відплúсти	to flow away, to swim away
допливáти: доплúсти	to approach by swimming

Drill #176

Choose the correct form of the verbs in parentheses:

1. Я люблю́ (літáти, летíти), алé я рíдко (літáю, лечý).
2. Я чув, що ви кудúсь (літáєте, летитé) сьогóдні ввéчорі.
3. Так, я (літáю, лечý) до Я́лти.
4. О котрíй годúні ви вчóра (прилітáли, прилетíли) до Торóнта?
5. Дя́дько Михáйло чáсто (прилітáв, прилетíв) до нас з Едмонтóну.
6. Собáка лю́бить (бíгти, бíгати).
7. Ця собáка (бíгає, біжúть) додóму.
8. Я рáнком бáчив Андрíя. Він кудúсь (бíгав, біг).
9. Він (прибігáв, прибíг) до мéне сьогóдні рáнком.
10. Він зáвжди (прибігáє, прибіжúть) назáд.
11. Я люблю́ (плáвати, плúсти).
12. Влíтку я щодня́ (плáвав, плив) в óзері.
13. Одногó рáзу, колú я (припливáв, приплúв) до бéрега, я побáчив рúбу, що (плилá, плáвала) до мéне. Вонá подивúлася на мéне і скóро (відпливáла, відпливлá) від мéне.

Drill #177

Translate into Ukrainian:

1. When I was running into the house, he ran out.
2. As I was approaching on the run the corner of the street, I ran (*flew*) into him.
3. Petro ran up to the house and saw the planes converging on the city.
4. Had father known that you would swim so far out, he would have never permitted you to go swimming.
5. Oksana influences me (*на + acc.*) by her good deeds.
6. First the bird ran up to the tree, then it flew up off the ground, and then it flew away.

7. Where did my paper plane land (*fly to*)?
8. The birds were flying south past my window.
9. Ihor swam across Lake Ontario.
10. When I opened the door the sound of water reached my ear. The house was full of water and more was flowing in.

Homework

a) Memorize the vocabulary in Lesson #21;
b) Review Lesson #20;
c) Translate the following sentences into Ukrainian:

1. If you want me to come on Tuesday, I shall come and read you the second part of the letter.
2. I asked Borys to write the director of your school. He hasn't answered his letter yet.
3. I want Olya to buy an evening dress.
4. If there were a park opposite our house, we would go there to walk.
5. Her brothers see each other very seldom.
6. If Oksana had had a choice, she would have chosen another apartment; but she had no choice.
7. He doesn't want me to go with him to the Middle East.
8. Take off your coat, put your wet umbrella in the corner and your wet hat on the table.
9. I shall take off my coat, put my hat on the table, and put my umbrella in the corner.
10. Don't put all these bottles on the floor. Put them in the cupboard, (there) where I usually put them.
11. I am sure that if he had wanted a good grade, he would have studied all day Sunday.
12. If they had always helped each other, their life would have been simple.
13. We would have helped them if we could have.
14. I would very much have loved to live in some eastern country.
15. The saleslady asked me if I wanted the black shoes or the blue ones.
16. We shall go to the country on Wednesday if the weather is nice.
17. We would have gone to the country if the weather had been nice.
18. I shall take off my hat.
19. I put the newspaper on the table underneath the book.
20. Your paper plane fell behind the piano.

ДВА́ДЦЯТЬ ПЕ́РШИЙ РО́ЗДІЛ

СЛОВНИ́К

Іме́нники жіно́чого ро́ду

Во́лга, -и	Volga
грани́ця, -і	boundary, border
двою́рідна сестра́, -ої -и	cousin
кузи́на, -и / кузи́нка, -и	cousin
люди́на, -и	person
ми́ля, -і	mile
Полта́ва, -и	Poltava
при́повідка, -и	proverb, saying
ху́стка, -и	kerchief, scarf

Іме́нники чолові́чого ро́ду

двою́рідний брат, -ого -а	cousin
квито́к, -тка́	ticket
кіломе́тр, -а	kilometer
клі́мат, -у	climate
кузе́н, -а	cousin
ме́шканець, -нця	inhabitant
Ха́рків, -кова	Kharkiv

Іме́нники сере́днього ро́ду

головне́, -но́го	main thing (adj. used as a noun)
завда́ння, -ння	assignment
запро́шення, -ння	invitation
зо́лото, -а	gold
майбу́тнє, -нього	future (adj. used as a noun)
срі́бло, -а	silver
Чіка́ґо	Chicago (indeclinable)

Прикме́тники

бли́зьки́й, -а́, -е́	near
божеві́льний, -а, -е	insane
відва́жний, -а, -е	valiant, courageous

дале́кий, -а, -е	far, distant
ду́жий, -а, -е	mighty
кра́сний, -а, -е	nice, beautiful
ле́гкий, -а, -е	easy, light
му́дрий, -а, -е	smart, intelligent
пі́зній, -я, -є	late
по́вний, -а, -е	full
пога́ний, -а, -е	ugly
рідки́й, -а́, -е́	thin, watery
різки́й, -а́, -е́	shrill, harsh
си́льний, -а, -е	strong
слаби́й, -а́, -е́	weak
те́плий, -а, -е	warm
швидки́й, -а́, -е́	fast, quick

Дієслова́

заси́джуватися: заси́дітися *(заси́джуюся, заси́джуєшся : заси́джуся, заси́дишся)*	to overstay

Прислі́вники

недоста́тньо	not enough, insufficiently

Ви́рази

в найгі́ршому ви́падку	at the worst
гра́ти в ша́хи	to play chess
ті́льки що	just now (+ *past of verb*)

GRAMMAR

The Comparative and Superlative Degrees of Adjectives and Adverbs — Сту̀пені порі́внення прикме́тників і прислі́вників (21.0—21.01)
Prefixes **по-, про-, за-** — *Пре́фікси* **по-, про-, за-** *(21.1—21.12)*
Verbs of Position (Review) — Дієслова́ мі́сця і кладі́ння (повто́рення) (21.2)

21.0 THE COMPARATIVE AND SUPERLATIVE DEGREES OF ADJECTIVES AND ADVERBS

1. The second (comparative) degree of Ukrainian adjectives is formed by adding to the stem of the adjectives the suffixes **-ш-** or **-іш-** plus the adjectival endings **-ий, -а, -е**. The suffix **-іш-** occurs usually when the stem ends in two or more consonants. This is not, however, a steadfast rule:

Positive		Comparative	
бага́тий, -а, -е	rich	бага́тший, -а, -е	richer
стари́й, -а́, -е́	old	ста́рший, -а, -е	older[1]
пові́льний, -а, -е	slow	пові́льніший, -а, -е	slower
пі́зній, -я, -є	late	пізні́ший, -а, -е	later
те́плий, -а, -е	warm	теплі́ший, -а, -е	warmer
		but	
ти́хий, -а, -е	quiet	ти́хший, -а, -е	quieter
		тихі́ший, -а, -е	quieter

2. Adjectives that have the suffix **-к-** or **-ок-** (*rarely* **-ек-**) drop this suffix before forming the comparative degree:

рідки́й, -а́, -е́	thin, rare	рі́дший, -а, -е	thinner, rarer
швидки́й, -а́, -е́	fast	шви́дший, -а, -е	faster
дале́кий, -а, -е	far	да́льший, -а, -е	farther
широ́кий, -а, -е	wide	ши́рший, -а, -е	wider
глибо́кий, -а, -е	deep	гли́бший, -а, -е	deeper

---

1 The comparative of стари́й, -а, -е is ста́рший, -а, -е when it is a question of age and authority, and старі́ший, -а, -е when it relates to time (aging). E.g.:

Богда́н ста́рший від Іва́на.	Bohdan is older than Ivan.
Цей буди́нок старі́ший від то́го.	This building is older than that one.

ле́гкий, -а, -е	light	ле́гший, -а, -е	lighter
		but	
м'яки́й, -а́, -е́	soft	м'я́кший, -а, -е	softer
різки́й, -а́, -е́	shrill	різкі́ший, -а, -е	shriller

3. The suffix **-ш-** changes to **-ч-** when preceded by a stem ending in **г, ж, зь** while the **г, зь** change to **ж**:

дороги́й, -а́, -е́	dear	доро́жчий, -а, -е	dearer
ду́жий, -а, -е	mighty	ду́жчий, -а, -е	mightier
близьки́й, -а, -е	near[1]	бли́жчий, -а, -е	nearer
низьки́й, -а, -е	low[1]	ни́жчий, -а, -е	lower

4. Some adjectives have irregular forms in the comparative degree. These should be memorized as such:

до́брий, -а, -е	good	лі́пший, -а, -е	better
		добрі́ший, -а, -е	better (morally)
		кра́щий, -а, -е	better (nicer)
га́рний	nice	кра́щий	nicer
and га́рний	nice	гарні́ший	nicer
зли́й, -а́, -е́	bad	гі́рший, -а, -е	worse
висо́кий, -а, -е	high	ви́щий, -а, -е	higher
вели́кий, -а, -е	big	бі́льший, -а, -е	bigger
мали́й, -а́, -е́	small	ме́нший, -а, -е	smaller
до́вгий, -а, -е	long	до́вший, -а, -е	longer

5. The third (superlative) degree of comparison is formed by the addition of the prefix **най-** to the comparative degree of the adjective:

Positive		Comparative		Superlative	
бага́тий	rich	бага́тший	richer	найбага́тший	richest
те́плий	warm	теплі́ший	warmer	найтеплі́ший	warmest
швидки́й	fast	шви́дший	faster	найшви́дший	fastest
висо́кий	high	ви́щий	higher	найви́щий	highest
низьки́й	low	ни́жчий	lower	найни́жчий	lowest

6. Another possible way to form both the comparative and the superlative degrees of adjectives is with the help of **більш, найбільш** (more, most) or negatively **менш, наймéнш** (less, least). This is the

1 The suffix **-к-** drops out as required in rule 2 above.

only way one can form the comparative and superlative of certain adjectives (such as those which describe materials, seasons, places — **залі́зний** "iron", **зимови́й** "winter", **міськи́й** "urban".) Note that very often in English nouns are used for adjectives in these cases. Likewise, the comparative and superlative of past passive adjectival participles (see Chapter 23) is formed with the help of **більш/ме́нш**:

спи́саний, -а, -е	більш спи́саний	найбі́льш спи́саний
written over	more written over	most written over

7. In sentences expressing comparison, the English "than" is rendered in Ukrainian by **ніж, як, чим** + *nom.*, **від** + *gen.*, or **за** + *acc.*

Я бага́тший, ніж він.	I am richer than he.
Я бага́тший, як він.	"
Я бага́тший, чим він.	"
Я бага́тший від ньо́го.	"
Я бага́тший за ньо́го.	"

При́повідки — Sayings

Бли́жча соро́чка ті́лу, як кожу́х.
Blood is thicker than water.
(Literally: The shirt is closer to the body than the sheepskin coat).

Час — найкра́щий лі́кар.
Time is the best healer.

Drill #178

Translate into Ukrainian:

1. In summer, nights are shortest, days longest.
2. Which scarf is more beautiful — the yellow or the green one?
3. Our car is bigger than yours.
4. Which is dearer: gold or silver?
5. The road to Kyiv is wider than the one to Lviv.
6. The widest and longest river in Ukraine is the Dnipro.
7. The greatest Ukrainian poet is Taras Shevchenko.
8. Poltava is smaller than Kharkiv.
9. New York is bigger than Chicago.
10. The most famous Ukrainian king was Danylo.
11. The cossacks were most valiant.

Drill #179

Complete the sentence:

Ку́дрики бага́тші від...	я, ти, він, вона́, ми, ви, вони́, до́ктор Чуб, на́ша нова́ вчи́телька, Іва́н, Дени́с Дени́сенко, на́ші дру́зі, ва́ші по́други
Ки́їв бі́льший за...	Оде́са, Львів, ва́ша столи́ця, це мі́сто, Торо́нто

Drill #180

Translate the words in parentheses:

1.	Котра́ ву́лиця ..... в цьо́му мі́сті?	(longest)
2.	Котри́й із цих буди́нків ..... ?	(oldest)
3.	Васи́ль учо́ра танцюва́в із ..... ді́вчиною.	(most pretty)
4.	Андрі́й лю́бить ..... ді́вчину з усі́х.	(the silliest)
5.	Я пишу́ цього́ листа́ до мого́ ..... това́риша.	(most intelligent)
6.	Я розка́зував про .... мого́ студе́нта.	(oldest)
7.	Володи́мир бага́то .... від Оста́па.	(taller)
8.	Оста́п бага́то ...., ніж Лі́на.	(smarter)

Drill #181

Supply the comparatives of the adjectives in italics and their antonyms according to the model:

Model: Іва́н *си́льний*, але́ Павло́ *сильні́ший* за Іва́на. Іва́н *сла́бший.*

1. Дніпро́ *до́вгий*, але́ Во́лга ..... Дніпро́ .....
2. Ми *бага́ті*, але́ Ро́кефелер ..... Ми .....
3. Володи́мир *висо́кий*, але́ Сла́вко ..... Володи́мир .....
4. Моя́ кварти́ра *га́рна*, але́ ва́ша ..... Моя́ кварти́ра .....
5. Оля *розу́мна*, але́ Зі́рка ..... Оля .....
6. Мені́ *вигі́дно* прийти́ о дру́гій, але́ о п'я́тій мені́ ..... Мені́ о дру́гій .....
7. Мій костю́м *дороги́й*, але́ твій ..... Мій костю́м .....
8. Я пишу́ *пога́но*, але́ ти пи́шеш ..... Я пишу́ .....
9. Ми живемо́ *дале́ко*, але́ ви живете́ ..... Ми живемо́ .....
10. Крамни́ця *бли́зько*, але́ апте́ка ..... Крамни́ця .....
11. Мій о́дяг *коро́ткий*, але́ твій ..... Мій о́дяг .....
12. Моя́ кімна́та *те́мна*, але́ твоя́ ..... Моя́ кімна́та .....

13. Сьогóдні *тéпло*, алá вчóра булó ..... Сьогóдні .....
14. Сúня спіднúця *ширóка*, алé чóрна ..... Сúня спіднúця .....
15. Дáрка співáє *гáрно*, алé ти співáєш ..... Дáрка співáє .....

Drill #182

Provide the comparative form of the adjectives in parentheses:

1. Дóктор Чуб (дóбрий) від дóктора Бýльби.
2. Я (погáно) варю́, ніж Івáнко.
3. Я живý (далéко) від університéту, чим ви.
4. Мені́ (лéгко) читáти по-украї́нському, ніж говорúти.
5. Цей вечі́рній óдяг (новúй), ніж той.
6. Олéг (мýдрий) за Микóлу.
7. Нáша вýлиця (вузькá) за вáшу.
8. Ваш дім (висóкий), чим наш.
9. Ця горá (низькá) від тiéї.
10. Нáша вітáльня (велúка) від ї́дáльні.

21.01 OTHER EXPRESSIONS WITH THE COMPARATIVE

The expression "how much + the comparative" is rendered in Ukrainian by **на скíльки**, which means literally "by how much". The answer to such questions must retain the "by" **на**; thus "by so much" is **на стíльки**:

> **На скíльки** дáльше ви живетé від університéту, ніж я ?
> (By) How much farther do you live from the university than I do?
>
> Я живý **на** п'ять миль дáльше.
> I live (by) five miles farther.

Such expressions as "the sooner the better" (*the + compar ... the + compar.*) are rendered in Ukrainian by **чим** + *compar ...* **тим** + *compar.*:

> **Чим крáще** ти вúвчиш цей вірш, **тим крáще** ти знáтимеш йогó.
> The better you learn this poem, the better you'll know it.

The expressions "more and more", "less and less" are translated into Ukrainian as **все** + *compar. of adverb* + **і** + *compar. of adverb*. Note that in negative comparisons one must use **менш** + *the positive degree of a given adverb*:

все більше і більше	more and more
все ме́нше і ме́нше	less and less
все частіше і частіше	more and more frequently
все менш і менш ча́сто	less and less frequently

Drill #183

Translate into Ukrainian:

1. How much younger is your brother than you are?
2. He is (by) two years younger than I am.
3. How much older is your son than mine? He is much older.
4. How much shorter is the second story than the first one?
5. How much closer do you live to the border than we do? Forty-two kilometers.
6. How many kilometers farther from the border is your town than theirs? Only a few (*several*) kilometers.
7. How many more books do you have now than you had before? Fifty or sixty.
8. The sooner you will finish this book, the sooner you will start another one.
9. The more often I see him, the less I like him.
10. He makes mistakes more and more often.
11. I like meat much more than fish.
12. He writes many more letters than I do.
13. The grandmother talks much more than the granddaughter.
14. She talks more and more.

21.1 VERBAL PREFIXES **по-, про-, за-**

As with other prefixes used to form perfectives, the prefix **по-** can be used to make a perfective of an imperfective verb without changing the verb's meaning in any way:

обідати	пообідати	to dine
снідати	поснідати	to breakfast
вірити	повірити	to believe

With many verbs, however, **по-** produces perfectives with a meaning of limited duration. An action has been performed, a state or condition has lasted "for a while" and was then terminated, but without any goal, result, or conclusion:

perfective:	почитáти	to read for a while
	попрацювáти	to work for a while
	поговори́ти	to talk for a while
	поспáти	to sleep for a while

Perfectives with **по-** are especially frequent in verbs describing actions that do not ordinarily lead to any result or completion; such are verbs of state or condition, particularly verbs of position (sitting, lying, standing):

сиді́ти — поси́діти
лежáти — полéжати
стоя́ти — постóяти

Unlike other prefixes, **по-** creates perfective verbs when added to indefinite imperfective verbs of motion:

прихóдити	(imperf.)	походи́ти	(perf.)
принóсити	(imperf.)	поноси́ти	(perf.)
привóзити	(imperf.)	повози́ти	(perf.)

Notice as well that, whereas all other prefixes use **-їжджáти**, **по-** uses the regular indefinite form **-ї́здити**:

приїжджáти	(imperf.)	пої́здити	(perf.)
від'їжджáти	(imperf.)	пої́здити	(perf.)

21.11 Verbs of state or condition (including sitting, lying, and standing) may also be prefixed with **про-**. Forms with **про-** are used when it is felt that the time spent in a state or condition (or position) has been long (sometimes excessively long). These verbs are transitive, and the time spent must always be indicated in the accusative (if the unit of time is expressed) :

Він проси́дів у нас увéсь вéчір.
He sat at our place the whole evening.

Він пролежáв два мі́сяці у шпитáлі.
He lay in the hospital for two months.

Він простóяв усю дорóгу.
He stood the whole journey.

Note:	пробу́ти	to stay for a given duration
	побу́ти	to stay for a while
	заси́дітися	to overstay

21.12 A special class of perfectives denotes only a start of an action. Such perfectives are known as inchoatives. They are formed with several prefixes, among which the most common is the prefix **за-**.

загра́ти	to start playing
заговори́ти	to speak up, begin speaking

Exceptions to the above use of **за-** are found mainly in the verbs of motion, where the prefix **за-** does not have an inchoative meaning.

thus:	зайти́	to drop in, to reach (on foot)
	заве́зти́	to deliver (by vehicle)
	зане́сти́ і т.д.	to deliver (to carry by hand), etc.

Drill #184

Translate into English:

1. Профе́сор ба́чив Василя́ і поговори́в з ним.
2. Львів бли́жче грани́ці, ніж Ки́їв.
3. Бага́то всі зна́ють про Володи́мира Вели́кого, найбі́льшого украї́нського кня́зя.
4. Як ті́льки верну́ся, я за́раз же про все це розкажу́ свої́м найкра́щим при́ятелям.
5. Ми зайшли́ в найбли́жчу крамни́цю, купи́ли найкра́ще вино́, яке́ в ній було́, і верну́лися додо́му.
6. Він відписа́в мені́ найдурні́шого листа́.
7. Я люблю́ всіх діте́й, але́ найбі́льше я люблю́ Ві́ру.
8. Ду́маю, що він поговори́в з ним про найважли́віше.
9. Нови́й словни́к доро́жчий від старо́го на шість до́ларів. Пра́вда, він гру́бший, то́бто повні́ший.
10. Він загра́в, вона́ заговори́ла, а ми заспіва́ли. Поси́діли і пішли́ додо́му, але́ зайшли́ на хвили́нку до Га́лі.

Drill #185

Translate into Ukrainian:

1. Most of all Chub likes to play chess. He plays the best (*better than anyone*) in our town.
2. Let's sit for a while.

3. He came to us and stayed with us for a whole month.
4. It seems that the music started playing by itself.
5. It would be nice to speak to him for a while.
6. At the worst, I shall be a few minutes late.
7. We ate our breakfast, sat for a while, and then left the house.
8. I read a bit and went to sleep.
9. I read the whole book.
10. Drop in on me on Thursday.

21.2 VOCABULARY REVIEW: VERBS OF POSITION

Being in a position	Assuming a position		Placing into a position
To stand			
стоя́ти: по/про/ пере/стоя́ти	встава́ти:	вста́ти	ста́вити: поста́вити
стою́	встаю́	вста́ну	ста́влю
стоі́ш	встає́ш	вста́неш	ста́виш
стоя́в	встава́в	встав	ста́вив
стій!	встава́й!	встань!	став!
To become	става́ти:	ста́ти	
and	стаю́	ста́ну	
To stop	стає́ш	ста́неш	
	става́в	став	
	става́й!	стань!	
To sit			
сиді́ти: по/про/ пере/си́діти	сіда́ти:	сі́сти	сади́ти: посади́ти[1]
сиджу́	сіда́ю	ся́ду	саджу́
сиди́ш	сіда́єш	ся́деш	са́диш
сиді́в	сіда́в	сів	сади́в
сиди́!	сіда́й!	сядь!	сади́!

1 Also means “to plant”.

To lie			**To lay**
лежáти: по/про/ пере/лежáти	лягáти:	лягти́	клáсти: поклáсти
лежу́	лягáю	ля́жу	кладу́
лежи́ш	лягáєш	ля́жеш	кладéш
лежáв	лягáв	ліг, ляглá	клав
лежи́!	лягáй!	ляж!	клади́!

Homework

a) Memorize the vocabulary in Lesson #22;
b) Review Lesson #21;
c) Translate the following sentences into Ukrainian:

1. How old is this little boy? He is only five years old. He is two years younger than my son.
2. The climate of that country is much worse and colder than the climate of our country.
3. We live a little closer to the border than you do.
4. His elder sister is seven years older than he is.
5. I have never heard him play, but they say he plays much better than his father.
6. He promised to return in an hour, but he returned much later.
7. He overstayed and came home later than usual.
8. She always used to go to bed late, but yesterday she went to bed even later.
9. Sit down beside me and let's have a talk.
10. We shall sit and smoke for a while until he returns.
11. He sat down at his table, worked for a while, and went to the restaurant.
12. The longer you (will) work on your novel, the better it will be.
13. I've read a most interesting story.
14. This is the most interesting story that I've read.
15. Let's go to the cinema this evening.
16. Let them pay for the tickets.
17. John is seventy-five years old; if he were younger he would travel more.
18. I paid $67.00 for this suit; formerly I used to pay much less for suits.
19. In our village there are 50 inhabitants; in yours 42. In your village there are 8 inhabitants fewer.
20. Everyone will think that you are crazy if you do not accept their invitation. Let them think what they wish.

ДВАДЦЯ́ТЬ ДРУ́ГИЙ РО́ЗДІЛ

СЛОВНИ́К

Іме́нники жіно́чого ро́ду

би́тва, -и	battle
біда́, -и́	misfortune
ви́ставка, -и	display, exhibit
Галичина́, -и́	Galicia (a region of Western Ukraine)
доба́, -и́	24 hours, era
Ки́ївщина, -и	Kyiv district
ку́рка, -и; ку́ри, -ре́й	chicken
орда́, -и́	horde
су́ка, -и	bitch
ті́тка, -и	aunt
шулі́ка, -и	hawk

Іме́нники чолові́чого ро́ду

кореспонде́нт, -а	correspondent
матема́тик, -а	mathematician
Петербу́рг, -у	St. Petersburg
пре́док, -дка	ancestor
про́від, -воду	leadership, (water/gas/electricity) main
рядо́к, -дка́	line, row
світ, -у	world
семе́стр, -у	semester
тип, -у	type

Іме́нники сере́днього ро́ду

відніма́ння, -ння	subtraction
ді́лення, -ння	division
додава́ння, -ння	addition
зни́щення, -ння	destruction
керівни́цтво, -а	leadership
мно́ження, -ння	multiplication
песеня́, -сеня́ти	puppy
товари́ство, -тва	company
хре́щення, -ння	christening, baptism

Прикме́тники

визначни́й, -а́, -е́	distinguished, noted
тата́рський, -а, -е	Tartar

Дієслова́

лиша́ти: лиши́ти *(лиша́ю, лиша́єш: лишу́, ли́шиш)*	to leave
лиша́тися: лиши́тися	to remain
наро́джуватися: народи́тися *(наро́джуюся, наро́джуєшся: народжу́ся, наро́дишся)*	to be born
ни́щити: зни́щити *(ни́щу, ни́щиш)*	to destroy
перемага́ти: перемогти́ *(перемага́ю, перемага́єш: перемо́жу, перемо́жеш)*	to overcome, conquer
рва́ти: порва́ти *(рву, рвеш)*	to tear

Прислі́вники

ко́ло	around, about
припадко́ве	by chance
чима́ло	quite a bit

Ви́рази

зна́чить	it means, that is
і... і	both... and

GRAMMAR

Numerals (Continuation and Review) — Числíвники (продóвження і повтóрення) (22.0—22.01)
Denoting Time — Ви́значення годи́ни (22.1)
Collective Numerals — Збíрні числíвники (22.2)
Fractions — Дрóби (22.3)
Indefinite Numerals — Неознáчені числíвники (22.4)
Other Numerical Expressions — Інші числівникóві ви́рази (22.5)
Ukrainian Terms for English Measures — Украї́нські нáзви для англíйських одини́ць ви́мірів (22.6)
Dates — Ви́слови на познáчення дат (22.7)

22.0 NUMERALS (CONTINUATION AND REVIEW)

40	сóрок	170	сто сімдеся́т
50	п'ятдеся́т	180	сто вісімдеся́т
60	шістдеся́т	190	сто дев'ятдеся́т/ сто дев'янóсто
70	сімдеся́т		
80	вісімдеся́т	200	двíсті
90	дев'ятдеся́т/ дев'янóсто	300	три́ста
		400	чоти́риста
100	сто	500	п'ятсóт
101	сто оди́н	600	шістсóт
102	сто два	700	сімсóт
110	сто дéсять	800	вісімсóт
120	сто двáдцять	900	дев'ятсóт
130	сто три́дцять	1000	ти́сяча
140	сто сóрок	2000	дві ти́сячі
150	сто п'ятдеся́т	100000	сто ти́сяч
160	сто шістдеся́т	1000000	мільйóн

1. The cardinal numeral **оди́н** "one" is used for the masculine, **однá** for the feminine, and **одне́/однó** for the neuter gender. All three forms are declined like hard-stem adjectives.

2. The cardinal numeral **два** "two" is used for the masculine and neuter genders; **дві** is used for the feminine gender. It is declined in the following way:

	Masc. & Neut.	Fem.
N.	два	дві
G.	двох	двох

D.	двом	двом
A.	два/двох	дві
I.	двома́	двома́
L.	(на) двох	(на) двох

The above declension also applies to the numeral **оби́два**, **оби́дві** "both", which in the oblique cases uses the former numeral **о́ба, о́бі** "both" as the stem for the declension. Hence:

	Masc. & Neut.	Fem.
N.	оби́два	оби́дві
G.	обо́х	обо́х
D.	обо́м	обо́м
A.	N./G.	N./G.
I.	обома́	обома́
L.	(на) обо́х	(на) обо́х

Drill #186

Translate into English:

1. Я прочита́в оби́дві газе́ти.
2. Га́ля Ма́рченко ма́є двох синів і двох дочо́к. Оби́два її́ сини́ живу́ть на полу́дні, а оби́дві дочки́ живу́ть з ма́тір'ю.
3. Я ду́же до́бре зна́ю обо́х синів і обо́х дочо́к.
4. Я вчи́вся у шко́лі з її́ обома́ сина́ми, а моя́ сестра́ вчи́лася з обома́ дочка́ми.
5. Вона́ ча́сто пи́ше до обо́х свої́х синів.
6. Вона́ ли́шить свої́м обо́м сина́м бага́то гро́шей.
7. Вона́ ча́сто дістає́ гро́ші від свої́х обо́х синів.
8. Бори́с і істо́рик, і матема́тик.

Drill #187

Translate into Ukrainian:

1. I liked both pictures.
2. I want to buy both tables.
3. I wrote to both sisters.
4. He loves both his mother and his father.

5. I spoke with both professors.
6. I was there with both my sisters.
7. I bought these briefcases for both our boys.

3. Cardinal numerals from **три** "three" to **дев'ятдеся́т де́в'ять** "ninety-nine" have the same form for all genders. They are declined in the following manner:

	three	four	five	seven
N.	три	чоти́ри	п'ять	сім
G.	трьох	чотирьо́х	п'ятьо́х	сімо́х
D.	трьом	чотирьо́м	п'ятьо́м	сімо́м
A.	N./G.	N./G.	N./G.	N./G.
I	трьома́	чотирма́	п'ятьма́	сімома́
L.	(на) трьох	(на) чотирьо́х	(на) п'ятьо́х	(на) сімо́х

The numerals **шість, де́в'ять, де́сять** are declined like **п'ять**; **вісім** is declined like **сім**.

4. In the genitive, dative, instrumental, and locative cases an alternate ending can be used for five and upward:

п'яти́	instead of	п'ятьо́х,	п'ятьо́м,	п'ятьма́
шести́	instead of	шістьо́х,	шістьо́м,	шістьма́
семи́	instead of	сімо́х,	сімо́м,	сімома́

5. In the nominative and accusative cases the cardinal numerals from **п'ять** "five" upwards require the genitive plural of the following noun.

Note: It is the last digit of a numeral which determines whether the numeral is five or above; thus twenty-*two* governs the *nominative plural*, while twenty-*five* governs the *genitive plural*.

П'ять лі́жок. Шість днів. Рік ма́є двана́дцять мі́сяців.
Йому́ бу́де вже три́дцять ро́ків. Йому́ три́дцять два ро́ки.
На світі живу́ть мільйо́ни люде́й.

6. The cardinal numeral **оди́н** behaves like a modifier and agrees with the noun; cardinal numerals **два, три, чоти́ри** in the nominative and accusative cases are followed by the nominative plural form of the noun, but with the accent being the same as that of the genitive singular.

Добá — це двáдцять чотѝри годѝни. Мíсяць трáвень мáє трѝдцять одѝн день. Скíльки тѝжнів у рóці? У рóці п'ятдеся́т два тѝжні. Скíльки тѝжнів в однóму мíсяці? Чотѝри тѝжні і два абó три дні. Ця книжка дешéва, вонá кóштýє тíльки два дóляри.

7. In oblique cases cardinal numerals modify the nouns. They are in the same case as the nouns but the nouns are plural:

Два дóляри. Трьом дівчáтам. Сімóх юнакíв.

8. Compound cardinal numerals (twenty-one, etc.) are declined only in the last part:

21: двáдцять одѝн, двáдцять одногó, двáдцять одномý...
134: сто трѝдцять чотѝри, сто трѝдцять чотирьóх, сто трѝдцять чотирьóм...

9. The numerals **сóрок** and **сто** have the following declensions:

Nom.	сóрок	сто
Gen.	сорокá	ста
Dat.	сорокá	ста
Acc.	сóрок	сто
Inst.	сорокá	ста
Loc.	сорокá	ста/стомá

Drill #188

Read the following in Ukrainian according to the model:

(a) Addition Додавáння

Model: 2+3=5 два й три є п'ять/два додáти три є п'ять

3+3 = 6	3+4 = 7	3+5 = 8
13+7 = 20	14+8 = 22	15+9 = 24

(b) Subtraction Віднімáння

Model: 5-3= 2 п'ять мéнше три є два/п'ять відня́ти три є два

17-2 = 15	22-10 = 12	25-10 = 15
78-23 = 55	94-55 = 39	125-42 = 83

(c) Multiplication Множення

Model: 3x3= 9 три рази три є дев'ять/три помножити на три є дев'ять

4x6	=	24	5x7	=	35	6x8	=	48
13x3	=	39	15x4	=	60	19x5	=	95

(d) Division Ділення

Model: 2/2 = 1 два поділити на два є один

6/2	=	3	8/4	=	2	12/6	=	2
35/7	=	5	44/11	=	4	66/3	=	22

22.01 ORDINAL NUMERALS

1. Ordinals are formed by the addition of the adjectival endings **-ий, -а, -е** to the stem of the cardinal numeral:

   five: п'ять fifth: п'ятий, п'ята, п'яте

2. The following cardinals have irregularly formed ordinals:

	Cardinals	Ordinals
1	один	перший, -а, -е
2	два	другий, -а, -е
3	три	третій, -я, -є
4	чотири	четвертий, -а, -е
6	шість	шостий, -а, -е
7	сім	сьомий, -а, -е
8	вісім	восьмий, -а, -е
40	сорок	сороковий, -а, -е
100	сто	сотий, -а, -е
1000	тисяча	тисячний, -а, -е

3. All ordinals are declined like hard-stem adjectives with the exception of **третій**, which is declined like a soft-stem adjective.

4. In ordinals formed from compounds (twenty-first, etc.) the adjectival endings are added only to the last digit:

два́дцять оди́н	два́дцять пе́рший
со́рок п'ять	со́рок п'я́тий

However, for ordinals which are formed from cardinal compounds written as one word (**двісті, три́ста**, etc.), adjectival endings are added to the last element of the compound **but** the first element is placed into the genitive case of the cardinal numeral.

Thus **двісті** (from **дві + сті** [*dual form of* **сто**]) places **дві** (*the first element of the compound*) into the genitive case — **двох** and changes the second element **сті** to the adjectival/ordinal form **со́тий,** hence **двохсо́тий** "two-hundredth".

300th	трьохсо́тий
400th	чотирьохсо́тий
500th	п'ятисо́тий
600th	шестисо́тий
700th	семисо́тий
800th	восьмисо́тий
900th	дев'ятисо́тий

By analogy to the above:

дві ти́сячі	=	двохти́сячний
три ти́сячі	=	трьохти́сячний
два мільйо́ни	=	двохмільйо́нний
п'ять мільйо́нів	=	п'ятимільйо́нний

Drill #189

Translate into English:

1. Рік 988-ий — це рік хре́щення Украї́ни.
2. В 1169-му ро́ці пре́дки сього́днішніх росія́н під про́водом Андрі́я Боголю́бського зни́щили Ки́їв.
3. Роки́ 1240-ий та 1241-ий — час по́вного зни́щення Украї́ни тата́рською ордо́ю.
4. В 1648-му ро́ці Богда́н Хмельни́цький переміг поля́ків.
5. В 1709-му ро́ці була́ би́тва під Полта́вою.

22.1 DENOTING TIME

The following forms are used to denote time:

Котрá годи́на?	What time is it?
О котрíй годи́ні?	At what time?
Тепéр дев'я́та годи́на.	It is now nine o'clock.
Пів (до) деся́тої/пів на деся́ту.	Half past nine.
Чверть на вóсьму.	Quarter past seven.
Три (чвéрті) на деся́ту.	Quarter to ten.
О пів на шóсту.	At five thirty.

		Котрá годи́на	О котрíй годи́ні
1	A.M.	пéрша годи́на нóчі	о пéршій годи́ні нóчі
2	A.M.	дрýга годи́на нóчі	о дрýгій годи́ні нóчі
3	A.M.	трéтя годи́на нóчі	о трéтій годи́ні нóчі
4	A.M.	четвéрта годи́на нóчі	о четвéртій годи́ні нóчі
5	A.M.	п'я́та годи́на нóчі	о п'я́тій годи́ні нóчі
6	A.M.	шóста годи́на рáнку	о шóстій годи́ні рáнку
7	A.M.	сьóма годи́на рáнку	о сьóмій годи́ні рáнку
8	A.M.	вóсьма годи́на рáнку	о вóсьмій годи́ні рáнку
9	A.M.	дев'я́та годи́на рáнку	о дев'я́тій годи́ні рáнку
10	A.M.	деся́та годи́на дня	о деся́тій годи́ні дня
11	A.M.	одинáдцята годи́на дня	об одинáдцятій годи́ні дня
12	Noon	пíвдень	о пíвдні
1	P.M.	пéрша годи́на дня	о пéршій годи́ні дня
6	P.M.	шóста годи́на вéчора	о шóстій годи́ні вéчора
11	P.M.	одинáдцята годи́на нóчі	об одинáдцтій годи́ні нóчі
12	Midnight	пíвніч	о пíвночі

4:15	чверть на п'я́ту	о чверть на п'я́ту
4:30	пів на п'я́ту	о пів на п'я́ту/пів до п'я́тої/ о пів до п'я́тої
4:45	три на п'я́ту	о три на п'я́ту
4:05	п'ять хвили́н по четвéртій	о п'ять по четвéртій
4:55	за п'ять хвили́н п'я́та	о четвéртій п'ятдеся́т п'ять

In schedules the 24-hour table is used:

0 hr./24 hr. : 12 P.M.	1 hr. : 1 A.M.	13 hr. : 1 P.M.
двáдцять четвéрта годи́на	пéрша годи́на	тринáдцята годи́на

Drill #190

Translate into English:

1. пів на пéршу (годи́ну)
2. о пів на пéршу
3. чверть на пéршу
4. три на пéршу
5. за двáдцять пéрша (годи́на)
6. дéсять по дрýгій (годи́ні)
7. двáдцять по пéршій
8. двáдцять п'ять по пéршій
9. за двáдцять п'ять дрýга
10. о пів на трéтю
11. за три хвили́ни трéтя
12. пів на п'я́ту
13. пів на сьóму
14. о пів на дев'я́ту
15. о пів на одинáдцяту
16. о три на одинáдцяту
17. за дéсять одинáдцята
18. двáдцять три по дев'я́тій
19. о чверть на одинáдцяту
20. о пів на дванáдцяту
21. за двáдцять три п'я́та
22. двáдцять три по п'я́тій

Drill #191

Read in Ukrainian and then translate into English:

Розмóва

— Ви́бачте, котрá тепéр годи́на?
— Прóшу дýже, тепéр дві хвили́ни по п'я́тій.
— Дýже дя́кую.
— Ах, ви́бачте! Мій годи́нник спіши́ть на дéсять хвили́н. Знáчить, тепéр тóчно за вíсім хвили́н п'я́та.
— Дýже дя́кую. Не знáєте, колú починáється вистáва в теáтрі?
— Десь кóло (бíля) вóсьмої годи́ни.
— Так, мені трéба о пів на вóсьму ви́йти з хáти.
— Ви так далéко живетé?

— Ні, але́ я му́шу о три на во́сьму зайти́ до бра́та.
— А так! Ви ма́єте ще дві й пів годи́ни ча́су.
— Ще раз ду́же дя́кую.

Drill #192

Read in Ukrainian:

	7:30	2:15	5:30		7:15		9:50
at	7:30	3:15	5:15		7:45		9:58
	1:30	3:30	5:45	at	8:30	at	11:00
at	1:30	3:40	6:30	at	9:30	at	10:50
	1:15	3:45	7:30	at	9:10	at	10:30

Drill #193

Translate into Ukrainian:

1. We live on the second floor.
2. Our house is number 12.
3. My father goes to the office at 8 o'clock, and we, children, go to school.
4. At 10 o'clock my mother goes to town.
5. We have our lunch usually at 2 o'clock.
6. In the evening at a quarter to eight we go to the theater.
7. We come back home at eleven and go to bed at half past eleven.

22.2 COLLECTIVE NUMERALS

Collective numerals **дво́є, тро́є** are declined similarly to the numeral **два: двох, трьох, двом, трьом**...

Collective numerals from **чоти́ри** and upwards are formed by means of the suffix **-еро** and are indeclinable: **че́тверо, п'я́теро, ше́стеро, се́меро, во́сьмеро, деся́теро.**

No collective numerals are formed from the cardinals 40 and 100, or from those indicating hundreds and thousands.

All collective numerals are followed by the gen. pl. of the noun:

двóє дітéй, трóє хлóпців, чéтверо курчáт, п'я́теро хлóпців і дівчáт

Collective numerals are used when referring to a company of persons of both sexes, and to young animals, and are also used with personal pronouns and with nouns that are always plural:

їх трóє ; п'я́теро граблі́в

Drill #194

Translate into English:

1. Нас булó п'я́теро в товари́стві: дві пáні й три пани́.
2. В пéршій кля́сі є тридця́теро дітéй, у тóму числі́ сімнáдцять дівчáт і тринáдцять хлóпців.
3. Кýрка ви́вела дев'я́теро курчáт; двóє з них порвáв шулі́ка, трóє кіт, а чéтверо і́нших живýть.
4. Нáша сýка мáє п'я́теро песеня́т.

22.3 FRACTIONS

Ukrainian fractions relate to the feminine noun for "part" части́на. They are formed by using cardinal numerals for the numerator and ordinal numerals for the denominator. The numerator always modifies (with "one") or governs (numbers "two" and higher) the noun части́на which, however, is only understood and not mentioned. Thus:

однá части́на	one part	(one modifies)
дві части́ни	two parts	(two + nom. pl.)
три части́ни	three parts	(three + nom. pl.)
п'ять части́н	five parts	(five + gen. pl.)
дéсять части́н	ten parts	(ten + gen. pl.)

The denominator, an ordinal numeral, agrees with the noun части́на in any fraction with "one" in the numerator:

однá трéтя (части́на), однá п'я́та (части́на), однá деся́та (части́на)

With numerators other than "one" the denominator is always in the genitive plural form:

2/3	дві тре́тіх (части́н)
3/4	три четве́ртих (части́н)
4/5	чоти́ри п'я́тих (части́н)
5/5	п'ять п'я́тих (части́н)
6/10	шість деся́тих (части́н)
9/10	де́в'ять деся́тих (части́н)
17/25	сімна́дцять два́дцять п'я́тих (части́н)

Fractions are followed by the genitive singular of the noun:

однá тре́тя (части́на) нáшого зо́лота
дві тре́тіх (части́н) всіє́ї землі

Note also the following:

1/2	пів, полови́на
1 1/2	півтора́ (*m.* + *n.*), півтори́ (*f.*)
2 1/2	два й пів
3 1/2	три й пів
1 1/4	оди́н і чверть (однá четве́рта)
23 4/5	два́дцять три й чоти́ри п'я́тих

N.B. 2 1/2 is also called півтретя́
3 1/2 is also called півчвертá

22.4 INDEFINITE NUMERALS

The indefinite numerals are:

чимáло	considerable, quite a bit
багáто	much
мáло	little
кілька	some
кільканáдцять	some teens (11 to 19)
кількадеся́т	some tens
кількасо́т	some hundreds

Чимáло and мáло are indeclinable; for the declension of **багáто, мáло, кілька** see 16.4 — 16.41, p.185. The oblique cases for **кільканáдцять, кількадеся́т, кількасо́т** are reduced to one form for each: кільканадцяти́, кількадесяти́, кількастá. This latter group, when used in the nominative or accusative, is followed by the genitive plural of the noun.

Я ба́чу кількана́дцять хло́пців, кількадеся́т хат і кількасо́т вікó́н. I see some teens of boys, some tens of houses and some hundreds of windows.

Drill #195

Translate into English:

1. У нас було́ вчо́ра бага́то госте́й.
2. Чима́ло біди́ в сві́ті.
3. Після кількадесяти́ ро́ків не бу́де вже ніко́го з нас.
4. Пе́ред кількана́дцяти́ рока́ми не було́ ще цього́ ти́пу літака́.
5. Кількасо́т літ мину́ло від то́го дня.
6. Пе́ред кількаста́ хло́пцями стоя́ло одне́ завда́ння - вчи́тися.

22.5 OTHER NUMERICAL EXPRESSIONS

Ukrainian	English
раз	one time, once
пе́рший раз	first time
дру́гий раз	second time
тре́тій раз і т.д.	third time, etc.
в/у/пе́рше	for the first time
вдру́ге	for the second time
втре́тє, вчетве́рте	for the third time, etc.
вдво́є, втро́є	doubly, trebly
по одно́му	one by one
по два, по три	in twos, in threes
раз	once upon a time

Ukrainian terms for English measures:

ounce	у́нція (0.65 гра́ма)
pound	фунт (453.5 гра́мів)
ton	то́на (1015 кілогра́мів)
inch	інч (2.5 центиме́трів)
foot	фут (30.4 центиме́трів)
yard	ярд (91.4 центиме́трів)
mile	ми́ля (1609.3 ме́трів)

pint	пайнт (0.56 літри)
gallon	ґальóн (4.54 літри)
bushel	бýшель (2 3/4 бýшлі = 1 гектолітр or 100 літрів)

In Ukraine a comma is used instead of a period for indicating decimals.

Drill #196

Translate the following cardinal and ordinal numerals into English:

1. двáдцять дéв'ять
2. сóрок вісім
3. сімдесят сім
4. дев'ятдесят сьóмий
5. сто дванáдцять
6. сто двáдцять дéв'ять
7. сóтий
8. сто сóрок дев'ятий
9. сто сімдесят дрýгий
10. сто сімдесят
11. двісті сорокóвий
12. двохсóтий
13. чотириста шістдесят чотири
14. чотирьохсóтий
15. чотириста шістдесят четвéртий
16. п'ятсóт два
17. п'ятисóтий
18. сімсóт сóрок дрýгий
19. восьмисóтий
20. тисяча дев'ятисóтий
21. тисяча дев'ятсóт шістдесят четвéртий
22. тисячний
23. двісті тисяч вісімсóт п'ятдесят один
24. шість тисяч двісті сóрок сьóмий
25. двісті трицять три тисячі сімсóт дев'ятдесят сім
26. три мільйóни вісімсóт сімдесят шість тисяч триста сóрок два
27. п'ять більйóнів шістсóт дванáдцять мільйóнів
28. двохмільйóнний
29. двохтисячний
30. дві тисячі вісімсóт п'ятдесят перший

Drill #197

Translate into English:

1. Я не розумію тих п'ятú рядків.
2. Ми зупинúлися на шістдесят четвéртому абó шістдесят п'ятому рядкý.
3. В тóму грýбому тóмі тúсяча трúста двáдцять сім сторінóк .
4. Я дýмаю, що тут мéнше, ніж тúсяча двáдцять сім сторінóк.
5. Прочитáйте тúсяча трúста двáдцять сьóму сторíнку.
6. Я прочитáв тúсячу сторінóк.
7. Ось статті нáших двох кореспондéнтів.
8. Це зóшити моїх трьох ýчнів.
9. Я даю лéкції трьом ýчням.
10. З тúми трьомá ýчнями я прочитáв почáток трéтьої лéкції нáшого підрýчника.
11. Я говорúв вам про моїх трьох ýчнів.
12. Ви, здаéться, знáєте моїх трьох ýчнів?
13. На тій вýлиці чотúри крамнúці з мéблями.
14. Ми булú в усíх чотирьóх крамнúцях, алé не знайшлú нічóго, чогó нам потрíбно.
15. Ми сподівáємося, що знáйдемо все в четвéртій крамнúці, бо вонá найбíльша зі всіх чотирьóх крамнúць.
16. Кость мáє п'ятьóх товаришів.
17. Він дістаé листú від своїх п'ятьóх товаришів і чáсто пúше своїм п'ятьóм товаришáм.
18. Він учúвся в школі з тúми п'ятьмá товаришáми.
19. Що мóжна зробúти з двáдцять п'ятьмá цéнтами?
20. Це селó мáє сто рóків, а це дéрево мáє більше двохсóт рóків.

Drill #198

Translate into Ukrainian:

1. She cannot live without her three dogs.
2. She buys the best meat for her three dogs.
3. These are the wives of their four sons.

4. Oksana is the wife of her fourth son.
5. Anna is their fourth daughter.
6. I didn't know the name of your fourth daughter.
7. I don't have $7.00 (gen. after negation).[1]
8. I don't have $25.00 (gen. after negation).
9. Why do you speak about $25.00?
10. In a year there are twelve months, or 52 weeks, or 365 days.
11. We have about $1,000,000.
12. Here is 102nd Street.
13. Who lives on 102nd Street?
14. Her husband is twenty years older than she is.
15. The new road is 139 kilometers longer than the old one.
16. In this city live 225,000 more inhabitants than in that one.
17. I read 1,010 pages less than Olya.
18. In this town there are 1,335 homes.
19. In this small village there are only 162 homes, and in ours there are 112 homes.
20. This church is 400 years old.

22.7 DATES

a) The day (number) and name of the month are expressed in the genitive:

Котро́го сього́дні?	Сього́дні пе́ршого кві́тня.
What is the date today?	It's the first of April.

b) The date of an occurance is also expressed in the genitive:

Два́дцять шо́стого че́рвня ми поі́демо додо́му.
We shall go home on the twenty-sixth of June.

c) The time period "from... to" is expressed by **від** + *gen*... **до** + *gen.*:

...від п'я́того тра́вня до пе́ршого се́рпня...
...from the fifth of May to the first of August...

1 "$" in Ukrainian text is written as "дол." after the numeral.

d) The time period from a certain date on is expressed by **від** + *gen.*:

Від пéршого вéресня ми бýдемо в мíсті.
From the first of September we shall be in the city.

e) Years are expressed by ordinals + **рік**:

1945 ти́сяча дев'ятсóт сóрок п'я́тий рік.

f) The year when something occurs is expressed by the preposition **в** + *loc.* of the year:

in 1945 — в ти́сяча дев'ятсóт сóрок п'я́тому рóці.

When a specific (complete) date in a year is given, then the whole date including the year is expressed in the genitive :

April 5, 1940 п'я́того квíтня ти́сяча дев'ятсóт сорокóвого рóку.

Drill #199

Translate into English:

1. Найбíльший украї́нський поéт Тарáс Шевчéнко народи́вся в селí Мóринцях на Ки́ївщині дев'я́того бéрезня ти́сяча вісімсóт чотирнáдцятого рóку, а помéр у Петербýрзі деся́того бéрезня ти́сяча вісімсóт шістдеся́т пéршого рóку.

2. Івáн Франкó — теж визначни́й украї́нський поéт — народи́вся в Галичинí в селí Нагуéвичах у 1856-му рóці, а помéр у Львóві 28-го трáвня 1916-го рóку.

Drill #200

Translate into Ukrainian:

1. Today is December 25th.
2. We are going abroad on December 25th.
3. We shall be in Italy from May 15th to June 6th.

4. Who said that yesterday was the 15th?
5. What date will it be tomorrow, the 21st or the 22nd?
6. Our exam is on the 22nd.
7. Where were you in 1945?
8. In August, 1945, I was in the south.
9. What date is it today? It is February 28th.
10. This semester began in September.
11. They say that it will rain from the 28th to the 30th.
12. It rained from the 15th to the 23rd.
13. In what month were you born?
14. I was born in April.
15. In what year and on what date? April 5, 1940.

Drill #201

Complete the sentence by translating the English phrase:

Я бýду/був у Львóві.

last year, last month, last January, last week, next week, this week, a month and a half, a week and a half, last summer, last winter, for the last time, for a whole week, the whole month of May, in May, next year, next spring, this Wednesday, this Sunday, on Tuesday.

Я ї́ду за грани́цю.

for the week, for two weeks, for two months, for a year and a half, for half a year, for five months, for three and a half years.

Drill #202

Write out the numerals in the correct case:

Йогó бю́ро на 15, 19, 20, 21, 27, 30, 40, 50, 102 пóверсі.
На котрíй це сторíнці? На 15, 19, 20, 30, 40, 50, 90, 102.
Він роди́вся 1.5.1923, 12.9.1847, 28.7.1942, 1962, 1951.
Ми від'їжджáємо на вакáції між 25 і 30, 1 і 5, 13 і 19.
Ми пробýдемо за грани́цею від 15 сéрпня до 27 вéресня, 1 жóвтня до 21 листопáда, 3 сíчня до 12 лю́того.

Homework

a) Memorize the vocabulary in Lesson #23;
b) Review Lesson #22;
c) Translate the sentences below into Ukrainian:

1. This year I am working much more than I worked last year.
2. I don't know yet what I will be doing next year.
3. Last month my sister arrived from China.
4. There will be many holidays this month.
5. I would like to go to the seashore next month.
6. It will be much warmer in a month.
7. We were at the seashore last week.
8. This week I must go to Kharkiv for two weeks.
9. I will return next week.
10. They told us that they were going to Vancouver for a week, and that in a week they would come back here.
11. I will return from there in three days.
12. Last time I explained the rule to you.
13. Last summer we spent the month in the Carpathians.
14. Next summer we'll go to the mountains.
15. Next spring we want to go to Ukraine.
16. I am going there for three days.

ДВА́ДЦЯТЬ ТРЕ́ТІЙ РО́ЗДІЛ

СЛОВНИ́К

Іме́нники жіно́чого ро́ду

па́ра, -и	pair, few

Іме́нники чолові́чого ро́ду

во́рог, -а	enemy
знíмок, -мка	photograph
паціє́нт, -а	patient
ха́рч, -у	provisions (*sing. in Ukrainian*)

Іме́нники сере́днього ро́ду

сторі́ччя, -ччя	century

Прикме́тники

гото́вий, -а, -е	ready
страшни́й, -а́, -е́	terrible, awful, frightful
сумни́й, -а́, -е́	sad

Дієслова́

жартува́ти: пожартува́ти *(жарту́ю, жарту́єш)*	to joke
забира́ти: забра́ти *(забира́ю, забира́єш: заберу́, забере́ш)*	to take away
забува́ти: забу́ти *(забува́ю, забува́єш: забу́ду, забу́деш)*	to forget
зде́ржуватися: зде́ржатися *(зде́ржуюся, зде́ржуєшся: зде́ржуся, зде́ржишся)*	to hold off
крича́ти: кри́кнути *(кричу́, кричи́ш: кри́кну, кри́кнеш)* (*imperative is* **кри́кни**)	to shout
оде́ржувати: одержа́ти *(оде́ржую, оде́ржуєш: оде́ржу, оде́ржиш)*	to receive
ото́чувати: оточи́ти *(ото́чую, ото́чуєш: оточу́, ото́чиш)*	to surround

підпи́сувати: підписа́ти to sign
(підпи́сую, підпи́суєш: підпишу́, підпи́шеш)
пла́кати: по/за/пла́кати to weep
(пла́чу, пла́чеш)
розгляда́тися: розгля́нутися to look around
(розгляда́юся, розгляда́єшся: розгля́нуся, розгля́нешся)
розка́зувати: розказа́ти to narrate
(розка́зую, розка́зуєш: розкажу́, розка́жеш)

Прислі́вники та і́нші слова́

бу́вши having been
бу́дучи being
в/у/горі́ above, upstairs
ви́дно apparently
внизу́ below, downstairs
назу́стріч towards, to go to meet, to meet half-way
посере́д in the middle (+ *gen.*)

GRAMMAR

Adjectival Participles — Дієприкме́тники (23.0)
Adverbial Participles — Дієприслі́вники (23.1)
Hypothetical Mood — Обме́жувально-допусто́ві констру́кції (23.2)

23.0 ADJECTIVAL PARTICIPLES

Participles are verbal adjectives. As adjectives they agree with the nouns they modify in case, number, and gender. As verbs they carry the verbal attributes of tense and voice. Thus, in a full participal scheme there can be present participles of both active and passive voice, as well as past participles of both active and passive voice. Ukrainian language has lost, however, the use of active participles both present and past.

A. Instead of using active participles in the present (former **-чий**, i.e., **колю́чий** no longer denotes "one who pricks" but one "with a prickly quality") Ukrainian uses relative clauses:

той (та, те), що	(+ *the pres. tense of the verb*)
той (та, те), хто	(+ *the pres. tense of the verb*)

той, хто пи́ше ці рядки́
the one who writes these lines

той учи́тель, що працю́є в шко́лі
the teacher that works in the school.

B. Instead of the past active participle (former forms with **-ший**) Ukrainian uses:

той (та, те), що/хто (+ *the past tense of the verb*)

Also, new forms ending in **-лий** (added to the past tense of the verb) are sometimes used to convey the past active participle:

пережи́/в/	:	**пережи́лий,**	**-ла, -ле**
зраді́/в/	:	**зраді́лий,**	**-ла, -ле**
недба́/в/	:	**недба́лий,**	**-ла, -ле**

зраді́лий хло́пець : той хло́пець, що зраді́в
the boy who became happy

C. Contemporary Ukrainian no longer has the present passive participles ending in **-мий**, although some forms still exist:

питóмий, відóмий, види́мий, знайóмий, рухóмий
(*but* only with adjectival meaning).

Instead of the present passive participle, Ukrainian uses a relative clause:

той (та, те), що йогó (її, їх) (+ *the pres. tense of the verb*):

Те мі́сце, що йогó опи́суємо.
The place which we are describing.

D. The only form still current in the Ukrainian language is the past passive participle. In meaning the past passive participle is equivalent to the use of the relative clause:

той (та, те), що йогó (її, їх) (+ *the past tense of the verb*)

There are basically three ways of forming the past passive participle:

1. Transitive verbs ending in **-ати** form past passive participles by adding the suffix **-н + -ий, -а, -е** to the infinitive stem:

читáти: чи́таний, -а, -е	read
знáти : знáний, -а, -е	known

2. Verbs ending in **-нути, -ити, -іти** form past passive participles by adding the suffix **-ен + -ий, -а, -е** to the first person sg. form of the verb minus the ending **-у/-ю**.

ходи́ти/ хóджу/ хóджений	walked
ї́здити/ ї́жджу/ ї́жджений	ridden
стри́гти/ стрижу́/ стри́жений	shorn
вози́ти/ вожу́/ вóжений	transported
пекти́/ печу́/ пéчений	baked
верті́ти/ верчу́/ вéрчений	drilled
масти́ти/ мащу́/ мáщений	greased

люби́ти/ люблю́/ лю́блений	loved
ліпи́ти/ ліплю́/ лі́плений	glued
лови́ти/ ловлю́/ ло́влений	caught

Some verbs ending in **-нути**. can have two forms of the past passive participle:

сти́снути: сти́снений/ сти́снутий	squeezed
ки́нути: ки́нений/ ки́нутий	thrown

3. Most verbs with monosyllabic stems form past passive participles by adding the suffix **-т + -ий, -а, -е** to the infinitive stem:

би́ти: би́тий**, -а, -е**	beaten
тя́ти: тя́тий**, -а, -е**	cut
те́рти: те́ртий**, -а, -е**	ground, pulverized

4. Stress. The syllable of the suffix **-ен** or the one immediately preceding the suffixes **-н/-т** is ordinarily never stressed.

Drill #203

Translate into English:

1. Я не мо́жу на ка́рті знайти́ **взя́того** мі́ста.
2. Куди́ ти положи́ла харчі́, **ку́плені** на за́втра.
3. **Оде́ржані** вчо́ра журна́ли лежа́ть на столі́.
4. На зні́мку дід і ба́ба **сфотографо́вані** з дітьми́ та вну́ками.
5. Стіл, **поста́влений** посе́ред кімна́ти, забира́є бага́то мі́сця.
6. Куди́ ви покла́ли **прочи́тані** газе́ти?
7. Я поба́чив на підло́зі кни́жку, що Іва́н забу́в.
8. Все було́ **зро́блене** вчо́ра.
9. Ця кни́жка була́ **напи́сана** в мину́лому сторі́ччі.

23.1 ADVERBIAL PARTICIPLES

Adverbial participles (sometimes called *gerunds* - not to be confused, however, with gerunds in English which are verbal nouns) are indeclinable, like adverbs, but, like verbs, have a tense.

Adverbial participles are said to be past when they refer to actions performed prior to the action of the main verb.

They are said to be present when they refer to actions performed simultaneously with the action of the main verb.

The present adverbial participle is formed by the addition of **-чи** to the third person plural of the present tense of the verb minus the ending **-ть.**

іду́(ть)	—	ідучи́
ба́ча(ть)	—	ба́чачи

If the verb is stressed on its ending, the **-чи** will be stressed; otherwise the stress will remain on the stem.

Він сиді́в, чита́ючи кни́жку.
He sat reading a book. (The action is *simultaneous*: while he sat he was reading the book).

The past adverbial participle is formed by the addition of **-ши** to the masculine past of a verb:

написа́в	—	написа́вши

Написа́вши статтю́, він ліг спа́ти.
Having written the article, he went to bed. (The action *precedes* the action of the main verb: first he wrote the article and then he went to bed).

Usually the present adverbial participle is formed from verbs of the imperfective aspect, while the past adverbial participle is formed from verbs of the perfective aspect. There are exceptions, however:

бу́дучи	being
бу́вши	having been

The particle **-ся** becomes **-сь** when the verb is formed into an adverbial participle:

смію́(ть)ся	—	сміючи́сь
засмія́вся	—	засмія́вшись

Drill #204

Replace the verbs by past adverbial participles and rework the sentence according to the model.

Model: Він *написа́в* свій рома́н і зра́зу став відо́мим.
Написа́вши свій рома́н, він зра́зу став відо́мим.

1. Він прожи́в па́ру ро́ків у Ки́єві і тепе́р га́рно гово́рить по-украї́нському.
2. Він оде́ржав телегра́му з Торо́нта і за́раз же туди́ пої́хав.
3. Він ви́пив до́сить бага́то горі́лки і поча́в го́лосно і ве́село співа́ти.
4. Я посні́дав і пішо́в пройти́ся.
5. Ми пообі́дали в рестора́ні і пішли́ до кі́на.
6. Я написа́в листа́ і пішо́в відпочива́ти.
7. Я прочита́в газе́ту і дав її́ Га́лі.
8. Ми скінчи́ли працюва́ти і почали́ чита́ти газе́ту.
9. Він запита́в мене́, чи гото́вий обі́д і пішо́в до ї́да́льні.
10. Вона́ почала́ говори́ти і не могла́ зде́ржатися.
11. Я відпові́в їй на пита́ння і ви́йшов з кімна́ти.
12. Зі́рка відчини́ла вікно́ і лягла́ на дива́н.

Drill #205

Replace the clauses with **коли́** by the present or past adverbial participle and rework the sentence according to the model:

Model: **Коли́ пацiє́нт говори́в з лі́карем**, він забу́в йому́ розказа́ти про найважливі́ше.
Говорячи́ з лі́карем, пацiє́нт забу́в йому́ розказа́ти про найважливі́ше.

1. Коли́ він жив у Ки́єві, він ча́сто ї́здив до Льво́ва.
2. Коли́ він гово́рить по телефо́ну, він за́вжди ку́рить.
3. Коли́ Га́ля розка́зує про свої́х діте́й, вона́ за́вжди сміє́ться.
4. Коли́ Андрі́й слу́хає му́зику, він відпочива́є.
5. Коли́ він відпочива́є, він слу́хає му́зику.
6. Коли́ вона́ ду́має про си́на, вона́ ча́сто пла́че.
7. Коли́ він працю́є, він ніко́ли не жарту́є.
8. Коли́ вона́ зняла́ плащ, вона́ ввійшла́ в ві́тальню.
9. Коли́ він відхо́див, він сказа́в, що ско́ро ве́рнеться.

Drill #206

Replace the first verb with a present or past adverbial participle, according to the model:

Model: Іва́н ішо́в по ву́лиці і співа́в.
Ідучи́ по ву́лиці, Іва́н співа́в.

1. Вона́ сиді́ла на крі́слі і говори́ла по телефо́ну.
2. О́ля чита́ла кни́жку і кури́ла.
3. Він прочита́в кни́жку і дав її́ мені́.
4. Він розповіда́в про своє́ життя́ в Кана́ді і кури́в цига́рку за цига́ркою.
5. Він розпові́в усе́ і ви́йшов.
6. Вона́ розгляда́лася і розмовля́ла із Зе́нею.
7. Вона́ говори́ла з Бори́сом і ве́село смія́лася.
8. Він сказа́в, що йому́ су́мно і пішо́в.
9. Вона́ поспа́ла і почала́ працюва́ти.
10. Вона́ гра́ла на фортепія́ні і співа́ла.

Drill #201

Translate into Ukrainian:

1. Speaking with me, she was looking at my husband.
2. Having said a few words, she left the room.
3. Having read the letter, he put it on the desk.
4. (*While*) reading the letter, he laughed.
5. Lying on the divan, he was looking at the wall.
6. While living with his family he never worked.
7. He said it without thinking.
8. He was walking along the street, not seeing anyone.
9. Not knowing what to do, she stood near the door.
10. Having finished our work, we went home.
11. I must finish the article begun last week.
12. He is a forgotten man.
13. Why does the woman speaking with your grandson shout so?
14. Tomorrow I will return the money taken by my cousin from the bank.

23.2 HYPOTHETICAL MOOD

The hypothetical mood corresponds to the English construction with *no matter* or with the suffix *-ever*. The hypothetical mood (similar in form to the conditional mood — past tense + **би/б**) with the particle **не** is used where English adds the suffix *-ever* to pronouns and adverbs:

> Когó **б** він **не просúв**, ніхтó йомý не хотíв помогтú.
> *No matter* whom he asked (*whomever he asked*), no one wanted to help him.
>
> Де **б** він **не жив**, він зáвжди був щаслúвий.
> *Wherever* he lived (*no matter* where he lived), he was always happy.

Drill #208

Translate into English:

1. Що б вонá не робúла, вонá все рóбить дóбре.
2. Комý б я про це не говорúв, ніхтó менí не вíрить.
3. Про кóго б він не говорúв, він усíх називáє дурнúми.
4. Кудú б вонú не приїжджáли, вонú всю́ди зустрічáли тогó самóго чоловíка.
5. Когó б я не питáв про Івáна, ніхтó нічóго про ньóго не знáє.
6. Колú б я їх не бáчив, вонú зáвжди кудúсь спішáть.
7. Що б я не купúла сестрí, їй зáвжди не подóбається.

Homework

a) Review Lesson #23;
b) Translate the following sentences into Ukrainian:

1. I know very well your cousin Hanya who lives in Poltava.
2. (*While*) living in the Kyiv district, I used to meet her and your cousin Paul quite often.
3. Not speaking Italian, I couldn’t explain to him the mistakes made by him in his speech.
4. Knowing that he would come at half past five, I placed the signed papers on the desk.

5. The director who signed them left the room without saying a word.
6. I saw a woman smoking a pipe.
7. Smoking, crying, and talking, she walked out of the room.
8. Do you know that the man who lives downstairs is my cousin?
9. Having heard [all of] the terrible news, they wept.
10. Having taken all our money, he went abroad.

APPENDIX

GRAMMATICAL TABLES

FIRST DECLENSION

Masculine Nouns Hard Type

Animate

N.	брат	брати́
G.	бра́та	браті́в
D.	бра́тові	брата́м
A.	бра́та	браті́в
I.	бра́том	брата́ми
L.	(на) бра́тові	(на) брата́х
V.	бра́те	брати́

Inanimate

N.	дім	доми́
G.	до́му	домі́в
D.	до́мові	дома́м
A.	дім	доми́
I.	до́мом	дома́ми
L.	(в) до́мі	(в) дома́х
V.	до́ме	доми́

Masculine Nouns Soft Type

Animate

N.	хло́пець	хло́пці
G.	хло́пця	хло́пців
D.	хло́пцеві	хло́пцям
A.	хло́пця	хло́пців
I.	хло́пцем	хло́пцями
L.	(на) хло́пці/-еві	(на) хло́пцях
V.	хло́пче	хло́пці

Inanimate

N.	край	краї́
G.	кра́ю	краї́в
D.	кра́єві	working
A.	край	краї́
I.	кра́єм	working
L.	(в) краю́/ кра́ї	(в) working
V.	кра́ю	краї́

Masculine Nouns Mixed Type

Animate

N.	хрущ	хрущі́
G.	хруща́	хрущі́в
D.	хруще́ві	хруща́м
A.	хруща́	хрущі́в
I.	хруще́м	хруща́ми
L.	(на) хрущі́	(на) хруща́х
V.	хру́ще	хрущі́

Inanimate

N.	ніж	ножі́
G.	ножа́	ножі́в
D.	ноже́ві	ножа́м
A.	ніж	ножі́
I.	ноже́м	ножа́ми
L.	(на) ножі́	(на) ножа́х
V.	но́же	ножі́

Feminine Nouns

Hard Type

N.	ха́та	хати́
G.	ха́ти	хат
D.	ха́ті	хата́м
A.	ха́ту	хати́
I.	ха́тою	хата́ми
L.	(в) ха́ті	(в) хата́х
V.	ха́то	хати́

Soft Type

N.	земля́	зе́млі
G.	землі́	земе́ль
D.	землі́	зе́млям
A.	зе́млю	зе́млі
I.	земле́ю	зе́млями
L.	(в) землі́	(в) зе́млях
V.	зе́мле	зе́млі

N.	наді́я	наді́ї
G.	наді́ї	наді́й
D.	наді́ї	наді́ям
A.	наді́ю	наді́ї
I.	наді́єю	наді́ями
L.	(в) наді́ї	(в) наді́ях
V.	наді́є	наді́ї

Mixed Type

N.	ро́жа	ро́жі
G.	ро́жі	рож
D.	ро́жі	ро́жам
A.	ро́жу	ро́жі
I.	ро́жею	ро́жами
L.	(в) ро́жі	(в) ро́жах
V.	ро́же	ро́жі

Neuter Nouns

Hard Type

N.	село́	се́ла
G.	села́	сіл
D.	селу́	се́лам
A.	село́	се́ла
I.	село́м	се́лами
L.	(в) селі́	(в) се́лах
V.	село́	се́ла

Soft Type

N.	місце	місця́
G.	місця	місць
D.	місцю	місця́м
A.	місце	місця́
I.	місцем	місця́ми
L.	(в) місці	(в) місця́х
V.	місце	місця́

Mixed Type

N.	прізвище	прізвища
G.	прізвища	прізвищ
D.	прізвищу	прізвищам
A.	прізвище	прізвища
I.	прізвищем	прізвищами
L.	(на) прізвищі/-у	(на) прізвищах
V.	прізвище	прізвища

SECOND DECLENSION

Neuter Nouns

	Singular	Plural
N.	весілля	весілля
G.	весілля	весіль
D.	весіллю	весіллям
A.	весілля	весілля
I.	весіллям	весіллями
L.	(на) весіллі/ю	(на) весіллях
V.	весілля	весілля
N.	ім'я́	імена́
G.	імени	іме́н
D.	імені	імена́м
A.	ім'я́	імена́
I.	ім'ям (іменем)	імена́ми
L.	(на) імені	(на) імена́х
V.	ім'я́	імена́

N.	лоша́	лоша́та
G.	лоша́ти	лоша́т
D.	лоша́ті	лоша́там
A.	лоша́	лоша́та
I.	лоша́м	лоша́тами
L.	(на) лоша́ті	(на) лоша́тах
V.	лоша́	лоша́та

THIRD DECLENSION
Feminine Nouns

	Singular	Plural
N.	по́вість	по́вісті
G.	по́вісти	по́вістей
D.	по́вісті	по́вістям
A.	по́вість	по́вісті
I.	по́вістю	по́вістями
L.	(в) по́вісті	(в) по́вістях
V.	по́вісте	по́вісті
N.	любо́в	любо́ви
G.	любо́ви	любо́вей
D.	любо́ві	любо́вам
A.	любо́в	любо́ви
I.	любо́в'ю	любо́вами
L.	(у) любо́ві	(у) любо́вах
V.	любо́ве	любо́ви
N.	ніч	но́чі
G.	но́чі	ноче́й
D.	но́чі	ноча́м
A.	ніч	но́чі
I.	ніччю	ноча́ми
L.	(у) ночі́	(у) ноча́х
V.	но́че	но́чі

ADJECTIVES

Hard

	Singular			Pl. for all
	Masc.	Fem.	Neut.	
N.	до́брий	до́бра	до́бре	до́брі
G.	до́брого	до́брої	до́брого	до́брих
D.	до́брому	до́брій	до́брому	до́брим
A.	N. or G.	до́бру	до́бре	N. or G.
I.	до́брим	до́брою	до́брим	до́брими
L.	(в) до́брому/-ім	(в) до́брій	(в) до́брому/-ім	(в) до́брих

Soft

N.	си́ній	си́ня	си́нє	си́ні
G.	си́нього	си́ньої	си́нього	си́ніх
D.	си́ньому	си́ній	си́ньому	си́нім
A.	N. or G.	си́ню	си́нє	N. or G.
I.	си́нім	си́ньою	си́нім	си́німи
L.	(в) си́ньому/-ім	(в) си́ній	(в) си́ньому/-ім	(в) си́ніх

PRONOUNS

Personal

N.	я	ти	він	вона́	воно́
G.	мене́	тебе́	його́, (у) нього	її́, (у) не́ї	його́, (у) нього
D.	мені́	тобі́	йому́	їй	йому́
A.	мене́	тебе́	його́, нього	її́, не́ї	його́, нього
I.	мно́ю	тобо́ю	ним	не́ю	ним
L.	(в) ме́ні	(в) то́бі	(в) ньо́му (в) нім	(в) ній	(в) ньо́му (в) нім

N.	ми	ви	вони́
G.	нас	вас	їх, (у) них
D.	нам	вам	їм
A.	нас	вас	їх
I.	на́ми	ва́ми	ни́ми
L.	(в) нас	(в) вас	(в) них

Possessive

N.	мій	моя́	моє́	мої́
G.	мого́	моє́ї	мого́	мої́х
D.	моє́му	мої́й	моє́му	мої́м
A.	N. or G.	мою́	моє́	N. or G.
I.	мої́м	моє́ю	мої́м	мої́ми
L.	(в) моє́му (в) мої́м	(в) мої́й	(в) моє́му (в) мої́м	(в) мої́х

N.	наш	на́ша	на́ше	на́ші
G.	на́шого	на́шої	на́шого	на́ших
D.	на́шому	на́шій	на́шому	на́шим
A.	N. or G.	на́шу	на́ше	N. or G.
I.	на́шим	на́шою	на́шим	на́шими
L.	(в) на́шому (в) на́шім	(в) на́шій	(в) на́шому (в) на́шім	(в) на́ших

Demonstrative

N.	цей	ця	це	ці
G.	цього́	ціє́ї	цього́	цих
D.	цьому́	цій	цьому́	цим
A.	N. or G.	цю	це	N. or G.
I.	цим	ціє́ю	цим	ци́ми
L.	(в) цьо́му (в) цім	(в) цій	(в) цьо́му (в) цім	(в) цих

N.	той	та	те	ті
G.	того́	тіє́ї/то́ї	того́	тих
D.	тому́	тій	тому́	тим
A.	N. or G.	ту	те, то	N. or G.
I.	тим	тіє́ю	тим	ти́ми
L.	(в) то́му (в) тім	(в) тій	(в) то́му (в) тім	(в) тих

VERBS

First Conjugation

Present tense: (consonant stem)

1.	несý	1.	несемó
2.	несéш	2.	несетé
3.	несé	3.	несýть

Past tense:

1.	я ніс, неслá, неслó	1.	ми неслú
2.	ти ніс, неслá, неслó	2.	ви неслú
3.	він ніс, вонá неслá, вонó неслó	3.	вонú неслú

Future tense:

1.	бýду нéстú / нéстúму	1.	бýдемо нéстú / нéстúмемо
2.	бýдеш нéстú / нéстúмеш	2.	бýдете нéстú / нéстúмете
3.	бýде нéстú / нéстúме	3.	бýдуть нéстú / нéстúмуть

Conditional mood:	я ніс би, вонá неслá б
Past cond. mood:	я ніс би був, вонá неслá б булá

Imperative:

		1.	несíм(о)!
2.	несú!	2.	несíть!
3.	хай несé!	3.	хай несýть!

Infinitive:	нéстú
Past pass. participle:	нéсений, -на, -не
Present adv. participle:	несучú
Past adv. participle:	нíсши

Present tense: (vowel stem)

1.	знáю	1.	знáємо
2.	знáєш	2.	знáєте
3.	знáє	3.	знáють

Past tense:

1. я зна́в, зна́ла, зна́ло	1. ми зна́ли
2. ти зна́в, зна́ла, зна́ло	2. ви зна́ли
3. він зна́в, вона́ зна́ла, воно́ зна́ло	3. вони́ зна́ли

Future tense:

1. бу́ду зна́ти/зна́тиму	1. бу́демо зна́ти/зна́тимемо
2. бу́деш зна́ти/зна́тимеш	2. бу́дете зна́ти/зна́тимете
3. бу́де зна́ти/зна́тиме	3. бу́дуть зна́ти/зна́тимуть

Conditional mood:	знав би, вона́ зна́ла б
past cond. mood:	знав би був, вона́ зна́ла б була́

Imperative:

	1. зна́ймо!
2. знай!	2. зна́йте!
3. хай зна́є!	3. хай зна́ють!

Infinitive:	зна́ти
Past pass. participle:	зна́ний, -на, -не
Present adv. participle:	зна́ючи
Past adv. participle:	зна́вши

Second Conjugation

Present tense:

1. хвалю́	1. хва́лимо
2. хва́лиш	2. хва́лите
3. хва́лить	3. хва́лять

Past tense:

1. я хвали́в, хвали́ла, хвали́ло	1. ми хвали́ли
2. ти хвали́в, хвали́ла, хвали́ло	2. ви хвали́ли
3. він хвали́в, вона́ хвали́ла, воно́ хвали́ло	3. вони́ хвали́ли

Future tense:

1. бу́ду хвали́ти / хвали́тиму
2. бу́деш хвали́ти / хвали́тимеш
3. бу́де хвали́ти / хвали́тиме

1. бу́демо хвали́ти / хвали́тимемо
2. бу́дете хвали́ти / хвали́тимете
3. бу́дуть хвали́ти/хвали́тимуть

Conditional mood:	я хвали́в би, вона́ хвали́ла б
Past cond. mood:	я хвали́в би був, вона́ хвали́ла б була́

Imperative:

	1. хвалі́м(о)!
2. хвали́!	2. хвалі́ть!
3. хай хва́лить!	3. хай хва́лять!

Infinitive:	хвали́ти
Past pass. participle:	хва́лений, -на, -не
Present adv. participle:	хва́лячи
Past adv. participle:	хвали́вши

Present tense:

1. люблю́	1. лю́бимо
2. лю́биш	2. лю́бите
3. лю́бить	3. лю́блять

Past tense:

1. я люби́в, люби́ла, люби́ло	1. ми люби́ли
2. ти люби́в, люби́ла, люби́ло	2. ви люби́ли
3. він люби́в, вона́ люби́ла, воно́ люби́ло	3. вони́ люби́ли

Future tense:

1. бу́ду люби́ти/люби́тиму
2. бу́деш люби́ти / люби́тимеш
3. бу́де люби́ти / люби́тиме

1. бу́демо люби́ти /люби́тимемо
2. бу́дете люби́ти / люби́тимете
3. бу́дуть люби́ти / люби́тимуть

Conditional mood:	я люби́в би, вона́ люби́ла б
Past cond. mood:	я люби́в би був, вона́ люби́ла б була́

Imperative:

		1.	любі́м(о)!
2.	люби́!	2.	любі́ть!
3.	хай лю́бить!	3.	хай лю́блять

Infinitive:	люби́ти
Past pass. participle:	лю́блений, -на, -не
Present adv. participle:	лю́блячи
Past adv. participle:	/по/люби́вши

ATHEMATIC CONJUGATION

Consists of four verbs and their derivatives: **бу́ти, ї́сти** are imperfective; **да́ти** and prefixed forms of **-ві́сти** are perfective.

Present tense:

1.	є;	їм	є;	їмо́
2.	є;	їси́	є;	їсте́
3.	є;	їсть	є;	їдя́ть

Past tense:

1.	я був, була́; їв, ї́ла	1.	ми були́; ї́ли
2.	ти був, була́; їв, ї́ла	2.	ви були́; ї́ли
3.	він був; їв, вона́ була́; ї́ла	3.	воні́ були́; ї́ли

Future tense:

1. бу́ду; бу́ду ї́сти / ї́стиму
2. бу́деш; бу́деш ї́сти / ї́стимеш
3. бу́де; бу́де ї́сти / ї́стиме

1. бу́демо; бу́демо ї́сти / ї́стимемо
2. бу́дете; бу́дете ї́сти / ї́стимете
3. бу́дуть; бу́дуть ї́сти / ї́стимуть

Conditional mood:	був би, була́ б; їв би, ї́ла б
Past cond. mood:	був би був, була́ б була́; їв би був, ї́ла б була́

Imperative:

	1. бу́дьмо!; ї́жмо!
2. будь!; їж!	2. бу́дьте!; ї́жте!
3. хай бу́де!; хай їсть!	3. хай бу́дуть!; хай їдя́ть!

Infinitive:	бу́ти; ї́сти
Past pass. participle:	/від/бу́тий, -та, -те; ї́джений, -на, -не
Present adv. participle:	бу́дучи; їдячи́
Past adv. participle:	бу́вши; /з/'ї́вши

Present tense: Does not exist for perfective verbs.

Past tense:

1. дав, дала́, /опо/ві́в, /опо/вілá
2. ти дав, дала́, /опо/ві́в, /опо/вілá
3. він дав, /опо/ві́в,
   вона дала́, /опо/вілá

1. ми дали́, /опо/вілú
2. ви дали́, /опо/вілú
3. вони́ дали́, /опо/вілú

Future tense:

1. дам /опо/ві́м 1. дамо́ /опо/вімо́
2. даси́ /опо/віси́ 2. дасте́ /опо/вісте́
3. дасть /опо/ві́сть 3. даду́ть /опо/відя́ть

Conditional mood:
дав би, дала́ б /опо/ві́в би, /опо/вілá б

Past cond. mood:
дав би був, дала́ б була́, /опо/ві́в би був, /опо/вілá б була́

Imperative:

	1. да́ймо! /опо/ві́жмо!
2. дай! /опо/ві́ж!	2. да́йте! /опо/ві́жте!
3. хай дасть! хай /опо/ві́сть!	3. хай даду́ть! /опо/відя́ть!

Infinitive:	да́ти /опо/ві́сти
Past pass. participle:	да́ний, -на, -не /опо/ві́джений, -на, -не
Present adv. participle:	Does not exist for perfective verbs.
Past adv. participle:	да́вши /опо/ві́вши

UKRAINIAN-ENGLISH VOCABULARY

А

а	and, but (5)[1]
абó	or (2)
абó ... абó	either . . . or (2)
авдитóрія, -ї	auditorium (9)
áвто, -а	automobile (2)
автóбус, -а	bus (13)
áвтор, -а	author (5)
адрéса, -и	address (3)
Áзія, -ї	Asia (13)
актóр, -а	actor (16)
алé	but (2)
Амéрика, -и	America (4)
американець, -нця	American (16)
американка, -и	American (female) (16)
англíєць, -лíйця	Englishman (16)
англíйка, -и	Englishwoman (16)
англíйський, -а, -е	English (6)
Áнглія, -ї	England (13)
Андрíй, -я	Andriy (1)
анекдóт, -а	anecdote (12)
апетúт, -у	appetite (7)
аптéка, -и	drugstore (8)
Аскóльд, -а	Askold(5)
аспірúна, -и	aspirin (13)
Áфрика, -и	Africa (13)
ах	Oh! (7)

Б

бабýня, -і	grandmother (13)
багáтий, -а, -е	rich, wealthy (6)
багáто	much, a lot (7)
багáто чогó	many things (16)
бáйка, -и	story, tale (5)
балерúна, -и	ballerina (4)
балéт, -у	ballet (4)
балькóн, -у	balcony (12)
банк, -у	bank (8)

---

1 All numbers in parentheses refer to Chapters.

батьки́, -ів	parents (fathers) (12)
ба́тько, -а	father (1)
ба́чити: поба́чити	to see, II conj. (3)
без	without (+ gen.) (6)
бе́рег, -а	shore, bank (8)
на бе́резі	on the shore (8)
бе́резень, -зня	March (19)
Берлі́н, -у	Berlin (17)
би́тва, -и	battle (22)
бібліоте́ка, -и	library (2)
бі́гати, бі́гти: побі́гти	to run, I conj., II conj. (20)
бі́гти see бі́гати	
біда́, -и́	misfortune (22)
бі́лий, -а, -е	white (3)
бі́ля	near, in the vicinity of (+ gen.) (12)
бі́льше	more (4)
бі́льше ні	no more, no longer (6)
біфсте́кс, -а	beef steak (16)
близьки́й, -а́, -е́	near (21)
бли́зько	near (2)
блонди́н, -а	blond male (4)
блонди́нка, -и	blonde female (4)
блю́зка, -и	blouse (12)
Бог, -а	God (20)
Богда́н, -а	Bohdan (5)
божеві́льний, -а, -е	insane (21)
болі́ти: поболі́ти	to hurt, intrans., II conj. (19)
Бори́с, -а	Borys (l)
Бори́ся, -і	dimin. of Boryslava, Borysya, (6)
борщ, -у́	borsch (7)
боя́тися: побоя́тися	to fear (+ gen.), II conj. (15)
брат, -а	brother (1)
брата́нка, -и	niece, daughter of brother (18)
брата́нок, -нка	nephew, son of brother (18)
бра́ти: взя́ти	to take, I conj. (4)
брудни́й, -а, -е	dirty (11)
брюне́т, -а	brunet male (4)
брюне́тка, -й	brunette female (4)
бу́вши	having been (23)
буди́нок, -нку	building (8)
буди́ти: розбуди́ти	to awaken, trans., II conj. (15)
бу́дучи	being (23)
бу́дьте такі́ до́брі	Please be so kind (14)
бу́ти	to be (no perfective) (2 & 10)
бю́рко, -а	desk (6 & 18)
бюро́, -а́	office (5)

В

важли́вий, -а, -е	important (9)
вака́ції, -й	vacation (plural only) (13)
валі́зка, -и	suitcase (18)
вальс, -у	waltz (15)
вари́ти: звари́ти	to cook, II conj. (16)
Васи́ль, -я́	Vasyl (5)
вбира́ти: вбра́ти/ убира́ти: убра́ти	to dress, trans., I conj. (15)
ввесь, вся, все: уве́сь, уся́, усе́	all, everything (3)
ввесь час	all the time (13)
вгорі́/угорі́	above, upstairs (23)
вде́ржати see **вде́ржувати**	
вде́ржувати: вде́ржати	to hold, I conj., II conj. (10)
вдово́лений/удово́лений	satisfied (+instr.) (6)
вдово́лення, -ня/ удово́лення, -ня	satisfaction (8)
вдо́ма/удо́ма	at home (1)
ве́зти́ see **вози́ти**	
вели́ке спаси́бі	many thanks (6)
вели́кий, -а, -е	big, large, great (2 & 14)
величе́зний, -а, -е	huge, enourmous (9)
вера́нда, -и	veranda (12)
ве́ресень, -сня	September (19)
верну́ти see **верта́ти**	
верну́тися see **верта́тися**	
верта́ти: верну́ти	to return, trans., I conj. (17)
верта́тися: верну́тися	to return, intrans. I conj. (17)
весе́лий, -а, -е	cheerful, gay (12)
ве́село	joyfully (1)
весна́, -и́	spring (7)
ве́сти́ see **води́ти**	
вече́ря, -і	supper (12)
вече́ряти: повече́ряти	to have supper, I conj. (12)
ве́чір, -чора	evening (3)
вечі́рка, -и	evening party (4)
вечі́рній, -я, -є	evening (adj.) (11)
взя́ти see **бра́ти**	
ви́бір, -бору	choice (20)
вивча́ти: ви́вчити	to study, to memorize, I conj., II conj. (19)
ви́вчити see **вивча́ти**	
вигі́дний, -а, -е	comfortable (3)

виголóшувати дóповідь	to deliver a lecture (8)
видéлка, -и	fork (12)
ви́дно	apparently (23)
визначни́й, -á, -é	distinguished, famous (22)
викладáти: ви́класти	to lecture, I conj. (19)
ви́класти see викладáти	
ви́мити see ми́ти	
винó, -á	wine (1)
випадкóво	by chance (15)
ви́падок, -дку	case, accident, incident, chance (16)
ви́пити see пи́ти	
ви́рости see рости́	
висóкий, -а, -е	tall, high (6)
вистáва, -и	display, exhibit, play (22)
ви́ставка, -и	exhibit (22)
вівтóрок, -тірка	Tuesday (14)
відвáжний, -а, -е	fearless, valiant (21)
віддавáти: віддáти	to give back, I conj. Athematic conj. (17)
віддáти see віддавáти	
ві́дділ, -у	department (9)
відійти́ see відхóдити	
від'їжджáти: від'ї́хати	to depart, I conj. (14)
від'ї́хати see від'їжджáти	
відкривáти: відкри́ти	to open, I conj. (14)
відкри́ти see відкривáти	
відмі́нний, -а, -е	excellent (14)
відмі́нно	excellently (14)
віднімáння, -ння	subtraction (22)
відóмий, -а, -е	known (12)
відповідáти: відпові́сти	to answer, I conj. Athematic conj. (11)
ві́дповідь, -і	answer (8)
відпові́сти see відповідáти	
відпочивáти: відпочи́ти	to rest, I conj. (4)
відпочи́ти see відпочивáти	
відпочи́нок, -нку	rest (4)
ві́дти/відтіля́	from there (13)
відчини́ти see відчиня́ти	
відчиня́ти: відчини́ти	to open, I conj., II conj. (4)
відхóдити: відійти́	to leave, II conj., I conj. (14)
війнá, -и	war (6)
вікнó, -а	window (2)
Вінніпéґ, -у	Winnipeg (8)
Ві́ра, -и	Vira (5)
ві́рити: пові́рити	to believe, II conj. (17)
вірш, -а	verse, poem (12)

вісь, óсі	axle (8)
вітáльня, -і	living room (6)
вíтер, -тру	wind (7)
вітрúна, -и	store/display window (20)
вмирáти: вмéрти/ умирáти; умéрти	to die, I conj. (17)
в найгíршому вúпадку	at the worst, in the worst case (21)
внизý/унизý	below, downstairs (23)
вночí/уночí	at night (15)
внук, -а	grandson (18)
внýчка, -и	granddaughter (18)
водá, -ú	water (2)
водúти, вéстú: повéсти	to lead, II conj., I conj. (18)
возúти, везтú: повéзти	to transport, II conj., I conj. (18)
вождь, -я́	leader (9)
Вóлга, -и	Volga (21)
волíти	to prefer, only imperf., I conj. (16)
волóсся, -я	hair (19)
вóрог, -а	enemy (23)
ворóта, ворíт	gates, pl. only (9)
воя́к, -á	soldier (12)
впáсти see **пáдати**	
впоря́дку/упоря́дку	in order (adv.) (15)
впрáва, -и	exercise (5)
все/усé	everything (3 & 4)
всі/усí	everyone, all (4)
вставáти: встáти/ уставáти: устáти	to arise, to get up, I conj. (12)
всю́ди/усю́ди	everywhere (7)
втомúтися see втóмлюватися	
втóмлюватися: втомúтися	to become tired, I conj., II conj. (17)
вузькúй, -á, -é	narrow (4)
вýйко, -а	uncle on mother's side (17)
вýлиця, -і	street (2)
вýхо, -а/ýхо, -а	ear (6)
вчúтися see учúтися	
вчóра/учóра	yesterday (2)
вчорáшній, -я, -є/ учорáшній, -я, -є	yesterday's (adj.) (6)

Г

газéта, -и	newspaper (1)
Галичинá, -ú	Galicia, western Ukraine (22)
Гáля, -і	Halya (14)

Га́ня, -і	Hanya (4)
гара́ж, -у	garage (9)
га́рний, -а, -е	nice, good, fine (2)
га́рно	nicely (1)
гаряче́	hot (adv.) (6)
гаря́чий, -а, -е	hot (3 & 17)
гаря́чка, -и	fever (19)
ге́ній, -я	genius (5)
герої́ня, -і	heroine (2)
геро́й, -я	hero (2)
гі́рше	worse (19)
гість, го́стя	guest (4)
гіта́ра, -и	guitar (5)
глибо́кий, -а, -е	deep (21)
говори́ти: поговори́ти/ сказа́ти	to speak, to talk, II conj. (2)
годи́на, -и	hour (10)
годи́нник, -а	watch, clock (13)
годи́нник пізни́ть	the watch is slow (13)
годи́нник спіши́ть	the watch is fast (13)
голова́, -и́	head (6)
головне́, -о́го	the main thing (21)
го́лос, -у	voice (7)
голосни́й, -а́, -е́	loud (7)
гора́, -и́	mountain (9)
горі́лка, -и	whisky (7)
горня́тко, -а	cup, small pot (6)
горо́д, -у	garden (2)
го́ряч, -і	heat (17)
господар, -я	host (7)
Го́споди!	Goodness! (5)
господи́ня, -і	hostess (5)
го́стрий, -а, -е	sharp (12)
готе́ль, -ю	hotel (3)
гото́вий, -а, -е	ready (23)
гото́вити: пригото́вити	to prepare, II conj. (10)
гра, -и	game (10)
граблі́, граблі́в (і грабе́ль)	rake, only pl. (9)
грама́тика, -и	grammar (4)
грани́ця, -і	boundary (21)
гра́ти: загра́ти	to play, I conj. (4)
гра́ти в ка́рти	to play cards (10)
гра́ти в те́ніс	to play tennis (10)
гра́ти в ша́хи	to play chess (21)

Гриць, -я	Hryts (5)
гріш, грошá	coin (11)
грóші, грóшей	money (11)
громадя́нин, -а	citizen (9)
громадя́нка, -и	citizen (female) (12)
грýбий, -а, -е	fat, thick (9)
грýдень, -дня	December (19)
грýди, грудéй	chest, pl. only (9)
гуля́ти: погуля́ти	to stroll, dance, I conj. (12)

Ґ

ґáнок, -нку	porch (12)

Д

давáти: дáти	to give, I conj. Athematic conj. (5)
давнó	long ago (adv.) (3)
далéкий, -а, -е	far (21)
далéко	far (2)
Дани́ло, -а	Danylo (3)
дарýнок, -нка	gift (5)
дáти see давáти	
дах, -ý	roof (15)
два, дві	two, m. & n., f. (9)
двéрі, дверéй	door, pl. only (9)
двір, дворá	yard, court (12)
двою́рідна сестрá	cousin (f.)
двою́рідний брат	cousin (m.)
де	where (1)
день, дня	day (3)
день нарóдження	birthday (19)
дéрево, -а	tree (9)
дерев'я́ний, -а, -е	wooden (12)
держáти: по/за/з/дéржати	to hold, II conj. (6)
дешéвий, -а, -е	cheap (3)
джаз, -у	jazz (5)
дзвони́ти: задзвони́ти	to ring, II conj. (5)
ди́вáн, -а	sofa, divan (7)
диви́тися: подиви́тися	to look, II conj. (15)
ди́вний, -а, -е	strange (10)
дирéктор, -а	director (5)
дити́на,-и	child (16)
дитя́, дитя́ти	infant, child (8)

дівчина, -и	girl (4)
дівчинка, -и	little girl (9)
дідо, -а	grandfather (17)
дійсний, -а, -е	true, real (11)
дійсно	indeed, really, truly (11)
ділення, -ння	division (22)
діло, -а	affair, matter, business (17)
діло в то́му	the matter is (11)
дім, до́му	home (9)
дістава́ти: діста́ти	to get (11)
діти, діте́й	children (9)
для	for, for the sake of (+gen.) (12)
Дніпро́, -а́	Dnipro (8)
до	to, up to (+ gen.) (6)
доба́, -и́	twenty-four hours, era (22)
добра́ніч!	Good night (17)
добри́день!	Good day (13)
до́брий, -а, -е	good (2)
добро́дій, -я	benefactor, sir (14)
до́вгий, -а, -е	long (9)
до́вго	for a long time (7)
дові́дуватися: дові́датися	to find out (17)
додава́ння, -ння	addition (22)
додо́му	homeward (13)
до́ктор, -а	doctor, Ph.D. (12)
докуме́нт, -у	document (6)
до́ляр, -а	dollar (10)
дома́шній, -я, -є	home, household (adj.) (11)
до́повідь, -і	report, speech, talk (8)
допомо́га, -и	help (6)
доро́га, -и	road, route, way (18)
дороги́й, -а, -е	dear, expensive (3)
до́сить	enough, rather, sufficient (6 & 15)
до́ти до́ки	until (17)
дочка́, -и́	daughter (1)
дощ, -у́	rain (13)
друг, -а	friend (4)
дру́гий, -а, -е	another, second (11)
дружи́на, -и	wife (1)
ду́же	very (4)
ду́жий, -а, -е	mighty (21)
ду́мати: поду́мати	to think, I conj. (2)
дурни́й,-а, -е	foolish, stupid (5)
дя́дько, -а	elder man, uncle (20)
дя́кувати: подя́кувати	to thank, I conj. (19)

Е

європе́йський, -а, -е	European (3)
Едмонто́н, -у	Edmonton (13)
еспа́нець, -нця	Spaniard (16)
Еспа́нія, -ї	Spain (16)
еспа́нка, -и	Spaniard (female) (16)
еспа́нський, -а, -е	Spanish (16)

Ж

жартува́ти: пожартува́ти	to joke, I conj. (23)
жест, -у	gesture (7)
жи́ти: пожи́ти	to live, I conj. (21)
життя́, життя́	life (8)
жі́нка, -и	woman (1)
жо́втень, -тня	October (19)
жо́втий, -а, -е	yellow (7)
журна́л, -у	journal, magazine (4)
журналі́ст, -а	journalist (male) (1)
журналі́стка, -и	journalist (female) (1)

З

за	in exchange for, for, (+acc.) (12)
заба́вка, -и	toy (18)
забага́то	too much (9)
забира́ти: забра́ти	to take away, I conj. (23)
забра́ти see забира́ти	
забува́ти: забу́ти	to forget, I conj. (23)
забу́ти see забува́ти	
завда́ння, -ння	assignment (21)
за́вжди	always (2)
за́втра	tomorrow (6)
за грани́цею	abroad (17)
за грани́цю	to go abroad (17)
загра́ти see гра́ти	
задава́ти: зада́ти	to assign, I conj. Athematic conj. (9)
зада́ти see задава́ти	
зада́ча, -і	assignment (9)
заде́ржати see держа́ти	
задзвони́ти see дзвони́ти	
задово́лений, -а, -е	satisfied (19)
заздалегі́дь	in advance (19)

зайти́ see **захо́дити**	
зако́н, -у	rule (of law) (17)
закури́ти see кури́ти	
заме́шкати see ме́шкати	
замика́ти: замкну́ти	to close, to lock, I conj. (15)
за мі́сто	to the suburbs (17)
замкну́ти see **замика́ти**	
запам'ята́ти see **запам'ято́вувати**	
запам'ято́вувати: запам'ята́ти	to memorize, to remember, I conj. (14)
записа́ти see **запи́сувати**	
за́пи́ска, -и	note (13)
запи́сувати: записа́ти	to note down, I conj. (9)
запита́ти see **пита́ти**	
запла́кати see **пла́кати**	
заплати́ти see **плати́ти**	
запро́шення, -ння	invitation (21)
заси́джуватися: заси́дітися	to overstay, I conj., II conj. (21)
заси́дітися see **заси́джуватися**	
засмія́тися see **смія́тися**	
заспіва́ти see **співа́ти**	
зателефонува́ти see **телефонува́ти**	
заува́жити see **заува́жувати**	
заува́жувати: заува́жити	to notice, I conj., II conj. (18)
захво́ріти see **хворі́ти**	
за́хід, -ходу	West (18)
захо́дити: зайти́	to drop in, II conj., I conj. (18)
захоті́ти see **хоті́ти**	
зача́ти see **зачина́ти**	
зачина́ти: зача́ти	to begin, I conj. (4)
зачини́ти see **зачиня́ти**	
зачиня́ти: зачини́ти	to close, I conj., II conj. (4)
звари́ти see **вари́ти**	
з ва́шої сторони́	on your part (14)
звича́йно	ordinarily, usually (5)
зви́чка, -и	habit (19)
звідкіля́	where from (11)
зві́дси	from here (18)
зві́дти	from there (18)
здава́ти: зда́ти	to pass, I conj. Athematic conj. (20)
здава́тися	to seem (imperf. only), I conj. (15)
зда́ти see **здава́ти**	
здержа́ти see **держа́ти**	
зде́ржатися see **зде́ржуватися**	
зде́ржуватися: зде́ржатися	to hold off, I conj., II conj. (23)

здіймáти: здійня́ти — to take off, I conj. (20)
здійня́ти see здіймáти
здорóвий, -а, -е — healthy (19)
здорóв'я, -я — health (19)
зелéний, -а, -е — green (9)
Зéня, -і — Zenya (13)
зимá, -и — winter (2)
зи́мний, -а, -е — cold (6)
зи́мно — cold (6)
зимови́й, -а, -е — winter (adj.) (3)
зібрáння, -ння — meeting (8)
Зірка, -и — Zirka (15)
з'ї́сти see ї́сти
злий, -а, -е — bad, evil, wrong (10)
змогти́ see могти́
змýсити see мýсити
знайóмий, -а, -е — acquaintance (noun), familiar (adj.) (16)
знайóмити: познайóмити — to acquaint, introduce, II conj. (16)
знайóмитися: познайóмитися — to become acquainted, II conj. (16)
знайти́ see знахóдити
знамени́тий, -а, -е — excellent, remarkable, wonderful (9)
знáти — to know (imperf. only), I conj. (2)
знахóдити: знайти́ — to find, I conj., II conj. (18)
знáчить — it means (22)
зни́щення, -ння — destruction (22)
зни́щити see ни́щити
знімáтн: зня́ти — to take off, I conj. (20)
знімок, -а — photograph (23)
знóву — again (10)
зóвсім — entirely, totally (7)
зóвсім ні — not at all (7)
зóлото, -а — gold (21)
зóшит, -а — note book (9)
зрáзу ж — right away (10)
зроби́ти see роби́ти
зрозуміти see розуміти
зупини́тися see зупиня́тися
зупиня́тися: зупини́тися — to stop, I conj., II conj. (18)

I

і — and (3)
Івáн, -а — Ivan (1)
Івáнко, -а — lvanko, dimin. of Ivan (4)
Íгор, -я — lhor (4)

ім'я́, і́мени	name (8)
інжене́р, -а	engineer (5)
і́нколи	sometimes (4)
і́ноді	sometimes (4)
і́нший, -а, -е	different, other (16)
і́спит, -у	exam, test (10)
істо́рик, -а	historian (7)
істори́чний, -а, -е	historical (9)
істо́рія, -ї	history (5)
італі́єць, -і́йця	Italian (male) (16)
італі́йка, -и	Italian (female) (16)
італі́йський, -а, -е	Italian (7)
Іта́лія, -ї	Italy (9)
іти́ see **ходи́ти**	

Ї

їда́льня, -і	dining room (6)
ї́здити, ї́хати: пої́хати	to travel, II conj., I conj., I conj. (13)
ї́сти: з'ї́сти	to eat, Athematic conj. (3)
ї́хати see **ї́здити**	

К

кабіне́т, -у	study (4)
ка́ва, -и	coffee (7)
Кавка́з, -у	Caucasus (8)
Кана́да, -и	Canada (4)
кана́дець, -дця	Canadian (male) (16)
кана́дка, -и	Canadian (female) (16)
кана́дський, -а, -е	Canadian (2)
кана́па, -и	sofa (20)
кані́кули, кані́кул	vacations (pl. only) (20)
капелю́х, -а	hat (20)
Карпа́ти, Карпа́т	Carpathians (9)
ка́рта, -и	card (12), map (2)
карти́на, -и	picture (12)
ка́ртка, -и	sheet of paper (2)
карто́пля, -і	potatoes (pl.) as well as potato (sg.) (7)
Катери́на, -и	Kateryna (6)
кварти́ра, -и	apartment (2)
квито́к, -тка́	ticket (21)
кві́тень, -тня	April (19)
кві́тка, -и	flower (18)

керівни́цтво, -а	leadership (22)
Ки́їв, Ки́єва	Kyiv (2)
ки́ївський, -а, -е	Kyivan (9)
Ки́ївщина, -и	Kyiv region (22)
ки́лим, -а	carpet, rug (6)
Кита́й, -ю	China (7)
кіломе́тр, -а	kilometer (21)
кі́лька	several (12)
кімна́та, -и	room (1)
кіне́ць, -нця	end (3)
кі́но, -а and **кіно́** (indeci.)	cinema (8)
кінча́ти: скінчи́ти	to finish, I conj., II conj. (11)
кінь, коня́	horse (12)
кіт, кота́	cat (12)
кла́с, -у	class (5)
кла́сти: покла́сти	to place in a lying position, I conj. (20)
клімá́т, -у	climate (21)
клюб, -у	club (8)
кля́са, -и	class (5)
книга́рня, -і	book store (6)
кни́жка, -и	book (1)
ковбаса́, -и́	kovbasa (16)
ко́жний, -а, -е	each, every (4)
коли́	when (1)
ко́лір, -льору	color (3)
ко́ло	near, about, around (+ gen.) (22)
конце́рт, -у	concert (4)
кореспонде́нт, -а	correspondent (22)
коридо́р, -у	corridor (12)
ко́рінь, -реня	root (3)
короле́ва, -и	queen (14)
коро́ль, -я́	king (14)
коро́ткий, -а, -е	short (9)
костю́м, -а	suit (5)
Кость, -я	Kost (17)
коха́ти: покоха́ти	to love, I conj. (15)
коштува́ти	to cost (imperf. only), I conj. (12)
край, -ю	edge, country (8)
крамни́ця, -і	store (4)
кра́сний, -а, -е	beautiful (21)
кра́ще	better (19)
кре́йда, -и	chalk (7)
кри́кнути see **крича́ти**	
Крим, -у	Crimea (8)

кричáти: кри́кнути	to shout, I conj., II conj. (23)
крім	besides, except (+ gen.) (6)
крíсло, -а	chair (2)
крóмка, -и	slice of bread (16)
кругóм	around (+ gen.) (12)
куди́	where to (13)
кузéн, -а	cousin (m.) (2)
кузи́на, -и, кузи́нка, -и	cousin (f.) (2)
купи́ти **see** купувáти	
купувáти: купи́ти	to buy, I conj., II conj. (4)
кури́ти: закури́ти	to smoke, II conj. (6)
кýрка, -и	chicken (22)
курчá, курчáти	chick (8)
кусóк, -скá	piece (3)
кут, -á	corner (as ofa room), angle (as in a triangle) (20)
кýхня, -і	kitchen (1)
кучеря́вий, -а, -е	curly (19)

Л

лазни́чка, -и	bathroom (6)
Левкó, -á	Levko (8)
лéгкий, -а, -е	easy, light (21)
це лéгко	that's easy (5)
лежáти: полéжати	to lie, II conj. (6)
лéкція, -ї	lesson (2)
Лéся, -і	Lesya (6)
летíти see літáти	
ли́пень, -пня	July (19)
лист, -á	letter (1)
листок, -ткá	leaf (9)
листопáд, -а	November (19)
ли́стя, -тя	leaves (collective) (9)
лицé, -я́	face (7)
лишáти: лиши́ти	to leave, I conj., II conj. (22)
лишáтися: лиши́тися	to remain behind, I conj., II conj. (22)
лиши́ти **see** лишáти	
лиши́тися **see** лишáтися	
лíвий, -а, -е	left (7)
ліжко, -а	bed (6)
лíкар, -я	doctor (5)
ліни́вий, -а, -е	lazy (6)
лíпше	better (19)

ліс, -у	forest (8)
літáк, -а	airplane (20)
літáти, летíти: полетíти	to fly, I conj., II conj. (20)
літератýра, -и	literature (17)
лíтній, -я, -є	summer (adj.) (7)
лíто, -а	summer (2)
ліфт, -у/-а	elevator (17)
лóжка, -и	spoon (12)
Лóндон, -у	London (14)
Люба, -и	Lyuba (8)
люби́ти: полюби́ти	to like, II conj. (7)
любóв, -и	love (8)
лю́ди, -éй	people (9)
люди́на, -и	person (21)
лю́лька, -и	pipe (7)
лю́тий, -ого	February (19)
ляборатóрія, -ї	laboratory (11)
лягáти: лягти́	to lie down, I conj. (16)
лягти́ see **лягáти**	
ля́мпа, -и	lamp (2)
Львів, Львóва	Lviv (4)

М

Мадри́д, -у	Madrid (16)
майбýтнє, -ього	future (21)
мáйже	almost (4)
мáйже нікóго	hardly anyone (4)
мáйже ніхтó	hardly anyone (4)
мáйже нічóго	hardly anything (4)
мáйже ніщó	hardly anything (4)
Макси́м, -а	Maksym (16)
малéнький, -а, -е	little (7)
мали́й, -á, -é	small (4)
мáло	little (2)
мáма, -и	mama, mother (2)
мáрка, -и	stamp (13)
Мáрта, -и	Marta (6)
Марýся, -і	Marusya(11)
мáсло, -а	butter (1)
математик, -а	mathematician (22)
математика, -и	mathematics (16)
мáти	to have (imperf. only), I conj. (10)
мáти рáцію	to be right (17)

ма́ти, ма́тері	mother (8)
ме́блі, -ів	furniture (pl.) (9)
межа́, -í	boundary (6)
мексіка́нський, -а, -е	Mexican (18)
мело́дія, -ї	melody (16)
ме́нше	less (4)
метро́	subway (indecl.) (8)
Ме́хіко	Mexico (indecl.) (13)
ме́шканець, -нця	inhabitant (21)
ме́шкати: за/по/ме́шкати	to inhabit, I conj. (15)
Мико́ла, -и	Mykola (4)
ми́лий, -а, -е	pleasant (5)
ми́ля, -і	mile (21)
мину́лий, -а, -е	past (8)
мир, -у	peace (6)
Миро́н, -а	Myron (5)
Миро́ся, -і	Myrosya (17)
ми́ти: ви́/об/ми́ти	to wash, I conj. (15)
між íншим	by the way (17)
міст, моста́/мо́сту	bridge (18)
мі́сто, -а	city (2)
мі́сце, -я	place (7)
мі́сяць, -я	moon (month) (4)
міськи́й, -а́, -е́	city (adj.), urban (17)
мно́ження, -ння	multiplication (22)
мо́ва, -и	language (10)
могти́: змогти́	to be able, I conj. (6)
мо́дний, -а, -е	fashionable (18)
мо́же бу́ти	maybe, perhaps (6)
мо́крий, -а, -е	wet (20)
молоди́й, -а́, -е́	young (3)
моло́дший, -а, -е	younger (4)
молоко́, -а́	milk (1)
мо́ре, -я	sea (8)
му́дрий, -а, -е	smart (21)
мужчи́на, -и	man (16)
музе́й, -ю	museum (4)
му́зика, -и	music (4)
музика́нт, -а	musician (5)
му́сити: зму́сити	to be obliged, must, II conj. (6)
му́ха, -и	fly (6)
м'ясни́к, -а	butcher (15)
м'яки́й, -а́, -е́	soft (15)
м'я́со, -а	meat (8)

Н

на́віть	even (2)
навча́ння, -ння	study, studying (14)
навча́ти: навчи́ти	to teach, I conj., II conj. (10)
навча́тися: навчи́тися	to learn, study (19)
навчи́ти see **навча́ти**	
навчи́тися see **навча́тися**	
наго́да, -и	opportunity (17)
надзвича́йний, -а, -е	extraordinary, unusual (11)
наді́ятися	to hope for (imperf. only), I conj. (15)
на жа́ль	unfortunately (19)
на́зва, -и	name, title (3)
назива́тися: назва́тися	to be called, named, I conj. (3)
назу́стріч	to meet, towards a meeting (13, 23)
найбі́льше	most (19)
найнові́ші журна́ли	the latest magazines (18)
напе́вно	for sure (11)
написа́ти see **писа́ти**	
напри́клад	for example (4)
напро́ти	across (+ gen.) (17)
наріка́ти: понаріка́ти	to complain (19)
наро́д, -у	a people, nation (16)
наро́джуватися: народи́тися	to be born, I conj., II conj. (19)
наро́дний, -а, -е і наро́дній, -я, -є	national, folk (17)
насту́пний, -а, -е	next (14)
Ната́лка, -и	Natalka (1)
нача́льник, -а	boss, chief (5)
на щá́стя	fortunately (19)
небага́то, небага́цько	a little (16)
не́бо, -а, небеса́, небе́с	sky, skies (12)
невдово́лений, -а, -е	dissatisfied (+instr.) (6)
неда́вно	recently (3)
недале́ко	near (2)
неді́ля, -і	Sunday (14)
недоста́тньо	not sufficient, not enough (21)
нема́ за́що	don't mention it (6)
не мо́же бу́ти	it can't be (6)
неважли́ве	unimportant, unnecessary (9)
не мо́жу не	I can't help but (+inf.) (6)
непотрі́бний, -а, -е	unnecessary, useless (12)
непра́вда, -и	falsehood, lie (4)
неприє́мний, -а, -е	unpleasant (4)

нéсти́ see носи́ти
низьки́й, -á, -é — low (6)
ни́щити: зни́щити — to destroy (22)
ніж, ножá — knife (12)
нíмець, -мця — German (male) (16)
нíмка, -и — German (female) (16)
Нíна, -и — Nina (10)
ніс, нóса — nose (7)
ніч, нóчі — night (8)
нови́й, -á, -é — new (2)
нови́на, -и — news (sing) (11)
ногá, -и́ — foot, leg (6)
нóжиці, -ць — scissors (9)
нормáльно — normally (2)
носи́ти, нéсти́: понéсти — to carry, II conj., I conj. (18)
нудни́й, -á, -é — dull, boring (4)
нýдно — dull, boring (adv.) (13)
нýмер, -а — number (10)
Нью-Йóрк, -у — New York (4)

О

Об'є́днані Нáції, -них -цій — United Nations (16)
обíд, -у — dinner (6)
обíдати: пообíдати — to dine, to lunch, I conj. (7)
обіця́ти: пообіця́ти — to promise, I conj. (18)
обми́ти see ми́ти
óбраз, -а — picture (3)
óбраз, -у — literary portrait, personage (3)
оголоси́ти see оголóшувати
оголóшувати: оголоси́ти — to announce, I conj., II conj. (10)
одéржати see одéржувати
одéржувати: одéржати — to receive, I conj., II conj. (11) (23)
Одéса, -и — Odesa (11)
однáково — alike (15)
óдяг, -у — clothing (14)
одягáти: одягнýти — to dress, I conj. (15)
одягнýти see одягáти
óзеро, -а — lake (9)
означáти: означи́ти — to define, I conj., II conj. (14)
означáє — it means (14)
означи́ти see означáти
óко, -а — eye (7)
Оксáна, -и — Oksana (5)

окуля́ри, -ів	eye glasses (pl. only) (9)
Олексі́й, -я	Oleksiy (6)
Оле́нка, -и	Olenka (3)
Оле́сь, -я	Oles (14)
оліве́ць, -вця́	pencil (6)
О́ля, -і	dimin. of Olha (3)
О́льга, -и	Olha (1)
о́пера, -и	opera (2)
оповіда́ння, -ння	story (8)
орда́, -и́	horde (22)
Оре́ст, -а	Orest (6)
оригіна́льний, -а, -е	original (5)
Ори́ся, -і	Orysya (6)
о́сінь, о́сени	autumn (7)
оста́нній, -я, -є	last (2)
Оста́п, -а	Ostap (5)
ось	here (1)
оточи́ти see очо́чувати	
ото́чувати: оточи́ти	to surround, I conj., II conj. (23)
оці́нка, -и	grade, mark (9)

П

Павло́, -а́	Pavlo (5)
па́дати: впа́сти	to fall, I conj. (9)
паку́нок, -нка	package (18)
па́лець, -льця	finger (7)
пальто́, -а́	coat (8)
пам'ята́ти: запам'ята́ти	to remember, I conj. (12)
па́м'ятник, -а	monument (8)
па́м'ять, -і	memory (8)
пан, -а	Mr. (7)
па́не добро́дію	dear sir, kind sir (14)
па́ні	Mrs. (indecl.), lady (7)
папі́р, -пе́ру	paper (6)
па́ра, -и	pair (23)
парасо́ля, -і	umbrella (20)
Пари́ж, -у	Paris (13)
парк, -у	park (9)
пасажи́р, -а	passenger (18)
паціє́нт, -а	patient (23)
па́чка, -и	package (18)
пе́вний, -а, -е	sure (20)
переписа́ти see перепи́сувати	

переписувати: переписáти	to copy, to rewrite, I conj. (11)
перéклад, -у	translation (6)
перекладáти: переклáсти	to translate, I conj. (2)
переклáсти see **перекладáти**	
перемагáти: перемогти́	to conquer, I conj. (22)
перемогти́ see **перемагáти**	
перéрва, -и	recess (15)
перó, -á	pen (1)
пéрший, -а, -е	first (2)
пес, пса	dog (6)
песеня́, -я́ти	puppy (22)
Петербýрг, -у	St. Petersburg (22)
п'єса, -и	play (8)
пи́во, -а	beer (16)
пи́льний, -а, -е	diligent (6)
писáти: написáти	to write, I conj. (2)
письмéнник, -а	writer (male) (2)
письмéнниця, -і	writer (female) (2)
питáння, -ння	question (8)
питáти: запитáти	to ask, I conj. (4)
пи́ти: ви́пити	to drink, I conj. (3)
півгоди́ни	half an hour (18)
південь	south (18)
північ, -ночі	north, midnight (18)
півні́чний, -а, -е	northern (18)
піджáк, -á	jacket (17)
підзéмка, -и	subway (8)
підлóга, -и	floor (9)
підписáти see **підпи́сувати**	
підпи́сувати: підписáти	to sign, I conj. (23)
підрýчник, -а	handbook, textbook (6)
пізнавáти: пізнáти	to recognize, I conj. (17)
пізнáти see **пізнавáти**	
пізній, -я, -є	late (21)
пізні́ше	later (11)
пізно	late (3)
після	after (+gen.) (6 & 11)
пісня, -і	song (12)
піти́ see **ходи́ти**	
плáвати,пли́сти́/пливти́: поплі́сти́	to swim, I conj. (20)
плáкати: за/по/плáкати	to cry, I conj. (23)
пожартувáти see **жартувáти**	
пожи́ти see **жи́ти**	

позича́ти: пози́чити	to borrow, I conj., II conj. (14)
пози́чити see **позича́ти**	
познайо́мити see **знайо́мити**	
познайо́митися see **знайо́митися**	
по́їзд, -у	train (8)
показа́ти see **пока́зувати**	
пока́зувати: показа́ти	to show, I conj. (5)
покла́сти see **кла́сти**	
покоха́ти see **коха́ти**	
по́ле, -я	field (1)
полє́жати see **лежа́ти**	
полеті́ти see **літа́ти**	
поли́ця, -і	shelf (4)
полови́на, -и	half (10)
Полта́ва, -и	Poltava (21)
полу́день, -дня	noon, South (18)
полюби́ти see **люби́ти**	
поля́к, -а	Pole (male) (16)
по́лька, -и	Pole (female) (16)
помага́ти: помогти́	to help, I conj. (5)
по́ми́лка, -и	mistake (10)
по́міч, -мочі	help (8)
помогти́ see **помага́ти**	
понеді́лок, -лка	Monday (14)
понести́ see **носи́ти**	
пообі́дати see **обі́дати**	
пообіця́ти see **обіця́ти**	
popла́кати see **пла́кати**	
попли́сти see **пла́вати**	
попрацюва́ти see **працюва́ти**	
попроси́ти see **проси́ти**	
пора́, -и́	season, suitable time (13)
пора́да, -и	counsel (15)
пора́дити see **ра́дити**	
порва́ти see **рва́ти**	
поро́жній, -я, -є	empty (20)
порозмовля́ти see **розмовля́ти**	
портфе́ль, -я	briefcase, wallet (18)
по́ряд	nearby, next in line (7)
посере́д	in the middle (23)
поси́діти see **сиді́ти**	
посила́ти: посла́ти	to send, I conj. (15)
пласти́нка, -и	phonograph record (4)
плати́ти: заплати́ти	to pay, II conj. (12)

плащ, -á	coat, windbreaker (8)
племíнник, -а	nephew (18)
племíнниця, -і	niece (18)
плечé, -á	shoulder (9)
пливтú see плáвати	
плúстú see плáвати	
плóща, -і	square, plaza (9)
плян, -у	plan (11)
плÿшка, -и	bottle (7)
по-англíйському	in English (2)
побáчити see бáчити	
побíгти see бíгати	
поболíти see болíти	
побоÿтися see боÿтися	
пóверх, -у	floor, story (14)
повéзти see возúти	
повéсти see водúти	
повечéряти see вечéряти	
повíльний, -а, -е	slow (9)
повíрити see вíрити	
повíтря, -я	air (8)
пóвний, -а, -е	full (21)
повóлі	slowly (4)
повтóрення, -ння	repetition (14)
повторúти see повторÿти	
повторÿти: повторúти	to repeat, I conj., II conj. (14)
погáний, -а, -е	bad, poor in quality, ugly (3)
погáно	badly (2)
поговорúти see говорúти	
погóда, -и	weather (2)
погулÿти see гулÿти	
подéржати see держáти	
подивúтися see дивúтися	
подíбний, -а, -е	similar (19)
подóбатися: сподóбатися	to appeal (intrans.), I conj. (15)
пóдорож, -і	journey, trip (16)
подорожувáння, -ння	travel (16)
пóдруга, -и	girl friend (4)
подýмати see дýмати	
подÿкувати see дÿкувати	
поéт, -а	poet (12)
послáти see слáти/посилáти	
послýхати see слýхати	
поснíдати see снíдати	

поспáти see **спáти**	
поспівáти see **співáти**	
постáвити see **стáвити**	
постоя́ти see **стоя́ти**	
пóсуд, -у	dishes (collective) (9)
потелефонувáти see **телефонувáти**	
потрíбний, -а, -е	necessary, needed (6)
по-украї́нському	in Ukrainian (2)
походи́ти see **ходи́ти**	
поцікáвитися see **цікáвитися**	
почáток, -тку	beginning (3)
починáти: почáти	to start, I conj. (19)
почувáтися	to feel (intrans. & imperf. only), I conj. (19)
почу́ти see **чу́ти**	
пóшта, -и	mail, post office (6)
пошукáти see **шукáти**	
поясни́ти see **поясня́ти/поя́снювати**	
поясня́ти: поясни́ти	to explain, I conj., II conj. (4)
поя́снювати see **поясня́ти**	
прáвда, -и	truth (2)
правди́вий, -а, -е	real, true (5)
прáвий, -а, -е	right (7)
прáвило, -а	rule (5)
прáвильно	correctly (13)
прáво, -а	law (17)
прáзник, -а	holiday (5)
працювáти: попрацювáти	to work, I conj. (4)
прáця, -і	work (6)
прéдок, -дка	ancestor (22)
президéнт, -а	president (7)
прекрáсний, -а, -е	beautiful (3)
прекрáсно	wonderfully (14)
привикáти: приви́кнути	to become accustomed, to get used to, I conj. (17)
приви́кнути see **привикáти**	
привíт, -у	greeting (5)
пригадáти see **пригáдувати**	
пригáдувати: пригадáти	to remind, to recall (6)
приготóвити see **готóвити**	
приє́мний, -а, -е	pleasant (3)
приє́мність, -ности	pleasure (17)
приї̈жджáти: приї́хати	to arrive, I conj. (14)
приї́хати see **приїжджáти**	

приймáти: прийня́ти — to entertain, receive, I conj. (17)
прийня́ти see приймáти
прийняттЯ́, -ттЯ́ — reception (16)
припадкóво — by chance (22)
при́повідка, -и — saying (21)
прирóда, -и — nature (12)
прихóдити: прийти́ — to come, II conj., I conj. (14)
при́ятель, -я — friend (male) (3)
при́ятелька, -и — friend (female) (3)
прíзвище, -а — surname (6)
про — about (+ acc.) (8)
пробáчте, пробáч — excuse me (14)
прóвід, -воду — leadership, water main
продавáти: продáти — to sell, I conj., Athematic conj. (11)
продавéць, -вця́ — salesclerk (9)
продавщи́ця, -і — sales girl (9)
продáти see продавáти
продóвжувати: продóвжити — to continue I, II (13)
проси́ти: попроси́ти — to ask, to beg, II conj. (14)
прóстий, -а, -е — simple, straight (8)
прóсто — straight, simply (6)
простýда, -и — a cold (19)
простýджуватися: простуди́тися — to catch cold, I conj., II conj. (19)
простуди́тися see простýджуватися
профéсор, -а — professor (4)
прохíд, -хóду — walk (15)
прочитáти see читáти
пря́мо — straight (6)
птах, -а — bird (12)
п'я́тниця, -і — Friday (14)

Р

рáда, -и — council, counsel (5)
рáдий, -а, -е — glad (6)
рáдити: порáдити — to advise, to counsel, II conj. (5)
рáдіо — radio (indecl. except for радіом in instr.) (5)
радя́нський, -а, -е — Soviet (9)
раз — once, one time (12)
рáзом — together (2)
рай, -ю — paradise (8)
ранíше — earlier (8)

ра́нній, -я, -є	early (12)
ра́но	morning (adv.) (3)
ра́нок, -нку	morning (5)
рва́ти: порва́ти	to tear, I conj. (22)
ревмати́зм, -у	rheumatism (19)
реда́ктор, -а	editor (14)
ресторА́н, -у	restaurant (3)
ре́чення, -ння	sentence (14)
ри́ба, -и	fish (5)
ріг, ро́га/ро́гу	corner, horn (8)
рідки́й, -а́, -е́	thin, not thick, watery (21)
рі́дкісний, -а, -е	rare (12)
рі́дко	rarely, seldom (5)
різки́й, -а́, -е́	shrill, harsh (21)
рі́зний, -а, -е	different, various (10)
рік, ро́ку	year (8)
ріка́, -и́	river (1)
річ, ре́чі	thing (9)
роби́ти: зроби́ти	to do, II conj. (2)
робо́та, -и	work (2)
роди́на, -и	family, relatives (6)
роди́тися: народи́тися	to be born, II conj. (19)
роже́вий, -а, -е	rosy (12)
розбуди́ти see **розбу́джувати**	
розгляда́тися: розгля́нутися	to look about, I conj. (23)
розказа́ти see **розка́зувати**	
розка́зувати: розказа́ти	to narrate, I conj. (23)
розмо́ва, -и	discussion (12)
розмовля́ти: порозмовля́ти	to discuss, I conj. (7)
розповіда́ти: розпові́сти	to narrate, I conj. Athematic conj.
розпові́сти see **розповіда́ти**	
розумі́ти: зрозумі́ти	to understand, I conj. (4)
розу́мний, -а, -е	intelligent (5)
Ро́ма, -и	Roma (5)
рома́н, -у	novel (4)
Ро́мко, -а	Romko (11)
росія́нин, -а	Russian (male) (16)
росія́нка, -и	Russian (female) (16)
рости́: ви́рости	to grow, I conj. (12)
рот, -а	mouth (7)
рука́, -и́	arm, hand (7)
рядо́к, -дка́	line (22)

С

сад, -у	orchard (8)
сала́та, -и	salad (7)
сам, -á, -ó	oneself (10)
самозрозумі́ло	self evidently, of course (11)
сві́жий, -а, -е	fresh (5)
світ, -у	world (22)
свя́то, -а	holiday (22)
секрета́рка, -и	secretary (1)
село́, -á	village (2)
селяни́н, -а	peasant, villager (male) (9)
селя́нка, -и	peasant (female) (9)
семе́стр, -у	semester (22)
середа́, -и́	Wednesday (14)
сере́ди́на, -и	middle (14)
серйо́зний, -а, -е	serious (7)
сере́дній, -я, -є	middle (18)
се́рпень, -пня	August (19)
сестра́, -и́	sister (1)
сестрі́нка, -и	niece (18)
сестрі́нок, -нка	nephew (18)
сиді́ти: поси́діти	to sit, II conj. (6)
си́льний, -а, -е	strong (21)
син, -а	son (1)
си́ній, -я, -є	blue (2)
сир, -у	cheese (3)
систе́ма, -и	system (14)
сіда́ти: сі́сти	to sit down, I conj. (16)
сім'я́, -ї́	family (8)
сі́чень, -чня	January (19)
сі́сти see сіда́ти	
сказа́ти see говори́ти	
ски́бка, -и	slice of bread (16)
скі́льки	how much (+ gen.) (3)
скінчи́ти see кінча́ти	
скля́нка, -и	glass (3)
скóро	fast, soon (2)
слаби́й, -á, -é	weak (21)
сла́ти: посла́ти	to send, I conj. (10)
Сла́вко, -а	Slavko (9)
словни́к, -á	dictionary (1)
сло́во, -а	word (2)
слов'яни́н, -а	Slav (16)

слов'я́нський, -а, -е	Slavic (14)
слу́хати: послу́хати	to listen, I conj. (2)
смак, -у́	taste (7)
смачни́й, -а́, -е́	tasty (7)
смета́на, -и	sour cream (8)
смерть, -и	death (8)
сміх, -у	laughter (12)
смія́тися: засмія́тися	to laugh, I conj. (15)
сніг, -у	snow (15)
сніда́ння,-ння	breakfast (8)
сні́дати: посні́дати	to breakfast, I conj. (7)
соба́ка, -и	dog (6)
со́нце, -я	sun (12)
соро́чка, -и	shirt (9)
спа́льня, -і	bedroom (6)
спа́ти: поспа́ти	to sleep, II conj. (3)
спе́ка, -и	hot weather (17)
спеція́льно	specially (8)
співа́к, -а́	singer (12)
співа́ти: за/поспіва́ти	to sing, I conj. (12)
співа́чка, -и	singer (female) (12)
спізни́тися see **спізня́тися**	
спізня́тися: спізни́тися	to be late, I conj., II conj. (5)
сподіва́тися	to expect (only imperf.), I conj. (18)
сподо́батися see **подо́батися**	
споча́тку	at first (7)
спра́ва, -и	matter (13)
спра́ва в то́му	the matter is (11)
спра́вжній, -я, -є	genuine, true, real (5)
срі́бло, -а	silver (21)
ستава́ти: ста́ти	to become, to stand, I conj. (16)
ста́вити: поста́вити	to place upright, II conj. (20)
ста́нція, -ї	station (8)
стари́й, -а́, -е́	old (2)
ста́рший, -а, -е	older (4)
ста́ти see **ستава́ти**	
статтяя́, -і́	article (2)
старомо́дний, -а, -е	old-fashioned (12)
сте́ля, -і	ceiling (15)
Сте́фа, -и	Stefa (5)
стипе́ндія, -ї	scholarship, stipend (19)
стіл, стола́	table (4)
сті́льки	so much (16)
стіна́, -и́	wall (2)

столи́ця, -і	capital (3)
столі́ття, -ття	century (14)
сторі́нка, -и	page (14)
сторі́ччя, -ччя	century (23)
сторона́, -и́	side (3)
стоя́ти: посто́яти	to stand, II conj. (2)
страшни́й, -а́, -е́	frightening, terrible (23)
стрі́нути see **стріча́ти**	
стріча́ти: стрі́нути	to meet, I conj. (12)
студе́нт, -а	student (male) (1)
студе́нтка, -и	student (female) (1)
субо́та, -и	Saturday (14)
суддя́, -і	judge (16)
су́ка, -и	bitch (22)
су́кня, -і	dress (2)
сумни́й, -а́, -е́	sad (23)
супере́чка, -и	argument (12)
сусі́д, -а	neighbor (male) (6)
сусі́дка, -и	neighbor (female) (6)
схід, схо́ду	east (20)
схо́дини, -дин	meeting (pl. only) (9)
сходи́ти: зійти́	arise (with sun), to come down (12)
схо́жий, -а, -е на	look like (+ acc.) (19)
схоті́ти see **хоті́ти**	
сюди́	hither (13)
сього́дні	today (2)
сього́днішній, -я, -є	today's (adj.) (6)

T

та	and (5)
табли́ця, -і	blackboard (2)
та́йна, -и	secret (11)
так	so, yes (1)
та́ко́ж	also (1)
таксі́	taxi, (indecl.) (8)
таксі́вка, -и	taxi (13)
так собі́	so-so (15)
talanови́тий, -а, -е	talented (5)
там	there (1)
Тама́ра, -и	Tamara (10)
та́нґо, -а	tango (10)
танцюва́ти: потанцюва́ти	to dance, I conj. (17)
тарі́лка, -и	plate (9)

тата́рський, -а, -е	Tartar (adj.) (22)
твари́на, -и	animal (domesticated) (19)
теа́тр, -тру	theater (4)
телеві́зор,-а	television set (5)
телегра́ма, -и	telegram (5)
телефо́н, -у	telephone (5)
телефонува́ти: потелефонува́ти	to phone, I conj. (5)
те́мний, -а, -е	dark (3)
температу́ра, -и	temperature (19)
тепе́р	now (4)
те́плий, -а, -е	warm (12)
терпели́вий, -а, -е	patient (14)
терпели́вість, -вости	patience (14)
ти́ждень, ти́жня	week (4)
тип, -а/-у	type (22)
ти́хий, -а, -е	quiet (4)
ті́льки	only (1)
ті́льки що	just now (21)
ті́тка, -и	aunt (22)
товари́ство, -а	company (22)
това́риш, -а	friend (12)
това́ришка, -и	friend (female) (12)
товсти́й, -á, -é	fat (4)
тоді́	then (6)
тому́	ago (12)
тому́ що	therefore (3), because (8)
тонки́й, -á, -é	thin (9)
Торо́нто, -а	Toronto (5)
то́чно	precisely (17)
тра́вень, -вня	May (19)
трамва́й, -я	streetcar (13)
тра́питися see трапля́тися	
трапля́тися: тра́питися	to happen, to occur, I conj., II conj. (16)
тре́тій, -я, -є	third (14)
три	three (9)
трудни́й, -á, -é	difficult (3)
туди́	there (13)
турке́ня, -і	Turk (female) (16)
ту́рок, -рка	Turk (male) (16)
тут	here (1)
тяжки́й, -á, -é	heavy, difficult (18)

У

убира́ти see **вбира́ти**	
убра́ння́, -ння́	clothing (11)
уве́сь see **ввесь**	
уве́чорі	in the evening (3)
угорі́ see **вгорі́**	
удово́лений see **вдово́лений**	
удово́лення see **вдово́лення**	
удо́ма see **вдо́ма**	
уже́/вже	already (3)
Украї́на, -и	Ukraine (4)
украї́нець, -нця	Ukrainian (male) (16)
украї́нка, -и	Ukrainian (female) (16)
украї́нський, -а, -е	Ukrainian (adj.) (2)
улю́блений, -а, -е	beloved (8)
Уля́нка, -и	Ulyanka (11)
умира́ти see **вмира́ти**	
унизу́ see **внизу́**	
університе́т, -у	university (12)
уночі́ see **вночі́**	
Ура́!	hurrah (14)
усе́ see **все**	
у́ступ, -у	chapter (10)
у́хо/ву́хо, -а	ear (6)
у́часть, -и	participation (17)
уче́ний/вче́ний	scholar (18)
учени́ця, -і	pupil (female) (6)
у́чень, -чня	pupil (male) (6)
учи́тель/вчи́тель, -я	teacher (male) (1)
учи́телька/вчи́телька, -и	teacher (female) (1)
учи́ти/вчи́ти: навчи́ти	to teach, II conj. (8)
учи́тися/вчи́тися: навчи́тися	to learn, study (19)
учо́ра see **вчо́ра**	
учора́шній see **вчора́шній**	

Ф

фа́брика, -и	factory (11)
фа́рба, -и	paint (19)
фільм, -у	film (8)
фортепія́но, -а	piano (2)

фотогра́фія, -ї	photograph (12)
Фра́нція, -ї	France (10)
францу́женка, -и	Frenchwoman (16)
францу́з, -а	Frenchman (16)
францу́зький, -а, -е	French (3)
фунт, -а	pound (3)

Х

хара́ктер, -у	character, disposition (6)
Ха́рків, -кова	Kharkiv (21)
харч, -у	provisions, victuals (collective) (23)
ха́та, -и	house (2)
хвили́на, -и	minute (14)
хворі́ти: захворі́ти	to be sick, I conj. (19)
хво́рий, -а, -е	sick (19)
хворо́ба, -и	sickness (19)
хліб, -а	bread (1)
хло́пчик, -а	little boy (9)
хма́ра, -и	cloud (15)
хмарочо́с, -а	skyscraper (17)
ходи́ти, йти́: піти́	to walk, I conj., II conj. (6)
хо́лод, -у	cold (17)
холо́дний,-а, -е	cold, cool (3)
хоті́ти: за/схоті́ти	to want, I conj. (6)
хоч/хоча́	although (6)
хре́ще́ння, -ння	christening (22)
Христи́на, -и	Khrystyna (8)
християни́н, -а	Christian (16)
Хри́стя, -і	Khrystia (dim. of Khrystyna) (8)
хрущ, -а́	beetle (6)
ху́стка, -и	kerchief, scarf (21)
ху́тір, -тора	summer home, villa (12)

Ц

центр, -у	center (3)
це́рква, -и	church (14)
сига́рка, -и	cigarette (18)
цитри́на, -и	lemon (7)
ціка́вий, -а, -е	interesting (5)
ціка́витися: поціка́витися	to be interested, II conj. (17)
ціка́во	interesting (2)
ці́лий, -а, -е	whole (4)

ціна́, -и́	price (3)
цуке́рок, -рка	candy (15)
цу́кор, -кру	sugar (7)

Ч

чай, -ю	tea (7)
час, -у	time (3)
части́на, -и	part (20)
ча́сто	often (5)
ча́шка, -и	cup (6)
чека́ти: за/почека́ти	to wait, I conj. (14)
че́рвень, -вня	June (19)
черво́ний, -а, -е	red (4)
череви́к, -а	shoe (9)
четве́р, -рга́	Thursday (14)
чи	if, whether (1) or (18)
чима́ло	quite a bit (22)
чи́стий, -а, -е	clean (11)
чита́ння, -ння	reading (8)
чита́ти: прочита́ти	to read, I conj. (2)
Чіка́ґо	Chicago (indeclinable) (21)
чолові́к, -а	husband, man, person (1)
чому́	why (1)
чому́сь	for some reason (11)
Чо́рне мо́ре	Black Sea (8)
чо́рний, -а, -е	black (7)
чоти́ри	four (9)
чужи́й, -а́, -е́	foreign (16)
чужи́нець, -нця	foreigner (16)
чу́ти: почу́ти	to hear, I conj. (6)

Ш

ша́бля, -і	sword (9)
ша́пка, -и	cap, hat (2)
ша́фа, -и	closet, cupboard (20)
швед, -а	Swede (male) (16)
шве́дка, -и	Swede (female) (16)
швидки́й, -а́, -е́	fast, swift (21)
широ́кий, -а, -е	wide (7)
шкільни́й, -а́, -е́	school (adj.) (19)
шко́да	it’s a shame, loss (adv.) (11)
шко́ла, -и	school (1)

Шопе́н, -а	Chopin (15)
шпита́ль, -ю	hospital (19)
штани́, -ів	pants (pl. only) (9)
шука́ти: пошука́ти	to search, I conj. (19)
шулі́ка, -и	hawk (22)
шум, -у	noise (12)
шумни́й, -а́, -е́	noisy (12)
шухля́да, -и	drawer (20)

Щ

ще	still, more (2)
ще ні	not yet (2)
що́	what (interr. pron.) (2)
що	that (relat. pron.)

Ю

Юрко́, -а́	Yurko (10)

Я

я́блуко, -а	apple (15)
як	how (1)
як тільки	as soon as (11)
якщо́	if (6)
я не мо́жу не...	I can't help but... (+ inf.) (6)
Я́лта, -и	Yalta (6)
Яри́на, -и	Yaryna (10)
я́сний, -а, -е	bright, clear (14)
я́сно	clearly (14)

ENGLISH-UKRAINIAN VOCABULARY

A

able, to be	могти́ (6)[1]
about	про (8)
about	ко́ло (22)
above	вгорі́, угорі́ (23)
abroad	за грани́цею (17)
to go abroad	за грани́цю (17)
accident	ви́падок (16)
acquaint, to	знайо́мити, познайо́мити (16)
acquaintance	знайо́мий (16)
acquainted, to be	знайо́митися: познайо́митися (з + **instr.**) (16)
across	напро́ти (17)
actor	акто́р (16)
addition	додава́ння (22)
address	адре́са (3)
affair	ді́ло (17)
Africa	А́фрика (13)
after	пі́сля (6)
again	зно́ву (10)
ago	тому́ (12)
air	пові́тря (8)
airplane	літа́к (20)
alike	одна́ково (15)
all	у/в/ве́сь, у/в/ся́, у/в/се́, у/в/сі́ (3)
all the time	у/в/ве́сь час (13)
almost	ма́йже (4)
already	уже́, вже (3)
also	та́ко́ж (1)
although	хоч, хоча́ (6)
always	за́вжди (2)
America	Аме́рика (4)
American (m.)	америка́нець (16)
American (f.)	америка́нка (16)
ancestor	пре́док (22)
and	і (3), та (5), а (5)
anecdote	анекдо́т (12)
angle	кут (20)

1 All numbers in parentheses refer to Chapters.

animal	твари́на (19)
announce, to	оголо́шувати: оголоси́ти (10)
another	дру́гий (11)
answer	ві́дповідь (8)
answer, to	відповіда́ти: відпові́сти (**на + acc.**) (11)
apartment	кварти́ра (2)
apparently	ви́дно (23)
appeal, to	подо́батися: сподо́батися (15)
appetite	апети́т (7)
apple	я́блуко (15)
April	кві́тень (19)
argument	супере́чка (12)
arm	рука́ (7)
arise, to	встава́ти: вста́ти (12), сходи́ти: зійти́ (about sun) (12)
around	ко́ло (22), круго́м (12)
arrive, to	приїжджа́ти: приї́хати (14)
article	статтяя́ (2)
Asia	А́зія (13)
ask, to	проси́ти: попроси́ти (favor) (14), пита́ти: запита́ти (question) (11)
aspirin	аспіри́на (13)
assign, to	задава́ти: зада́ти (9)
assignment	зада́ча (9), завда́ння (21)
as soon as	як ті́льки (11)
at first	спочатку (7)
at home	вдо́ма, удо́ма (15)
at night	вночі́, уночі́ (15)
at the worst	в найгі́ршому ви́падку (21)
auditorium	авдито́рія (9)
August	се́рпень (19)
aunt	ті́тка (22)
author	а́втор (5)
automobile	а́вто (2)
autumn	о́сінь (7)
awaken, to	буди́ти: розбуди́ти (15)
axle	вісь (8)

B

bad	злий (10), пога́ний (3)
badly	пога́но (2)
balcony	бальќо́н (12)
ballerina	балери́на (4)

ballet	бале́т (4)
bank	банк (8)
bathroom	лазни́чка (6)
battle	би́тва (22)
be, to	бу́ти (2)
beautiful	кра́сний (21), прекра́сний (3)
because	тому́ що (8)
bed	лі́жко (6)
bedroom	спа́льня (6)
beef steak	бі́фстекс (16)
beer	пи́во (16)
beetle	хрущ (6)
beg, to	проси́ти: попроси́ти (14)
begin, to	зачина́ти: зача́ти (4), почина́ти: поча́ти (17)
beginning	поча́ток (3)
being	бу́дучи (23)
believe, to	ві́рити: пові́рити (17)
beloved	улю́блений (8)
below	у/в/низу́ (23)
benefactor	добро́дій (14)
Berlin	Берлі́н (17)
besides	крі́м (6)
be so good as to	бу́дьте такі́ до́брі (14)
better	кра́ще (19)
big	вели́кий (14)
bird	птах (12)
birthday	день наро́дження (19)
bitch	су́ка (22)
black	чо́рний (7)
Black Sea	Чо́рне мо́ре (8)
blond/blonde	блонди́н, блонди́нка (4)
blouse	блю́зка (12)
blue	си́ній (2)
board	табли́ця (2)
book	кни́жка (1)
book store	книга́рня (6)
boring	ну́дно (13), нудни́й (4)
born, to be	наро́джуватися: народи́тися, роди́тися: народи́тися (19)
borrow, to	позича́ти: пози́чити (14)
borsch	борщ (7)
boss	нача́льник (5)
bottle	пля́шка (7)

boundary	грани́ця (21), межа́ (6)
boy, little	хло́пчик (9)
bread	хліб (1)
breakfast	сніда́ння (8)
breakfast, to	сні́дати: посні́дати (7)
bridge	міст (18)
briefcase	портфе́ль (18)
bright	я́сний (3)
brother	брат (1)
brunet/brunette	брюне́т, брюне́тка (4)
building	буди́нок (8)
bus	авто́бус (13)
business	ді́ло (17)
but	а (5), але́ (2)
butcher	м'ясни́к (15)
butter	ма́сло (1)
buy, to	купува́ти: купи́ти (4)
by chance	припадко́во (22)
by the way	між і́ншим (17)

C

Canada	Кана́да (4)
Canadian	кана́дський (2), кана́дець, кана́дка (16)
candy	цуке́рок (15)
capital	столи́ця (3)
card	ка́рта (12)
Carpathians	Карпа́ти (9)
carpet	ки́лим (6)
carry, to	носи́ти, не́сти: поне́сти (18)
cat	кіт (12)
Caucasus	Кавка́з (8)
ceiling	сте́ля (15)
center	центр (3)
century	столі́ття (14), сторі́ччя (23)
chair	крі́сло (2)
chalk	кре́йда (7)
chance	ви́падок (16)
chapter	у́ступ (10)
character	хара́ктер (6)
cheap	деше́вий (3)
cheerful	весе́лий (12)
cheese	сир (3)

chest	гру́ди (9)
Chicago	Чіка́ґо (21)
chick	курча́ (8)
chicken	ку́рка (22)
chief	нача́льник (5)
child	дитя́ (8), дити́на (16)
children	ді́ти (9)
China	Кита́й (7)
choice	ви́бір (20)
Chopin	Шопе́н (15)
christening	хре́щення (22)
Christian	християнин (16)
church	це́рква (14)
cigarette	цига́рка (18)
cinema	кі́но, кіно́ (**indecl.**) (8)
citizen	громадя́нин (19), громадя́нка (12)
city	мі́сто (2)
class	кля́са (5)
clean	чи́стий (11)
clear	я́сний (3)
clearly	я́сно (14)
climate	клі́мат (21)
clock	годи́нник (13)
close, to	зачиня́ти: зачини́ти (4), замика́ти: замкну́ти (15)
closet	ша́фа (20)
clothing	убра́ння́, вбра́ння́ (11), о́дяг (14)
cloud	хма́ра (15)
club	клюб (8)
coat	плащ (8), пальто́ (8)
coffee	ка́ва (7)
coin	гріш (11)
cold	зи́мно (5), хо́лод (17), зи́мний (6), просту́да (19)
cold, to catch a	просту́джуватися: простуди́тися (19)
color	ко́лір (3)
come, to	прихо́дити: прийти́ (14)
comfortable	вигі́дний (3)
company	товари́ство (22)
complain	нарі́ка́ти (19)
concert	конце́рт (4)
conquer, to	перемага́ти: перемогти́ (22)
contain oneself, to	зде́ржуватися: здéржатися (23)
continue, to	продо́вжувати: продо́вжити (13)

conversation	розмо́ва (12)
converse, to	розмовля́ти: порозмовля́ти (7)
cook, to	вари́ти: звари́ти (16)
cool	холо́дний (3)
correctly	пра́вильно (13)
corner	ріг (8), кут (20)
correspondent	кореспонде́нт (22)
corridor	коридо́р (12)
cost, to	коштува́ти (12)
council	ра́да (5)
counsel	ра́да (5), пора́да (15)
counsel, to	ра́дити: пора́дити (5)
country	край (8)
court	двір (12)
cousin	двою́рідна сестра́, двою́рідний брат, кузи́на, кузи́нка, кузе́н (21)
Crimea	Крим (8)
cry, to	пла́кати: попла́кати (23)
cup	горня́тко, ча́шка (6)
cupboard	ша́фа (20)
curly	кучеря́вий (19)

D

dance, to	танцюва́ти: потанцюва́ти (17), гуля́ти: погуля́ти (12)
dark	те́мний (3)
daughter	дочка́ (1)
day	день (3)
dear	дороги́й (3)
dear sir	па́не добро́дію (14)
death	смерть (8)
December	гру́день (19)
deep	глибо́кий (21)
define, to	означа́ти: означи́ти (14)
deliver, to (talk)	виголо́шувати: ви́голосити (до́повідь) (8)
depart, to	від'їжджа́ти: від'ї́хати (14)
department	ві́дділ (9)
desk	бю́рко (6)
destruction	зни́щення (22)
destroy, to	ни́щити: зни́щити (22)
dictionary	словни́к (1)
die, to	вмира́ти: вме́рти; умира́ти: уме́рти (17)

different	рíзний (10), íнший (16)
difficult	трудни́й (3), тяжки́й (18)
diligent	пи́льний (6)
dine, to	обíдати: пообíдати (7)
dining room	їда́льня (6)
dinner	обíд (6)
director	дире́ктор (5)
dirty	брудни́й (11)
discuss, to	розмовля́ти: порозмовля́ти (7)
discussion	розмо́ва (12)
dishes	по́суд (9)
display	виста́ва (22)
dissatisfied	невдово́лений (6)
distinguished	визначни́й (22)
divan	дива́н (7)
division	дíлення (22)
Dnipro	Днiпро́ (8)
do, to	роби́ти: зроби́ти (2)
doctor	лíкар (5), до́ктор (12)
document	докуме́нт (6)
dog	соба́ка (6), пес (6)
dollar	до́ляр (10)
don't mention it	нема́ за́що (6)
door	две́рі (9)
downstairs	у/в/низу́ (23)
drawer	шухля́да (20)
dress	су́кня (2)
dress, to	одяга́ти: одягну́ти (15), вбира́ти: вбра́ти (15)
drink, to	пи́ти: ви́пити (3)
drugstore	апте́ка (8)

E

each	ко́жний (4)
ear	ву́хо/у́хо (6)
earlier	ранíше (8)
early	ра́нній (21), ра́но (3)
east	схід (20)
easy	ле́гкий (21)
that's easy	це ле́гко (5)
eat, to	ї́сти: з'ї́сти (3)
editor	реда́ктор (14)
Edmonton	Едмонто́н (13)

either ... or	абó ... абó (2)
elder man	дя́дько (20)
elevator, lift	ліфт (17)
empty	порóжній (20)
end	кінéць (3)
enemy	вóрог (23)
engineer	інженéр (5)
England	А́нглія (13)
English	англі́йський (6)
English, in	по-англі́йському (2)
Englishman	англі́єць (16)
Englishwoman	англі́йка (16)
enormous	величéзний (9)
enough	дóсить (6)
entertain, to	приймáти: прийня́ти (17)
entirely	зóвсім (7)
era	добá (22)
European	европéйський (3)
even	нáвіть (2)
evening	вéчір (3), вечі́рній (11)
in the evening	увéчорі (3)
evening party	вечі́рка (4)
every	кóжний (4)
everything	все (3)
everywhere	у/в/сю́ди (7)
exactly	тóчно (17)
exam	íспит (10)
excellent	відмі́нний (14), знамени́тий (9)
excellently	відмі́нно (14)
except	крім (6)
excuse me	пробáчте, пробáч (14)
exercise	впрáва (5)
exhibit	ви́ставка, вистáва (22)
expect, to	сподівáтися (18)
expensive	дороги́й (3)
explain, to	поя́снювати/поясня́ти: поясни́ти (1)
extraordinary	надзвичáйний (11)
eye	óко (7)

F

face	лицé (7)
factory	фáбрика (10)
fall, to	пáдати: впáсти (9)
falsehood	неправда (4)

familiar	знайо́мий (16)
family	сім'я́ (8)
famous	визначни́й (22)
far	дале́ко (2), дале́кий (21)
fashionable	мо́дний (18)
fast	швидки́й (21)
fat	гру́бий (9), товсти́й (4)
father	ба́тько (1)
fear, to	боя́тися: побоя́тися (15)
fearless	відва́жний (21)
February	лю́тий (19)
feel, to	почува́тися (19)
fever	гаря́чка (19)
field	по́ле (1)
film	фільм (8)
find, to	знахо́дити: знайти́ (18)
find out, to	дові́дуватися: дові́датися (17)
fine	га́рний (2)
finger	па́лець (7)
finish, to	кінча́ти: скінчи́ти (11)
first	пе́рший (2)
fish	ри́ба (5)
floor	підло́га (9), по́верх (14)
flower	кві́тка (18)
fly	му́ха (6)
fly, to	літа́ти; леті́ти: полеті́ти (20)
folk	наро́дній і наро́дний (17)
foolish	дурни́й (5)
foot	нога́ (6)
for	для (12), за (12)
forefather	пре́док (22)
foreign	чужи́й (16)
foreigner	чужине́ць (16)
forest	ліс (8)
for example	напри́клад (4)
forget, to	забува́ти: забу́ти (23)
fork	виде́лка (12)
for some reason	чому́сь (11)
for sure	напе́вно (11)
fortunately	на ща́стя (19)
four	чоти́ри (9)
France	Фра́нція (10)
French	францу́зький (3)
Frenchman	францу́з (16)
Frenchwoman	францу́женка (16)

fresh	сві́жий (5)
Friday	п'я́тниця (14)
friend	друг, по́друга, това́риш, това́ришка (12), при́ятель, при́ятелька (3)
frightening	страшни́й (23)
from here	зві́дси (18)
from there	відтіля́, ві́дти (13); зві́дти (18)
full	по́вний (21)
furniture	ме́блі (9)
future	майбу́тнє (21)

G

Galicia	Галичина́ (22)
game	гра (10)
garage	гара́ж (9)
garden	горо́д (2)
gate	воро́та (9)
gay	весе́лий (12)
genius	ге́ній (5)
genuine	спра́вжній (5)
German	ні́мець, ні́мка (16)
gesture	жест (7)
get, to	дістава́ти: діста́ти (11)
get used to, to	привика́ти: приви́кнути (17)
gift	дару́нок (5)
girl	ді́вчина (4), ді́вчинка (9)
girl friend	по́друга (4)
give, to	дава́ти: да́ти (5)
give back, to	віддава́ти: відда́ти (17)
glad	ра́дий (6)
glass	скля́нка (3)
glasses	окуля́ри (9)
go, to	і/й/ти́, ходи́ти: піти́; ї́здити, ї́хати: пої́хати (13)
God	Бог (20)
gold	зо́лото (21)
good	га́рний (2), до́брий (2)
good day	добри́день (13)
Goodness	Го́споди! (5)
good night	добра́ніч (17)
grade	оці́нка (9)
grammar	грама́тика (4)
granddaughter	вну́чка (18)
grandfather	ді́до (17)

grandmother	бабу́ня (13)
grandson	внук (18)
great	вели́кий (2)
green	зеле́ний (9)
greetings	приві́т (5)
grow, to	рости́: ви́рости (12)
guest	гість (4)
guitar	гіта́ра (5)

H

habit	зви́чка (19)
hair	воло́сся (19)
half	полови́на (10)
half an hour	півгоди́ни (18)
hand	рука́ (7)
handbook	підру́чник (6)
happen, to	трапля́тися: тра́питися (16)
hardly anyone	ма́йже ніхто́, ма́йже ніко́го (4)
hardly anything	ма́йже нішо́, ма́йже нічо́го (4)
harsh	різки́й (21)
hat	ша́пка (2), капелю́х (20)
have, to	ма́ти (6)
having been	бу́вши (23)
hawk	шулі́ка (22)
head	голова́ (6)
health	здоро́в'я (19)
healthy	здоро́вий (19)
hear, to	чу́ти: почу́ти (6)
heat	го́ряч (17)
heavy	тяжки́й (18)
help, to	помага́ти: помогти́ (14)
help	допомо́га (6), по́міч (8)
here	тут (1), сюди́ (13), ось (1)
hero	геро́й (2)
heroine	геро́їня (2)
high	висо́кий (6)
historian	істо́рик (7)
historical	істори́чний (9)
history	істо́рія (5)
hold, to	держа́ти: поде́ржати (6)
hold off, to	зде́ржуватися: зде́ржатися (23)
holiday	свя́то (12), пра́зник (5)
home	дім (9)
home (adj.)	дома́шній (11)

homeward	додо́му (13)
hope for, to	наді́ятися (15)
horde	орда́ (22)
horse	кінь (12)
hospital	шпита́ль (19)
host	госпо́дар (7)
hostess	господи́ня (5)
hot	гаря́чий (3), гаряче́ (6)
hotel	готе́ль (3)
hot weather, heat	спе́ка (17)
hot weather	го́ряч (17)
hour	годи́на (10)
house	ха́та (2), дім (9)
how	як (1)
how much	скі́льки (3)
huge	величе́зний (9)
hurrah	ура́ (14)
hurt, to	болі́ти: поболі́ти (19)
husband	чолові́к (1), дружи́на

I

I can't help but	не мо́жу не... (+inf.) (6)
if	чи (1), якщо́ (6)
important	важли́вий (9)
in advance	заздалегі́дь (19)
incident	ви́падок (16)
indeed	ді́йсно (11)
inhabit, to	ме́шкати: заме́шкати (15)
inhabitant	ме́шканець (21)
in order	у/в/поря́дку (15)
insane	божеві́льний (21)
insufficient	недоста́тньо (21)
intelligent	розу́мний (5)
interested, to be in	ціка́витися: поціка́витися (17)
interesting	ціка́вий (5)
interestingly	ціка́во (2)
in the worst case	в найгі́ршому ви́падку (21)
introduce, to	знайо́мити: познайо́мити (16)
invitation	запро́шення (21)
Italian	італі́єць, італі́йка (16), італі́йський (7)
Italy	Іта́лія (9)
it can't be	не мо́же бу́ти (6)
it means	означа́є (14)

J

jacket	піджáк (17)
January	сíчень (19)
jazz	джаз (5)
job	прáця (2)
joke, to	жартувáти: пожартувáти (23)
journal	журнáл (4)
journalist	журналíст, журналíстка (1)
journey	пóдорож (16)
joyfully	вéсело (1)
judge	суддя́ (16)
July	ли́пень (19)
June	чéрвень (19)
just past	тíльки що (21)

K

kerchief	хýстка (21)
Kharkiv	Хáрків (21)
Khrystyna, Khrystia	Христи́на, Хри́стя (8)
Kyiv	Ки́їв (2)
Kyivan	ки́ївський (9)
Kyiv region	Ки́ївщина (22)
kilometer	кіломéтр (21)
king	корóль (14)
kitchen	кýхня (1)
knife	ніж (12)
know, to	знáти (2)
known	відóмий (12)
kovbasa	ковбасá (16)

L

laboratory	ляборатóрія (11)
lake	óзеро (9)
lamp	ля́мпа (2)
landlady	господи́ня (5)
language	мóва (10)
large	вели́кий (2)
last	остáнній (2)
late	пíзній (21), пíзно (3)
late, to be	спізня́тися: спізни́тися (5)
later	пізнíше (11)
latest magazines	найновíші журнáли (18)
laugh, to	смія́тися: засмія́тися (15)
laughter	сміх (12)

law	пра́во (17)
lay, to	кла́сти: по кла́сти (20)
lazy	ліни́вий (6)
lead, to	води́ти: ве́сти́: пове́сти́ (18)
leader	вождь (9)
leadership	про́від, керівни́цтво (22)
leaf	листо́к (9)
leave, to	лиша́ти: лиши́ти (22), відхо́дити: відійти́ (14)
leaves	лист (9)
lecture, to	виклада́ти: ви́класти (11, 19)
left	лі́вий (7)
leg	нога́ (6)
lemon	цитри́на (7)
less	ме́нше (4)
lesson	ле́кція (2)
letter	лист (1)
Levko	Левко́ (8)
library	бібліоте́ка (2)
lie	непра́вда (4)
lie, to	ляга́ти: лягти́ (16), лежа́ти: полежа́ти (6)
life	життя́ (8)
light	ле́гкий (21)
likewise	тако́ж (1)
line	рядо́к (22)
listen, to	слу́хати: послу́хати (2)
literature	літерату́ра (17)
little	мале́нький (7), небага́то, небага́цько (16), ма́ло (2)
live, to	жи́ти: пожи́ти (2)
living room	віта́льня (6)
lock, to	замика́ти: замкну́ти (15)
London	Ло́ндон (14)
long	до́вгий (9)
long ago	давно́ (3)
long time	до́вго (7)
look, to	диви́тися: подиви́тися (15)
look around, to	розгляда́тися: розгля́нутися (23)
look like	схо́жий на, поді́бний до (19)
loss	шко́да (11)
loud	голосни́й (7)
love, to	коха́ти: покоха́ти (15), люби́ти: полюби́ти (16)
love	любо́в (8)
low	низьки́й (6)
Lviv	Львів (4)

M

Madrid	Мадри́д (16)
magazine	журна́л (4)
main thing	головне́ (21)
man	чолові́к (1), мужчи́на (16)
many thanks	вели́ке спаси́бі (6)
many things	бага́то чого́ (16)
map	ка́рта (12)
March	бе́резень (19)
mark	оці́нка (9)
master	госпо́дар (7)
mathematician	матема́тик (22)
mathematics	матема́тика (16)
matter	спра́ва (13), ді́ло (17)
matter is, the	ді́ло в то́му (спра́ва в то́му) (11)
May	тра́вень (19)
maybe	мо́же бу́ти (6)
means, it	зна́чить (22)
meat	м'я́со (8)
meet, to	стріча́ти: стрі́нути (12)
meeting	схо́дини (9), зібра́ння (8)
meeting, half-way	йти назу́стріч (23)
melody	мело́дія (16)
memorize, to	запам'ято́вувати: запам'ята́ти (14)
memory	па́м'ять (8)
Mexican	мексіка́нський (18)
Mexico	Ме́хіко (13)
middle	середи́на (14), сере́дній (18)
middle, in the	посере́д (23)
midnight	пі́вніч (18)
mighty	ду́жий (21)
mile	ми́ля (21)
milk	молоко́ (1)
minute	хвили́на (14)
misfortune	біда́ (22)
mistake	по́ми́лка (10)
Monday	понеді́лок (14)
money	гро́ші (11)
month	мі́сяць (4)
monument	па́м'ятник (8)
moon	мі́сяць (4)
more	ще (2), бі́льше (4)
morning	ра́но (3), ра́нок (5)

most	найбі́льше (19)
mother	ма́ти (8), ма́ма (2)
mountain	гора́ (9)
mouth	рот (7)
Mr.	пан (7)
Mrs.	па́ні (7)
much	бага́то (7)
multiplication	мно́ження (22)
museum	музе́й (4)
music	му́зика (4)
musician	музика́нт (5)
must	му́сити (му́сіти) : зму́сити (зму́сіти) (6)

N

name	на́зва (3), ім'я́ (8)
narrate, to	розка́зувати: розказа́ти (23), розповіда́ти: розпові́сти (11)
narrow	вузьки́й (4)
national	наро́дній (наро́дний) (17)
nature	приро́да (12)
near	бли́зько (2), бі́ля (12), близьки́й (21)
nearby	по́ряд (7)
needed	потрі́бний (6)
neighbor	сусі́д (6), сусі́дка (6)
nephew	племі́нник, брата́нок, сестрі́нок (18)
new	нови́й (2)
news	нови́на (11)
newspaper	газе́та (1)
New York	Нью-Йо́рк (4)
next	насту́пний (14)
next door	по́ряд (7)
nice	га́рний (2)
nicely	га́рно (1)
niece	племі́нниця, брата́нка, сестрі́нка (18)
night	ніч (8)
noise	шум (12)
noisy	шумни́й (12)
no longer	бі́льше ні (6)
no more	бі́льше ні (6)
normally	норма́льно (2), звича́йно (5)
north	пі́вніч (18)
northern	півні́чний (18)

nose	ніс (7)
note	за́пи́ска (13)
note down, to	запи́сувати: записа́ти (9)
not far	недале́ко (2)
notice, to	заува́жувати: заува́жити (18)
not yet	ще ні́ (2)
novel	рома́н (4)
November	листопа́д (19)
now	тепе́р (4)
number	ну́мер (10)

O

obey, to	слу́хати: послу́хати (2)
occur, to	трапля́тися: тра́питися (16)
October	жо́втень (19)
Odesa	Оде́са (11)
of course	самозрозумі́ло (11)
office	бюро́ (5)
often	ча́сто (5)
oh	ах (7)
old	стари́й (2)
older	ста́рший (4)
old-fashioned	старомо́дний (12)
once	раз (12)
oneself	сам (10)
only	ті́льки (1)
on your part	з ва́шої сторони́ (14)
open, to	відкрива́ти: відкри́ти (14), відчиня́ти: відчини́ти (4)
opera	о́пера (2)
opportunity	наго́да (17)
or	або́ (2), чи (18)
orchard	сад (8)
ordinarily	звича́йно (5)
original	оригіна́льний (5)
other	і́нший (16)
overstay, to	заси́джуватися: заси́дітися (21)

P

package	па́чка, паку́нок (18)
page	сторі́нка (14)
paint	фа́рба (19)
pair	па́ра (23)

pants	штани́ (9)
paper	папі́р (7)
paradise	рай (8)
parents	батьки́ (12)
Paris	Пари́ж (13)
park	парк (9)
part	части́на (20)
participation	у́часть (17)
pass, to	здава́ти: зда́ти (іспит) (20)
passenger	пасажи́р (18)
past	мину́лий (8)
patience	терпели́вість (14)
patient	паціє́нт (23), терпели́вий (14)
pay, to	плати́ти: заплати́ти (12)
peace	мир (6)
peasant	селяни́н, селя́нка (9)
pen	перо́ (1)
pencil	оліве́ць (6)
people (nation)	наро́д (16)
people	лю́ди (9)
perhaps	мо́же бу́ти (6)
person	люди́на (21)
personage	о́браз (3)
phone, to	телефонува́ти: потелефонува́ти (5)
phonograph record	пласти́нка (4)
photograph	фотогра́фія (12), зні́мок (23)
piano	фортепія́но (2)
picture	о́браз (3), карти́на (12)
piece	кусо́к (3)
pipe	лю́лька (7)
place	мі́сце (7)
place, to	ста́вити: поста́вити, кла́сти: покла́сти (20)
plan	плян (11)
plate	тарі́лка (9)
play	виста́ва (22), п'є́са (8)
play, to	гра́ти: загра́ти (4)
play cards	гра́ти в ка́рти (10)
play chess	гра́ти в ша́хи (21)
play tennis	гра́ти в те́ніс (10)
plaza	пло́ща (9)
pleasant	ми́лий (5), прие́мний (3)
pleasure	прие́мність (17)
poem	вірш (12)

poet	поéт (12)
Pole	поля́к, пóлька (16)
Poltava	Полтáва (21)
poor (bad)	погáний (21)
porch	ґáнок (12)
post office	пóшта (6)
potato	картóпля (7)
pound	фунт (3)
precisely	тóчно (17)
prefer, to	волíти (16)
prepare, to	готóвити: приготóвити (10)
president	президéнт (7)
price	цінá (3)
professor	профéсор (4)
promise, to	обіця́ти: пообіця́ти (18)
provisions	харч (23)
pupil	ýчень, учени́ця (6)
puppy	песеня (22)

Q

queen	королéва (14)
question	питáння (8)
quick	шви́дко, швидки́й (2)
quiet	ти́хий (4)
quite a bit	чимáло (22)

R

rain	дощ (13)
radio	рáдіо (5)
rake	граблí (9)
rare	рíдкісний (12)
rarely	рíдко (5)
rather	дóсить (6)
read, to	читáти: прочитáти (2)
reading	читáння (8)
ready	готóвий (23)
real	спрáвжній, правди́вий (5), дíйсний (11)
really	дíйсно (11)
recall, to	пригáдувати: пригадáти (6)
receive, to	одéржувати: одéржати (11) (23)
receive guests, to	приймáти: прийня́ти (17)

recently недáвно (3)
reception прийняттЯ́ (16)
recess перéрва (15)
recognize, to пізнавáти: пізнáти (17)
red червóний (4)
relatives роди́на (6)
remain, to лишáтися: лиши́тися (22)
remarkable знамени́тий (9)
remember, to пам'ятáти: запам'ятáти (17)
remind, to пригáдувати, пригадáти (7)
repeat, to повторя́ти: повтори́ти (14)
repetition повтóрення (14)
report дóповідь (8)
rest відпочи́нок (4)
rest, to відпочивáти: відпочи́ти (4)
restaurant ресторáн (3)
return, to вертáтися: вернýтися, вертáти: вернýти (17)
rewrite, to перепи́сувати: переписáти (11)
rheumatism ревмати́зм (19)
rich багáтий (6)
right прáвий (7)
right, to be мáти рáцію (17)
right away зрáзу ж (10)
ring, to дзвони́ти: задзвони́ти (5)
river рікá (18)
road дорóга (18)
roof дах (15)
room кімнáта (1)
root кóрінь (3)
rosy рожéвий (12)
route дорóга (18)
row рядóк (22)
rug ки́лим (6)
rule прáвило (5)
rule of law закóн (17)
run, to бíгати, бíгти: побíгти (20)
Russian росія́нин, росія́нка (16)

S

sad сумни́й (23)
St. Petersburg Петербýрг (22)
salad салáта (7)
salesclerk продавéць (9)

sales girl	продавщи́ця (9)
satisfaction	у/в/дово́лення (8)
satisfied	задово́лений (19), у/в/дово́лений (6)
Saturday	субо́та (14)
saying	при́повідка (21)
scarf	ху́стка (21)
scholar	в/у/че́ний (18)
scholarship	стипе́ндія (19)
school	шко́ла (1)
school (adj.)	шкільни́й (19)
scientist	в/у/че́ний (18)
scissors	но́жиці (9)
sea	мо́ре (8)
search, to	шука́ти: пошука́ти (19)
season	пора́ (13)
second	дру́гий (11)
secret	та́йна (11)
secretary	секрета́рка (1)
see, to	ба́чити: поба́чити (3)
seem, to	здава́тися (15)
seldom	рі́дко (5)
sell, to	продава́ти: прода́ти (11)
semester	семе́стр (22)
send, to	посила́ти: післа́ти (15)
sentence	ре́чення (14)
September	ве́ресень (19)
serious	серйо́зний (7)
several	па́ра (23), кі́лька (12)
shame	шко́да (11)
sharp	го́стрий (12)
sheet (of paper)	ка́ртка (2)
shelf	поли́ця (4)
shirt	соро́чка (9)
shoe	череви́к (9)
shore	бе́рег (8)
short	коро́ткий (9)
shoulder	плече́ (9)
shout, to	крича́ти: кри́кнути (23)
show, to	пока́зувати: показа́ти (5)
shrill	різки́й (21)
sick	хво́рий (19)
sick, to get	хворі́ти: захворі́ти (9)
sickness	хворо́ба (19)
side	сторона́ (3)

sign, to	підпи́сувати: підписа́ти (23)
silver	срі́бло (21)
similar	поді́бний до, схо́жий на (19)
simple	про́стий (8)
simply	про́сто (6)
sing, to	співа́ти: за/по/співа́ти (12)
singer	співа́чка, співа́к (12)
sister	сестра́ (1)
sit, to	сиді́ти: поси́діти (6)
sit down, to	сіда́ти: сі́сти (16)
sky	не́бо (12)
skyscraper	хмарочо́с (17)
Slav	слов'яни́н (16)
Slavic	слов'я́нський (14)
sleep	спа́ти: поспа́ти (3)
slice (of bread)	кро́мка, ски́бка (16)
slow	пові́льний (9)
slowly	пово́лі (4)
small	мале́нький (7), мали́й (4)
smart	му́дрий (21)
smoke, to	кури́ти: закури́ти (6)
snow	сніг (15)
so	так (1)
sofa	дива́н (7), кана́па (20)
soft	м'яки́й (15)
soldier	воя́к (12)
sometimes	і́нколи, і́ноді (4)
so much	сті́льки (16)
son	син (1)
song	пі́сня (12)
soon	ско́ро (2)
so-so	так собі́ (15)
sour cream	смета́на (8)
south	пі́вдень, по́лудень (18)
Soviet	радя́нський (9)
Spain	Еспа́нія (16)
Spaniard	еспа́нець, еспа́нка (16)
Spanish	еспа́нський (16)
speak, to	говори́ти: поговори́ти/сказа́ти (2)
specially	спеція́льно (8)
spoon	ло́жка (12)
Spring	весна́ (7)
square	пло́ща (9)
stamp	ма́рка (13)

stand, to	стоя́ти: постóяти (2)
stand up, to	става́ти: ста́ти (16)
station	ста́нція (8)
stipend	стипе́ндія (19)
stop, to	зупиня́тися: зупини́тися (18)
store	крамни́ця (4)
store/display window	вітри́на (20)
storey	пóверх (14)
story	оповіда́ння (8), ба́йка (5)
straight	прóстий (8), пря́мо (6)
strange	ди́вний (10)
street	ву́лиця (2)
streetcar	трамва́й (13)
stroll, to	гуля́ти: погуля́ти (12)
strong	си́льний (21)
student	студе́нтка, студе́нт (1)
study	кабіне́т (4)
study, to	вивча́ти: ви́вчити, в/у/чи́тися/ навча́тися: навчи́тися (19)
studying	навча́ння (14)
stupid	дурни́й (5)
subtraction	відніма́ння (22)
suburbs	за мíстом (17)
subway	підзе́мка, метрó (8)
sufficient	дóсить (6)
sugar	цу́кор (7)
suit	костю́м (5)
suitcase	валíзка (18)
summer	лíто (2), лíтній (7)
summer home	ху́тір (12)
sun	сóнце (12)
Sunday	недíля (14)
supper	вече́ря (12)
supper, to have	вече́ряти: повече́ряти (12)
sure	пе́вний (20)
for sure	напе́вно (11)
surname	прíзвище (6)
surround, to	отóчувати: оточи́ти (23)
Swede	швед, шве́дка (16)
swim, to	пла́вати, пли́сти/пливти́: попли́сти/попливти́ (20)
sword	ша́бля (9)
system	систе́ма (14)

T

table	стіл (4)
take, to	бра́ти: взя́ти (4)
take away	забира́ти: забра́ти (23)
take off, to	здійма́ти: здійня́ти, зніма́ти: зня́ти (20)
tale	ба́йка (5)
talented	талановúтий (5)
talk, to	говори́ти: поговори́ти (2)
talk	до́повідь (8)
tall	висо́кий (6)
tango	та́нґо (10)
Tartar	тата́рський (22)
taste	смак (7)
tasty	смачни́й (7)
taxi	таксі́ (8), таксі́вка (13)
tea	чай (7)
teach, to	навча́ти: навчи́ти (10), учи́ти: навчи́ти (8)
teacher	учи́тель, учи́телька (1)
tear, to	рва́ти: порва́ти
telegram	телегра́ма (5)
telephone	телефо́н (5)
telephone, to	телефонува́ти: потелефонува́ти (5)
television set	телеві́зор (5)
tell, to	розповіда́ти: розпові́сти (11), розка́зувати: розказа́ти (23)
temperature	температу́ра (19)
textbook	підру́чник (6)
thank, to	дя́кувати: подя́кувати (19)
theater	теа́тр (4)
then	тоді́ (6)
there	там (1), туди́ (13)
therefore	тому́ що (3)
thin	тонки́й (9), рідки́й (as of gruel) (21)
thing	річ (9)
think, to	ду́мати: поду́мати (2)
third	тре́тій (14)
three	три (9)
Thursday	четве́р (14)
ticket	квито́к (21)
time	час (3), пора́ (13), раз (12)
tire to	вто́млюватися: втоми́тися (17)
to	до (6)

today	сьогóдні (2)
today's	сьогóднішній (6)
toe	пáлець (7)
together	рáзом (2)
tomorrow	зáвтра (6)
too much	забагáто (9)
Toronto	Торóнто (5)
towards a meeting	назýстріч (23)
toy	зáбавка (18)
train	пóїзд (8)
translate, to	перекладáти: переклáсти (2)
translation	перéклад (6)
transport, to	возúти, вéзтú: повéзтú (18)
travel	подорожувáння (16)
tree	дéрево (9)
true	спрáвжній (5), дíйсний (11), правдúвий (5)
truly	дíйсно (11)
truth	прáвда (2)
Tuesday	вівтóрок (14)
Turk	тýрок, туркéня (16)
twenty four hours	добá (22)
two	два (9)
type	тип (22)

U

Ukraine	Украї́на (4)
Ukrainian	украї́нець, украї́нка (16), украї́нський (2)
Ukrainian, in	по-украї́нському (2)
umbrella	парасóля (20)
uncle	вýйко (17), дя́дько (20)
understand, to	розумíти: зрозумíти (4)
unfortunately	на жаль (19)
unimportant	неважлúве (9)
United Nations	Об'є́днані Нáції (16)
university	університéт (12)
unnecessary	непотрíбний (12)
unpleasant	неприє́мний (4)
until	дóти, дóки (17)
unusual	надзвичáйний (11)
upstairs	в/у/горí (23)
urban	міськúй (17)
usually	звичáйно (5)

V

vacations	вака́ції (13), кані́кули (20)
valiant	відва́жний (21)
various	рі́зний (10)
veranda	вера́нда (12)
verse	вірш (12)
very	ду́же (4)
victuals	харч (23)
villa	ху́тір (12)
village	село́ (2)
villager	селяни́н (9)
voice	го́лос (7)
Volga	Во́лга (21)

W

wait, to	чека́ти: зачека́ти (14)
walk	про́хід (15)
walk, to	ходи́ти, і/й/ти́: піти́ (6)
wall	стіна́ (2)
wallet	портфе́ль (18)
waltz	вальс (15)
want, to	хоті́ти: за/с/хоті́ти (6)
war	війна́ (6)
warm	те́плий (12)
wash, to	ми́ти: ви́мити, обми́ти (15)
watch	годи́нник (13)
water	вода́ (2)
water main	про́від (22)
way	доро́га (18)
weak	слаби́й (21)
wealthy	бага́тий (6)
weather	пого́да (2)
Wednesday	середа́ (14)
week	ти́ждень (4)
weep, to	пла́кати: запла́кати (23)
well	га́рно (1)
West	за́хід (18)
wet	мо́крий (20)
Western Ukraine	Галичина́ (22)
what	що (2)
when	коли́ (1)
where	куди́ (13), де (1)

where from звідкіля́ (11)
whether чи (1)
whisky горíлка (7)
white бíлий (3)
whole ціли́й (4)
why чому́ (1)
wide широ́кий (7)
wife дружи́на (1)
wind вíтер (7)
windbreaker плащ (8)
window вікно́ (2)
window display вітри́на (20)
wine вино́ (1)
Winnipeg Вінніпе́ґ (8)
winter зима́ (2), зимови́й (3)
without без (6)
woman жíнка (1)
wonderful знамени́тий (9)
wonderfully прекра́сно (14)
wooden дерев'я́ний (12)
word сло́во (2)
work робо́та (2)
work, to працюва́ти: попрацюва́ти (4)
world світ (22)
worse гíрше (19)
write, to писа́ти: написа́ти (2)
write down, to запи́сувати: записа́ти (9)
writer письме́нник, письме́нниця (2)
wrong злий (10)

Y

Yalta Я́лта (6)
yard двір (12)
year рік (8)
yellow жо́втий (7)
yes так (1)
yesterday вчо́ра (2)
yesterday's вчора́шній (6)
young молоди́й (3)
younger моло́дший (4)

GRAMMATICAL INDEX

ABBREVIATIONS

acc., A.	accusative
adv.	adverb
adj.	adjective
athem. verb	athematic verb
conj.	conjunction
dat., D.	dative
demonstr.	demonstrative
dem. pron.	demonstrative pronoun
dim.	diminutive
f., fem.	feminine
gen., G.	genitive
imper.	imperative
imperf.	imperfective
indecl.	indeclinable
inf.	infinitive
intrans.	intransitive
interrog.	interrogative
interr. pron.	interrogative pronoun
instr., I.	instrumental
loc., L.	locative
m., masc.	masculine
n., neut.	neuter
nom., N.	nominative
pass.	passive
perf.	perfective
pers.	person
pl.	plural
poss. pron.	possessive pronoun
prep.	preposition
pres.	present
pron.	pronoun
sg., Sing.	singular
subj.	subject
trans.	transitive
voc., V.	vocative